Y0-AQW-914

CONTESTED POWER IN ANGOLA, 1840S TO THE PRESENT

Women Agricultural Laborers, Jamba, Early 1990s. From UNITA,
Unita: Identité d'un Angola libre, Jamba: UNITA, 1995. Used by permission.

CONTESTED POWER IN ANGOLA, 1840S TO THE PRESENT

Linda Heywood

UNIVERSITY OF ROCHESTER PRESS

First published 2000
by the University of Rochester Press

The University of Rochester Press is an imprint of Boydell & Brewer, Inc.
668 Mt. Hope Avenue, Rochester, NY 14620, USA
and of Boydell & Brewer, Ltd.
P.O. Box 9, Woodbridge, Suffolk 1P12 3DF, UK

ISBN 1–58046–063–1
ISSN 1092–5228

Library of Congress Cataloging-in-Publication Data
Heywood, Linda Marinda, 1945–
    Contested power in Angola, 1840s to the present / Linda Heywood.
      p. cm. — (Rochester studies in African history and the diaspora,
    ISSN 1092–5228 ; v. 6)
    Includes bibliographical references and index.
    ISBN 1–58046–063–1 (alk. paper)
    1. Angola—Politics and government—1855–1961. 2. Angola—Politics and government—1961–1975. 3. Angola—Politics and government—1975–.
    4. Mbundu (African people)—Politics and government. I. Title. II. Series.

DT1373.H49 2000
323.1′19639320673′09—dc21   00–027765

British Library Cataloguing-in-Publication Data
A catalogue record for this book is available from the British Library

Designed and typeset by ISIS-1 Corporation
Printed in the United States of America
This publication is printed on acid-free paper

CONTENTS

ROCHESTER STUDIES in
AFRICAN HISTORY and the DIASPORA

(ISSN: 1092-5228)

MAPS

TABLES

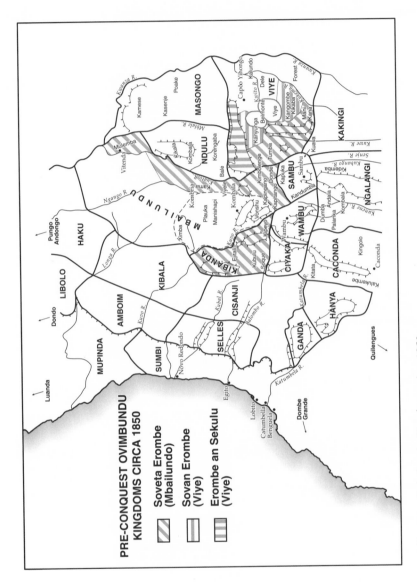

Pre-Conquest Ovimbundu Kingdoms, circa 1850

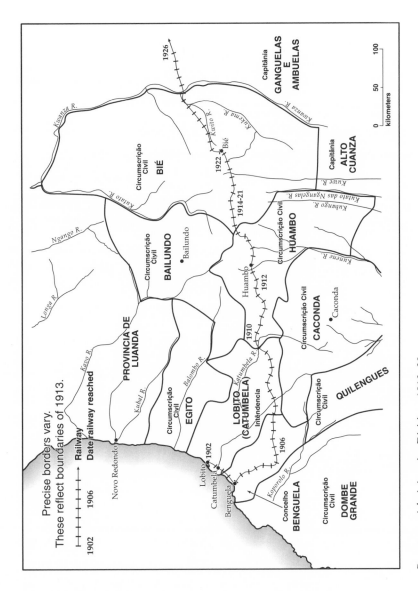

Portuguese Administrative Divisions 1913–30

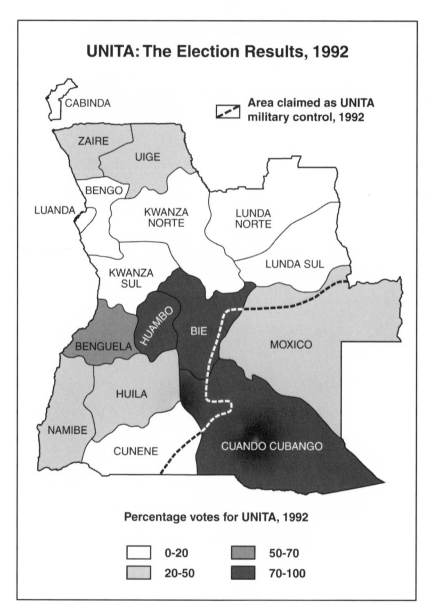

UNITA: The Election Results, 1992

ABBREVIATIONS

DISA   Direcção de Informação de Segurançã Angola/
            Angolan Department of Security
FAA   Forças Armadas Angolanas/
            Angolan Armed Forces
FALA   Forças Armadas de Liberação de Angola/
            Armed Forces for the Liberation of Angola
FAPLA   Forças Armadas Popular para a Liberação de Angola/
            Popular Armed Forces for the Liberation of Angola
FNLA   Frente Nacional de Liberação de Angola/
            National Front for the Liberation of Angola
GRAE   Governo Revolucionário de Angola no Exilo/
            Angolan Revolutionary Government in Exile
JMPLA   Juventude do Movimento Popular de Liberação de Angola/
            The Youth of the Popular Movement for the Liberation of
            Angola
MFA   Movimento das Forcas Armadas/
            Movement of the Armed Forces
MINSE   Ministerio de Segurança Angolana/
            Angolan Ministry of Security
MPLA-PT   Movimento Popular de Liberação de Angola—Partido dos
            Trabalhadores/
            Popular Movement for the Liberation of Angola—Workers'
            Party
OMA   Organização das Mulheres Angolanas/
            Angolan Women's Organization
PIDE   Polícia Internacional e de Defesa do Estado/
            International Police for the Defense of the State
SADF   South African Defence Force
SWAPO   Southwest Africa People's Organization
UNITA   União Nacional de Independência Total de Angola/
            National Union for the Total Independence for Angola
UPA   União das Populações de Angola/Union of Angolan Populations
ZANU   Zimbabwe African National Union

INTRODUCTION AND ACKNOWLEDGMENTS

This book is a testament to the African search for the proper balance between centralizing institutions and local autonomy in a region whose history has been linked to the global market and international politics from the late sixteenth century onwards. The book deals with the relationship between the villager subjects of the historical Ovimbundu kingdoms and their rulers, and between the former rulers and ruled and the succession of Angolan regimes which have claimed and, to a greater or lesser degree, exercised authority over them from the 1840s to 1997. Their experience provides a window for understanding the tortured history of Angola.

The study shows how local and regional identities gave way to Angolan nationalism as the people participated in the nineteenth century commercial revolution, experienced colonial conquest and colonialism, and fought for representation in the modern Angolan state. This transformation occurred as a result of both local and international developments taking place over more than a century and a half.

The work begins in the 1840s when the Ovimbundu occupied several kingdoms in central Angola. Despite their linkages to the international economy and a level of ethno-linguistic homogeneity that caused others to regard the population as having a common identity, the people had strong ties to kin and locality. They jealously guarded local prerogatives, and although they were subjects of the various Ovimbundu kingdoms the before Portuguese conquest (1890), local and regional tendencies were paramount.

When the Portuguese conquered the states and imposed their own structures of colonial rule between 1890 and 1975, they retained many features of Ovimbundu village institutions, but instituted their own system of rule that threatened local autonomy. As a result, throughout the colonial period, tensions between local prerogatives and state (central) authority continued. They took the form of heightened regional and ethnic identities that reinforced Ovimbundu separateness from the state and from other African populations of Portuguese Angola.

With the outbreak of the nationalist struggle (1961–75) Ovimbundu leaders (led by Protestant-trained cadres, like other Angolans who rose against the colonial state), formed their own liberation movement, UNITA (União Nacional de Independência Total de Angola) and conducted a liberation war against the colonial state. During the anticolonial struggle, and the vicious civil war (1975–92) which followed the MPLA's (Movimento Popular de Liberação de Angola) conquest of the colonial state, the ethnic and regional tendencies which had been promoted but controlled by the colonial regimes since 1890 finally surfaced. This development involved a significant percentage of the Ovimbundu population. At the same time, however, the civil war had the positive effect of helping to break down Ovimbundu localism, ruralism, and ethnic cohesion. The experiences forced the Ovimbundu leadership and people to confront the issue of their role in the creation of modern Angolan nationalism. By the time of elections of 1992, the divide between the Ovimbundu population and the state was the narrowest it had ever been under all the various regimes that had exercised authority over the population from the 1840s.

The concept of the "state" adopted here draws on recent Africanist writings that have stressed the coercive and autocratic nature of formal state systems in Africa. It also entails the notion that these formal systems, even though dominant, existed alongside less formal local village systems, civic societies which had more democratic and participatory features.[1] In the studies which deal with autocratic state systems, the "state" is regarded as a bureaucracy run by its agents having the power to dominate and to impose its will on a population. In keeping with this focus, this study uses the term "state" to indicate the administrative apparatus that rulers with sovereign power exploited. The study argues that by skillfully restructuring and manipulating judicial, military, fiscal, and other administrative mechanisms during the precolonial, colonial, and independence periods, rulers and their representatives used the state to benefit a select group among the population. Autocratic principles were always paramount, even when democratic notions were proclaimed or were nominally implemented. This situation did much to create tensions between the Ovimbundu and the state, this being more evident when the Ovimbundu kingdoms gave way to the various colonial regimes and the postcolonial state. Throughout the period of the study, however, the many segments of the Ovimbundu population looked to local/civic institutions rather than to larger regional or state ones.

Included in this definition of the state are the concepts of resistance as well as compromise on the part of those dominated. At various times (the Mbailundu war of 1902, the civil war) when those in power threatened local autonomy, resistance to state policies was commonplace. On the whole, however, compromises and subordination were the norm, allowing local institutions to adapt and ethnic identity to consolidate.

A history of the administrative changes and political culture in the central highlands from the 1840s to 1997 shows how both these strategies worked. Before the central highland region became part of the Portuguese colony of Angola, a variety of political tendencies flourished within the various Ovimbundu kingdoms. Both the rulers and ruled accepted a body of political ideas that included both autocratic and proto-democratic principles of governance which allowed both local and centralizing political tendencies to coexist. The rulers of the kingdoms, however, were never strong enough to impose central authority over all the subjects of their kingdoms. Local political interests were always paramount.

Portuguese conquest (1890–1902) changed the status quo, as the Ovimbundu kingdoms disappeared and with them the ideology which had supported local and regional political systems. In place of the plurality of Ovimbundu states, the Portuguese set up between 1902 and 1975 an integrated, comprehensive regime based on autocratic principles, forming the basis of the modern Angolan state. They used the colonial state in Angola and elsewhere to give supremacy to their language and culture, while at the same time exploiting the pre-existing local, regional, and ethno-linguistic divisions among their various African and Afro-Portuguese subjects in the colony.

Between 1961 and 1975, as Ovimbundu nationalists joined with other Angolans to spearhead armed resistance against the Portuguese, they became mired in an internecine struggle triggered by the continuing ability of the Portuguese to exploit the ethnic and regional differences between Africans and Afro-Portuguese in the colony. Imported ideologies and foreign military support (which kept the anticolonial forces afloat) also reinforced these ethnic and regional divisions. When independence came in 1975, the anticolonial leadership was ill-prepared to manage the colonial administrative structures they had inherited. They sought allies among the former colonial rulers, socialist and democratic governments, and the Apartheid regime in South Africa which had supported them during the anticolonial struggle. Two clear sets of contestants for control of the state emerged by 1976. On the one side were partisans of the MPLA, who wanted to use the state, autocratically once again, to impose their socialist vision on the population; on the other side were the supporters of UNITA, whose leaders, having been ousted from central and southern Angola to which they had laid claim, and seeing no possibility of compromise, began a seventeen-year civil war to wrest control of the state from the MPLA. In 1992, with a military stalemate and massive economic destruction all around, the competitors participated in United Nations–supervised elections. After another burst of vicious fighting in the aftermath of election results which UNITA had condemned as fraudulent, the competitors entered a prolonged process of working through agreements based on the principle of power sharing, modeled in part on postapartheid South Africa. Through this period, contests over control of the administration (state) and competing political aspirations at various levels dominated the Ovimbundu relationship with the state.

Dealing with a period that spans more than one hundred and fifty years allows for a study of the way in which political traditions developed over time in Angola. It includes those critical moments (the 1840s, 1902, 1927, 1961, 1975, 1992), when contenders for state power made war or manipulated economic and political institutions to achieve their goals. It also provides a basis an for analysis of the contradictions inherent in the Ovimbundu (and Angolan) experience, as the rulers of the precolonial kingdoms, Portuguese colonial administrators, and leaders of the MPLA and UNITA have attempted, during more than a century and a half, to consolidate state power, push political programs, and promote political ideas at the expense of local ethnic and regional interests. Furthermore, it reveals how global geopolitical issues play a role in national and local political developments.

The issues of the state, resistance, and compromise also permit us to focus on internal developments in order to explain how initially weak colonial and later national states turned integral, local, civic societies into regional, often ethnic, rivals, to achieve degrees of autocracy that they could not otherwise have managed. First, such an approach identifies the continuities between the precolonial state structures and the colonial state, and between the colonial and postcolonial states. Second, it addresses the problem of the connections between economic control and autocracy. Third, it connects the increasing autocracy of the colonial state with the ability of Portuguese officials to extend state protection and support to specially favored groups.

The implications of this study go far beyond Angola and touch on the crucial issue of modern African nationalism. The study helps us understand why modern African nationalism, when local communities temporarily submerged their divisions to get rid of colonial regimes which had capitalized on the divisions of subject peoples to maintain their autocracy, was a fleeting moment. Paradoxically, the same divisions which the colonial state had used to advance its goal, and which nationalists kept in bounds during the anticolonial struggle, surfaced at independence, leaving the way open for the reappearance of the autocratic state only decades after the achievement of independence. This study of the Ovimbundu goes a long way to explain the interdependence of weak states, autocracy, and ethnic hostilities, all familiar aspects of modern African nations.

Although no single study deals with the Ovimbundu and their relationship to precolonial Ovimbundu kingdoms, and to the colonial and postcolonial state, several works provide background for some of the issues raised in this book. Among the more important are Gladywn Murray Childs's *Umbundu Kinship and Character* (1949); René Pélissier's *Guerres grises: Résistance et révoltes en Angola (1845–1941)* (1977), and *Colonie du Minotaure: Nationalismes et révoltes en Angola (1926–1961)*; Gerald Bender's *Angola under the Portuguese: The Myth and the Reality* (1978); John Marcum's two-volume work, *The Angolan Revolution* (1969 and 1978); and James Martin III's *Political History of the Civil War in Angola 1974–1990* (1992).

Ultimately this book rests on a wide range of primary documentation and secondary material. For the precolonial period, the diaries and published writings of the Hungarian László Magyar and the Portuguese António da Silva Porto were invaluable. Both of these Europeans resided among the Ovimbundu for fifty or more years, beginning in the 1830s,[2] and were astute observers of and participants in the politics of several of the Ovimbundu kingdoms.[3] In addition, the substantial corpus of letters, published works, reports, collections of folklore, and other material from the diverse group of missionaries originating from Canada and North America (Congregationalists, later United Church of Christ), England (Plymouth Brethren), and France and Portugal (Holy Ghost Fathers) who worked in the region after 1880 give valuable insights into local political culture and life.

A rich body of correspondence between precolonial central African rulers and the Portuguese, written between 1880 and 1895, shows the African perspective on the ominous eve of colonial rule. The published and unpublished letters and reports of various European explorers, travelers, and missionaries enhance the documentation. For the colonial and postcolonial periods (1902–95), the diverse and voluminous documentation available in various archives in Angola, Europe, and North America provides added richness.[4] African, American, and European newspapers offer other insights on the nationalist and the postindependence struggles. Finally, interviews and correspondence I conducted with several Angolans, and with foreigners with Angolan experience, provide additional local perspective.

Acknowledgments

Many institutions and individuals have made this work possible. My greatest gratitude goes to the archivists and others in Europe, Africa, the United States, and Canada who, over the years, have assisted me in locating material relevant to the study. Financial support came from the Whiting Foundation of Columbia University, the Fundação Calouste Gulbenkian of Lisbon, and Howard University. I owe special thanks to the government and people of Angola, who in 1979–80 allowed me to work in the state as a *cooperante científica* at the Centro de Documentação e Investigação Histórica, and who also gave me the opportunity to experience life as an Angolan in the immediate postcolonial period. Finally, I would like to express my appreciation of the Angolans and North American missionaries who shared their recollections, insights, and correspondence with me, even when painful.

My thanks also go to John Thornton of Millersville University, who has shared many lengthy discussions about the manuscript; and to Joseph Miller and Elliot Skinner who read earlier drafts of the manuscript and provided me with detailed and helpful questions, criticism, and advice. Joseph Miller, Susan Broadhead, and John Thornton also provided useful comments on this final draft.

I am particularly grateful to John Thornton, Marlene Courtney, and Claudia Thomas for their help in typing earlier drafts of the manuscript. I would not have completed the project without the understanding and loving support of my family—John, Amara, and Amanda.

1

THE COMMERCIAL REVOLUTION IN THE OVIMBUNDU STATES, 1840S–1904

Introduction

In the 1840s, twenty-two independent Umbundu-speaking African kingdoms of various sizes dominated the central highland region of what is now Angola. They were located in naturally protected fortresses on a plateau which stands between 1,000 and 2,000 meters above sea level, and their populations enjoyed one of the healthiest climates found in Angola, where temperatures which today average 80.6 degrees Fahrenheit, but which also sees frosts and hailstorms.[1] The area contained then, as it does today, the highest population density in Angola. The kingdoms were also strategically located (see map—Preconquest Ovimbundu Kingdoms circa 1850), being at the center of a commercial zone which covered 400,000 square kilometers. The rulers of the kingdoms had commercial and other relations with each other, and with the Portuguese colony of Angola; the still independent Kimbundu kingdoms; the Lunda Kingdom (now in the Shaba Province of southeastern Democratic Republic of the Congo); the Kwanyama populations (Nhaneca–Humbe–Ovambo) in the south of Angola; and the Lozi, Luena, Chokwe, and other peoples of eastern Angola and western Zambia.[2]

Although the nineteenth century ruling lineages of some of the king-doms acknowledged their indebtedness to the Portuguese, who had helped their eighteenth-century ancestors take control, the kingdoms were inde-pendent. Indeed, Portuguese officials were reluctant to incorporate the king-doms into the colony, and as late as the 1870s they reaffirmed an earlier policy of limiting their sovereignty to "no more than 90 to 100 leagues" from the coast.[3] Thus unlike some their Kimbundu neighbors to the north, whose once independent states had been integrated into Portuguese Angola, and who were theoretically subject to Portuguese overrule, the Ovimbundu kingdoms retained their political autonomy.

The subjects of all the kingdoms were Umbundu speakers, but the peoples of each kingdom were known by its name, i.e., the Viyenos (Bienos), Wambus (Huambos), and Mbailundus (Bailundus) were subjects of the Kingdoms of Viye (Bié), Wambu (Huambo), and Mbailundu (Bailundu) respectively. Although the kingdoms were not politically unified, they had a common set of political traditions and cultural beliefs and an ethno-linguistic identity which set their peoples apart from their non-Umbundu-speaking neighbors. Since the seventeenth century, outsiders had recog-nized the peoples of the central highlands as being different; this was not unlike the situation in the neighboring Kimbundu region, where the sense of Kimbundu linguistic unity among the people of then Ndongo kingdom linked them with neighboring Kimbundu states.[4]

During the seventeenth century, political authorities connected with the Imbangala (mobile military units that often served as mercenaries for anyone who would compensate them for their services)[5] and local elites in the region initiated military and commercial relations with the Portuguese from their strongholds in the highlands. In time, rulers of the various king-doms that emerged retained economic and political control over the states and the relationship with the Portuguese deepened. Although they engaged in other activities, the rulers were also major slave raiders and slave traders who supplied slaves to the Atlantic slave trade.[6] By the 1840s, however, the end of the Atlantic slave trade, the effects of the Industrial Revolution, the availability of cheap manufactured foreign imports, and the demand for African raw materials shifted economic control from the ruling groups to the lower classes in the kingdoms. This was especially because of the hun-dreds of thousands of non-Ovimbundu slaves brought into the states, who were owned by ordinary subjects after the end of the slave trade. The politi-cal and social disruption engendered by this development facilitated the Portuguese conquest of the kingdoms between 1890 and 1904. During this period, the once proud and independent rulers and the subjects of the kingdoms were incorporated into the Portuguese colony of Angola.

Studies of the effects of the ending of the Atlantic slave trade and the shift to commodity export, Portuguese military conquest and the establishment of the colonial state; Portuguese colonialism; and the notoriety the Ovimbundu attained as a result of the civil war give only a partial history of the group from the 1840s to 1997. Local factors including political culture, leadership, and the pervasiveness of local rather than pan-ethnic or national identities are also integral parts of their experiences. This was true for a time even after the Portuguese conquest and the disappearance of the political boundaries that had served to separate the subjects of the kingdoms. During this period, the ethno-linguistic identity that outsiders had used to separate the subjects of the different kingdoms assumed a greater importance.

The growth of pan-Ovimbundu ethnic consciousness and the role of local rather than nonlocal factors are among the most salient aspects in the recent history of the Ovimbundu. These local factors had defined and shaped Ovimbundu political culture and identity in the precolonial period, just as they influenced the rise of modern Ovimbundu nationalism during the colonial and nationalist periods.

Political Ideology in the Ovimbundu States

Large political entities may have emerged in the central highlands before the seventeenth century (when they first appear in the first written records).[7] Several of these kingdoms survived into the 1840s, and in some, including Ngalangi, Mbailundu, and Bié, new ruling families came to power in the late eighteenth century when they secured Portuguese military assistance for their claims. In return, the rulers signed vague and unenforceable vassalage treaties similar to those the Portuguese had with rulers in the Kimbundu-speaking area, allowing a Portuguese *capitão-mor* to reside in their *ombala* (heavily fortified capital, usually located at the highest elevation and sometimes hewn out of rock)[8] to represent official Portuguese interests. The rulers also agreed to provide military assistance to the Portuguese in wars against neighboring states.[9] Apart from new ruling families that came to power between the 1780s and 1840s, the shift did not result in any new political realignments among the Ovimbundu states. During the period, however, the rulers of the two largest states, Viye and Mbailundu, claimed overrule over several of the smaller states, including Wambu, Ngalangi, Sambu, Ndulu, Ciyaka, and Civulu.[10]

Although the kingdoms did not constitute a large Ovimbundu state, the individual ruling lineages intermarried, had political and commercial ties, and possessed a common political ideology which rationalized their right to inherit control of these states. They adhered to several general principles, which manifested themselves in each of the states. Some of the most important ideas that governed their political culture were the belief in hereditary rights, the idea that rulers had supernatural powers, and the belief that the ruler was the highest judge in the kingdom, since he was the repository of traditional knowledge and wisdom. The subjects (commoners) of the various kingdoms also accepted these ideas as valid.

Hereditary rights did not imply primogeniture, however, and candidates from eligible lineages gained their positions through elections. These elections gave the states an appearance of limited monarchy or at least pluralism, in process if not in authority, which in Europe was the springboard for evolving democracies. Indeed, one nineteenth-century European observer noted this principle when he wrote of Mbailundu at election times:

> the government . . . is democratic. These heathens mix with the infamous humiliations of the orientals (despotism) the unabridged coarseness of the English people at election time in England. The kings defer to and flatter their counsellors, these are those who elevate a king to the throne and also those who cast him down.[11]

The Ovimbundu believed that their rulers (olosomas;[12] Portuguese—sobas) possessed supernatural powers, but there were limits to their authority. The *impunga* court and the *erombe sekulu* in Mbailundu, and the *chindur* in Sambo, were all popular organs which had the power to dethrone the olosoma, even to force him to commit suicide in some cases.[13] The ocimbandas also helped to check the rulers' power. They were the repositories of religious and secular traditions, and arbiters and upholders of morality for the society at large, a position which put them potentially at odds with the rulers. In cases where rulers gravely contravened the consensual laws and customs, ocimbandas could call for the death of an olosoma by accusing him of witchcraft.[14] This sentence would be carried out if they had the necessary political support from the electors.

The legacy of the Imbangala mentality of pillage, the history of incessant warfare between the kingdoms, the population density, the persistence of local identities, and the almost total absence of state bureaucracies also limited the power that Ovimbundu rulers exercised. For example, although the inaccessible location and fortified perimeter of a capital (*ombala*) gave the appearance of invincibility, it effectively cut rulers off from most of their population. This was because *ombalas* were strategically located to take advantage of a physical environment offering both protection and sustenance, but which limited communication between the ruler and the majority of the population, whose villages were far away from the capital. Wambu's capital was typical. An 1803 report observed that it was "like a castle hewn out of rocks surrounded by trees."[15] In 1962, when a ground plan of the city was made sixty years after the *ombala* was abandoned, workers pinpointed its location at 1851 meters high. The ruler's house, the houses of his wives, caves, ancestors' houses, houses for the rulers' personal guards, people's walkway and the like were all located here.[16] The numerous villages of the commoners were always in the lowlands away from the capital. Village elders also chose defensible, fortress-like sites as their centers, a practice that recalled the history of slave raiding by the ruling groups from their defensive residential sites. The fact that local fortresses provided security against slave raiding, and also ensured protection for those engaged in subsistence bred a fierce attachment to locality. Most pan-Ovimbundu initiatives occurred when war threatened, or for the purpose of slave raiding and trading. This situation favored the emergence of an Ovimbundu identity when subjects joined rulers in wars and raids or in trade with outsiders, but otherwise promoted intense loyalties to local community.

The large size of the kingdoms and their population density (high by Angolan standards but relatively low when compared with population densities in Europe at the time) also presented formidable obstacles to rulers seeking to strengthen the state bureaucracy. In the 1840s, Mbailundu, the largest state, covered about 85,000 square kilometers (about the size of modern Portugal) but had only 450,000 people or one-eighth of Portugal's 3.5 million population.[17] At that time, the ruling lineage did not have effective rule in power in every part of the kingdom, and there were still several districts with populations—as high as 20,000 whose representatives (erombe sekulus or olosomas) were unrelated to the ruling lineage. Strong olosomas were sometimes successful in replacing local rulers, however.

The Ovimbundu kingdoms were essentially pre-industrial states. As with states in other parts of the pre-industrial world, none of them had reached a level of development at which the presence of an independent bureaucracy, a common language, and a religion or culture had led to a national identification of the populace with the kingdom.[18]

Despite the lack of a modern state apparatus and the absence of national identity from any of the Ovimbundu kingdoms, rulers in the larger states of Mbailundu and Viye had officers and a chain of command which allowed the state to collect taxes, mobilize the population for war, and impose sanctions on their subjects. Moreover, the rulers could resort to autocratic methods of maintaining the integrity of their states. Each state had a permanent army which enforced order at home and expanded the range of the ruler's power. Furthermore, rulers manipulated the supernatural symbols which the population believed they possessed, exploited judicial and other privileges, and enlarged their own lineages by accumulating slaves, bribing clients and buying pawns, and engaging in trade with the Portuguese and with neighboring African peoples.

The permanent armies were ordinarily small, but when expanded by general conscription, could be quite large—in mid-century Viye's reached 20,000 men out of a total population of 150,000,[19] and in 1870 Wambu led a force of 30,000 combined Ovimbundu troops against Luso-Brazilian plantations near the coast at Mossamedes.[20] The rulers used their armies to attack the lands of insolent regional authorities or other states or Portuguese and Luso-African outposts in the region. The armies also imposed a forced taxation system by raiding passing commercial caravans. Between the 1840s and 1880, central Angola became famous in Portuguese annals for the "Nano wars," seasonal incursions by combined Ovimbundu armies (led by Mbailundu) that the Portuguese blamed for the general political instability and insecurity of the region.[21] The use of the army both at home and abroad enhanced the rulers' ability to keep order within their lands and to protect the integrity of their states. Furthermore, the armies enabled astute rulers to enrich their lineages by increasing their supplies of cattle and slaves, the two most important forms of wealth in the kingdoms.[22]

Other essential elements of state power included the many opportunities that rulers had to exploit the wide range of beliefs associated with their supernatural powers. In Viye, for example, these beliefs were reiterated when rulers inaugurated their reign with a general hunt which honored the gods, the real and mythical hunters and warriors who founded the kingdom, and the mythical hunter Embelengenje who was supposed to possess supernatural strength and agility.[23] Indeed, the candidate who was elected king was considered legitimate only after he had eaten "the old one"—a captured enemy/slave—at the completion of the inaugural hunt. If elections highlighted the democratic features of Ovimbundu political ideology, ritual cannibalism imposingly laid bare its autocratic features.[24] The cannibalism of the rulers after the hunt shows how the concept of "hunter-king" served to strengthen the state by ritually investing rulers with despotic powers.[25] The wide range of other ritual behavior and taboos, including special dress, food, and religious practices that rulers were subject to, also helped to maintain the integrity of the state by drawing a symbolic distinction between rulers and ruled.

The idea of the ruler as interpreter and enforcer of the law through his control of traditions and taboos was also an essential feature of Ovimbundu political ideology. Added to this were the rights of rulers to impose taxes, their rights of primacy and eminent domain, and their opportunities to accumulate capital as a representatives of their lineages.

The Ovimbundu did not possess a set of written statutes but adhered to customary precedents—*Kesila* codes—which rulers were expected to use to settle conflicts between competing parties. One crucial feature of the *Kesila* codes was a judicial procedure (*mucano*) which comprised the accusation, the judgment, and the payment of fines for those convicted (or their enslavement). Imprisonment was not an option.[26] Rulers' control over the legal system and the other rights and privileges of rulers and their representatives made the Ovimbundu kings much like others in Africa at the time.

Social Structure in the Ovimbundu States

The ruling lineages comprised the dominant groups in the Ovimbundu kingdoms. Their members were distinguished from their fellow Ovimbundu by the positions they held in the state, the rights and privileges they exercised, and the number of dependents in their households. The olosomas were at the top of the prestige ranking and lived in their *ombalas* with their retainers, titled officials, and dependents. Olosomas also had direct control over a number of outlying districts, and the villages of their counsellors, slaves, and wives. Lineage heads from nonruling lineages, but who were titled officials of the state or leaders of districts, also comprised part of this dominant group. In Viye they were called erombe sekulu or sovan erombe. Some of the titled officials included Kesongo (the public crier or advance guard of the army), Ukuasapi (guardian of the *ombala*), and the Uyahu (the tax receiver).[27]

Members of this dominant group were distinguished from the rest of the population by their status and their privileged access to resources. For example, when a ruler made war he kept half of all booty for consumption in the *ombala*. Moreover, members of the dominant group also collected fines from litigation (*mucano*), received goods—cloth, guns and other imported items—in exchange for slaves, cattle, and agricultural products from a system of reciprocal exchange called *ocibanda*, and had a variety of ways to acquire additional resources from the rights of primacy that they enjoyed. For example, during planting and harvest-time they received taxes in kind or corvée labor, and those in the larger states also received yearly tributes in the form of local and imported goods from outlying provinces and smaller Ovimbundu and neighboring states (whose subjects were open to attack by the marauding armies of the larger states).[28] Control over the state also provided members of the dominant groups with an access to surplus that was not available to the rest of society. This included the right to farm some of the most fertile land, the right to purchase and own slaves and other dependents, and opportunities to participate in long-distance trade. Their control of large numbers of dependents (whom they used to organize their own trading caravans and to protect those of their Portuguese allies), plus their ability to maintain security along the trade routes, and to exploit the labor of their dependents to supply the caravans with provisions allowed members of this group to monopolize the slave-trading activities for which the region was famous. The wide range of rights and privileges they enjoyed put them at a distinct advantage when compared with the freeborn commoners, clients, slaves, and foreigners who were the other major social group in the state.[29]

The freeborn population (*mukwendye*), clients (*hafuka*), and slaves (*pika*) accounted for the majority of the people in the kingdoms, their lives more influenced by daily and seasonal routines than by the demands of rulers. The freeborn population enormously outnumbered the ruling groups but was outnumbered in turn by the large numbers of unfree people in the villages. Each village contained about thirty to fifty households, whose members were related by blood and marriage. An elder, called a sekulu (according to a modern day Ocimbundu "the wisest person in the village, with experience of the social, family, and tribal life, capable of governing or at least influencing society by his counsel that he carries and transmits") whose lineage went back to its founders was the village head.[30] The sekulu was elected to his position from among eligible kinsmen identified with the founders of the village. Sekulus along with the ocimbandas (religious practitioners) and other titled individuals, comprised the village leadership and managed its affairs. They were the people who represented the villages when state officials visited, organized labor or military details when required by the state, distributed land to villages, and dispensed justice. All freeborn male villagers, however, had the right to participate in village affairs as part of their membership in the kin group at its core. As one sekulu explained in the early twentieth century, "In our Umbundu country people do not build together unless we are blood relatives."[31]

Like the members of the ruling groups who derived their status by descent from the founders of the state or villages, freeborn commoners gained their status because they were descended from the oldest lineages associated with their village. Although both patrilineal and matrilineal lines of reckoning descent existed, as in other African societies at the time, freeborn commoners derived rights, privileges, and status from the matrilineage. For example, they inherited usufruct rights to land in the villages, and they could sit on village councils at the *onjango*, or freemen's meeting house, where men trained their sons and nephews in the traditions and in marriage and kin values through proverbs. Learning the traditions through proverbs such as "kinship is half full, sharing makes it overflow," or "the head of an adult is full with wisdom, as the cave is full with leaves" ("ocisitalungi pelete amela, utue wutulu pelete olodunge"), strengthened the bond between younger and older males and tied young men to their maternal kin group. A man who did not join in discussions in the *onjango* left a stain on his maternal kin, and was called *ocimbalakoko*—unsociable— and ridiculed.[32] All freeborn men were eligible for various positions of authority in the village. The title of sekulu, for instance, always went to freeborn males of eligible families who had demonstrated upright character by their participation in activities at the *onjango*.[33]

The two most significant factors distinguishing life in the village from the life of members of the ruling group were the sexual division of labor and free and unfree status. In the villages, women and slaves were responsible for farming, the mainstay of the village economy. They farmed the lands of their male kinsmen, husbands, and masters; they did not have direct rights to the land they farmed. Freeborn men were only marginally involved in agriculture, clearing new plots for cultivation but neither planting nor harvesting. Indeed, their abhorrence of farming was so pronounced that a popular way to ridicule a man was to assert, "You are not a man, take up a hoe" "Ove si lume, kái-ko".[34] Male slaves, however, farmed alongside free and slave women.

Farming techniques were rudimentary. The plough was unknown, and in any case was useless in most parts of the plateau, where the women and slaves used a simple hoe and "sedentary-shifting cultivation." The yield, however, compared favorably with that of Portugal because of the good climate, the rarity of droughts, and the intensive cultivation. The techniques which the villagers had developed for exploiting the range of land types in the plateau, that is, staggered plantings in four plot types (*ocumbu*—house garden, *onaka*—low-lying lands along streams, *ombanda*—plots sloping up from the river, and *epia*—clearings in the forest) were quite sophisticated and accounted for the agricultural productivity.[35] Women and slaves also foraged to supplement the diet with the wide variety of animal and plant products which were available.

Apart from farming, villagers engaged in a wide range of economic activities, but participation in these also depended on one's gender and civil status. Hunting, iron and woodworking, carpentry, locksmithing, tanning, and weaving were occupations for freeborn men. Many prized hunting and ironworking, because these activities brought both material benefits and social prestige. As a result of the heavy demand in Europe for ivory from the 1850s, elephant hunters' skills were in demand by members of the ruling groups, who sent them out on long hunting expeditions. Because of their expertise, elephant hunters had close ties to the ruling groups and thus to the state.[36] Ovimbundu blacksmiths were famous in the region; and in Ndulu, where there were "mines of iron and steel," local blacksmiths fulfilled a regional demand.[37] Although freeborn lineages owned cattle, animal husbandry was not significant, and the Ovimbundu were not well known as cattle breeders like their neighbors to the south and east.

Long-distance trading also attracted freeborn Ovimbundu males. Caravan organizers (called *pombeiros*) were often sekulus, and they were renowned for their expertise as caravan organizers and as the leaders of the long-distance caravans which traversed the region. The items of trade included skins, ivory, domestic animals such as pigs and sheep, locally made axes and hoes, slaves, guns, salt, maize and other agricultural items, local and imported textiles, as well as other local and imported products. The trading took place along the caravan routes between the Benguela coast and the Shaba region of the present-day Democratic Republic of the Congo, in the villages or at markets (*feiras*) which rulers established to supervise trading with the Portuguese and Afro-Portuguese.[38]

Freeborn women and children also had defined roles in the village. While freeborn men moved between the village and the regional economy, the occupational specialization based on gender and status confined freeborn adult women and their unmarried children to the home and village, insulating them from the state and the regional economy. They formed the mainstay of the subsistence economy, being responsible not only for farming but also for foraging, pottery making, dyeing of textiles, brewing the variety of beverages for every day and festive occasions, and for collecting firewood and water. Moreover, as in other pre-industrial agricultural communities, they were obligated to join in inter-village economic activities such as clearing the land for planting, plus communal hunting and fishing. Freeborn women also prepared the daily meals that freeborn males enjoyed in the *onjango*, which was off-limits to women. Indeed, the ability to cook well gained women great respect in the village. They were also responsible for training their and their brothers' children (girls until marriage and boys up to the age of six), and they might serve as helpers to freeborn men who were specialists or traders. Nineteenth-century observers who witnessed the system functioning concluded that the obligations and the gender and status distinctions made freeborn women virtual slaves to their husbands' and brothers' kin, and estimated that well over half the people (that is, freeborn women and slaves) were slaves to the rest of society.[39]

The presence of slaves in the households of freeborn women could amend this arrangement substantially. Married women expected their husbands to give them their monthly ration of cloth and often received other commodities, including jewelry or a young slave. These slaves performed daily activities like collecting firewood and water, and some observers believed that a slave in the household allowed free-born women to "live in idleness."[40] Freeborn women, however, like their male counterparts, fulfilled a wide range of lineage obligations. Owning slaves meant that freeborn women could spend more time planning and participating in the numerous ceremonies and rituals involving singing, dancing, naming of babies, and initiation. These activities were essential to life as an Ocimbundu and helped preserve the distinctiveness of Ovimbundu language, religion, folklore, and culture.[41]

Purchased slaves (*pika*) occupied the lowest position in the village. Unlike the pawns (*háfuka*), and other dependents who were part of kin groups of their own, slaves were non-Ovimbundu, purchased or obtained through raids.[42] These slaves were branded with hot irons, could be resold, and were subject to extreme and humiliating demands (male slaves had to do women's work) and physical punishments. Apart from the small death fee which slave owners had to pay to the ruler at the death of a slave, slaves had absoutely no means of influencing their owners.[43]

Slaves born in the household were called *ocilitumbihe* (child by good will) or *omolo okuakua* ("the child I bore in my arms"), were often integrated into the lineage, and enjoyed many of the rights of freeborn people.[44] They were not eligible to inherit titles but could inherit moveable property from their masters. Many freemen married female slaves as second wives to enlarge the kin group, a system that may have prevented the rise of competing slave sub-lineages.

The Transformation of the Regional Economy and Society to 1890

From the 1840s to 1890, the expansion of non-slave commodity trade and the end of the Atlantic slave trade had major economic and social repercussions in the states, ultimately challenging the ability of the rulers to retain power. The changes also pushed the Portuguese to reassess their presence in central Angola and to redefine their relationship with the Ovimbundu states. The rulers' failure to adapt their political culture to the new realities, their decreasing legitimacy at home, and their lack of adequate military technology and training allowed the Portuguese to gain the upper hand and to begin the conquest of the Ovimbundu states in 1890.

When Portugal officially abolished the Atlantic slave trade from Portuguese Angola in 1836, following the Anglo-Portuguese Treaty of 1830 that banned the trade, the ruling Ovimbundu lineages had been deeply involved in the slave trade for over half a century. Between 1741 and 1828, Portuguese and Brazilian buyers had exported a total of 399,267 slaves, an average of 4,869 a year, from the southern port of Benguela.[45] Most of these slaves were purchased from or through Africans who were associated with the Ovimbundu states. During the height of the trade, the *feiras* that the rulers hosted guaranteed them a monopoly over the commerce, for they enabled the rulers to dictate where trade took place and who could engage in it, and guaranteed them a part of the revenues. Moreover, they were able to sell their own slaves at controlled prices and impose taxes on the Portuguese and Afro-Portuguese who traded at the *feiras*.[46] The rulers were in a good position to obtain slaves because of their power (control over armies). Slaves they captured in war, obtained as tribute, or kidnapped could either be sold or retained and used to enhance their wealth.

The end of the Atlantic slave trade and the more democratic organization of commodity trade witnessed a shift from state-controlled trade in slaves at the *feiras* to a more competitive long-distance market. Although the rulers continued to obtain slaves for the illegal export market (in Brazil and Cuba) and to meet the expanding regional demand, the American and European buyers now wanted ivory, beeswax, gum copal, and later rubber, all of which the Ovimbundu had to purchase from African producers in the interior. This shift in demand lost the rulers their ability to monopolize trade. Between 1830 and 1857, for example, ivory exports from the ports of Luanda and Benguela went from 2,300 kilograms to 76,455 kilograms. Gum copal and beeswax experienced even more dramatic increases, going from 64,935 kg in 1830 to 327, 416 kg in 1857, and from 106,000 kg in

1830 to 773,000 kg in 1857.[47] The Ovimbundu states supplied a large percentage of these exports.[48]

For a while, the members of the ruling lineages retained their dominant role in the international trade, as Portuguese and Brazilian trading partners continued to supply them with imports—muskets, gunpowder, and the wide range of textiles in demand in the markets in the African interior.[49] In 1846 the Portuguese and Afro-Portuguese community in Viye totalled one hundred traders. Many members of the ruling lineages, including a daughter of Viye's ruler Riambulla, who was married to the Hungarian merchant-adventurer László Magyar, had close ties to the foreign traders. The ruling lineages' ability to develop marriage and other personal ties with foreign traders enabled them to retain a prominent place in the new trade.[50] Mbailundu's rulers capitalized on the new opportunities offered by commodity trade by agreeing in the early 1850s to the request of the Portuguese trader Silva Porto to allow a major trade route to pass through their kingdom. By the 1870s, Mbailundu, Viye, Ndulu, Ciyaka, and Civulu were at the center of four major trade routes which linked the central highlands to the Portuguese import-export houses on the coast, the Kimbundu region to the north, and the markets in Shaba Province (Democratic Republic of Congo) and Western Province (Zambia).[51] Moreover, the rulers imposed fees on foreign traders passing through their lands.

The ruling lineages also initially retained their dominant role in trade because they could supply the expert ivory hunters and caravan organizers—skilled hunters to track down the elephants, and reliable men who could trade on their behalf. Their slaves and clients allowed them to mobilize the labor needed to transport the products between the coast and the interior. Some of their expeditions required major planning and organizing, as evidenced by the eight hundred-person caravan that Soba Riambulla of Viye sent to conduct trade in Benguela in 1846. Large caravans always had a broker (*enzálo* or *pombeiro*) who negotiated terms, as well as an armed contingent for security.[52]

Members of the ruling lineages were initially able to retain dominant places in the market because they could use their privileged position to limit competition; but from the 1870s onwards international developments such as the depression and the rise of new firms had their effects on the regional trade. Between the 1870s and 1890, rulers witnessed trade conditions shifting against them and their local Portuguese and other foreign allies. By 1890 in both Viye and Mbailundu, for example, rulers lost a major source of income due to the closing of *feiras*, which itself was due to the steady decline of the foreign merchant community. Many of the merchants had become bankrupt, and some, like Silva Porto, with thirty-eight years experience in the region, carried an 18,624,175 *reis* debt to his coastal suppliers. Although the merchants blamed their situation on the high taxes local officials imposed on them, their decline was in part the consequence of the competition resulting from the entrance of new firms in the local market, firms that were more willing to sidestep both the rulers and the Portuguese inland traders.[53] More significant, however, was the undermining of the monopoly the ruling lineages had exercised in the trade due to the competition they faced from nonruling titled lineages and the rise in the numbers of freeborn commoners who directly challenged the status quo.

The dominant role which the freeborn population came to play in the trade by 1890 was due to the ability of Ovimbundu entrepreneurs (mostly members of nonruling titled lineages and freeborn commoners) to respond creatively to the new labor and trading requirements of the commodity era. Unlike the slave trade era, when rulers and foreign traders organized raids or conducted state-to-state business to purchase slaves, the purchasing of small quantities of ivory, wax, and later rubber from individual producers in the interior required individual drive, astuteness, and access to kin labor. Many members of the nonruling titled and nonroyal population capitalized on the new opportunities which commodity trade presented.[54] The group came to dominate the trade between the 1870s and 1890, as the states became the central point for organizing caravans to the interior to obtain ivory, gum copal, beeswax, and other items for export.

From the 1860s, sekulus and some members of nonruling titled lineages were the first to enter the trade alongside the rulers and the foreign traders, becoming *pombeiros*, and playing a crucial role in recruiting porters, possibly because rulers could not provide enough, due to the numbers required and the speed of expansion of the trade. They also became the main organizers of trading caravans. These men exemplified a new entrepreneurial spirit among the population, and their kinship ties, organizational skills, knowledge of local languages, and local understanding proved essential to the growing Ovimbundu involvement in long distance commodity trade. The caravans which they organized and managed, either on their own behalf or on behalf of the few remaining Portuguese traders, made journeys as far as Katanga and Lunda. Some were large—between five hundred and a thousand people—and brought profits to the organizer, the *sertenejos* (Portuguese inland traders) and the coastal merchants because of the leaders' entrepreneurial drive.[55] In 1875, the English explorer Vernon Cameron met a Viye broker called Kindele (an African with European ways) in Lozi country; he employed a white clerk and could speak several of the languages of central Africa, in addition to Kiswahili and Portuguese. His caravan included a hundred hired porters and several personal slaves, and Cameron speculated that such ventures made enormous profits.[56]

Some sekulus became successful traders by investing their earnings in slaves and ivory, and received credit from coastal traders. The 14,000 *reis* which Silva Porto's *pombeiro* received in credit from a coastal firm was a significant amount for a person who was not part of the ruling group.[57]

Other members of the freeborn population who followed sekulu into the trade as porters also became deeply involved. The majority began as humble porters who made verbal contracts with the sekulus to join the caravan and received twenty yards of cloth as wages and to pay tolls. Instead of using their payment to cover costs, however, most of them brought their own food and other items to cover the cost of the journey, and invested the cloth in a young slave that could be exchanged for a tusk of ivory or a load of wax for resale on the coast. Like the sekulus, freeborn Ovimbundu who had made several trips as porters turned to trading in their own right. Many gained the confidence of coastal suppliers who advanced them goods on credit (as much as 5,000 *reis*, and by the 1880s, caravans composed entirely of porters turned traders dominated the trade between the highlands, the interior, and the coast.[58]

This transformation was particularly evident after the 1870s when rubber became a viable export crop and there was a small boom in the domestic sale of slaves in central Africa. Exports of rubber from the port of Benguela rose from thirty-three tons in 1870 to ninety-one tons in 1885 and continued to rise until 1914.[59] Reports from the 1870s onward point to the number of Ovimbundu villagers (men, women, and children) who joined caravans to the interior with cloth, beads, alcoholic beverages, and guns to exchange for ivory, wax, slaves, hides, gum copal, or honey.[60] In 1874, a United States consular report on Benguela noted that the caravan trade was in the hands of "Bihe and Bailundu natives who occasionally come in gangs from 3,000 to 5,000 bringing ivory, cattle, and some gum copal."[61]

Many other Ovimbundu simply joined the caravans to take the opportunity of participating in kidnapping raids for slaves, whom they exchanged for ivory or rubber or put to farming in the highlands to meet the rising Portuguese demand for maize and other locally grown products in the coastal settlements. These activities not only gained them an infamous reputation as slave traders, but also set them on the road to becoming the dominant traders and laborers between the Benguela coast and central Africa.[62]

By the end of the 1880s, perhaps more than fifty thousand Ovimbundu from the various states participated annually in the various aspects of the long-distance trade.[63] Thousands of females, children, and slaves also became active. Villagers lined the caravan routes to sell "sweet potatoes, mandioca, bananas, and corn meal" as well as meat to travelers on their way to the interior. Others carried maize and cassava to the coast, where Portuguese settlers bought them as food for their servants and slaves.[64]

Social and Political Changes in the Era of Long Distance Trade

The integration of members of the nonruling titled lineages and freeborn Ovimbundu into the circuit of long-distance trade had major repercussions in the Ovimbundu kingdoms. With the wealth they gained from trade, these men were able to purchase titles and challenge the status of the ruling groups. The transformations opened the way for foreigners—Portuguese traders, government officials, and North American missionaries to become more deeply involved in the internal politics of the states. By the time the Portuguese moved to conquer the states as a way to secure the colony of Angola against challenges from the British and Germans, the Ovimbundu state system had been undermined. As a result, the Portuguese were able to subdue all the kingdoms by 1904 and integrate them into the colony of Angola.

The first evidence that the trade was having an impact on the social and political institutions of the Ovimbundu kingdoms was the increase in the number of Ovimbundu obtaining titles. This was because freeborn commoners who gained wealth—slaves, cattle, guns, cloth—invested it in social capital by purchasing titles, thus acquiring the right to exercise the judicial privileges that had previously been the prerogative of members of the ruling lineages. As one observer noted as early as the 1860s, a few successful sekulus were already purchasing lifetime titles such as "*macotas, sargents* and *quinduras*." By the 1880s even a simple porter who had some success in trade could set himself up as a "*pombeiro*, magnate at court or seculu, chief of a small settlement". The greatest desire of the newly titled trader was to conduct *mucanos* and become richer from the fees he collected.[65] Indeed, the period witnessed the proliferation of *mucanos*, as accusations and counter-accusations of witchcraft became common. Rulers of the kingdoms were unable to stop the process, because the administrative mechanisms were weak. This social upheaval slowly eroded the authority of the ruling lineages. As observers described the situation, in many villages "the most trivial mistake or breach of etiquette is a crime and has to be paid for dearly"—in the form of one's wife—as one observer noted.[66]

The new opportunities which allowed members of the nonruling titled lineages and freeborn Ovimbundu commoners to succeed in trade worked in other ways to undermine the old order and weaken the Ovimbundu states. Men enriched by trade flaunted their new wealth by marrying additional wives, accumulating slaves and cattle, and hoarding cloth (a major sign of wealth). Many also purchased guns, and a few even adapted some aspects of Western design to the traditional house, buying prestigious items of local and foreign origin, and wearing European clothing and other symbols of European civilization.[67] Silva Porto, whose forty-year residence in the highlands made him an acute commentator on Ovimbundu society, described these men as upstarts who sported "trousers," and who possessed "many slaves and large herd[s] of cattle, sheep, and goats." Years later, Canadian missionary John Tucker, relying on letters from earlier missionaries who were eyewitnesses to the changes, concluded that during the days of the rubber boom, the average Ovimbundu villager who still had access to ivory, slaves, and rubber from the interior was "rich in this world's goods according to African standards. Spirit huts were full of tusks of elephants, rubber and bales of cloth . . . slaves abounded."[68]

The changing situation also allowed the freeborn population more access to slaves and more opportunities to improve their social position at the expense of members of the ruling lineage. During the period of the Atlantic slave trade, members of the ruling lineages had more access to slaves than ordinary Ovimbundu. From the 1830s, slave holding among ordinary villagers increased steadily. The slaves not only relieved freeborn women of many agricultural tasks, but shifted the population center from the *ombalas* to other localities. Thus, the 232,000 people that the *olosoma* of Mbailundu controlled in the 1850s would have been outnumbered by the total number of freeborn people and slaves in Mbailundu who lived in the lands of the nonruling titled lineages, or by the slaves owned by freeborn commoners. Similar power shifts took place in all the other kingdoms, as slaveholding became widespread. This process weakened the power of the ruling lineages as against the nonruling titled lineages and freeborn commoners.[69] Indeed, ownership of slaves and livestock became real symbols of wealth across the social divide in the Ovimbundu states.

The material improvement among ordinary Ovimbundu led to new social realignments in Ovimbundu society. Ocimbandas, for example, may have experienced the greatest shift in their position as they gained more from the fees they obtained for judging the many lawsuits (*ocimbu*) involving witchcraft which less fortunate kinsmen brought against their more successful kin. Missionary eyewitnesses reported that at the public trials, where the accused faced trumped-up charges of exploiting the spirit world for personal enrichment and not for the kin, the dice loaded, defendants faced guilty verdicts, and swift sentencing (usually the loss of their material wealth) was assured. In the majority of cases in the villages from the 1880s onwards, rulers or their representatives were not involved as they became less and less able to exert direct influence on local affairs.[70]

Ocimbandas also improved their economic and social standing as more people came to rely on them for psychological and health services during this period of economic and social transformation. They acquired wealth and prestige from making and selling the charms traders carried for protection, and from the herbs and potions they concocted to keep men healthy during their stay at the hot, humid, malaria-infested coast. The demand for ocimbandas' services also increased as more villagers were able to pay them to conduct the ceremonies associated with the traditional birth, death, and initiation rites, and for the ceremonies that grew out of the long-distance trade.[71] The widespread and growing role of the ocimbandas did much to undermine the spiritual authority of olosomas.

The most serious aspect of these economic and social transformations, however, was the change in the relationship between village elders and villagers, and between localities and members of the ruling lineages. The first evidence of the new attitudes can be seen in increased reports of sekulus who could not get young men to comply with labor requests or military conscription for raiding parties. Some who were called up refused to obey, while others could not be found because they were away from the village. Moreover, olosomas, unable to raise sufficient troops, could not even get their own slaves to comply with their orders. For example, in July 1886 when Ekwikwi II (1876–93), the olosoma of Mbailundu, insisted that the two slaves, Mosu and Samba, whom he had loaned to the Protestant missionaries, must return to the court to join a war party, they refused to go, complaining that they regarded such "wars" as "bad."[72] Rulers were also unable to enforce compliance on recalcitrant sekulus and leaders of localities who refused to pay tribute.[73] In 1888, Ekwikwi again had to send some of his soldiers to attack and burn the village of Ocimbombo, located only a short distance from the *ombala*, to ensure the compliance. The villagers resisted and killed two of his soldiers.[74] Similar acts by individuals and localities reported during the 1880s suggest an assertion of local autonomy which severely challenged the authority of the ruling lineages in the Ovimbundu kingdoms.

To try and prevent the steady erosion of their power, members of the ruling lineages adopted several strategies. In Viye, where rulers faced the greatest threat from social upheaval, from a population integrated into the long-distance trading economy from its very inception, the olosomas sometimes took extraordinary measures to weaken the social forces which threatened their authority. An extreme case may have occurred there in 1875 when the olosoma was reported to have hidden himself for four days and had it rumored that he had died. He reappeared on the fifth day and swore that he had brought himself back to life by his special powers.[75] More typically, however, the ruling lineages used the tried and true: marriages, diplomatic alliances, personal threats, and haranguing of foreigners, and invasions of communities to maintain control.

The ruling lineages also made numerous alliances with influential foreigners and neighboring non-Ovimbundu rulers. For example, in 1849 Olosoma Kanyangula of Viye married his daughter Osoro to the Hungarian trader Lázsló Magyar, to strengthen his ties with foreign traders and to enhance his standing among his nobles and the population at large.[76] Similarly, there was the forty-year relationship the olosomas of Mbailundu and Viye maintained with Silva Porto. Silva Porto persuaded Mbailundu's ruler to open his lands to a major caravan route and resided for many years in Viye where he was treated as a member of the ruling lineages. This relationship also served the interests of the Ovimbundu rulers. Indeed, Porto had several children by local women.[77] The ruling lineages in the various states had similar relationships with interior rulers, including the Lozi rulers and Msiri of Garanganza (Katanga).[78] However, a more competitive commercial environment, together with the increasing involvement of the British and Boers in the politics of central African states, limited the ability of the Ovimbundu ruling elites to capitalize on these ties.

The hold which the ruling lineages had over the states, and which had been maintained in part through marriage and commercial ties, thus came under intense strain as a result of the expansion of commodity trade. The period from the 1840s to the 1890s witnessed an increase in political rivalries and conflicts over territorial sovereignty and trade between Ovimbundu kingdoms; this also weakened the states.[79]

These pressures help explain why, from the 1840s, the rulers appeared more eager to renew ties with Portuguese officials in the colony of Angola (up to that time made up of parts of the Kimbundu-speaking region and parts of the coastal and sub-plateau areas of central and southern Angola), and to welcome North American Protestant missionaries who came to the region in 1880. Ovimbundu rulers may have regarded the Portuguese and missionary alliances as other guarantees of power, but in fact the presence of the foreigners heightened the tensions among factions in the states and ultimately facilitated Portuguese conquest.

Changing Ovimbundu-Portuguese Relations

The relationship between the kingdoms and the Portuguese colony, maintained through the years by the various rulers through diplomatic and commercial ties, began to shift as a result of the end of the Atlantic slave trade, as the ruling lineages faced the uncertainties of shifting prices and new demands for exports of legitimate commerce. Increasingly, the olosomas turned to Portuguese officials to resolve conflicts with the newer group of foreign merchants who came to dominate the legitimate commerce, and even to resolve conflicts over trade between the rulers of the various kingdoms and neighboring states. For example, in 1845 the Olosoma Riambulla requested the Portuguese governor in Luanda to look into a case involving the kidnapping of his porters trading in Pungo Ndongo. On other occasions the rulers helped the Portuguese put down uprisings, or clear caravan routes of the highway robbers and bandits who attacked caravans and kidnapped porters along the unprotected routes.[80]

The pressures the olosomas faced at home as a result of the new social forces unleashed by legitimate trade also helped to push them into alliance with officials in the colony. Beginning in the 1840s, the rulers of both Viye and Ngalangi swore formal vassalage to the Portuguese crown, with Ngalangi's ruler Dom Pedro Dumba actually converting to Catholicism. Like vassals in Portuguese controlled Angola, he received the honorific title of "Colonel of the Portuguese Auxiliaries." The vassalage terms also guaranteed protection and certain trading privileges for the two rulers in the lands under their control.[81]

By the 1870s and 1880s as the trade expanded, along with increased social tensions and conflicts over trading and security between Portuguese and Ovimbundu and between one Ovimbundu kingdom and another, the rulers sought to maintain their legitimacy by seeking support from the Portuguese for their domestic aims. For example, in 1886 Olosoma Ekwikwi sent a letter to the Portuguese official at Catumbela reminding him that he, Ekwikwi, "as a vassal and Portuguese subject," sought permission to "make war in the interior of Quibula [Civulu] because they are highwaymen who rob merchants and *sertenejos* [Portuguese colonists] of their goods". He also asked permission to invade "Quissama" (Kisama) to the north.[82] The moves by the ruling elites did not bring the advantages the rulers hoped for, because Portuguese aims conflicted with Ovimbundu ones. The ruling lineages wanted to protect Ovimbundu independence and retain control over the trade; but security of trade and the extension of real Portuguese control over the region also dominated Portuguese official thinking. The Portuguese regarded vassalage treaties with the Ovimbundu rulers as one means to achieve their aims. Thus, when Wambu's rulers indicated they were ready to renew their acts of vassalage or signalled their desire to be on better terms with the *presídio*, Portuguese officials willingly complied. They believed that it was essential to maintain "the friendship and expertise of the soba,"[83] despite Wambu's rulers being openly hostile towards the Portuguese, who indeed considered them "rebels and aggressive" and "pouco submisso" ("not submissive").

These two competing goals which emerged during the 1870s and 1880s changed the political status quo in the highlands. During this period, the ruling lineages became deeply involved in diplomatic attempts to secure formal Portuguese recognition and alliance with Protestant missionaries, to counteract the social consequences of the commodity trade in rubber. By 1880s they were facing a new "boom" in the commodity trade as rubber replaced ivory as the export par excellence from central Africa. At the same time, the Portuguese decision to protect their Angolan and Mozambican possessions from other European powers led them to change their policies towards the highland kingdoms, claiming more sovereignty over them and demanding obedience from the rulers. These opposing goals led inevitably to war and the consequent loss of Ovimbundu political independence.

The decision of the Ovimbundu elites to renew ties of vassalage with the Portuguese and to welcome Protestant missionaries rested on the belief that this would increase their role in trade, allow them to collect more tribute, obtain the coveted luxury items so essential for retaining their power and prestige, and regulate the spread of western ideology among their subjects and those of neighboring African states. A series of despatches from the rulers of Viye and Mbailundu to the Portuguese illustrate how much the changing commercial environment shaped Ovimbundu rulers' policy decisions, and how this eventually led them to compromise Ovimbundu political independence. An 1884 despatch from Njambajamina, the ruler of Viye, clearly indicates a shift from the earlier policy which had held official Portuguese involvement in the internal affairs of the kingdom to a minimum. In the despatch, the olosoma swore allegiance and obedience to the Portuguese, recalling the debt his lineage owed them for assisting his grandfather Dom Soba Congombe to gain power in the late eighteenth century. He also swore to "obey all the orders you send me."[84]

Similarly, the 1886 letter that Ekwikwi of Mbailundu—honored by some Angolans for his resistance against the Portuguese[85]—sent to the Portuguese, in which he acknowledged his allegiance to the Portuguese king, sought permission to make war against his neighbors, and even stressed that his aim was to "civilizar", shows a similar concern. In his long correspondence with Angolan officials during the period Ekwikwi often requested gifts, supplies, teachers, and priests.[86]

The relationships which the ruling lineages developed with Protestant missionaries, who came from North America and England and who established the first Protestant missions in the kingdoms in 1880, were also intended to enhance the lineages' prestige, legitimize their power, and give them a central role in the advance of western ideas and expertise. The Portuguese feared that the missionaries were really looking for the legendary gold mines that the Portuguese still believed to exist in Angola. They attempted to prevent the rulers from opening their lands to the missionaries, by spreading rumors that the missionaries wanted Ovimbundu land. However, the leaders of Mbailundu, Viye, Ndulu, and other smaller states welcomed the missionaries, and as their Kongo counterparts in the north, hoped that the Protestant missionary presence would act as a counterweight to the Portuguese. Both Ekwikwi II of Mbailundu and Njambajamina of Viye attempted to use them to bargain with the Portuguese. Thus Ekwikwi, perhaps influenced by Portuguese rumors about the motives of the missionaries, who he noted, did not come to buy "wax, rubber, or slaves," the same Ekwikwi who even encouraged his people to destroy the mission and plunder its goods, still allowed the missionaries to build a mission station near his *ombala*. He even sent two of his children to the school they established. Njambajamina also gave the missionaries land, while both he and Ekwikwi simultaneously pressured the Portuguese to send Roman Catholic missionaries and to nominate a political representative to their kingdoms.[87] In 1886 the Portuguese finally responded to the rulers' request by nominating Silva Porto, a now-bankrupt Portuguese slave trader who had resided in the region for more than three decades, as *capitão-mor* of Viye and Mbailundu. They also assigned two priests to open Catholic missionary stations in the kingdoms.[88]

Although these initiatives were intended to reinforce and publicize the Ovimbundu rulers' control over the state and enhance their prestige locally, they actually compromised Ovimbundu independence. Although a North American official in Luanda wrote perceptively in 1885 that, "in Bailundu and Bihe . . . although considered vassals of the Portuguese government . . . they [the Portuguese] do not have the power to compel them to do as they would like . . . ," the situation was changing.[89] By 1890, when the Portuguese invaded Viye and took steps to end Ovimbundu independence and incorporate the kingdoms into the colony of Angola, the rulers found it difficult to mount any effective resistance.

Portuguese Conquest and the Making of the Early Colonial State

The attempts of the ruling Ovimbundu lineages to bolster their position by opening their lands to outsiders only resulted in further undermining of their control over the state and the deterioration of their status. This was because as legitimate trade expanded and more of the population became involved in it, the role the ruling lineages had played in the organization of exports and the supply of labor and services declined. Portuguese traders and other foreigners increasingly bypassed them and developed ties with heads of competing lineages or sekulus who were less demanding and more eager to use their ties to outsiders to strengthen their position in the kingdoms. This resulted in the emergence of pro-foreign factions and traditionalist factions in the ruling lineages, factions which competed to have a supportive candidate elected as olosoma. These developments helped to undermine the ruling lineages and weaken the state.

The weakening of the old order began first in Viye in the mid-1880s, when eligible lineages with competing ideologies fought for control of the state by supporting their own candidates for the olosoma position. At the root of the conflict was the tension between traditionalists, who wanted to retain the old order and restrict the activities of outsiders in the kingdoms, and pro-trade factions who wanted to expand the contacts. In 1886 when Njambajamina, whose tentative attempts to strengthen ties with the Portuguese and other outsiders had alienated some segments of the ruling lineages, was overthrown, the tensions between the various factions increased. The situation became more complicated when Kapoko of Chisamba, Njambajamina's rival (who was of slave origin and therefore without strong traditional ties among the electors), also failed in his attempts to win nomination. Apparently, traditionalists among the electors derailed his nomination because of his foreign birth and humble origin, and they resented his close ties to Portuguese traders and Protestant missionaries.[90]

The nomination of Ciyoka (1886–88), a man with legitimate claims (he was the nephew of a former olosoma), but also a well-known trader and supporter of Portuguese interests, also failed to stop the decline. His assassination in 1888, presumably because he had refused to lead the postelection raid against the Ngangelas and "eat the old one" (participate in ritual cannibalism), contributed to the further erosion of the state.[91]

When an unknown sekulu called "Chindunduma-wa-Ndumisa-Ofeka" (Ndunduma) was nominated in 1888, the state was ready to collapse. In his short time as olosoma (1888–90), Ndunduma's pro-traditionalist, anti-foreign policy and opposition to social mobility heightened even further the tensions among the ruling lineages and alienated many freeborn and slaves. This situation created a vacuum in the ruling lineages, it led to the first direct Portuguese military intervention in the Ovimbundu kingdoms since the eighteenth century, and resulted in their conquest and absorption into the colony of Angola by 1904.

Hoping to broaden his base among the traditionalists and to restrict the activities of outsiders, Ndunduma began his reign by reinstating raids, which threatened the interests of both Ovimbundu and Portuguese. He also harassed and expelled the Protestant missionaries and subjected Silva Porto, the official Portuguese representative, to public humiliations.[92] His policies not only failed to broaden his support inside Viye but also alienated Portuguese traders and officials, Protestant missionaries, and rulers of neighboring states, including Ekwikwi in Mbailundu who feared that Ndunduma's actions could derail his own pro-Portuguese policies.

In January, 1890, Ndunduma, with little popular support, expelled the members of a Portuguese expeditionary force. This had camped in Viye before making its way to Cubango in eastern Angola to begin Portuguese occupation and forestall British inroads. He also refused to acknowledge the new representative, Martin Teixeira da Silva, who replaced Silva Porto, and harangued the old trader Silva Porto by accusing him of keeping the ruler ignorant of Portuguese plans to incorporate Viye into the colony. Although Ndunduma had many detractors, his pro-Ovimbundu stand resonated among important segments of the Ovimbundu in neighboring states, especially Wambu and Ciyaka, whose people were regarded as bandits and anti-Portuguese. Ndunduma's actions thus directly undermined Portuguese overlordship and impelled them to take action against him.

The Portuguese invasion of Viye in the middle of 1890 was a direct response to the suicide of Silva Porto in March 1890. The bankrupt and disillusioned former slave trader had wrapped himself in a Portuguese flag and blown himself up. The fever-pitch jingoism which this event generated in Portugal pushed reluctant officials to take up arms against the Ovimbundu. They blamed Ndunduma for Porto's suicide and for damaging Portuguese prestige in the region. The official plan of the Portuguese Overseas Minister was not limited to the Viye operation: Artur de Paiva, the leader of the expedition, was ordered to "imprison the *soba* and substitute another as head of state and . . . militarily occupy the region and conquer the native tribes."[93]

The Ovimbundu did not "rise with one mind" against the Portuguese.[94] As the expeditionary forces, consisting of more than a thousand regular metropolitan troops, Angolan and Mozambican soldiers, South African mercenaries, and locally recruited porters, made their way to Viye, they found little resistance from a population intimidated by their terrorist tactics. In Viye, where Ndunduma could muster only two thousand soldiers to defend the capital out of a potential fighting population of twenty thousand, the invaders quickly demolished the fortified *ombala* with their modern artillery and automatic machine guns, and overpowered the lightly armed and ineffective soldiers who were defending it.[95]

No doubt his military weakness made Ndunduma's stance unpopular among influential sections of the population in Viye. When he sought refuge in Ngangela after the bombardment of the *ombala*, the leading men in Viye had no trouble in putting together a force of a thousand men with eight hundred rifles to bring him back and turn him over to the Portuguese, who sent him and his close associates into exile in São Tomé. Ndunduma died there in 1903.[96] Neighboring rulers such as Ekwikwi II also remained aloof from the events in Viye and hostile to Ndunduma, refusing to support his initial anti-Portuguese campaign. Indeed, Ekwikwi threatened to invade Viye if harm came to the Portuguese representative and urged the Portuguese authorities to discipline Viye, so that the Ovimbundu would not lose respect "for the maniputo" (the Portuguese king).[97] Ekwikwi's position not only demonstrated his diplomatic skills, but also reveals much about Ovimbundu (and, more generally African) theories of political power at the time, when the concept of "respect" for duly constituted rulers was sacrosanct.

Even before the power of the ruling lineage in Viye began to disintegrate in the mid-1880s, Portuguese colonial policy had undergone some fundamental shifts. By the 1870s the Portuguese were reluctant to respond to Ovimbundu overtures for a greater official Portuguese presence in the kingdoms. By 1890, however, they were committed to follow a more aggressive African policy. This change was in direct response to the theory of effective occupation the Berlin Conference, dominated by Portugal's European competitors, imposed on countries with claims to African territories. The Ovimbundu highlands figured prominently in their plans to legalize their Angolan boundaries and forestall German, Belgian, and British designs. Their old relations with the ruling Ovimbundu lineages had to give way to the new imperial demands.[98]

With the 1890 conquest, the Portuguese began to implement their proven colonial techniques in the region. Although they allowed the electors in Viye to nominate a new soba (the Portuguese term for olosoma) after Ndunduma's exile, political power shifted from the *ombala* to the new military fort they had established at Silva Porto's old residence at Belmont. Here a military representative, the *capitão-mor*, supported by a small force, worked to implement Portuguese policies not only in Bié (the Portuguese spelling of Viye) but also in the still nominally independent states.

The Portuguese faced few obstacles in Bié, especially after the death of Ekwikwi in 1893 and the subsequent weakening of the control of the ruling lineages over their kingdoms as a result of similar pressures pitting traditionalists against pro-Portuguese factions there.[99] Thus while the ruling factions in each state fought over titles, Portuguese representatives consolidated their power in the region. They set up rudimentary administrative structures at the forts, and the *capitães–mores* who manned them slowly took over some of the functions of the olosomas and sekulus. They relied on the small military force they kept at the fort to force titleholders to send porters, to respond to official requests, to intervene in the internecine conflicts between factions, and to keep the caravan routes open. In this way they further eroded the authority of the ruling lineages.

Between 1890 and 1902, Portuguese presence expanded in both Bié and Bailundu (the Portuguese spelling of Mbailundu), as traders, settlers, and adventurers from the colony flocked to the highlands. While the *capitão-mor* set about establishing a rudimentary administration, the settlers and traders competed with the Ovimbundu in the caravan trade and in supplying the demand for agricultural products at the coast. At the same time, both Catholic and Protestant missionaries expanded their work in the states, and soldiers implemented new orders. The growing power of the outsiders resulted in a steady decline in the power and privileges of the ruling lineages.

By 1902 the Portuguese, through the *capitão-mor*, exercised a wide range of powers including levying tribute, demanding labor, enforcing military conscription, and ensuring security and order on the caravan routes to end brigandage. The *capitão-mor* had not only supplanted the ruling lineages in controlling their states, but he had become the most powerful political figure in the entire central highlands. In addition, the Portuguese had expanded their power beyond the highlands, conquering and integrating into the colony parts of the vast Chokwe-Lunda region which Ovimbundu caravans had first pioneered.[100] While the Portuguese authorities tried to create the economic and political environment for their advancement, the Ovimbundu states collapsed, and the commercial revolution they had spearheaded slowly began to decay.

Establishing Portuguese hegemony after the conquest of Bié proved to be a protracted affair which did not end until 1904. Along the way, however, the Portuguese found as many collaborators in the other Ovimbundu kingdoms as resisters. In Ndulu and Ngalangi, for example, the ruling lineages never openly rejected the growing Portuguese influence, and some members worked closely with the *capitães-mores*. The collaboration of the ruling factions in the two kingdoms was undoubtedly easier since their ruling lineages had not been dominant players in the commodity trade or in the regions' politics. Besides, the relationship between the Portuguese and ruling lineages of Ngalangi (who had converted to Catholicism) was more like the classic Luso/African model found in the Kimbundu-speaking region than the relationship between the Portuguese and Bailundu, Huambu (the Portuguese spelling of Wambu), and Bié, for example. In these latter states, where important segments of the ruling lineages and their supporters were deeply involved in the trade and exercised some forms of sovereignty over smaller states like Civulu, the ruling lineages remained hostile to all foreigners, denying both officials and traders access to their states, and taking up arms against the Portuguese.

Thus, many of the resources the Portuguese invested in the central highlands between 1890 and 1904 did not go into setting up a colonial administration but went instead into maintaining security and putting down several Ovimbundu uprisings. The Portuguese struggled relentlessly against Ovimbundu guerrilla bands, whose members conducted raids against caravans and supply convoys. The most formidable threat to Portuguese power from the Ovimbundu was the "Bailundu war" of 1902, when significant numbers of the leadership and the people rebelled. Although the Ovimbundu lost the war, this uprising was the first pan-Ovimbundu attempt to put an end to the Portuguese presence in the highlands and rebuild the old political order under the leadership of surviving members of the preconquest lineages.

The 1902 Bailundu war was led by the traditionalist segments of the ruling lineages in Mbailundu and Wambu, who resented the Portuguese presence and the loss of their own sovereignty. They also had the support of a cross section of the population in the still independent kingdoms who had been enriched by trade and wanted to go back to the preconquest status quo. There were several reasons why the war united leaders and peoples from different Ovimbundu states. Part of the explanation lay in the grudge which some members of the Bailundu ruling lineages bore against the Portuguese, whom they regarded as responsible for the deteriorating state of their affairs in the region. This feeling was especially evident after 1896 when the Portuguese invaded Mbailundu, seized the *ombala* and made it into a fort, and foisted a pro-Portuguese olosoma onto the population. Some of the leaders of the 1902 revolt were men who had fled to the mountains of Bimbe after this event and carried out acts of sabotage against the Portuguese.

In Wambu and Ciyaka, where the ruling lineages were still in power and where there was a long legacy of anti-Portuguese sentiment, many people also joined the revolt. Indeed, when the *capitão-mor* of Bailundu organized a military campaign against Wambu in 1896, Samakaka of Wambu, identified as one of the principal leaders of the 1902 revolt, led the traditionalist forces in publicly denouncing Portuguese intervention and the local Ovimbundu collaborators. He and his followers kept up a steady campaign of economic sabotage against the traders, and political harassment of the *capitão-mor*. They openly defied his orders, and Samakaka several times boasted that although the "maniputo" had conquered Viye and Mbailundu, "in our lands he cannot enter."[101]

The 1902 rebellion also had widespread support among freeborn commoners, especially in Bailundu, Wambu, Soque, and Ciyaka. After the expansion of Portuguese authority in 1890, the economic prospects and social aspirations of many freeborn people were frustrated, as the growing demands of *capitão-mores*, settlers, and missionaries threatened the commoners' dominance in the trade. Many ordinary people resented the newcomers who were demanding cheap local labor (porters and unfree laborers). Before 1890, many freeborn commoners simply refused to work for the outsiders and continued their own trading activities. By 1902, however, they were finding it more difficult to avoid the demands of Portuguese traders, who had the support of the *capitão-mor*. Many ordinary villagers in Bailundu who participated in the 1902 war resented the growing competition and abuse they suffered from Portuguese traders.[102] They, like the olosomas and sekulus who led the uprising, hoped to return to the old days when they had few obligations to the state and little competition from outside.

Although members of the ruling lineages from eight Ovimbundu kingdoms (Wambu, Mbailundu, Soque, Civulu, Civanda, Ngalangi, Cipeyo, and Sambu), with an estimated 40,000 men under arms, were involved in the 1902 uprising, the Ovimbundu lost the war. The collapse of the resistance effort was due in large part to the massive show of men and arms with which the Portuguese put down the revolt in order to keep the area within the colony. The 1902 campaign was one of the largest military operations in southern Angola that the Portuguese had undertaken in over a century. In a three-pronged attack that included more than six hundred metropolitan troops, thousands of porters, Boer wagons, and the latest 70 mm mountain guns, the highly mobile Portuguese units quickly outmaneuvered and outgunned the Ovimbundu armies in their mountain redoubts. The army's intimidation of the civilian population with terror tactics (which included burning villages) is a further reason why the resistance collapsed.[103]

The uprising also failed because of shortcomings on the Ovimbundu side. These included inadequate military planning, training, or defense, the absence of a unified Ovimbundu offensive due to local, regional, and other cleavages, and the continuing ideological differences between traditionalists and pro-trade factions among the Ovimbundu leaders. The actions of Ovimbundu collaborators and missionaries, who supplied food to the besieged Portuguese fort at Bailundu and provided the invading forces with crucial intelligence about the rebellion, also explain why the uprising failed.[104]

The experiences of one leader of the rebellion illustrate how factionalism, the intrigues of collaborators and missionaries, and a yet undeveloped pan-Ovimbundu identity undermined the attempt to show a united front against the Portuguese. Before the 1902 Bailundu war against the Portuguese, the ruling lineages enforced their political authority on their own subjects and on some of the neighboring states through a combination of force, the awarding of titles, marriages, and their status as members of a noble group. The attempt to transform this into some kind of larger symbolic "Ovimbundu" unity made little sense to most members of the ruling lineages in the individual states or to their subjects. Mutu-ya-Kavela, a counselor of olosoma Hungungulu of Mbailundu and one of the most competent military strategists on the Ovimbundu side, is a case in point. He failed to generate the widespread support of the Mbailundu leadership and people. At a crucial point during the uprising (when the Portuguese stormed the *ombala*), the electors rejected Mutu-ya-Kavela's bid to become olosoma, because he did not have the right lineage connections. Some of his detractors betrayed his guerrilla base to the Portuguese captain Paes

Brandão, who attacked the camp and captured and killed Mutu-ya-Kavela. Although his supporters mounted a counter-attack against the Portuguese fort, they were routed and Mbailundu's resistance crumbled.[105]

Neither was Samakaka of Wambu allowed to play a leading role in the uprising. He was rejected in his attempt to be nominated as olosoma because of his beginnings as a humble *pombeiro*. Wambu's Olosoma Libongo who was the legitimate ruler was eventually captured and sent to Luanda, along with thirteen other leaders of the uprising. In Civanda, Joaquim Camcheque, one of the leading sekulus, betrayed the olosoma to the Portuguese in return for 100 *reis*.[106]

Conclusion

The 1902 war brought an end to the preconquest Ovimbundu kingdoms. However, as the Portuguese state took shape from 1902, local European officials kept many features of the Ovimbundu state system alive by incorporating them into the emerging colonial administrative structure. In order to adjust to the colonial state between 1902 and 1926, the Ovimbundu people gradually replaced the local/lineage loyalties and identities of the preconquest period with a pan-Ovimbundu identity, and Ovimbundu language and culture became potent forces in shaping a new identity.

2

THE POLITICS OF PACIFICATION AND COLONIZATION: THE EARLY COLONIAL STATE, 1904–1926

Introduction

Between the 1902 Bailundo War and 1926, when António de Oliveira Salazar established the *Estado Novo* (New State), the central highlands presented special problems for the staff of the Portuguese Overseas Office and the military and government officials in Angola. The challenge for the state was to control those elements of the various kingdoms who had been enriched by the commercialization of commodity trade and early peasant initiatives, and who now sought ways to counter the state. Throughout the period the colonial government—first under the monarchy (up to 1910) and then the Republic (1910–26)—relied heavily on military initiatives and sheer force, through an alliance of local officials and settlers, to advance its policies. Its main successes in the highlands were the completion of the conquest, the expansion of the colonial bureaucracy, and the introduction of limited economic initiatives. Despite these, however, state/society relations in the highlands were developing as a dynamic process in which various segments of the former kingdoms adapted their civic/local institutions and created new ones in the struggle against the state.

Theory and Reality in Central Angola

The most important element in the Portuguese program was the military emphasis, both at the formal level of colonial policy and by necessity in the subjugation strategies that officials followed. The conquest of the central highlands between 1890 and 1904 had not been not an isolated event, but was part of a plan to extend Portuguese military rule to regions of Angola that were still under African control. These included traditional African client states like Kongo and Kasanje, and independent regions such as the Chokwe-Lunda lands east of the central highlands, the Libolo-Nsele region between the Kimbundu and the Ovimbundu highlands, and the Kwanyama lands to the south. The "pacification" and subjugation strategies which formed the colonial thrust continued until the end of the First World War. During this period, local officials also laid down the foundations of a Portuguese administrative structure.

In addition, to get access to the population, colonial authorities hoped to build a revenue base and create conditions which would advance Portuguese settler interests in the region. As in most other recently conquered African territories, social planning involving the health, religious, and educational development of the conquered population received little attention.

The conquered peoples of the various Ovimbundu kingdoms did not immediately conform to Portuguese expectations, as the colonial state's long period of gestation after the 1904 conquest allowed some of them to seek access to the levers of political power. Thus, although the conquest and the expansion of a colonial bureaucracy meant that an increasing number of Ovimbundu had to face the administrative, fiscal, and labor demands of the colonial state, until the mid-1920s many Ovimbundu were not directly affected by these developments. For these latter, responding to the continuing intrusion of the world economy, and adapting their beliefs and values to those of the Catholic and Protestant missionaries who came in increasing numbers were more pertinent issues than Portuguese colonialism. They were able to exercise this autonomy because the Portuguese administration in the highlands remained financially and bureaucratically weak up to 1926, and officials failed to implement most of the labor and fiscal regulations which would have dislocated hundreds of thousands of Ovimbundu. In fact, Ovimbundu involvement in the colonial economy increased as the demand for their agricultural products grew. For these Ovimbundu peasant producers, Christianity and the transformation of culture presented the appearance of progress, even as their economic and political options narrowed.

In 1904, as the Portuguese moved to establish the modern boundaries of Angola after the conquest of the central highlands, their weakness and the exaggerated notions of Ovimbundu power shaped their attempts to ensure that these boundaries would include the recently conquered Ovimbundu kingdoms. For more than a decade after the war, local authorities and settlers were convinced that the Ovimbundu were planning another revolt. Rumors detailing plans for the revolt circulated in the local newspapers, and one report sent to the governor noted that despite the ban on Africans purchasing weapons, the Ovimbundu were the best-armed Africans in the colony, possessing an estimated 150,000 guns, and were hostile to Portuguese rule.[1]

In reality, however, in the early years after conquest the concern of many of the remaining Ovimbundu rulers to find ways of gaining access to the levers of political power led them to collaborate with the Portuguese. Ovimbundu military expertise and labor helped the Portuguese to achieve their military objectives in central and southern Angola. This allowed the Portuguese to shift their focus from the Ovimbundu to the problem of subjugating the peoples northwest and south of the highlands. The still independent status of these peoples made a mockery of Portuguese control.

The Portuguese found Ovimbundu collaborators among the hand-picked sekulus and sobas whose nomination as leaders they had promoted. These individuals provided men and local expertise to help the Portuguese conquer other Angolan peoples and states. Their actions, which recalled the Portuguese-Ovimbundu collaboration in the preceding period, created a colonial precedent for the Ovimbundu-Portuguese alliance in the decades to come.

Ovimbundu assistance was crucial in the eleven military engagements the Portuguese led against Africans in central and southern Angola between 1904 and 1918. The 1915 southern campaign against the Kwanyama was part of World War One against the Germans and was the largest such operation, with some 5,000 Ovimbundu serving as conscripted porters.[2] The Portuguese also recruited Ovimbundu as mercenaries. In 1917, for example, local Portuguese officials recruited more than 2,000 Ovimbundu "auxiliaries" who fought with colonial forces in the Nsele-Amboin campaign. This campaign was one of the most brutal of the period, and the terror and destruction it caused among the civilian population were indelibly imprinted in the memory of survivors. Years later the terror was remembered with the dreaded phrase, "To see a Bailundu is to see death."[3] The Portuguese victory in the Nsele-Amboim region stabilized the political situation within Angola at a crucial point, while their success against

German–South African threats secured Portuguese sovereignty in southern Angola.

As they were completing the conquest, the Portuguese were also making tentative attempts to adapt the political and economic policies on which they had come to rely in governing the older parts of the colony to the recently pacified Ovimbundu region. Here also, although their aims conflicted with those of their Ovimbundu allies, the status quo was more one of collaboration than of conflict.

José Mendes Ribeiro Norton de Matos, who served as High Commissioner for Angola from 1912 to 1915 and 1921 to 1923, came closest to articulating a colonial policy at variance with the expectations of the various Ovimbundu populations. In outlining the long-term objective of colonization, he stressed that after the necessary violent military occupation, when collaborating local leaders had replaced resisters who had been imprisoned or killed, the essentials for a rational system of occupation were

> general disarmament, the obligation to paid employment in works of the state, the facility of recruiting well paid workers for private works, military recruitment, agricultural and commercial development of the region occupied, the collection of the hut tax and the necessary transformation of *capitães-mores* for civil circumscription.[4]

As Overseas Minister and High Commissioner of Angola, Norton de Matos pushed his colonial objectives. As a result, by the mid-1920s Angola was much more an integral part of Portugal[5] than during the century before, and his ideas continued to affect developments in Angola long after his time.

Colonial officials in the highlands failed to achieve all of de Matos' goals, but their actions did lead to a real colonial presence which brought revenues to the state, set up the mechanisms for the growth of a state-controlled labor force, and initiated a white settler policy in the region. Even with these few accomplishments, however, the Portuguese relied on local Ovimbundu institutions, and retained Ovimbundu collaborators whose aims were not always consistent with those of the state.

Creating Colonial Order

Towards a New Bureaucracy

The Portuguese took several important steps towards replacing the administrative structure of the Ovimbundu kingdoms with their own model.

This began soon after the 1902 war when all the former Ovimbundu king-doms became part of the province of Benguela (which until 1910 consisted of the districts, Benguela and Bié, each with its own governor).[6] Further administrative changes took place between 1912 and 1926, as the Lunda and Choke regions became provinces, thus extending Angola's frontier to the borders of Northern Rhodesia and of Katanga Province in the Belgian Congo. The establishment of the colonial boundaries in the east connected the various Ovimbundu populations politically to the Lundas, Chokwes, Luvales, and other peoples with whom they had maintained the trade con-nections initiated during the period of commodity trade.[7]

The administrative restructuring within the highlands, which involved establishing a Portuguese administrative structure over the Ovimbundu one, also affected the various Ovimbundu population groups. The new Portuguese structure which took shape after 1910, and which made the bureaucratic divisions in the highlands more like those of rest of the colony, integrated the formerly independent Ovimbundu kingdoms of Viye, Mbailundu, Wambu, Ndulu and others into the three provinces of Huambo, Bié, and Benguela. These large administrative units were subdivided into smaller divisions, variously called *concelhos* or *circumscrições civis*, each headed by a Portuguese administrator. Other changes followed, and the military positions of the *capitães-mores* became *postos civis* (civil posts), and *chefes de posto* became *chefes* or civil servants. All *chefes* had a corps of African sol-diers and policemen (*cipaes*) who were part of the Portuguese bureaucracy.

Below this Portuguese structure were the older Ovimbundu adminis-trative divisions some of which the Portuguese attached to their own, but with some important changes. The Portuguese abolished the kingdoms and districts. They took over the *ombalas* and made the *ombalas* or loca-tions near to them the capitals of *concelhos*, and constructed new *postos civis* on the site of, or near to the residence of, every soba or important sekulu, thus linking them to the Portuguese *chefe* and the *posto civil*. Each *posto civil* incorporated up to 100 or more villages. The groups of villages were called *sobado* or *sobeta*. The *chefes* regarded the hand-picked sobas and im-portant sekulus (sometimes called *sobas grandes*), whom they allowed to carry the traditional titles, as the representatives of the *sobados* or *sobetas*. In this way, the Portuguese integrated the sekulus and sobas into the colonial bureaucracy and achieved one of their objectives, that is, using loyal sobas and sekulus to maintain control over the rest of the population. Without the traditional prestige of the former rulers, the new men whom the *chefes* nominated as sekulus and sobas could not serve as a magnet for anti-Portu-guese activities. They did, however, bring their expertise (knowledge of local languages, law, and customs) which helped to consolidate Portuguese rule in the region and allowed the new men to be near to the new levers of power.[8]

The early colonial bureaucracy departed from the old system of the Ovimbundu kingdoms in some fundamental ways. For example, in comparison with the precolonial period, when olosomas and provincial rulers found it difficult to impose their demands on the sekulus who had more local sympathies, the new *chefes* exercised more power than their Ovimbundu predecessors. With the power to remove recalcitrant Ovimbundu officials or physically brutalize them, the *chefes* were able to get sobas and sekulus to comply with their demands. Moreover, by intervening in the election of sobas and sekulus they effectively weakened the bonds which linked the sobas and sekulus to particular communities. These collaborating Ovimbundu representatives gained their positions more from their willingness to go along with the colonial administration than from local lineage and other sympathies. Thus, the *chefe* was the real political force.

In other ways, however, the system had much in common with the Ovimbundu system it replaced. For instance, most *sobados* conformed to the small districts in the former Ovimbundu states, albeit with a much smaller population—no more than five hundred to six hundred people. In some cases, however, the authorities allowed collaborating sobas to represent as many as two thousand people.[9] Even though sobas and sekulus had to win the approval of the *chefe*, they were often members of the precolonial ruling lineages who had proved their loyalty to the government.[10] Ovimbundu village organization also differed little before the conquest. *Chefes* conducted most of their work with the sobas and sekulus through a translator and used Ovimbundu rather than Portuguese customs. Neither Portuguese officials nor Ovimbundu representatives were required to know each other's language, laws, or customs. Sobas and sekulus continued to handle day-to-day business, hear cases through their own courts (except where customary law ran counter to "civilized" [Portuguese] civil codes),[11] distributed land, settled land use claims, received customary gifts, and imposed fines and fees on villagers.

Unlike the situation in the preconquest period, however, *chefes* held the real power. With their small contingent of conscripted soldiers (sobas and sekulus could not keep retainers), they could order the latter to recruit workers, collect taxes, conscript soldiers, and in other ways relay colonial demands to the population.[12] From 1911, *chefes* could call on the *cipaes* (African policemen) and soldiers to assist them in enforcing labor requirements, collecting taxes, taking the census,[13] and ensuring that sekulus and sobas carried out official orders.[14] This administrative arrangement allowed the Portuguese to extend their control over most segments of the Ovimbundu population.[15]

In 1914, the Portuguese attempted the first major overhaul of the system by establishing the Department of Native Affairs (*Departamento dos Negocios Indigenas*) to coordinate native labor policy,[16] and to reduce some of the autonomy of the *chefes*, sobas, and sekulus.[17] Although it undertook a few cadastral surveys and gathered data on the political divisions, judicial institutions, commercial practices, and the social and cultural differences among the various African peoples, this department's work did not lead to any real changes in the bureaucracy in the highlands.[18] After 1918, the department became moribund, and sobas and sekulus continued to carry on much as before.[19]

Taxation and Labor

In the years immediately after 1902, the Portuguese did little to interfere with Ovimbundu sovereignty with regard to customary law and social practices, since their priority was to avert the collapse of the colonial economy. The taxation and labor initiatives they pursued, however, directly affected significant numbers of Ovimbundu producers and traders. Even though the authorities presented the initiatives in political terms, the result of them was to undermine the Ovimbundu population economically. This was a critical step in changing the beneficiaries of the trade by using the state's legislative power to redistribute profits to itself and to favored Portuguese groups.

The first tax collection legislation that affected the Ovimbundu was passed in 1906, when the government imposed a hut tax (*imposto de cubatas*) on Ovimbundu who lived near civil posts. The tax was not much different from the labor dues and goods that the precolonial leaders had required, and it gave the colonial regime revenues equal to those that rulers of the precolonial kingdoms had received. The law required men to pay a tax of 600 *milreis* on every hut that they owned, which was in effect a tax on women and dependents, for polygamous men had to pay taxes on the houses of each of their wives. Although sekulus and sobas were personally exempt, they had to pay the taxes for their dependents (wives, servants, clients, and slaves).[20]

After the Republic was established in 1910, officials in the Overseas Ministry pushed for higher taxes and a stricter tax collection policy, stressing that colonial authorities must link payment of the hut tax to capitulation to the state.[21] Norton de Matos expressed the new policy best in a

1913 memo, in which he argued that the purpose of the tax was more political than financial, since it "ought to be considered as a final act of occupation, pacification and administration of the regions of the interior."[22]

The push to use the collection of revenue as the starting point of sovereignty was evident in the four increases in the taxes between 1906 and 1926. In 1913, when a monetary reform changed the currency unit from *reis* (which had royalist implications) to *escudos*, the tax went from 600 *milreis* to 3 *escudos* (equal to 3 *reis* or a fivefold increase). In 1919 the amount was raised to 5 *escudos*,[23] and from 1919 to 1926 it fluctuated between 40 and 80 *escudos*.[24] Even with the changes in the value of the *escudo* between 1919 and 1926, these increases were steep for the average Ovimbundu household; they did not replace existing taxes but were intended to make the population prostrate before the administration. They also hit the population at a time of great economic downturn.

Linking taxation to political subordination was not the only motivation behind the taxes, because the Portuguese also needed money for use in extending their administration.[25] Thus, after pacification in 1918, the tax became a personal tax on African men and women, still at increased amounts even after women were removed from the tax rolls in 1925.[26]

These polocies signaled a real change from 1904. Between 1919 and the mid-1920s, the regime succeeded in raising the number of Ovimbundus who paid taxes from 197,204 to 279,900.[27] The taxes actually collected in the 1920s, however, suggested that no more than 15 to 20 percent of the eligible males actually paid them.[28] Even with such a low level of compliance, income derived from taxes came to represent a significant portion of local receipts, the rest coming from tariffs, business taxes, and fines.[29] Ovimbundu taxpayers paid a substantial part of the taxes collected in the colony as a whole.

In line with the strategy of other colonial regimes to transfer revenue from colonial subjects to the colonial state through labor control, the Portuguese implemented several labor initiatives. These also affected Ovimbundu agriculture, since this was the occupation of the majority of the people. Since the central highlands were the most densely populated region of Angola (in 1914, the population in the highlands totaled well over one million, making the Ovimbundu the largest ethnic group in the entire colony)[30] and the people were involved in porterage, trading, agriculture, and other labor-intensive activities, competition for labor in the highlands was intense. Officials pushed to promote state-private collaboration in labor recruiting, because they believed that this could bring huge financial gains.

The labor policy the regime implemented in the highlands was not new, since Portugal had a long history of using corvée and slave labor in the regions of Angola they had alrady controlled. As early as 1899, forced labor legislation had been on the books in all of Portuguese Angola. The basic philosophy underlying the labor laws was that conquered peoples had a legal obligation to work, stated as a moral premise, but in fact meaning an obligation to work for the state or its chosen beneficiaries.[31] Before 1910, slaves—called *libertos* and *serviçaes* after the 1880s—comprised a significant percentage of the Africans recruited in Portuguese Angola. After the Republic abolished slavery in Portuguese Africa in 1910, a system of *corvée* labor replaced it.

The establishment of the Department of Native Affairs in 1914 was another step in bringing African labor under state control. Its major role in the highlands was to classify the African population into "civilized" or assimilated (*assimilado*), and "non-civilized" or nonassimilated (*não-assimilado*) to facilitate recruiting and to designate who were collaborators. "Non-civilized" Africans were supposed to earn their "civilized" status by working for the state or for a settler.[32] Although a 1921 decree outlawed forced labor in the colony, it remained in place in the highlands.

Here, local authorities attempted to use the labor legislation to divert labor from Ovimbundu households to state and private concerns in the highlands and elsewhere in the colony which suffered from serious labor shortages.[33] They assessed each *sobado* or group of villages, and came up with a quota of workers who, they decided, could be withdrawn without damaging agricultural production.[34] The workers were then sent out to state projects and settler businesses.[35]

Economic Initiatives

Besides administrative restructuring, new taxation, and new labor policies, colonial officials made tentative steps to promote the economic development of the highlands under state and private European control. This involved improving infrastructure, promoting commerce, and encouraging settler agriculture. The intention was to alter market forces in order to create an environment in which the state and favored Portuguese settlers would benefit.[36] This was not, as some apologists for the Portuguese have argued, to encourage "liberal" or market–oriented policies, but to undermine the Ovimbundu role in the local economy.

The first state priority was the modernization of the infrastructure to reduce the dependence on human porterage. Colonial officials took the first steps towards solving this problem in 1902 by granting a concession to the British investor Robert Williams, who had links to South African, Rhodesian, and Katangan investors and who agreed to build a railroad through central Angola.[37] Construction of the railroad from the Benguela–Lobito port started in 1902, reached Huambo in 1911, crossed Bié by 1926, and reached the Northern Rhodesia/Katanga frontier in 1929.[38] Local authorities helped recruit laborers for the project, and provided *corvée* labor with which to construct the network of feeder roads and numerous bridges.

But the main concern of officials was to reserve the central highlands for Portuguese settlement and they frustrated the attempts of the owners of the Benguela Railway Company made to develop plantations and launch stock–raising ventures in the highlands.[39] Having already opened up portions of southern Mozambique to British and South African capital, the Overseas Office was under pressure from metropolitan interests to retain Angola for Portuguese capital and settlers.[40]

The first attempt at attracting white settlers occurred in 1909, when a commission earmarked the entire highlands for European settlement, stressing the region's temperate climate and fertile soil.[41] From then until the mid–1920s, local officials used Ovimbundu corvée laborers to construct the city of Nova Lisboa (now Huambo) and several smaller towns all along the railroad, and to build a network of roads to connect them to each other and to the railroad.[42] Although at a high human cost to the Ovimbundu, by 1926 the policy had resulted in one of the best transportation centers in the colony and a city surpassing, in the view of many, the old colonial capital of Luanda.[43]

Legislation enacted to control trade also advanced the regime's goal of bringing all economic activities under Portuguese state and settler control. The section of the legislation that affected the Ovimbundu directly required all traders to purchase commercial licenses (*guias de marcha*) in order to conduct business or travel from one area of the highlands to another. In fact the policy made most Ovimbundu trading activities illegal, since European traders received most of the *guias* issued.[44] The laws that restricted human porterage to areas outside the range of wagons, railroads, and trucks (all areas where settlers circulated) were intended to change the natural force of the market away from favoring independent Ovimbundu traders and agriculturalists towards strengthening the state and the settlers. The laws did not cover Ovimbundu who worked for settlers or the state.[45]

Initially, the new directives did not affect many producers, who continued to carry their goods to the railroad and avoid Portuguese "bush" traders (who set up shop in the villages to purchase products direct from the peasants).[46] Before long, however, the old methods of transport (caravan, tipoia, and bush car)[47] which the Ovimbundu had monopolized gave way to the bicycle, motorcycle, car, train and truck, all of which the state, private enterprises and settlers owned and operated. No Ovimbundu could compete in the new transport market and their economic options became narrower and narrower.

Beyond the State

Ovimbundu Producers

The agricultural experience of the Ovimbundu under the Portuguese colonial state up to the mid–1920s parallels some of the experiences of Africans in other colonies. In settler colonies such as Kenya, the Belgian Congo, and the Rhodesias, for example, Africans were initially able to maintain sufficient economic leverage and social distance from the colonial regime to exercise some local autonomy, despite the loss of their political independence.[48] An assessment of the economic, political, and social experiences of the Ovimbundu during the first two decades of Portuguese rule in the highlands suggests a similar situation. The major contradiction here was the conflicting interests of the state during a period when the objective was still military, and of Ovimbundu factions, especially the dynamic peasant sector in which producers were still responding to an expanding world economy.

The rise of peasant agriculture among the Ovimbundu—especially the peoples of the former kingdoms of Mbailundu, Viye and Wambu and Ndulu—demonstrates the resilience of the population in the face of state imperatives which sought to impose a new order in the highlands from 1902 to the mid–1920s. The dynamics of peasant development in the area lay in the transformation which household production had undergone since the 1840s, and especially during the period of the rubber boom when women and slaves produced agricultural surpluses to satisfy the demands of caravans and coastal consumers. Beyond that, the demand for grains during the First World War and the simultaneous collapse of rubber prices on the world market confirmed the region's status as one of mixed subsistence and market–oriented farming, as men entered agricultural production on a massive scale.[49] Railway propaganda and the expertise and training provided provided by missionaries to converts were also important.

Maize, the crop responsible for the transformation, began to appear as a significant export from central Angola only after 1913—only half a ton was exported in 1901, and exports remained low for the next decade. Exports increased to 13,000 tons in 1914 and continued to rise.[50] The local sale of ground maize (*fuba*) in the highlands and coastal ports also increased. By the mid–1920s, between 150,000 and 200,000 hectares (or about 20 percent of the cultivable land in the district of Benguela, which included the former kingdoms of Wambu and Mbailundu) were planted with maize.[51] In 1925 Angola exported 25,703 tons of maize, double the amount exported in 1914.[52] The Ovimbundu region was responsible for most of the maize exported.

The soaring price of maize in the central highlands was primarily responsible for the increase. While in 1914, 15 kilograms of maize brought the producer between 30 and 37 *centavos*, in the mid–1920s the same amount of maize sold for 5 *escudos*. This was a substantial increase, even in view of the rampant inflation that the colony was experiencing. According to reports from the mid–1920s, even unripe and poorly selected maize sold for 4 *escudos* per 15 kilograms.[53]

Maize production increased without the Ovimbundu receiving expert advice from Portuguese officials, and without much change in farming methods. In the first part of the period, women, mostly descendants of captives brought to the highlands as slaves from the 1870s, were responsible for the increase. Eyewitness accounts of the transformation suggest that farming for the market by women was the norm. In 1908 Alexandre Malheiro commented on the farming methods in the region of Viye which he visited; he observed that farming was "exclusively left to women," who prepared the land and had a large enough harvest that they were able to meet basic village consumption needs and sell the surplus to settlers who used it to feed their *serviçaes*.[54] An Italian agricultural commission, led by Dino Taruffi who visited the highlands in 1916, to gauge the region's suitability as a site for Italian settlers confirmed this. Taruffi noted that women had farms of 10 to 12 hectares in size, and planted maize, beans, manioc, potatoes and legumes; and he expressed amazement at the high yields they obtained.[55]

Women's involvement in both subsistence and commercial farming continued when men took to farming on a massive scale after 1914, when rubber prices fell from a high of 2.75 *escudos* per kilogram to .75 *escudos*.[56] Many Ovimbundu men had relied on their income from the sale of rubber to meet their tax obligations, so they went into farming as an alternative. Women also exercised some control over the land they farmed. In 1914 the

Protestant missionary John T. Tucker paid the mother of Pastor Macedo Mbonga Chesungu, a convert, "two eighths of cloth plus an *elasola*" (a length of cloth measuring four yards)[57] for the purchase of her "worn–out field" (*ochipembe*) on which he intended to build the future Means School for girls.[58]

By the 1920s, more land was devoted to farming and men were working alongside women in the fields. Each household planted an average of 2.5 hectares of maize interspersed with beans, but the sexual division of labor remained the same, and women continued to use the method of staggered planting. Although most households harvested anywhere from 600 to 900 kilograms per hectare,[59] some harvested as much 2,290 kilograms of maize and 210 kilograms of beans in excess of household needs.[60]

Some of the most successful male farmers were Ovimbundu Protestants who had benefited from the agricultural training and advice they received from Protestant missionaries, the main providers of agricultural training available to the Ovimbundu. The access Protestant converts had to high–yielding grain, to information on crop diversity, and to training on the use of the plow enabled Protestant peasant families to prosper.[61] The only role the state played was that of tax collector and labor recruiter.

Thus, although African peasant production and settler farming offered a more fruitful alternative for the state to achieve its goals, the authorities pursued plans which concentrated on heavy taxation of peasant farmers and supporting large estates and public works through corvée labor. This strategy did not work and ultimately was at variance with constructive African peasant development.

Missionary reports provide some insight into the effects of government taxation policy. In 1918, for example, when the tax went to 5 *escudos* in addition to the one month's *corvée* labor,[62] men easily raised the money. Women and girls, who were still responsible for feeding the household, found it harder to meet their tax obligations.[63] The apparent ability of the men to pay the taxes without overt resistance helped explain in part why the government plans made modest inroads. Thus in 1924 when the taxes were raised from 40 to 80 *escudos*, even though there was an outcry in some quarters against the increase, officials and settlers rationalized it by arguing that since the Ovimbundu harvested up to 1,000 kilograms per harvest, and many had two harvests, they should have no difficulty meeting the new tax requirements.[64]

During the drought of 1925 when missionaries pointed out that many people were able to pay taxes only by selling their seeds and even children, *chefes* still required the people to meet their obligations.[65] They remained blind to the plight of families whose ability to keep together was threatened when men had to absent themselves for long periods to earn money to pay taxes.[66] *Chefes* also illegally inscribed the names of underage boys on the tax rolls in order to increase the taxes they collected.[67]

The regime made some headway in implementing its labor regulations because of the role of Ovimbundu collaborators.[68] Without the African policemen, soldiers, sobas and sekulus carrying out directives, the authorities would have found it impossible to implement its tax and labor requirements.[69] Many of the African collaborators complied with orders to fill out labor quotas because they feared physical punishment from *chefes*.

Sobas and sekulus met their quota of laborers largely by sending dependents and slaves whom officials and settlers openly accepted despite the official end of slavery.[70] Indeed, the slave population in the highlands had actually increased as a result of the influx of refugees from eastern Angola made destitute as a result of the Spanish Influenza outbreak in the early part of the century, and the deadly famines of 1913–16 and the mid–1920s.[71] As the Ovimbundu heartland was largely unaffected by these natural disasters, and as the refugee population increased, slave holding remained steady.[72] Slaves were a crucial asset to the Ovimbundu, representing a labor force that they controlled and whose labor no doubt was responsible for much of the increase in maize production.

This was particularly true after the drought in 1924–25, when the population in the highlands swelled with refugees who were integrated into the households as new kin.[73] The pressure on the Ovimbundu to meet the obligation to work for the state led some Ovimbundu men to organize caravans to purchase slaves in the interior.[74] As late as 1926, the German traveler Willem Jaspert met an Ovimbundu caravan of fifty people north of Caconda bound for the interior, who were willing to buy and sell slaves.[75] Moreover, many Ovimbundu bought slaves locally—a slave cost 15 kilograms of corn in the highlands—and also used them in their households.[76] In 1913, soba Ngoya of Chisenda boasted about the one hundred slaves who worked for him.[77] Many of the slaves in the highlands were from the interior—some from as far away as Katanga (Shaba Province of the present–day Democratic Republic of the Congo)—and simply remained in the households of their former masters after the Portuguese abolished slavery.[78]

Just as the state took over the taxes Ovimbundu rulers had formerly collected, so the Portugueses colonial labor system turned Ovimbundu slaves into state slaves. The highlands also became a prime target for recruiters from other regions of the colony because of its high population density and the presence of large numbers of slaves.[79] During the period, the pre–existing slave and dependent system of labor of the Ovimbundu gradually merged into the colonial forced labor system. Administrators and *chefes* in the highlands perfected the system by improving techniques for calculating the size of the pool of male laborers to meet government and settler demands. As early as 1914, more than 5,000 laborers from the highlands were recruited to work on public projects and in private businesses. By the 1920s, thousands more Ovimbundu were working in private concerns and public agencies throughout the colony.[80]

Many women also entered the forced labor circuit as able–bodied freemen evaded the dragnet, and *chefes* turned to females and dependent males to meet their quota. By the early 1920s women and children were doing road work details, and under–aged boys fourteen to seventeen years old were forced to do corvée or contract labor to fulfill tax obligations.[81] This practice enabled the state to siphon off up to three years of labor from Ovimbundu households at a time when boys were beginning to work alongside the women in agriculture.[82] *Chefes* also compelled adult males in their late fifties to perform *corvée* labor, disregarding existing legislation that stipulated that contract labor should be performed by adult males between eighteen and fifty–five years old.[83]

Officials also devised a system to guarantee that the population fulfilled its tax and labor obligations, by allowing private agencies to recruit laborers using their own labor agents. In exchange, the firms forwarded up to 80 percent of the recruits' wages to the *chefes*, who were supposed to deduct unpaid taxes and turn over the remainder to the repatriated workers.[84]

Despite the fact that private recruiting was wracked with abuses at all levels, with physical ill–treatment of workers, especially those on small farms,[85] and with employers who seldom followed the minimum requirements the law set down concerning housing, health, and wages, the system took root. Settlers and businesses were guaranteed forced and cheap labor from the highlands while expending a minimum cost on wages, clothing, food, and housing for the workers.[86]

By 1926, the authorities were still short of their goal of implementing an efficient taxation policy that would cover all Ovimbundu and controlling the labor market. For example, in 1918 when one of the censuses showed an adult male population in central Angola eligible for recruitment as numbering about 247,903 persons, or nearly half of all eligible laborers in Angola,[87] less than a third of the eligible workers were in public or private service. This situation had not changed in 1923 when a more comprehensive census was undertaken. At that time the authorities were able to recruit only between 10 and 30 percent of the eligible laborers.[88] In 1924, officials estimated that between 53,061 and 64,061 men would be required to fulfill the demands from the private sector for laborers in trade, industry, and agriculture, plus the demand for public works, but admitted that they could not guarantee that many men.[89]

Their actual success rate was not impressive. In 1923, officials recruited only 5,803 contract workers from Bailundo, with 1,292 of these destined for work outside the highlands, a figure far lower than the authorities had anticipated.[90] Moreover, in Huambo, a region much smaller than Bailundo—and also with a high density and a strong official presence—the administrator recorded in 1924 that only 30 percent of all eligible laborers worked "regularly on their own or for a salary." He noted that the remaining 70 percent were not working and had not been recruited that year.[91] The shortfall was most likely due to the fact that former freeborn men were able to evade the authorities, while slaves or those with slave ancestry could not.

Traders

Another local development which conflicted with Portuguese aims was the continuing pull of regional commerce on the Ovimbundu, especially those from Huambo, Bié, and Bailundu. The experiences of the Ovimbundu in commerce suggest that local prerogatives threatened to derail state objectives and afforded the Ovimbundu some economic leverage, even as the state was implementing a new economic order. As they had done during the era of commodity trade, freeborn Ovimbundu continued to dominate local and regional commerce, mainly because of the rise in the price of rubber between 1902 and 1913 and the increased demand in the world market. They controlled local and regional trade because of the slow development of the infrastructure and the lack of major investments by the state or settlers. Estimates suggested that as many as 100,000 Ovimbundu per year participated in the rubber trade as late as 1910,[92] when 6,258 tons of rubber were exported from Angola.[93] Moreover, privately recruited porterage was still important in the trade between the highlands and the coast up to 1911, and Ovimbundu porters transported 479 tons of rubber, even as the Benguela railroad transported a total of 2,694 tons from its Huambo station.[94] In 1911, at least 77,000 Ovimbundu were employed as porters and petty traders between the highlands and the coast.[95]

The Ovimbundu also continued to participate in and profit from the trade in domestic slaves. Certainly many Ovimbundu caravans brought slaves into the highlands after the authorities had abolished domestic slavery in 1910, and both Ovimbundu and Portuguese traders owned them.[96] Gervase Clarence–Smith put the number of slaves for the whole of Angola in the 1910s at 20,000, and many of these were in the highlands.[97]

The rubber crash of 1914, which left many Ovimbundu destitute, increased the prospect of the Portuguese gaining control over Ovimbundu labor and thus defining their role in the local economy.[98] Even with the new administrative policies, however, local officials were unable initially to break the Ovimbundu dominance of local porterage and commerce. Many Ovimbundu men continued their petty trading[99] and porterage up to the early 1920s.[100]

The Settler Factor

The government's limited plans for Portuguese settlers, who, officials in the colonial office envisioned, would advance the state's objectives, also failed to break the local dynamics which had come into play since the era of commodity trade. Unwilling to make the long–term monetary investment in settler programs, the state never attracted suitable candidates in large enough numbers to develop white farming and undermine the direction Ovimbundu farming had taken. In 1911 when the railway reached Huambo, which was declared a city, the white population in the highlands had grown only to 2,000, in 1918 the number had increased only to 3,000. As late as the mid–1920s, the white settler population in the highlands numbered only 5,268, 3,336 of whom lived in Nova Lisboa.[101]

The make–up of the settlers who came to the highlands was mainly responsible for the limited impact of the government's policies. Instead of being the compliant white yeoman class who would serve de Matos' goal of development under Portuguese tutelage, settlers fought with the state for the right to shape their own development, and in some instances damaged the efforts of the authorities to bring the Ovimbundu population under tighter administrative control.[102] For example, as the Benguela Railway made its way across the highlands, it not only displaced African traders, but also the Boer carts that many settlers had used to compete with Ovimbundu porters. Again, many enterprising settlers suffered economically when the 1910 law abolishing slavery was passed and their small rum–making operations, which relied on slave labor, collapsed.[103] A few who opposed the measure continued to rely on unfree labor[104] to make alcohol for sale to Africans, despite a 1911 law that prohibited such sales.[105] Only the better–capitalized businesses made the transition to sugar manufacturing, relying on large concessions and state–supplied corvée laborers.

The fact that settler farming failed to take off also undermined the state's plans to redirect the regional economy for its benefit and for favored settlers. The most elaborate plans for settler farming came from the Benguela Railway Company, which from 1914 to 1922 attempted to develop plantation farming on the 250,000 hectares of land which it had leased from the state. After spending large amounts of money on land surveys and other technical studies, the company concluded that plantation agriculture was too expensive because of the cost of annual fertilization.[106] By 1922, the company was forced to sell two of its largest farms, which had proved incapable of sustaining either plantation agriculture or cattle ranching.[107]

Portuguese investors in plantation agriculture made only limited headway.[108] An official survey of 1923–24 showed that only 10 percent of the land earmarked for European farming had been transferred and most of this—about 280,000 hectares—was the concession given to the Benguela Railway Company and its English subsidiary, Benguela Estates Ltd.[109]

Settlers, who had come to the central highlands to farm, quickly switched to commerce as interest–free or low–interest long–term loans through the colonial bank were unavailable.[110] With short–term commercial credit they set up small shops called *quitandeiras* near villages and sold salt, cloth, wine, and oil in exchange for the maize and other products supplied by Ovimbundu producers.[111] To undercut competitors, they offered incentives (*otingo*) that ran as high as 50 percent or more to the producers, and they undermined efforts of local authorities to end the system which, the authorities argued, encouraged unnecessary competition between Portuguese and allowed Africans to break the law and benefit into the bargain.[112]

The Precolonial Social Order

Although local Portuguese officials implemented few social initiatives, their "pacification" and subjugation techniques helped undermine the old social order that had survived the conquest. This impact was evident in the early decline in the status of the descendants of preconquest Ovimbundu ruling lineages who collaborated with the regime. Unlike the situation in the Kongo region or the Dembos area in the north, where the king and members of the ruling lineages retained prestige and legitimacy among the population,[113] many Ovimbundu titleholders who collaborated with the Portuguese suffered a loss of status.

Chefes and administrators arbitrarily removed collaborating Ovimbundu representatives from office, physically abused, intimidated, and humiliated them, or had them imprisoned if they failed to comply with demands for workers.[114] In 1915, for example, soba Chipalo of Huambo was imprisoned and fined for failing to comply with orders to recruit men for the southern campaign.[115] Similarly, in 1920 soba Mabongo of Huambo, who had long been an ally of the Portuguese (refusing to join in the 1902 war), and who was well respected by the local merchants, was driven to commit suicide because he was unable to send the number of contract workers which the *chefe* had ordered, and he could not face the popular scorn of the villagers who ridiculed him for his collaboration.[116] In 1926, six years after his suicide, the local people remembered him as a man who had sold out to the Portuguese.[117]

For others, escape to the mountains was the only way to avoid imprisonment.[118] Indeed, as late as the 1960s popular Ovimbundu belief in Huambo was that soba Livonge (Samba Iolundungo), the ruler in 1902, had actually escaped and lived in hiding in the nearby rocky fortresses for several years. The official Portuguese belief was that Livonge, who in 1902 had publicly threatened to "cut off the heads" of all the whites in the region, had died defending his *ombala* at Samisasa.[119]

The loss of status of the former members of the Ovimbundu ruling groups was also due to the fact that they derived few material benefits from their position in the administration.[120] The sobas and sekulus and their group seldom received monetary compensation, and many lost income and power when *chefes* required them to pay a tax (*imposto de jango*), which was actually a tax on the village meeting house, or imposed heavy labor quotas on them.[121] The 420 *escudos* that one hundred of them from Huambo received in 1921–22 (as a percentage of the taxes collected) was an exception.[122]

Moreover, although some were involved in trade, owned slaves,[123] and were exempt from forced labor, *chefes* strictly monitored their behavior to prevent their becoming wealthy and powerful.[124] Most sobas and sekulus lost the livestock and slaves[125] which had set them apart from freeborn commoners up to and during the period of commodity trade. Agricultural surveys of the early and mid–1920s, for example, showed no sharp material differences among the Ovimbundu population as measured by ownership of livestock, and number of wives and dependents.[126] The laws of the colony, which forbade the private ownership of land by Africans, meant that the descendants of the precolonial ruling lineages and village elders could not accumulate wealth by putting lineage land on the market, as happened in other colonies or as settlers were doing.[127] Those who still held dependents accumulated land indirectly. But for the most part, they lost the most desirable land to which they had traditionally had access, as was the case in

Bié when settlers took over the large plantation that the soba and his relatives had once managed.[128] Thus, the Portuguese owners gained access to
the slaves and dependents of the former Ovimbundu rulers. Another instance of outright loss of land by the members of the precolonial ruling
elites involved the collaborating Huambo soba Khala II, who in 1903 was
forced to move his *ombala* next to the Portuguese fort which had been built
near his capital. This became the site fort the Portuguese city of Nova Lisboa.
Similarly, in 1912 the site of the *ombala* of soba Kachivungo of Dondi,
where he had been captured and sent into exile for his participation in 1902
revolt, and which had been abandoned by the six or seven villages which
were attached to it, became the site of the Protestant Dondi Institute.[129]

Besides undermining Ovimbundu leadership, the arm of the state
reached into some Ovimbundu villages and enforced tax and labor obligations in a more brutal manner than had been the case under the former
Ovimbundu regimes. This development left some Ovimbundu prostrate
before the state and gained the Portuguese the reputation of condoning
modern–day slavery. Although few of them left written records, word of
their plight reached far beyond Angola as missionaries revealed details of
forced labor practices that the Portuguese sanctioned. The writings of the
American Edward Ross, who condemned the slave labor system in 1925,[130]
and the investigation of the English Anti-slavery and Aborigines Protection Society, which detailed the brutality of the labor practices in central
Angola, provided chilling details of the abuses suffered by workers from the
central highlands.[131] Critics accused the authorities of condoning state slavery by requiring African males to pay taxes as well as to perform forced
labor, noting that the part of the workers' salaries transferred by private
businesses to the state was just a way for the state to enrich itself further by
"keeping four–fifths of the laborers' pay."[132] Even the British–owned
Benguela Railway Company did not escape criticism. When officials at the
company were accused of giving thirty lashes each to two Ovimbundu
employees who had each worked over twenty years for the company, they
argued in their own defense that such treatment was normal, even for long–
serving loyal employees.[133]

The barrage of international criticism pushed the Overseas Minister
to order reform of the labor practices in all Portuguese colonies, and the
authorities in Angola passed several statutes prohibiting the recruitment of
minors and of natives who were gainfully employed on their own farms.
The statutes also forbade physical abuse and required companies to enforce
the state guidelines covering the health, rations, lodging, and medical care
of contracted workers. In the central highlands, the reforms remained on

paper only, and the status of the Ovimbundu who were subject to the abuses did not change, as local officials lacked the funds and the inclination to enforce the laws.[134]

Survival or Collapse:
The Origins of Modern Ovimbundu Identity

The Catholic Factor

Despite the fact that the early colonial state left few opportunities for descendants of the former Ovimbundu ruling groups to recover from the military defeat, and altered the economic and social position of this group and of other Ovimbundu, the limitations of the colonial state were evident in the novel ways in which the various segments of the Ovimbundu population interacted with it. These ways, in large measure, reflect the ability of some Ovimbundu to adapt older civic/local institutions and create new ones, in order to cope with the changes which conquest and the establishment of the colonial state had brought.

The Ovimbundu coped with the increasing demands of the regime in both organized and individual ways. Those Ovimbundu who were connected to the Catholic and Protestant missionaries were in the best position, generally speaking, to interact creatively and cope with the pressures coming from the state. Even here, however, distinctions arose, as the Ovimbundu who developed ties with the with the Catholic Church were not in as favorable a situation to interact independently and creatively to the state as those who had connections to the Protestant missionaries. This was because officials in the Overseas Office regarded the Catholic Church in Angola as an arm of the state and as the official agency responsible for transforming African society. They expected the missionaries to spread the Catholic faith, offer the African population training in agriculture and the arts, and spread Portuguese culture in the colony. This official status and the hierarchical nature of the Catholic Church, however, limited the ability of Ovimbundu Catholics to put a distance between themselves and the state.

In any event, the Catholic missionaries who worked among the Ovimbundu failed to meet any of the goals the state had set. Most of the fault lay with the government's inability to provide the missionaries (the majority of whom were non–Portuguese) with the resources to advance the educational, religious, and social work they wished them to undertake.

The missionaries faced the same kinds of financial and personnel problems as other state sectors.

The achievements of the Catholics were not impressive. In 1925, the French Holy Ghost Fathers who ran the Catholic operations had trained only two Ovimbundu priests and forty male catechists. Up to that time the burden of conversion and social transformation fell on forty–two European priests, lay brothers, and nuns who ran the ten mission stations Catholics operated in the central highlands. According to their records, they taught 40,000 children in the 300 rural schools they operated, and served 50,000 to 70,000 Ovimbundu converts and European settlers.[135] Yet they complained about underfinancing (they received no government funds), competition from Protestant missionaries,[136] and the forced labor system which pulled away promising Ovimbundu catechists and impoverished the population.[137] Here too, most of the converts who, the missionaries hoped, would become catechists and advance the work of evangelizing the rest of the population did not live up to expectations. They regarded the missionaries as little more than a ticket to assimilation, and broke their ties with the missions as soon as they found better–paying jobs in trading houses which gave them an easier ticket to assimilation.[138] The church made few attempts to recruit and cultivate descendants of the precolonial ruling group, and most of those who, like soba of Ngalangi, were nominal Catholics, gained no special privileges from their ties to the church and state. The church was not an institution where Ovimbundu Catholics found opportunities to continue the innovative adaptations that had become a distinguishing factor in the lives of both ruling elites and others since the beginning of commodity trade. Thus, the rise in the number of Ovimbundu Catholics had little impact on the rest of the Ovimbundu population. In particular, Catholic converts did not adopt a pattern of behavior or challenge the state in such a way as to make them stand out from of nonconverted Ovimbundu population.

The Protestant Factor

The same was not true of Ovimbundu converts, who were linked to the Protestant missionaries (overwhelmingly North Americans but with some Europeans) who arrived in the highlands in the 1880s, and who by 1926 shared the work of "civilizing" the population with the Catholics. Unlike the Catholics, the growth in the number of Ovimbundu Protestants led to some fundamental changes in Ovimbundu civic/local institutions and Ovimbundu identity in response to Portuguese conquest and the establishment of the early colonial state. As a result, the group not only informed state/society relations up to 1926 but contributed significantly to what became the modern Ovimbundu identity.[139]

Protestant missionaries ran a well–funded mission organization and outperformed their Catholic counterparts. Their goals were to provide Ovimbundu converts with education, health, and social services, to establish a network of institutions which the Ovimbundu could help manage, and to represent the concerns of their Protestant community to the state. These goals served as a base from which converts could adapt to early Portuguese colonialism but find protection from the direct control and abuse that the state and settlers perpetrated against the rest of the Ovimbundus population.

The Protestant missionaries were in a unique position to provide this space to their converts. Despite the suspicions of officials their work was a threat to Portuguese sovereignty in the highlands, the state tolerated them because their work put a positive face on Portuguese colonialism. Indeed, in the early years Protestants received official permission to purchase choice lands for their mission stations and were allowed to expand their educational, social, and religious work at a time when social expenditure by the colonial state was almost nonexistent.[140] In 1914, for example, High Commissioner Norton de Matos himself approved the sale of 9,000 acres of prime land in Dondi (formerly Kachivungu) which became the site of the Currie Institute for boys and the Means School for Girls. At the time, he reminded the missionaries that the state wanted "a spacious mission, none of your wattle and daub or adobe shacks, but schools and houses of brick, well laid out."[141] By the mid–1920s, a total of 132 British, Canadian, and American Protestants worked to fulfill De Mato's dream among the Ovimbundu. They managed 26 mission stations, and operated 215 rural schools. In addition they had established the Currie Institute for boys at Dondi, which they started in 1914 with a class of 26 young men drawn from all classes and regions of the former kingdoms, and the Means School for Girls whose students had a similar profile. The converts to their churches numbered in the thousands, including 27,000 in Bailundu alone.[142]

Like their Catholic counterparts, Ovimbundu Protestant converts represented a cross section of the population of the former Ovimbundu kingdoms, but the group counted among their numbers many descendants of sobas and sekulus who had gone against the older status quo and welcomed the first Protestants. Soba Kanjundu of Bié and the sobas of Andulu, Chissamba, Chiyuku had disregarded both the power of the precolonial rulers and the warnings of Portuguese who attempted to frustrate the work of the Protestant missionaries, and allowed the Protestants to open mission stations in the lands they controlled. In Bié the three mission stations which the Protestants established—at Chissamba, Kamundongo, and Chilesso— were all on land that the precolonial Ovimbundu rulers had ceded, sold, or given to the early Protestant missionaries.[143]

Many of the sobas and sekulus who attached themselves to the missionaries were self-made men of the commodity era, who regarded the Protestants, not the representatives of the state or the Catholic missionaries, as reasonable guardians of their land. In 1912, for example, two years before Norton de Matos formally sold Dondi to the Protestants, Soba Mutandavantu, a former porter, agreed to the proposals of Protestant missionaries Henry Neipp and William Bell to establish the Dondi mission at the abandoned *ombala* of soba Kachivungo, whose dependents had abandoned it after the Portuguese had captured and exiled the soba.[144] The decision to pass it over to the Protestant missionaries was an excellent move by soba Mutandavantu. For the time being he preempted its takeover by the state or settlers and guaranteed that the Ovimbundu would continue to have access to this strategic and well-watered site, located on the route of the Benguela Railway and near the Kutato River, a potential source of electricity.

These decisions which members of the Ovimbundu ruling elites made, even as the early colonial state was expanding, strengthened rather than weakened their relationship with the Protestants by the early 1920s.[145] Indeed, several Ovimbundu who became Protestants during the period, and who were in line to become titleholders, chose to remain with the Protestants rather than risk filling positions that exposed them to the power of the state. In 1914, for example, Sekulu Ganga, who was the grandson of the last king, Chipata, of the Ndulu kingdom and who was in line to inherit the title, chose to keep his position as a carpenter at the Protestant mission in Ndulu.[146] Many others in the Protestant community were children of the early converts. For example, in 1920, Dorina, one of the daughters of Kanjundu of Bié who had given up all his wives but one when he converted, attended the Means School for girls. The missionary Leona Stukey described her "a real princess, for her mother was one of the great wives of the great Kanjundu of Bié and she was the wife he kept when he became a Christian and put away the rest of his wives."[147]

Sobas and Sekulus were not the only Ovimbundu who hitched their wagons to Protestants. Slaves (especially the foreign-born ones who hailed from the Luimbe and Katanga–Shaba–region), porters, traders, and even kimbandas (ocimbandas) became Protestants. For example, Albert Katema Kanyanga, who converted in 1924, served for many years as a slave to his non-convert Ovimbundu master and was a skilled herder, weaver of mats, and drummer.[148] A court crier of the soba of Galangue became the official who called the people to Sunday service after the king became a Protestant;[149] while kimbandas who were associated with sobas who converted and who publicly burnt their divining baskets received special favors.

With so many members of the former ruling elite connected to the Protestants, the effect was very different from the hopes of the authorities, and had become a source of conflict by the mid–1920s. For one, *chefes* resented the attempts of the missionaries to protect the population from the exactions of Portuguese officials and settlers.[150] However, in areas where Portuguese civil authority was still weak, sobas and sekulus continued to favor an alliance with the missionaries as in Galangue and Andulu.[151]

By the mid–1920s, Ovimbundu Protestants comprised the most prosperous and forward–looking members of rural society. The Currie Institute and Means School trained small groups of Ovimbundu young people in a wide variety of skills, preparing them to be better farmers and to work as pastors, teachers, health care workers, carpenters, and railway attendants. This group also used and promoted the "court" Umbundu that they had helped the missionaries to put to writing, and they used the Umbundu Bible in village churches. The use of the Umbundu language served as a key to an evolving modern Ovimbundu identity.[152] Moreover, many adopted the plough that missionaries at Dondi mission had introduced in 1914,[153] became fluent in English, French, and Portuguese, and learnt the manners and cultural norms of Europeans.

Those who were trained to be pastors became missionaries, and built Christian villages throughout the highlands, establishing model Christian communities all along the railroad.[154] As Protestants were always ready with their taxes, some officials supported them, and their training and modern outlook set them apart from Ovimbundu Catholics and non–Catholics. Many of them had little difficulty in qualifying for *assimilado* status.[155] In many villages and urban centers, Protestant pastors, teachers, and other workers, many of them the children of the former ruling groups, but some also of more modest backgrounds, began to replace the nonconverted sobas and sekulus in leadership positions.

The Ovimbundu Protestant leaders imposed strict moral and social codes of behavior on fellow Ovimbundu who professed conversion, including monitoring the behavior of prospective candidates and converts to prevent them succumbing to the efforts of "their heathen relatives who try in every way to get them back to their way of life".[156] In 1920 the Dondi mission alone catered to some 15,000 Ovimbundu "communicants, preparants and hearers".[157]

Between 1902 and 1926, Ovimbundu Protestants seemed to have weathered the trauma of conquest and were adapting to the expansion of the state. Although their numbers were smaller than those of the Catholics, the ties which bound them to the former kingdoms gradually began to give way an Ovimbundu Protestant tie. But the social transformation was far from complete, and old rivalries, based on identity with kingdoms and cultural differences, surfaced often and were fiercely defended, as in 1920 when a group of Kamundongo students from Bié angrily withdrew from the Currie Institute, convinced that the missionaries were favoring the students from Bailundu.[158]

But the social transformation that came with the growth of Ovimbundu Protestants was visible in other ways. For example, by the mid–1920s Ovimbundu Protestants used the term "Ovimbundu" instead of Bieno, Bailundu, Ndulu and other names associated with the nineteenth–century kingdoms, when referring to their ethnic identity.[159] Moreover, they formed a distinct social group whose members were distinguished by their dress, deportment, lifestyle, and houses.[160] The Protestant Soba Chiyuka was a representative of this group. In 1920, for example, he had "a nine room house made of burnt bricks", but still delighted in reminiscing about the ceremonies related to the burials of past kings and the life the people led in the "old days" before the Portuguese and missionaries appeared.[161] The Protestants, unlike their Catholic counterparts, developed a tight network through camp meetings, Sunday services, and other church–related activities including a short–lived newsletter published in Umbundu called *Ndaka*, which students at the Dondi mission edited.

In some respects this was a social revolution reminiscent of the upper mobility that porters and traders had experienced during the period of commodity trade. The first graduates of Dondi became the railway workers, pastors, clerks, and teachers who gave stimulus to numerous Protestant congregations in the central highlands, especially in the settlements that sprang up along the Benguela Railway beyond the central highlands, in Lobito and other urban coastal areas of Angola, and in neighboring countries where Ovimbundu Protestants settled.[162] Among this dynamic group of Protestant Ovimbundus were Lott Malheiro Savimbi and Jesse Chipenda, whose sons Jonas Malheiro and Jesse and Daniel Chipenda would later play a major role in the anticolonial struggle and the growth of modern Ovimbundu nationalism.

It was to forestall the prospect of Ovimbundu Protestants emerging as the magnet of Ovimbundu opposition to the colonial state that local officials stepped in to stop some of the activities of the Protestants and to limit their influence. The concern was evident before the 1920s. Norton de Matos spearheaded official efforts to blunt the impact of Protestant missionaries, and to eliminate the nascent Ovimbundu solidarity which was surfacing among Ovimbundu Protestants. He first moved to protect Portuguese sovereignty against the foreign Protestants, whose influence he believed was "more powerful" than the state's, in 1911 by creating the town of Nova Lisboa (Huambo) on the eve of the arrival of the railway.[163]

Local officials and settlers also sounded the alarm as the following two incidents involving Soba Kanjundu of Chiyaka and Sekulu Jerry, both Protestant converts, demonstrate. Before Kanjundu, an early Protestant convert, died in 1913, he named as executor of his estate (which was quite substantial and included "gold sovereigns from Rhodesia and a big Rhodesian saddle back dog with chain") not the local *chefe* but the missionary John Tucker. When word of the late soba's bequest leaked out, local officials were incensed and began to press for restrictions on the Protestants, even calling for them to stop work in the villages. Tucker's attempts to carry out the wishes of the deceased led to his denunciation in an article in the *Jornal de Benguela*, which accused the Protestants of taking over functions reserved for state officials.[164]

In a 1915 incident, Protestant Sekulu Jerry of Chileso and 110 of his villagers were sent off to forced labor because the sekulu had written a letter in Umbundu, informing the *chefe* that he was unable to send the men who had been requested to act as porters to the visiting governor of Benguela, because they were at church services.[165] The governor informed Tucker (who attempted to plead the sekulu's case) that as a representative of the colonial state, he had the authority to send the Ovimbundu to any part of the colony he wished. He also warned Tucker that he should "give better instructions to your people that when the governor is around they should not place the orders of a simple missionary above those of the authorities".[166]

Faced with this dynamic rise of an Ovimbundu group with the ability to act as a magnet for other Ovimbundu with anti–state sentiments, the authorities continued to attack the Protestants. In 1916 they suppressed the newspaper *Ndaka* under the Defense of the Realm Act, accusing the students of anti–state activities because the paper contained an article critical of Portugal's participation in World War One.[167] In addition, they pressed the Catholic missionaries to open more centers in the highlands to compete with the Protestants, and passed several anti–foreign laws to restrict the work of foreign Protestant missionaries.[168]

The most serious attack on the group occurred in 1921, when Norton de Matos implemented the infamous Decree 77 which required that Portuguese be spoken in all schools in the colony and that all teachers pass an examination in Portuguese. His purpose was to end the practice of using African languages as the medium of instruction in schools and churches in the colony. In the case of the highlands, this meant ending the use of the Umbundu language and replacing it with Portuguese in Protestant schools and churches. De Matos had long been concerned that the Protestant practice of teaching in Umbundu was leading to "denationalization," and had often urged the missionaries to integrate Portuguese history into their sermons, in order to further government objectives.[169]

Local officials and settlers welcomed De Matos' initiatives, seeing in Decree 77 the legitimacy they craved to weaken the influence Ovimbundu Protestants were beginning to exert on the non–Christian Ovimbundu. After the decree was promulgated, *chefes* and settlers deliberately targeted Dondi students and other Protestants; they arrested and sent off to the army or *corveé* labor many Dondi students, some of them simply because they were away from the mission without their *guias de marcha* (travel permit).[170] They also closed hundreds of Protestant outstations that Ovimbundu converts ran.[171] The immediate result of this was that many Protestants found it harder to take advantage of the social and material opportunities the missionaries offered, and saw their status temporarily decline.[172] Local *chefes* even made it mandatory for converts who had passed the first part of the primary school examination (*primiera grau*) to do contract labor and pay hut tax.[173]

Moreover, in 1925 de Matos pointedly refused the appeals of the Protestants who wanted *chefes* to stop sending elementary school graduates and pastors off to forced labor, and drafting catechists into the army.[174] Officials also ignored the complaints of the missionaries about physical and sexual abuse of female students by soldiers, *cipaes*, and officials.[175] The policy was to force the Ovimbundu Protestants to assimilate on Portuguese terms.

By the mid–1920s, some converts were reacting to the increased official pressure by affectionately recalling the "good old days" of the precolonial kingdoms. As one stressed, in the former period when slavery was legal "slaves were fed and those left behind were unmolested except for some calls for carriers."[176] In 1926, the missionary Henry S. Hollenbeck, writing from Bié, also contrasted the convert's lot with the past, noting that the "restriction of trade by the authorities and a steady increase in taxes have nearly exhausted their capital".[177] He added that labor policies were also having a terrible impact on agriculture, as people were leaving fields "uncultivated or so poorly cultivated as to give inadequate crops and the people could not make up the difference in livestock because they had also disappeared."[178]

Nevertheless, Ovimbundu Protestants had already established themselves as a distinct and important social group in the colony. The network that they developed as a result of their association with the foreign Protestant missionaries also reinforced their new form of consciousness. For one thing, although arguments over the correct pronunciation of Umbundu (which included "court" Umbundu, promoted at Dondi Institute, and regional variations) sometimes led to physical attacks, for the first time Ovimbundu from different kingdoms were working together, not as Bienos, Bailundus, Ndulus, Kamundungos, and the like but as Ovimbundus.[179] Moreover, other activities, such as traveling to villages other than their own to recruit villagers to Protestantism, enabled young Protestants to become familiar with an Ovimbundu world beyond their own village and region. This new identity proved a powerful psychological weapon against the attacks from the state.

Nonconverted Ovimbundu

Many nonconverted Ovimbundu rivaled the Protestants in developing novel ways in which to respond to demands and to the increasing role of the colonial state in setting up a new social order in the highlands. Many nonconverted Ovimbundu attempted to retain control over local/civic institutions by adapting them in profound ways, to counter the pressures of the early colonial era. They were able to do this because, despite the state's efforts to make model Catholics out of a small percentage of Ovimbundus who were officially accepted into the faith and to suppress the Protestants, local Portuguese officials seldom intervened in the social life of the villages once sekulus and sobas collected the requisite taxes from villagers and sent out men and women for *corveé* labor when requests came in. As a result, in many parts of the highlands a dynamic interaction between colonizer and colonized was taking palace.

For example, one could still find in the highlands Ovimbundu who asserted a degree of pride in Ovimbundu customs which went counter to both colonial laws and Christian teachings, and who recalled the defiance of some leading precolonial Ovimbundu rulers who resisted the Portuguese and scorned the teachings of the missionaries. One such individual was Soba Ngoya of Chisende, who, in 1913, after listening to the Protestant missionary Tucker preach, stood up and asserted proudly, "I have no sin, adultery I do not commit, I have ten wives. Stealing is not mine. I have one hundred slaves to work for me."[180] Others were men like Lott Savimbi's father, whose pride in the precolonial political order and faith in the traditions of his youth held up against political pressures from the authorities and spiritual pressures from his devoutly Protestant son.[181]

Likewise, many ordinary Ovimbundu who were neither Catholic nor Protestants exercised some autonomy over their social institutions and cultural practices. They continued to consult the kimbandas for potions they provided for protection and good luck at home and work, and listened to sobas and sekulus and their titled assistants who dispensed local justice and distributed land much the same as in former days.[182] Despite the scorn which some of them suffered because of their ties to the administration, many Ovimbundu titleholders continued to play a central role in cultural practices that strengthened lineage and ethnic ties, including marriage, naming, feasts of the dead (*ochisunji*), circumcision and initiation ceremonies, purification rites to solve interpersonal and societal problems, witchcraft trials, and others, as they had done before the conquest.[183]

Missionaries provide many details on rural life during the period, describing the annual burning of grasses before planting, ironmaking, and many other activities essential to rural life. Their interest in eliminating what they believed were "devilish" practices associated with witchcraft led them to describe these in more detail than the other cultural practices they noted. Their reports suggest that people sought explanations for the changes in the Ovimbundu moral universe that came with the conquest, and some noted that in particular villages people stopped planting new crops for fear of retribution from their ancestors.[184] In other cases, kinsmen resorted to witchcraft accusations to stop their members from converting.[185] In 1913, the missionary Tucker recorded the plan that members of a secret society (Chiyuka) of Bié had devised to take the body of Soba Kanjundu and give it a traditional burial, having rejected a Protestant service.[186] Some Ovimbundu whose kinsmen converted also blamed the government, settlers, and missionaries for promoting Western culture, and believed that witchcraft was involved in conversion.[187] Sekulu Chamuanga, a former slave dealer, concluded in 1914 that "the country is in bad shape . . . Witches and sorcerers abound. Formerly we burnt alive such people on top of the Chimabango mountain."[188]

Although it has been common to link incidents of witchcraft and other precolonial practices that occurred throughout Africa during the early colonial period to an African inability to cope with the dramatic alienation (anomie) which conquest and colonialism had brought, the case of the

Ovimbundu suggests otherwise.[189] The reports of witchcraft trials and ceremonies which came to the attention of the authorities and missionaries rather suggest the profound ambivalence some Ovimbundu had to the changing political, economic, and social order.

As they had done during the period of commodity trade, some people turned to the kimbandas, the religious practitioners who, they believed, could restore moral order and reinforce the moral universe that was under attack. In fact, the kimbandas proved adept at adapting to the changed situation. When one old kimbanda was questioned as to why he had a Portuguese flag and an old copy of St. John's Gospel in his divining basket, he replied, "When it is anyone connected with the Ombange [fort] who is guilty of witchcraft [umbanda] . . . we can't get him unless we have the Portuguese flag," noting also that he needed the book to "catch those Christians. Without it we have no power over them."[190]

A 1921 incident involving a soba who threatened to burn down the house of a Christian convert, because he believed that Christians have "the rain in a box in their houses," also suggests that some individuals who had formerly wielded power did not hesitate to attempt to harness ideological and religious beliefs to maintain autonomy against the forces of change, whether they originated from the Portuguese or from their own kin. This might explain why many people in the area were attracted to the African independent church movements that emerged in the neighboring Belgian Congo, especially those that preached that God was about to drive whites out of the country and give their possessions to Africans.[191]

Conclusion

Although by 1926 the state's labor and taxation policies created economic insecurity for the masses of Ovimbundu, and begun to derail the progress the forward–looking Protestant Ovimbundu had made, there were powerful forces supporting local autonomy among all groups of Ovimbundu. The fact that most Ovimbundu continued to use their own language, even while some adjusted their beliefs and kept control over their social institutions and cultural practices, reinforced rather than weakened an emerging modern regional and ethnic identity that all Ovimbundu shared by the mid–1920s.

This cultural cohesion served as a psychological shield which gave the population a level of self–respect and allowed them to confront the reduced political and economic opportunities, even though it was formulated in ethnic terms. The 1926 army coup in Portugal that set in place the *Estado Novo* and the re–formulation of colonial ideology and programs allowed state power to intrude on civic/local institutions in more decisive ways, however. All Ovimbundu—Catholic, Protestants, non–converted Ovimbundu, rural and urban, assimilated and nonassimilated—1926 to 1960 faced a state more challenging and formidable than anything they had experienced in the past.

3

THE ESTADO NOVO (NEW STATE) AND THE POLITICS OF ECONOMIC SUBJUGATION, 1926–1960

Introduction

On 28 May 1926, leaders of an army coup in Portugal brought down the Republic, proclaimed the birth of the *Estado Novo* (New State) and appointed Dr. António de Oliveira Salazar, former Minister of Finance and a fiscal conservative, as head of the government. Salazar and his supporters were fascists who believed that an authoritarian-administrative state would bring economic prosperity to Portugal through more efficient exploitation of the Overseas Territories. They also intended to restore Portugal's image in the world.[1] Despite the criticism that the dictatorship represented "nativistic" tendencies,[2] the leaders succeeded where their predecessors had failed, and transformed Angola into a preserve in which Portuguese capitalism was nurtured on the labor and agricultural surplus of the African people.[3]

The impact of the political and economic policies of the New State on the Ovimbundu villagers during the period from 1926 to 1960 contrasted dramatically with both the policies of the former Ovimbundu kingdoms and the monarchist and republican regimes which preceded the New State. In part, the success of the New State policies was due to the absence in Angola of the type of conflict which pitted metropolitan and colonial interest groups in other settler colonies, like the Rhodesias and Kenya, against each other over issues dealing with the political and economic status and role of Africans in the colony. In Angola the contradictions between the colonial state and metropolitan, settler, and African colonial subjects were never sufficiently decisive to alter the policies of the Salazar dictatorship, which by 1960 had perfected one of the most oppressive regimes that the Ovimbundu had ever experienced. Unlike the former Ovimbundu states, whose leaders had been unable to contain the various social forces that emerged during the period of commodity trade, or the politically weaker but militarily intrusive early colonial state, between 1926 and 1960 the *Estado Novo* regime succeeded in using the state to advance its goals of promoting the political and economic interest of its metropolitan supporters.

Remaking the Bureaucracy

Colonial legislation passed between 1926 and 1960, dealing with administrative reforms, laid out the strategy of the New State ideologues. Some of the legislation and policies the Portuguese implemented reflected their empire-wide preoccupations, others reflected their concerns specifically with the colony of Angola, while all had region-specific effects in the highlands. The most far-reaching were the *Estatuto Político, Civil, e Criminal dos indígenas das colónias dos Angola, Guiné e Moçambique* (Political, Criminal, and Civil Statute of the Natives of Angola, Guinea, and Mozambique), published in 1926 and revised as the Colonial Act of 1930, the 1954 Organic Law of the Colonies, and several decrees of the mid-1950s dealing with "Rural Well-Being". The historic Missionary Accord of 1940 based, on the Concordat between the Vatican and the Portuguese, and the Missionary Statute of 1941 were also important. These laws spelled out the subordinate but vital role the colonies and colonial peoples were to play in the new Portuguese Empire, and the duty of the government towards the "native" populations.[4] The laws stressed the moral obligation the Portuguese had to "promote, by all means, the moral improvement and material life of the [native] population,"[5] and the Africans' duty of assuming their legal status in Portuguese colonial society.

The 1926–1930 legislation intended to the overhaul colonial bureaucracy was the first that had a colony wide and region-specific impact in Angola. Throughout the colony it led to the dismissal from the colonial service of most Angolan-born Portuguese, creoles, and *assimilados* and their replacement with pro-Salazar, Portuguese-born individuals.[6] In the highlands, this bureaucratic reshuffling strengthened the position of Portuguese *chefes*, decreased the role of sobas and sekulus, and increased the role of soldiers, *cipaes* (policemen), *cantoneiros* (road crew heads),[7] *regedores* (Portuguese-nominated rulers who the population referred to as "*Katamajila*"), and catechists and priests, over whom *chefes* could exercise more control. A 1944 law was more specific to the highlands and resulted in narrowing the local autonomy that sobas and sekulus retained, by reorganizing pre-conquest borders and making it illegal for more than four great sobas to live in the preconquest capitals of any civil post. The law also stipulated that a soba should be responsible for no more than five hundred taxpayers unless he was so well-respected that he would encounter no difficulties in collecting taxes.[8] The aim was to weaken but not eliminate the sobas and sekulus, whose knowledge of customary law saved the authorities the cost of codifying African law and training Portuguese civil servants to replace them.[9] This bureaucratic reshuffling was meant to bring a more metropolitan-centered political order to bear on the colonial regime and to reduce local political initiatives.

Fiscal Reorientation and Development Initiatives

New State officials took several steps to bring Angola's economy under control and to benefit the state and its supporters. In 1926 when Salazar became head of Portugal, he was convinced that he could rein in the runaway inflation that burdened Angola and improve its economic performance. For several years Angola had been unable to meet its operating costs, had experienced chronic deficits in both the budget and the balance of trade, and suffered from hyperinflation (one estimate put the inflation rate at the time at 7000 percent). Blaming fiscal mismanagement, and unwilling to use public funds from Portugal to save the colony from economic ruin, the Oversees Minister took over fiscal management of the colony.[10] The goal was to run the economy for the benefit of Portugal to a greater extent than ever before. The regime implemented a series of reforms intended to achieve this aim.

The first priority was monetary reform, which the Overseas Minister achieved by substituting for the Portuguese *escudo* (the currency in use in the colony) a new currency, the *angolar*, valued at 80 percent of the metropolitan *escudo*.[11] This meant a 20 percent devaluation of all stocks in the colony, as everyone was forced to bring in their *escudos* to exchange for *angolares* one-to-one.[12] The government also created a new bank (*Banco de*

Angola) to handle transfers and commercial transactions (but not savings and credit).[13] In addition, the authorities implemented several other fiscally conservative measures aimed at decreasing imports (which dropped by half in less than five years), and imposing stricter controls over colonial spending.[14]

The regime followed this with measures that favored private Portuguese investments in the plantation sector, and a state supported yeoman settler initiative, while giving lip service to plans promoting African peasant production. Land reform, including laws that allowed alienated African lands to go to Portuguese settlers and businesses, was at the heart of the initiative. The land reforms and settler programs had special ramifications in the highlands which were still high on the government list for Portuguese yeoman farming. By the mid-1940s the state had transferred over 3,126,925 hectares of land in the highlands and sub-plateau regions to Portuguese businesses for the development of plantations.[15] In addition, small-scale Portuguese farmers obtained concessions, and small grants were made to Boer settlers.[16] Also, the state reserved land for agricultural experiments, new municipalities, and the urban and semiurban settlements which were springing up in the highlands. Catholic missionary groups received large donations of land, and even Protestant missionaries received permission to purchase plots.[17]

Likewise, the dream of building a strong, corporately directed economy in Angola and of transforming the colony into a real province of Portugal also led the authorities to favor policies intended to promote an investment climate in which plantations and parastatals would play a dominant role.

Government spending on the infrastructure and on public works projects became significant after the Second World War, when Portugal received money from the Marshall Plan and the International Corporation Administration. The initiatives included new roads, railways, drainage and irrigation works, and hydroelectrical schemes. In 1956, newly appointed Governor General Rapelo spelled out the commitment of the colonial government to the economic transformation of Angola by promising to ". . . carve out new roads . . . cultivate new land . . . explore more mines . . . intensify development works."[18]

The transformation was evident in the economic activities which the colony witnessed between 1945 and 1960, when Angolan government expenditure on infrastructure rose from $10.7 million (U.S,) to $142 million (U.S.). Most of the funds were spent on bridge construction, opening up new sources of electrical energy, ports, telecommunications, agricultural and veterinary research, and European settlements.[19]

Although the government initially excluded foreign capitalists, giving preference to state and private Portuguese investments, after the Second World War it allowed American, Belgian and some South African capital to be invested in the colony. Foreign investors pioneered the petroleum industry and expanded the mineral and plantation sectors. Foreign companies also opened new import firms and supplied the colony with machinery, petroleum, chemical products, and some consumer products. By 1960, Portuguese and foreign investors had sunk millions of dollars into oil and mineral ventures, textiles, cotton, cement, and other industries.

The more open investment climate was reflected in the remarkable growth in the colony's economy by the 1950s. Between 1953 and 1955, capital investments amounted to 28 million pounds sterling ($48 million U.S.) per annum, with the state accounting for 40 percent, and private investments, especially in mining, accounting for the rest.[20] In 1955 yearly industrial activity was valued between 600,000 and 700,000 *contos* ($2,400,000 to $2,800,000 U.S.), a level never before achieved.[21]

The plantation sector was one of the most dynamic, and one whose growth had major consequences for the Ovimbundu. Output increased significantly, with coffee going from a few tons in the 1930s to 58,860 tons by 1950; by 1960 Angola produced 87,217 tons of coffee. The area devoted to coffee plantations also increased, from 125,251 hectares in 1950 to 266,185 hectares in 1960.[22] Sisal production in the sub-plateau region reached 41,369 tons in 1955 compared with 6,198 in 1940.[23] One hundred and seventy planters owned the 50,000 hectares of land where sisal was planted. The fishing industry experienced a massive expansion in the late fifties, with 300 factories employing 15,000 African workers.[24]

Anti-foreign propaganda and state preferences which favored wealthy Portuguese investors, and all but excluded foreign investments in the colony, also led parastatal agencies to consolidate their position in the highlands during the 1930s and early 1940s. Even the Benguela Railway was forced to sell its land and machinery to Portuguese investors because of the increased official bias against foreign-owned and firms,[25] while metropolitan Portuguese firms were expanding their presence in the highlands. For example, up to 1930 there were only four Portuguese businesses, holding titles to between 400,000 and 500,000 hectares of land, in Bailundo and Huambo.[26] By 1938 Portuguese investors owned seventeen cotton, palm oil, sugar, and sisal plantations in the highlands, sub-plateau region, and Cuanza Sul, valued at a total of 15 million *contos* or 15 billion *angolares*.[27]

This economic transformation had major consequences for the Ovimbundu, since most of the operations relied almost exclusively on the hundreds of thousands of Ovimbundu contract workers provided by the state, plus voluntary Ovimbundu migrant laborers. The Ovimbundu were also affected by the authorities' allocation of funds to several projects in their region. These included funds for public buildings, road works, and improvements in veterinary, agricultural and agriculture-related research centers in and around Nova Lisboa.[28]

White Immigration

The *Estado Novo* authorities also pursued a more aggressive settler policy which had major ramifications for the Ovimbundu. Convinced that Angola was crucial to crucial to its plans to advance Portugal's domestic development, the dictatorship initially promoted the idea of a white yeoman class in Angola, particularly in the central highlands. The regime argued that settlers would provide the human capital needed to manage the modern sector, and would help African subsistence and peasant farming to improve under state and private Portuguese guidance.

The concept of managed colonial development through government-supported peasant immigration was first emphasized in the 1930 Colonial Act, which noted that "the State, as a sovereign entity, assumes the function of promoting, orienting, and disciplining the people [of the colonies] by a new nucleus of Portuguese settlers of metropolitan origin."[29] Although the Act had as one of its aims the improvement of African peasant farming, the emphasis was on Portuguese tutelage of African peasants.[30]

Later legislation elaborated on the role of Portuguese colonization[31] and stressed that this was essential to guarantee Portuguese (as opposed to non-Portuguese and indigenous) exploitation of the rich resources in Angola. With reference to the central highlands, the authorities argued that Portuguese "colonists [who were] accustomed to hard work" would promote a more efficient "cereal cultivation" there.[32]

White immigration to central Angola from 1926 to 1960 proved disastrous to the Ovimbundu population. The negative impact on the Ovimbundu developed slowly, since the early attempts at encouraging white yeomen farmers to the region failed. In 1935, for example, when the administration set aside 4,066,200 (*escudos*) or about $300,000 (U.S.) to cover the expenses for transporting and settling forty colonists in the highlands, the scheme attracted few eligible families.[33] By 1940 only two hundred and fifty white farmers were involved in export agriculture, far below the numbers the authorities had expected. Even an investment of $2.8 million (U.S.)

which the Benguela Railway authorities spent on white settlement between 1935 and 1949 attracted only nineteen colonists, and only nine of these were still farming when the company ended the project in 1949.[34]

Many of the immigrants pushed out Ovimbundu entrepreneurs from the position they had retained in commerce in the highlands. In the latter part of the 1930s, the *concelho* of Huambo alone boasted 290 small settler businesses, and Bailundu had 151. By 1943, Nova Lisboa (Huambo) alone had more than 509 retail shops,[35] and Caala had 137 stores in 1946.[36]

White immigration jumped after the Second World War, when the government stopped attempting to develop a white yeoman class and recruited–middle class Portuguese to fill mid-level management positions in both private and state concerns. In 1948 civil servants and military personnel numbered 7,284 persons, or more than 60 percent of all Portuguese settlers coming to the colony.[37] The government also encouraged settlers from Belgium, Germany, and Italy, hoping that these immigrants would help Portugal strengthen its control in Angola.[38]

These later immigration initiatives also had region-specific ramifications for the Ovimbundu, since officials continued to regard the central highlands as a major center for white settlement. By the 1950s, a number of peasants from northern Portugal and Madeira took advantage of new government incentives and settled in Angola. The region of Cela, some 240 kilometers from Nova Lisboa, eventually hosted the largest state-run settlement program in the colony with an area totalling one and a quarter million acres.[39] By 1955 the state was spending an average of 150,000 *escudos* per family,[40] and three hundred Portuguese were actually living in Cela in 1960.[41]

The government's open-door immigration policy also led to a fourfold increase in voluntary white immigration, with the total numbers growing from 44,000 in 1940 to 173,000 by 1960.[42] Cities in the southern part of the colony mainly benefitted from increased immigration. Between 1940 and 1960, the white population of Benguela and Lobito increased by 70 percent and 75 per cent respectively, numbering 10,474 and 24,000 persons by 1960.[43] Nova Lisboa's white population rose by more than 70 percent, standing at 28,000 persons in 1960 and continuing to increase; it was second only to Luanda's.[44]

This explosion in the white population further marginalized the Ovimbundu, who occupied the areas that many white settlers coveted. The availability of jobs and government services made Nova Lisboa a magnet for the white population. Not only was the city the seat of the district of Huambo, with oversight over the Concelho of Huambo and five administrative posts, but the Benguela Railway and other businesses centered their operations there. The whites who monopolized the jobs in government and private establishments occupied what became the best real estate in the city and pushed the Ovimbundu residents into what became an expanding *bairro indigena* (black slum). Indeed, in 1955 the soba of Huambo was forced to move his residence from Congolala, where it had been since 1903, to some kilometers away because of quarrying of rock for buildings in the expanding city.[45]

A New Deal For Africans? Taxation, Labor, Marketing, and Agriculture

The colony-wide restructuring of the bureaucracy and the economic initiatives that the New State encouraged also had region-specific ramifications for the Ovimbundu population. The initiatives which most directly affected the population were those dealing with the taxation, labor, marketing, and agricultural policies they intended to apply to the African population. Officials were convinced that government control over these four areas was essential if they were to establish an authoritarian state in the colony and drain the colony of its resources.[46]

The taxation burdens Africans were supposed to bear figured prominently in the government's plans. New State bureaucrats wanted Africans to cover "their quota of the general budget,"[47] and matched projected expenses to projected tax receipts from the African people.[48] Writing in 1938, the governor of Benguela emphasized the official position, stressing that "the natives should pay back for the protection which they receive [by] . . . helping in the collection of the *imposto de capitação* [tax of submission or head tax] . . . helping in their fiscal obligations by finding work, and by identifying those who have not paid."[49]

New State officials also strengthened the procedures for controlling African labor. They incorporated elements of the 1899 labor legislation into the 1930 Colonial Act and put additional regulations on the books, linking the welfare of Africans to their work for Europeans. A 1933 despatch from Manuel Vicente de Almeida de Neves, Director of Native Affairs, set out the core ideology: that Africans had to work for Europeans in order to become civilized, a position also adopted by other colonial governments in their colonies. As in other colonies, the real motive of New State officials was not the "civilizing mission" but the subordination of Ovimbundu labor to the state. In a circular sent to administrators, who were required to publicize it among "all natives in Angola," work by Africans in Angola was identified as an essential part of life. The circular emphasized that "in the past the natives stopped working and let their children live in misery, even to the point of starvation which is still evident today," It concluded that if the "black man wishes to have equal rights with the white man . . . he must work."[50]

Peasant farming did not qualify as work guaranteeing "civilized" status; as only work done for the colonial state and for private concerns fulfilled the state criteria.[51] Officials also argued that by requiring Africans to work for Europeans they guaranteed that Africans would pay taxes, and legislation spelled out the amount of work adult Africans had to perform in order to meet their "natural fiscal obligation."[52] Decrees from the 1930s required administrators and *chefes* to facilitate labor recruiting for public and private use,[53] and gave the state a much larger role in recruiting African labor, overriding directives that the Overseas Office had passed in 1926 making it illegal for officials to be involved in labor recruiting.

As part of their plan to bring the economy under government and settler control, officials in the Overseas Office laid down other regulations dealing with African farming. From the beginning, government economists were ambivalent about the future of African agriculture. While a few wanted to promote African peasant farming and praised the progress that had been made up to that time,[54] the majority felt that the needs of Portugal would be best served by settler farming.

Two issues dominated the discussions concerning the future of African agriculture. The first focused on how government could maximize profits from the peasantry, and the other dealt with how to create the conditions which would allow settler farmers and plantations access to African labor. The first concern, maximizing profits from African peasants, could take the form of modernizing African agriculture. In this scenario, the state could give producers access to loans and extension services (that is, promote an African peasantry) and regulate the marketing of African-grown products through marketing boards (really a disguised means of raising taxes). The second issue, concerning the labor needs of the state and the private sector, dealt with whether this could be achieved by allowing Africans to be producers using traditional methods while still fulfilling settler and state labor demands. In the end, the government need for revenues and for cheap African labor in settler businesses favored regulating marketing and increasing production at the cost of modernizing African agriculture.

During the 1930s New State officials targeted the African peasant sector, which they regarded as vital in the efforts to maximize state revenues and eliminate African profit. To this end they set up marketing boards—the *Grémio do Milho Colonial* (Colonial Maize Board, 1933) and the *Junta de Exportação dos Cereais* (Organization of Cereal Export, 1938)[55] to begin operations in the colony, and especially in the central highlands. While these parastatal corporations were meant to help Portugal out of the Depression, and to achieve Salazar's goal for cereal self-sufficiency in the Portuguese empire, their impact on the Ovimbundu peasants was to undermine, in large part, the advances that had made before the 1930s.

The boards were established because of pressure from wholesale purchasers of colonial products in Portugal, who believed that backward marketing practices in the colonies were responsible for the low quality of colonial exports. They blamed the hundreds of petty Portuguese traders in Angola, in particular, for the situation. Other critics pointed out that the state agency (*Agência Commercial dos Productos Agricolas*)[56] that was established in 1928 to monitor coffee and maize destined for export had done little to improve the situation.[57]

The marketing boards became the main instrument for implementing the regime's agricultural program in the highlands. One of the four offices the *Grémio* set up in Angola was in Nova Lisboa. It was initially responsible for regulating all aspects of production, marketing, and exporting of maize in the region. When the *Junta* was established in 1938, responsibilities were split between the two agencies, with the *Junta* coordinating all activities linked to marketing and export, especially setting and implementing export standards, while the *Grémio's* main function was to provide high-grade seeds to African producers.[58]

The Vision Realized: The Ovimbundu Undermined

Taxation

New State success in the highlands was largely due to the ability of local officials to extend administrative control to Ovimbundu villages and to direct the economy away from Ovimbundu control to state and settler control. The government policies had an evident impact on Christian (largely Protestant) Ovimbundu, on collaborating Ovimbundu representatives, and on the masses of non-Christian Ovimbundu producers who had responded to the increase in demand for export products up to 1926. Between 1926 and 1960 New State policies transformed Ovimbundu producers and traders into a variety of different economic groups including migrant laborers, rural

producers, Christian farmers, urban proletarians and government functionaries. This division of the population into distinct economic groups (yet
unified by culture, language and region) served the different economic needs
of the state and parastatal organizations, private businesses, and settlers.

The colony-wide goals that New State officials established for dealing
with the African population had an immediate impact on the Ovimbundu.
The population first confronted the new policy in 1927, when new fiscal
measures to fight inflation led to a 20 percent devaluation of the currency
when the *angolar* replaced the *escudo*. In that year, prices for consumer
goods (salt, dried fish, palm oil, wines) rose by 20 percent, while maize and
beans brought in only 80 percent of their 1926 value. Taxes on the group
also rose. In 1929–30, the taxes on Africans increased from 40 to 80
angolares.[59] Taxes also increased in 1937 when the tax year was changed
from a fiscal year starting in July to a calendar year starting in January.[60]
Furthermore, in 1940, in response to settler lobbying for increased taxes on
the Ovimbundu (the argument was that higher taxes would force them to
work for settlers), the administration raised taxes by a steep 35 percent to
108 *angolares*.[61]

The Ovimbundu also felt the effects of government taxation policies
as local officials redoubled their efforts to add more Ovimbundu taxpayers
to the rolls. Putting more pressure on their hand-picked sekulus, and sobas
who feared the public whippings and ridicule, led to the numbers of eligible Ovimbundu taxpayers climbing rapidly. Officials also made businesses
withhold taxes from migrant workers' wages. Furthermore, they increased
taxes by imposing residential and personal property taxes on Africans and
assimilados residing in urban and semiurban areas and requiring African
craftsmen to purchase licenses.[62] By the 1950s, every eligible Ovimbundu
male (who met the minimum age requirement) was listed on the tax rolls.
On paper the only people exempt from paying head taxes were rural producers who "regularly farm an area of not less than 10 hectares where animal or mechanical implements are used."[63] This group made up less than
one percent of the African population of the central highlands.

This comprehensive approach to African taxation showed results as
early as 1930, when "native taxes" became the largest single contribution to
the colony's budget, amounting to nearly 2,000,000 pounds sterling (ap-
proximately $4,000,000 U.S.).[64] In the 1948 Angolan budget, native taxes
accounted for 65 percent (60,000,000 *angolares* out of the total 91,855,000
angolares or ($1,650,000 U.S out of $2,530,000).[65] For most Ovimbundu,
tax day exposed them to some of the worst aspects of government exploitation
of village communities, as *chefes* intimidated, threatened, and brutalized

them to make them pay the taxes. Tax collection measures often resulted in a general exodus of men, as *cipaes* (policemen) arrested defaulters and sent them for corvée labor and subjected sobas and sekulus to public beatings and imprisonment.[66] In 1945 the tax amounted to about five months' wages for an individual.[67]

A significant part of the increase in the taxes came from first-time Ovimbundu tax-payers. Success was also evident in the numerical increase in the number of Africans from the highlands listed on the tax rolls. Between the 1928–29 tax year and 1939, a period for which figures are available, a total of 238,387 men were listed as being eligible to pay taxes annually.[68] Figures collected for the *concelho* of Bailundu in 1936 recorded a total of 55,000 eligible (by virtue of age) male taxpayers, of which 18 percent were listed as exempt (by virtue of the amount of land they farmed, old age, etc.). By 1942, figures for the same *concelho* identified more than 105,260 males who were subject to pay hut taxes, while a paltry 11,393 or 9 percent of African males in the area were exempt for reasons of old age and *assimilado* status.[69] The number of Ovimbundu tax-payers rose rapidly after the Second World War. In 1948, some 345,000 Africans in the *concelho* of Huambo alone were listed as eligible to pay taxes.[70] The figures for the region as a whole continued to increase after that year.

Labor

The comprehensive colony-wide labor reform strategy that New State officials put into place from 1926 to 1960 also dovetailed with their tax initiatives. In the highlands, it succeeded in dragooning Ovimbundu men, and ultimately women and children, to work in public and parastatal organizations. The laws which the New State regime implemented required all able-bodied men who were unable to convince local officials that they were able to take care of their families while working on their own account to work for a white employer for nine months a year. If the men did not find work, they were liable to be conscripted to work for the government or for a private employer of the government's choice.[71]

The policies also increased the numbers of Ovimbundu males who became migrant workers in the privately owned plantations and industries (coffee, fisheries, sugar, sisal, and palm oil) throughout the colony. With male and female recruiting rising to meet the nationwide demand for labor, the Ovimbundu peasant and subsistence economy rapidly collapsed.[72]

Labor censuses for the central highlands reflect the trend. For example, as shown in Table 3.1, between 1935 and 1937 Benguela and Bié

Table 3–1 (a)
Men Eligible for Recruitment

Provinces	1935	1937
Benguela	27,591	37,502
Bié	29,.401	40,141

Table 3–1 (b)
Worker Profile, 1936

Workers	Benguela	Bié
Total No.	208,595	167,795
Self-employed	99,229	118,755
Privately employed	71,864	21,449
Available for Recruitment	37,502	27,591

provinces showed a 30 to 35 percent increase in the number of males listed as eligible for recruitment, allowing officials to respond more efficiently to labor demands.[73]

The number of Ovimbundu recruited continued to rise. In 1946, public works and 99 private agencies[74] recruited over 80,000 Ovimbundu workers;[75] between 1949 and 1954 the number of workers recruited went from 150,000 (or slightly more than 20 percent of the local male labor force) to 379,000.[76] By the late fifties, nearly four of every five Ovimbundu males did migrant labor.

By the 1940s Ovimbundu migrants dominated the labor forces of Portuguese-run fisheries from Mossamedes to the Bahia dos Tigres bordering South West Africa (Namibia), and of coastal and São Tomé plantations and other businesses on the coast; in addition, several thousand Ovimbundu men worked in public and port services in Luanda and other regions of the colony.[77] In 1941, Ovimbundu men working as contract laborers in the plantations and fisheries numbered 17,556, while between 1955 and 1957 the majority of the 42,181 workers employed in the sisal and sugar plantations of the sub-plateau region were Ovimbundu.[78] They also accounted for a large percentage of the 9,000 to 10,000 men working on the northern coffee plantations.[79] Other large employers of Ovimbundu labor during the 1950s were the Benguela Railway (just under 12,000 in 1955) and the fisheries, which employed nearly 15,000 migrants.[80] Officials in other parts of the country favored Ovimbundu workers, and requests for them came from all over the territory.[81]

The success of the migrant labor system was tied to the campaign to collect taxes from the population, and *chefes* relied on private businesses to round up tax evaders. In the 1935–36 tax year, for example, the administrator in Bailundo estimated that he would use about 25–30 percent of the eligible male population, or about 60,000 men, in local public works and for contract labor outside the *concelho*.[82] Another 1936 report noted that 15,000, or 30 percent of the men on the tax rolls in Bailundu, had not paid their taxes, and that officials were looking for prospective employers for them.[83]

As businesses in the colony came to rely on the state or private recruiters to provide them with contract laborers, they closed off the opportunities that had allowed the Ovimbundu to operate in a free labor market. Statistics available for a few of the larger companies illustrate this. In 1935 for example, more than half the workers at the Portuguese owned sugar plantation—*Sociedade Agrícola Cassequal*—were contract laborers from the highlands.[84] In 1936 the English-owned Benguela Estates Company obtained one thousand to twelve hundred contract workers and local forced laborers to fell trees at its plantation at Capoco. The yearly reports of the company noted that *chefes* were willing to supply men whenever the need arose.[85]

This labor system, like its predecessors, became riddled with abuses, and the men faced exploitation exceeding anything found in other European colonies in Africa.   Labor laws which linked work that Africans performed for Europeans with acquisition of civilization, which banned trade unions, and which depended on employers to withhold taxes allowed many of them to disregard government regulations concerning salary, rations, and housing of workers without fear of penalty and still be guaranteed their labor supply. Since local officials disregarded the laws intended to protect the welfare of "native" workers and peasants, once employers were passing on taxes collected from the workers to the state, Ovimbundu workers had few means to report abuses, to sue and receive redress, or access private benevolent groups that might act as watchdogs.

Ovimbundu migrants suffered the worst of the abuses. Descriptions of the recruiting practices of state and private agencies include instances in which laborers were recruited and transported under circumstances reminiscent of the worst aspects of the Atlantic slave trade. Scenes of "long lines of men tied neck to neck with rope . . . marching to collection points where they would be put into box carts or trucks and shipped to the point of work" were not uncommon.[86]

Private recruiters, many of them recently landed settlers, published advertisements in the colony's newspapers promising to supply businesses—many of them disreputable, unlicensed, and undercapitalized—with a certain number of workers (a hundred or so) for an agreed-upon amount. One advertisement in a Luanda daily newspaper promised to bring laborers to any coffee plantation for 500 *escudos* per man, which was to cover recruitment cost, transport, food, and the recruiter's salary.[87]

Corruption was rampant throughout the system, and many poorly paid government officials succumbed to the bribes recruiters offered them to supply workers.[88] José de Jesus Pires, an old settler in Dondi, admitted to the missionary John Tucker that the contract labor system was worse for the Africans than the slavery of the past. He recalled that, in the old days, "I went to the interior and bought slaves with goods . . . they were my own risk . . . I fed them well, I medicined them well . . . If I didn't do so, my capital would shrink." With the contract system, however, he simply went to the "*chefe do posto*", gave him his *mata-bicho* (tip), so much per head, and "get my needs supplied, 20, 30, 50, 100 *contractos*."[89]

The system remained much the same when the British consul, S.P. House, observed it in 1951. He wrote: "The price paid to the administration in bribes for forced labor has reached extraordinary heights. It goes up to 1500 *angolares* a head for men, and 1000 *angolares* for little boys of ten or twelve."[90] Many recruits were simply rounded up in nightly kidnapping forays.[91] *Chefes* often filled quotas with exempt individuals, including catechists and even lepers.[92]

Recruiters also enlisted underage boys and older men and advanced them a hundred to two hundred *angolares* to pay delinquent taxes. In many instances, no taxes were paid or, if they were, the money went to pay other debts incurred during the worker's contract. Fear of being replaced led many sobas and sekulus to buy into the system, and some carried out personal vendettas against villagers, sending innocent men to forced labor for "disobeying" their orders.[93]

Migrants were also abused in other ways, receiving inadequate food, housing, and rations, despite official requirements stipulating that employers should spend up to three hundred and eighty *escudos* per recruit for transport, clothing, taxes, vaccination, and rations.[94] By the 1950s, when the laws changed and required employers to pay migrants on two-year labor contracts between one hundred and one hundred and fifty *escudos* per month before taxes, in addition to housing, rations, and clothing, many recruits were lucky if they received even one issue of clothing.[95]

Physical mistreatment of Ovimbundu migrants by employers was widespread in both rural and urban areas, as state monitoring was nonexistent. Eyewitnesses noted that it was common to see white employers physically punish African workers even in the presence of state officials. A 1960 report of an incident on the docks of Lobito spoke of a Portuguese foremen who "kicked and cuffed" African laborers under the eyes of Portuguese policemen, without any intervention by the latter.[96]

Despite the concerns of sympathetic observers who warned against sending Ovimbundu migrants to coastal fisheries because of the high mortality rate, the number of contract laborers from the highlands increased in the fisheries.[97] Here, a sixteen-hour work day became the norm, and many workers who were unable to keep up were flogged with the *jambok* (a long whip made of rolled hippopotamus hides). A number of them died from overwork. Conditions remained terrible even after officials inspected these operations.[98] In 1945, mortality rates of contract workers were more than 40 percent, and by the 1950s more than 50 percent according to unofficial estimates.[99] Not even the threat of international censure stopped the New State's drive to control Ovimbundu labor. Until 1960 the labor abuses continued openly, despite international condemnation. Portuguese officials simply ignored complaints, since Portugal was not a signatory to the Abolition of Penal Sanctions Act and the Abolition of Forced Labor Act which the International Labor Organization (ILO) had passed in 1955 and 1957 to put an end to abuses of workers in colonized areas.[100]

Many Ovimbundu males turned to migrant labor as an alternative to *corvée* labor, and by the 1940s they went voluntarily to urban centers in the colony and abroad. In 1941, for the *concelho* of Bailundo alone, 10,000 males had secretly left their villages.[101] Many of them went to Northern Rhodesia (now Zambia), where working conditions were better and wages higher. Indeed, Ovimbundu refugees accounted for a significant percentage of the more than 300,000 Angolan refugees (locally called "Wawiko") in Northern Rhodesia during the Second World War. One Protestant missionary wrote that he was in contact with more than 20,000 Ovimbundu in Northern Rhodesia at the time.[102]

The trend continued after the war, as thousands of Ovimbundu voluntarily joined the growing numbers of Africans moving between the urban centers inside Angola and the mining centers of Katanga, the Rhodesias, and South Africa to avoid the forced labor system.[103] During the mid-fifties an urban-rural divide among the Ovimbundu population was evident, with 12,000 Ovimbundu men residing in Luanda, 12,000 on the Rand in South Africa, 30,000 in the city of Nova Lisboa, 25,000 in Lobito, and smaller numbers in the small European centers scattered along the railroad. By 1960 the Ovimbundu, mostly men, made up a significant percentage of the more than one half million Angolans living in neighboring colonies.[104] Many no longer had to be coerced into leaving the village for work, as most boys as young as twelve years old "volunteer[ed] to go to Gabela and other centers that need labor."[105]

The labor system also affected women and children, who were required to do unpaid labor for the state, to fulfill the terms of the 1933 Colonial Charter. By the 1950s with males away on migrant labor, officials turned to women and children to build and maintain roads and bridges for the expanding white settler population.[106] British consular and missionary reports for the 1950s provide vivid pictures of pregnant women, many with babies strapped to their backs, and children as young as six, who performed roadwork in many parts of the highlands. The situation had worsened by 1960, when reports of "gangs of small children and . . . a gang of young women doing heavy (road) work" became more numerous.[107]

Marketing and Agriculture

The program which the marketing boards (the *Junta* and the *Grémio*) pursued also directly weakened the economic autonomy of the Ovimbundu peasant and subsistence producers. Through the boards, the state intervened in the marketing, export, and production sectors of the peasant economy, and imposed a new regime on the peasants. This included setting and implementing standards, providing high-grade seeds to African producers, providing ploughs to producers at cost, promoting experimental work with cereals, and advising subsistence producers on ways to improve their farming techniques and increase output.[108]

The ultimate aim of the *Grémio* was not to develop African peasant agriculture, but to exploit African producers more efficiently by requiring producers to grow the high-quality grains which would meet export standards. Although in 1932 the Benguela Railway Company donated 50,000 *escudos*' worth (15,000 kilograms) of different varieties of high-grade wheat seeds to *chefes* and Catholic missionaries for distribution to Ovimbundu living along the railroad, the general quality of exports remained low.[109]

By the early 1940s, agents of the *Grémio* and *Junta* decided that distributing high-quality seeds to the Ovimbundu was crucial for maize to become a competitive export. They pressed *chefes*, sobas, sekulus, missionaries, and other local leaders into distributing several tons of high quality and fast-maturing imported maize seeds to Ovimbundu peasants.[110] The recipients were obliged to give back to the agency the amount they had received, plus 10 percent commission.[111] The *Grémio* also supplied Portuguese-made plows to Africans at cost on the same terms.[112] Between 1939 and 1940, the agents also ran campaigns to encourage the population to grow rice and wheat, and distributed 7,096 tons of wheat seed to Europeans and Africans[113] to capitalize on the rise in wheat prices caused by the war. Wheat at this point was selling at twice the price of maize.[114]

Because the maize distribution promoted a crop whose export the Ovimbundu had initiated after the collapse of rubber as an export crop in 1914, the program had a dramatic and long-lasting impact on agriculture in the highlands. It encouraged producers to increase the amount of land devoted to maize cultivation. In the *concelho* of Huambo, for example, government surveys in the 1930s indicated that a total of 17,000 Ovimbundu producers farmed 57,000 hectares of land, or a little over 3 hectares per farmer, one hectare more than the average household had farmed, according to government surveys in 1923–24.[115] The amount of land under maize cultivation, specifically, in the provinces of Bié and Benguela rose by over 30 percent between 1934 and 1941—going from 503,885 hectares in 1935 to 714,444 hectares in 1941.[116]

The growing economic importance of maize was reflected in export statistics, in which it accounted for 17.1 percent of the value of Angola's exports in 1932.[117] By the 1940s, maize growing and trading dominated "the entire economic life of vast regions of the province."[118] In 1942 the estimated harvest in the highlands was put at 200,000 tons [119] and the region's export rose significantly after 1945. The amount of maize exported from Angola between 1926 and 1960 rose from under 40,000 tons to 137,800 tons, and attests to the success of the measures implemented by the marketing agencies. In addition, the *Junta* became the final purchaser of African maize geared for export and built warehouses to clean, husk, and store it.[120]

The marketing boards also attacked the barter system of trade between Europeans and Africans, with the aim of pushing both groups out of trade and into the roles the government wanted them to play in the economy: Africans as producers of cash exports and laborers and Portuguese as yeoman farmers.[121] The boards implemented new measures which required traders to use money instead of barter to purchase African-grown maize, and imposed numerous regulations for disinfecting, cleaning, and processing the maize before export.[122] They created commercial zones, forced Portuguese and Afro-Portuguese to purchase licenses, and regulated the annual markets. They also set a limit on the amount per kilo that African producers could receive for their maize.[123]

In the 1940s, laws excluded African producers from engaging in any other economic activity aside from growing maize and becoming migrant laborers. For example, decrees made it illegal for African producers to husk corn or rice before sale, and required them to transport their produce to a European-run business with husking machines. In 1944, the *Junta* required small-scale Portuguese and Afro-Portuguese merchants to make manifests identifying the amount of maize they purchased from Africans. Its agents also set the times (twice yearly) for purchasing honey, and required wax and honey collectors to buy honey extractors, a move which eventually resulted in a significant decline in the number of Ovimbundu extracting honey on a part-time basis because of the high cost of the device.[124] The *Junta* also made it illegal for Africans to brew traditional beverages (*okacipemba* and *ocimbombo*) from sweet potatoes and maize.[125] In cities such as Lobito, local statutes criminalized retail trade by Africans, as did the 1943 statute which could be used to bring criminal charges against anyone who purchased imported items from Africans. The law stipulated that Africans could sell only those goods that they had made themselves.[126] African producers who sold their produce themselves received lower prices than Europeans who resold African-grown products.[127]

Although these measures were economically inefficient, officials defended them, arguing in the mid-1930s that the Depression, locust invasions, droughts, and backward trading practices called for government intervention. In the long run, the restrictions served to strengthen the authority of the state and allowed the redistribution of profits from Africans to colonial officials and selected settlers.

While they pushed maize production and attempted to bring marketing under their control, agents of the boards did little to improve the peasant sector, despite the desire in some official circles to support African property rights. They argued that examples from developments in peasant agriculture in the French and British colonies[128] augured well for Ovimbundu peasant producers, but their concerns went no further than being incorporated into the 1933 Colonial Act. A stipulation exempted Africans farming ten hectares of land and using modern methods from hut tax and forced labor.[129]

Those ordinary Ovimbundu who wanted to buy land were unable to do so, because sobas and sekulus frustrated their efforts in an attempt to protect their rights to distribute lineage lands. They also feared the growth of a class of Ovimbundu property owners who could challenge some of their privileges. Moreover, many *chefes* also did not support the idea of the growth of an Ovimbundu Kulak class. In 1935 only 12,834 hectares of the land Ovimbundu farmed were privately owned,[130] while 503,885 hectares were farmed under land tenure practices in existence prior to the establishment of the New State.[131]

Moreover, Ovimbundu who owned land outright faced settler hostility and official neglect.[132] Indeed, in 1936 when Portugal was expecting an international loan, the government refused to support a proposal which would have led to the establishment of an agricultural bank to provide credit to African farmers. The British consul in Angola observed that "the poor negro is not to have his slice of the cutting up of this juicy melon . . . although [he is the] backbone of the agricultural system." The pro-peasant sentiment in the administration was evident in the 1940s, however, when a program established in 1949 promoting an African peasantry proved moderately successful (see below).[133]

Thus, besides responding to the taxation and labor demands of the state, the Ovimbundu grew cash crops (mainly maize) for a colonial regime more interested in the profits it made from local and export sales than in modernizing production and opening options to the producers. By the 1950s, some five hundred thousand rural producers supplied the colony with more than 95 percent of the maize used locally and exported.[134] An official report of 1953 noted that "women and children" were the reason behind the supply, since the labor migrancy system diverted men and boys from farming.[135] Because most of their income from migrant labor went to taxes, migrants had neither the inclination for farming nor the knowledge, skills, or resources to become independent peasants. Unlike the porters and petty traders who had prospered during the caravan trade, Ovimbundu migrants returned to their villages after two or three years with little more than funds to cover back taxes and here and there to buy a radio, bicycle, or sewing machine.[136]

Yet agents of the marketing boards did not consider women and children suitable subjects to be trained in "modern farming," taking the position that any change would be disastrous to Portuguese economic objectives. In fact, they reasoned that the women ought to be able to sustain expected production levels with existing methods.[137] As with taxes and labor migrancy, the rise in maize production came at a tremendous cost to the Ovimbundu. Among the more serious issues were the use of more marginal land, the widespread adoption of the plow, and the lack of agricultural assistance from the state. The state's labor requirements, which prevented producers from leaving sufficient time between harvest and fallow, also undermined the rural economy.[138]

The first warning of problems appeared with a precipitous drop in yield per acre. In 1942 the average yield from a hectare of land was only four to five hundred kilograms, half of what it had been in the 1920s.[139] Furthermore, land erosion occurred at an alarming rate as the more marginal land was cultivated without regard to conservation and rehabilitation.[140] To halt the decline, the government promoted "rural well-being" campaigns, focusing mainly on soil conservation measures and targeting Ovimbundu men. In 1956, the *Junta* even earmarked 240,000 hectares of land in Huambo and Bié so that agricultural agents could undertake experiments with the peasants to stem the "destructive agriculture."[141] This belated attempt failed because the men who were the targets of the campaign were not present long enough to benefit—and were not farmers either.

The marketing policies of the *Grémio* and *Junta* also severely undermined Ovimbundu agriculture.[142] Before 1945, villagers living within a fifty-mile radius of the railroad were always assured of a viable return for their maize crop, despite being cheated by unscrupulous Portuguese traders. By the late forties the price controls set by the *Grémio*[143] put producers at an economic disadvantage. In 1949, for example, producers received only 27.1 percent of the price that the Portuguese consumer in Lisbon paid for a kilo of Angolan maize. By 1954, Ovimbundu peasants still received only 70 *centavos* per kilo for their maize, at a time when peasants in Mozambique received 155 *centavos* per kilo. This was less than 30 percent of the price the metropolitan consumer paid.[144] Despite the additional marketing, processing, and transport costs involved, the marketing agencies still profited from the price controls.

The decline of the rural economy was also due to the state's taxation and labor policies, which kept the earnings of migrants low and thereby lessened their ability to contribute to the village economy. In 1945, for example, when inflation in the colony stood at 300 percent, a contract laborer received 100 *angolares* a day, the same as in 1937.[145] Moreover, contractees received 2½ times less per day than free laborers.[146] Since their wives and children did unpaid work for the state, they also contributed less than before to household income.

The state's policy condoning private-sector exploitation of Africans also undermined the Ovimbundu village economy.[147] The downturn was evident from the 1940s, when the financial shoestring on which the colonial government was operating, as well as Salazar's immigration policies for dealing with the economic and social problems in Portugal, also led poor, desperate, and unprepared peasants as well as some criminals and other undesirables to settle in the colony.[148] Many of the newcomers who flocked to the highland were unscrupulous, and soon followed the time-tested practice of opening up small businesses, especially private credit outlets, and advancing credit (*otingo*) at outrageous rates to Africans who needed cash to cover taxes. At the end of the harvests, or when migrants returned from contract labor, debtors handed over entire harvests and wages to cover their debt (*fuca*).[149] The loan sharks did not hesitate to take livestock, implements, and even wives and children from a peasant who was unable to repay his debt.[150] Others cheated the population by fixing weights and imposing their own form of private justice on creditors,[151] knowing full well that they would not be prosecuted.

The status of urban Ovimbundu, who were officially prevented from making inroads in the urban economy, also demonstrates how far-reaching New State initiatives were and how much they helped to explain why the Ovimbundu became a subjugated labor force and impoverished rural producers during the period. By the 1950s more than sixty five thousand Ovimbundu lived in the various urban centers of the colony, including Luanda, Lobito, Benguela, and Nova Lisboa.[152] Before the Second World War the majority were day laborers, but a minority worked as interpreters, nurses, teachers, and pastors in mission schools and health clinics, while some worked as carpenters and masons. Others were petty entrepreneurs making a living as fishmongers, washerwomen, shoe shine boys, and handymen.[153]

By 1960, however, settlers had displaced the Ovimbundu from service and skilled occupations in Nova Lisboa, Benguela, and Lobito. Most craftsmen lost their Portuguese customers, and employers laid off or demoted long-serving Ovimbundu employees and replaced them with Portuguese-born settlers.[154] The group witnessed a dramatic decline in their status as many found themselves competing with cheaper contract labor or poor Portuguese laborers. In 1960, the average wage of an assimilated African worker (who represented the most prosperous of African households) in Lobito was 200 to 250 *escudos* (about 7.00 to $10.00 U.S. per month). In 1958 the average monthly wage of white workers in the same position was 1500 *escudos* (about $52 U.S.), over six times the amount the Ovimbundu worker received.[155] Urban Ovimbundu also paid higher taxes, faced racial quotas, and suffered from an official labor policy which gave the state the right to Ovimbundu labor. In Lobito and Novo Lisboa, long-term Ovimbundu residents were often picked up by soldiers and policemen and sent out as contract workers or were forced to do unpaid labor for the state if found without a residential pass.[156]

"Coping with the Contradictions": Decline or Survival?

As studies of settler colonies like Kenya and the Rhodesias have shown, the road toward the authoritarian state was not without its contradictions. In the central highlands the contradictions were evident at both the political and the economic levels and allowed some Ovimbundu a certain degree of local autonomy.

African Titleholders

In comparison with the former monarchist and republican regimes, the New State government made significant advances in their plans to develop a group of Ovimbundu representatives who would be loyal to the state. Depite the individual resistance that titleholders like Sakaita Savimbi waged against the state,[157] between 1926 and 1960 local officials had identified and eliminated a significant number of sekulus and sobas they suspected of being anti-Portuguese. The bureaucratic reorganization had also resulted in a nomination process which allowed only a few collaborating Ovimbundu to function as government-approved traditional titleholders.[158] In many cases, *chefes* nominated *regedores* (African government representatives) who, along with Ovimbundu catechists, priests, and other assimilated Africans carried out the government's directives. These Africans served as brokers, and saved the state the expense of employing Portuguese civil servants.[159]

Yet the system still relied on Ovimbundu traditional titleholders in order to function. New State bureaucrats were convinced that using Ovimbundu who had links to the precolonial ruling lineages was sound policy, since the goal was to create African Portuguese collaborators who knew the laws and language of the Ovimbundu. Thus, sekulus and sobas continued to settle disputes in the villages, in addition to collecting taxes and sending out contract labor.[160] The number of those serving in the government was high, for among the administrative posts of Bailundu alone some 280 sekulus and 10 sobas were listed in 1944.[161] In 1948 the *concelho* of Huambo (later included in the province of Huambo) had 495 traditional authorities—sobas and sekulus—who worked with the administration to manage an adult male taxpaying population totalling 345,000 persons (not including women, children and the elderly).[162]

What local officials attempted to ensure, however, was that no strong, independent-thinking candidate was confirmed as soba or sekulu. Ovimbundu who served in these capacities were a far cry from the proud men who had resisted the Portuguese. Although many lived in fear of physical punishment and public humiliation[163] and were ignorant of Portuguese language and customs, the prestige of others among the Ovimbundu population remained high. The case of the *concelho* of Bailundo is instructive. Here, descendants of the precolonial rulers retained the title of *soba grande* and had immense influence on Bailundo's population.[164] New State policies deprived the *soba grande* of the rights that precolonial Ovimbundu rulers had exercised, yet local Portuguese *chefes* were dependent on his prestige, which enabled labor recruiting, military conscription, and tax collection to take place in his jurisdiction.[165]

Thus, despite government laws to the contrary, in some areas of the highlands a system of indirect rule survived well into the fifties. The British anthropologist Adrian Edwards recorded how the system worked in 1956–57 in Bimbe where he spent a year doing research. He noted that in the villages where he undertook research there was hardly any Portuguese administrative presence. He wrote that the "*chefe de posto* visits each subchief" once a year, and that the relationship between *chefes* and the people usually concerned taxes, labor recruitment, and judicial matters.[166] These same collaborating traditional titleholders proved crucial, from the 1960s onwards, to the gains that the anticolonial forces made among the Ovimbundu population.

The contradictions were also evident in the regime's approach to military recruitment. When the colony-wide policy of conscription of eligible males came into effect, Ovimbundu soldiers became one of the fastest growing groups in the colonial army. In 1959, 67,813 men, or 25 percent of the 188,408 Africans recorded in the military census, were from the provinces of Benguela, Bié–Cuando–Cubango, and Huambo, which were overwhelmingly Ovimbundu.[167] When the recruits were called up, the highlands and other rural areas contributed far more than did urban areas. Thus, while only 13 percent of the males aged twenty to twenty-nine from Luanda were judged eligible for the army in 1959, more than 47 percent from Huambo province were.[168] Even though few of the recruits who registered actually served in the armed forces—fewer than eight thousand men were called up at the time—the number of Ovimbundu was significant.[169] Their numbers also increased in 1960 when a draft was passed requiring all men between the ages of twenty to twenty-nine to serve in the colonial army. But the government never had the full loyalty of many of the Ovimbundu conscripts, many of whom would later use their military expertise to contribute to the anticolonial resistance forces that became active in the 1960s.

The African Peasantry

The most pronounced contradiction was between the concerns of the parastatals, plantation owners, and metropolitan industrialists and transporters who wanted producer prices in the colony to remain very low, and small-scale settlers who wanted higher prices and freedom to purchase and market African-grown products. Their desire to push for higher prices in order to retain their retail trade pitted them against the larger trading concerns and the Benguela Railway, against whom they could not compete.

Another area of conflict involved those members of the administration and settlers who believed that the growth of a pro-Portuguese Ovimbundu peasantry would serve as a useful counterpoint to the impoverished rural producers and settlers who favored a pro-migrant policy. The former group did not view the growth of migrancy and an impoverished rural population as developments which would promote the state and settler interests. These contradictions allowed a small group of Ovimbundu to retain some economic independence.[170]

Even the official push to modernize African farming by establishing model peasant villages did not have the desired effect, because of the inherent contradictions. One of the more progressive programs required the government to fund pilot projects to study how to "stabilize African agriculture."[171] The influence of the pro-peasantry group was evident in a plan that went into effect in 1949 when officials in Caconda initiated a model agricultural project. The scheme eventually included a total of eight hundred resident African peasants occupying about 250,000 hectares. The project got off to an excellent start, and the British consul who visited it in 1950 concluded that the peasants were "two or three times better off than the peasants of Bulgaria, which was my last post."[172]

Another model, which was made public in 1950, called for the appointment of an administrator to be in charge of establishing and supervising a group of modern, monogamous African peasant households. The plan envisioned each household as being headed by a "native couple" living in a "hygienically constructed" house, with a small garden around it and with land (five hectares) set aside for cultivation. The authorities were to provide each model couple with "sanitary, social, technical and spiritual assistance."[173] The project was attempted only in 1956, among non-Christian villagers but failed to get off the ground since the women who were the target group had no respect for the *regedores* and *cipaes* whom the Portuguese *chefe* chose to implement the program.[174] They preferred to avoid state representatives while still complying with the regulations regarding taxation.[175] Up to 1960, the program did not expand much beyond the original plan.

Some Ovimbundu managed to avoid government controls. This was particularly the case with the marketing boards, whose policies many small-scale Portuguese settlers opposed. Their opposition at times created a breach in the state's plans and allowed some Ovimbundu to evade the measures the marketing agencies imposed. For example, in 1940, when taxes on the Ovimbundu were raised, some Portuguese merchants who relied on the annual maize sale came out publicly against the increase and also disregarded the policy and openly traded with farmers. In 1943, merchants with the same sentiments brazenly established their own marketing board, while in 1944 others held up a train carrying forced laborers to the coast, arguing that such emigration was "excessive and injurious to their trade."[176]

The Ovimbundu used these opportunities to hold their own economically. At least through the 1930s, and perhaps much later, some Ovimbundu continued to trade on their own, and did not hesitate at the thought of "walking one or two days to find markets to sell their goods and purchase the items which [they needed]".[177] Well into the 1950s, unlicensed Ovimbundu petty traders with "no overhead cost" sold their products in Nova Lisboa and Silva Porto, and many went as far as the Guanhamas to exchange tobacco for cattle.[178] Many of the thirty thousand Africans (mostly Ovimbundu) who lived in the crowded, unsanitary, squalid conditions in Nova Lisboa continued to practice their skills, living off the earnings they obtained from making dresses and suits and repairing shoes for settlers.

Some producers openly challenged the regulations that the marketing agencies imposed. In 1940, for example, some producers in Bailundo openly refused to sign up for government wheat seeds. When confronted by the *chefes*, they defended their action by arguing that they saw no reason why they should give back the seeds and 10 percent surplus to the authorities, when they could do better by planting their own crops.[179] These were the same producers who studied the annual prices listed by the marketing agencies and when prices were set too low, switched to other crops for the next season. For example, in 1943 when *Portaria* no. 4373 led to a reduction in maize prices, the tonnage for the reported harvest fell by nearly half, declining from 131,913 tons in 1942 to 78,060 tons in 1943. As officials suspected, the farmers deliberately made alcohol and ground maize (*fuba*) and sold them to settlers at higher prices.[180] Similarly, rural producers harvested 50 percent fewer beans in 1944 than they had in 1940, because the *Junta* had decreased the price.[181] Moreover, in 1945 when the local newspapers reported that there was a shortage of sweet potatoes in the Belgian Congo, the people responded by growing less maize and more sweet potatoes.[182]

Another glaring contradiction between official policy and reality was the support the state gave for a time to Protestant missionaries who supplied extension and other services to the rural population. The beneficiaries of this policy were mainly Protestant farmers, a group that officials viewed with distrust, but who accounted for a significant percentage of the 365,000 Protestants documented as ethnic Ovimbundu in 1960. Protestant farmers were able to achieve what the *Grémio* and *Junta* had failed to do, by joining a network of Protestant missions that provided them with extension services, training, and expertise.[183]

Although they did not do as well as settler farmers who went into stock breeding or interbreeding, and they seldom used fertilization to increase yields, this group of Ovimbundu peasants was faring well until the 1930s. Figures available for Bailundo clearly identified the trend. They showed that out of 210,619 Ovimbundu living in the *concelho* in 1935–36, a total of 42,253 (or about 20 percen)t were farmers who held title to their land. Furthermore 2,714 were skilled traders and craftsmen including masons, sawyers, and carpenters.[184] These families grew most of the rice, wheat, and varieties of fruits and vegetables that supplied the local market,[185] and they were quite innovative, planting bottom lands, deepening rivers, draining swamps, and generally bringing new land under cultivation.

Ownership of plows was also the hallmark of the progressive farmers, especially Protestants.[186] In Huambo, for example, African farmers (Christian and non-Christian alike) purchased a total of 2,270 plows between 1939 and 1943,[187] despite a price of $17.00 (U.S.) in 1940.[188] A missionary visiting a Christian village in 1935 commented that "the Christians own a large number of plows . . . these Christians are always ready with their money when the government *chefe* calls for the head tax, and are among the best givers to the work of the Lord both in cash and in workers."[189] Moreover, in 1939 alone a number of Ovimbundu Protestant farmers in Sambo and Cuima bought over "200 plows," in addition to "hundreds of heads of cattle" from the Guanhamas.[190]

The increasing number of settlers who came to this region of the highlands, and the effectiveness of the state's labor and taxation policies adversely affected Protestant farmers: only a small percentage of the group (numbering no more than nine hundred in the early 1940s)[191]survived into the 1950s. The father of Aarão Cornelio, a Protestant convert, was typical

Table 3–2
Maize Exports from Angola, 1926–1959

Year	Tons	Year	Tons
1926	37,606	1943	66,013
1927	67,034	1944	70,575
1928	63,211	1945	98,795
1929	53,956	1946	117,592
1930	71,250	1947	43,395
1931	55,336	1948	33,149
1932	54,448	1949	91,944
1933	90,968	1950	189,363
1934	86,198	1951	133,592
1935	46,193	1952	91,241
1936	115,136	1953	77,015
1937	114,586	1954	98,288
1938	128,745	1955	51,892
1939	114,581	1956	132,363
1940	97,581	1957	30,964
1941	151,463	1958	161,201
1942	124,098	1959	137,888

of the successful Christian farmer. In the mid-1950s, Senhor Cornelio owned as many as twelve oxen, as well as plows and other agricultural implements. In addition to his income from selling his crops, he profited by employing hands who prepared the fields of families who did not own plows.[192] Many less successful farmers sent their oxen to the missionary agronomist for training and paid the required fees.[193]

Women in these households supplemented the family income with salaries from teaching, nursing, and farming. The few reports on their activities show that they skillfully manipulated the colonial and gender barriers which they confronted in their homes and in the larger colonial society. One of the most successful used the money earned from the sale of her "superior" corn and her "bran-fed pigs" to put a son through university.[194] Moreover most of these women kept kitchen gardens where they grew lettuce, tomatoes, carrots, cabbages, and other vegetables for home consumption and local sale.[195]

Conclusion

The architects of the New State largely achieved their goal of taking over the reins of political power in the colony and putting in place an economic program which guaranteed the dominance of pro-Salazar Portuguese. In so doing, they closed off any avenue for meaningful political participation by the Ovimbundu in the colony and reduced their economic roles to those of migrant laborers, state slaves, and rural producers. As the largest ethnic group in the colony, the Ovimbundu felt the full impact of government policies.

New State architects were not satisfied with running the colony as an exploitable backwoods of Portugal; they also had a social and cultural agenda. This favored Portuguese over African, urban over rural, Catholic over Protestant, and assimilation over association, and demanded total loyalty to the dictatorship. The Ovimbundu experiences with the social and cultural programs of the New State provide another perspective on the group's relationship with the state, and give some background to the tensions between the Ovimbundu and the state during the anticolonial struggle and the postindependence period.

4

SOCIAL CHANGE AND THE NEW STATE, 1926–1960

Introduction

Even though up to 1960 New State officials stressed their political and economic initiatives, they also had a social agenda which was meant to strengthen the corporatist state centered in Portugal. In 1948, Governor Valdez Thomas dos Santos articulated the central tenet that shaped the thinking of New State architects who pushed the "colonial pact." He wrote that the dictatorship's policies would lead to a "close union of races of different degrees of civilization that help and support each other loyally."[1] Salazar and his advisors believed that state-supported white immigration would advance Portuguese civil and social institutions and make Portuguese culture to become dominant in Angola. The designers of the New State had no interest in integrating African beliefs and customs into the colonial fabric. This position clearly contradicted the multicultural image (*lusotropicalismo*), with its emphasis on the mutuality and intermingling of African, Afro-Portuguese (creole), and Portuguese institutions, that New State propaganda publicized as the ideal of Portuguese colonialism.[2] The social structure New State architects really envisioned was to be molded almost entirely by Portuguese history, culture, and social mores.

In this scheme, the administration divided the population of Angola by race, civil status, and class, with people of visible European racial stock and heritage at the top of the civil and social hierarchy. All nonwhites were in the "uncivilized" category at the bottom of the heirarchy. Civil law accorded "civilized" status to Africans of mixed ancestry and those Africans who achieved *assimilado* (assimilated) status. The majority of the subject African population (natives/*indígenas*) made up the "uncivilized" bottom stratum.[3]

Each stratum was also hierarchically arranged according to class. Among the "civilized" population, metropolitan-born civil, military, and security personnel, along with members of banking, marketing, and large business concerns comprised the top layer, with a middle stratum made up of white settlers, Angolan-born whites, and a minority of Afro-Portuguese professionals and civil servants. The lower segment of the westernized social stratum consisted of poor settlers. The majority of the Afro-Portuguese and assimilated Africans were at the bottom of the "civilized" population. The nonwesternized African masses occupied the lowest position in the colonial social order.

F. W. Heimer has suggested an alternative structure, arguing that the dictatorship's policies created less subtle social divisions. He concluded that only two competing classes actually emerged in Angola, one consisting of a "central society," composed of white settlers, the state and its representatives, and the other consisting of "tributary societies," which included the various African ethnic groups.[4] The analysis here, however, challenges Heimer's, detailing a much more complex structure among the Ovimbundu, where the Protestant Congregational network continued to provide the opportunities for the reformulation of Ovimbundu civil society alongside the social requirements of the New State. This development weakened the hegemony that the state was attempting to impose and further distanced some members of the Ovimbundu population from the state.

Social Engineering: Legislating Status

The most important initiative of the social agenda of New State authorities was the co-option of the Roman Catholic Church and its transformation from an overwhelmingly missionary institution with mostly foreign personnel to a state-controlled organization managed by supporters of the regime. Salazar turned to the Catholic Church soon after the coup in 1926, when he signed a Missionary Act with the Holy See in Rome on behalf of the Portuguese Empire. This Act again gave to the Roman Catholic Church in Portugal and its colonies the formal recognition it had once held as an arm of Portuguese colonization.[5] One article of the Act required the government to pay the salaries of Catholic missionaries in the colonies.[6] In order to show that Portugal still respected the earlier international agreements to allow all denominations to carry out religious work in its African colonies, the Act also guaranteed religious liberty to the peoples of the colonies.[7] Colonial legislation of 1930 reinforced the relationship between the Catholic Church and the state, by stipulating that the goal of the government was to unite Church and state. The 1940 Concordat and Missionary Agreement signed with Rome further strengthened Catholic Church/state relations. In outlining the official role the state envisioned the Catholic Church would play in Portugal and its colonies, the Concordat made the Catholic Church a branch of the government, with one of its main purposes to educate and socialize Africans for eventual assimilation into Portuguese society. The Church was required to follow a program that served the national interests of the New State.[8] This document finally, officially united Church and state as the 1930 Colonial Act had stipulated.[9]

Another major social initiative was embarked on during the 1950s with the passage and implementation of several statutes aimed specifically at the African population. Perhaps the most important of the statutes was the 1954 *Estatuto dos Indígenas das Províncias de Guiné, Angola e Moçambique* (Native Law of the Portuguese Provinces of Guinea, Angola, and Mozambique), which revised older laws and implemented new ones. The law called on the colonial governors to "promote, by all means, the improvement of the moral and material life of the [native] population."[10]

Although the ideas behind the Colonial Act and the statutes were not new in Portuguese thinking, they reached a new orthodoxy during the period of the New State.[11] Armando de Castilho Soares, a respected scholar of the regime, argued that the colony was an enormous cultural laboratory in which the state had to fight valiantly "to attain spiritual unity which would enhance the national integrity of the Portuguese people."[12] Again, these ideas helped legitimize the social engineering that was intended to make Portuguese institutions and values dominant in Angola.

Angolan State Initiatives

Between 1926 and 1954, Angolan officials implemented several social policies in Angola, but before the 1940s they had a difficult time putting the social agenda in place. This was because of the colony's budgets failed to set aside adequate funds for social programs. They began by imparting new life to the legislation that Republican Governor Norton de Matos had initiated in 1921, giving primacy to Portuguese language and civilization. The government's adaptation of the earlier legislation appeared as part of the Colonial Act of 1930, and in legislation of the 1940s and 1950s.

A new push came with the passage of the 1954 Native Law, as the Angolan authorities responded with several decrees on the role of the government in the moral and material uplifting of the African population. For example, a 1955 decree required uniformity in the policies aimed at "civilizing the African population."[13] In 1956, the authorities established the "Provincial Commission of Rural Well-Being" or *bem-estar*. The phrase came to refer to government initiatives dealing with African agriculture, health, religion, and education which were used to divert criticism of the negative impact that the state's economic and political programs were having on the African population. The authorities argued that the rural "well-being" initiative would strengthen the African family and prepare the population for eventual assimilation into white society, even though as a subordinate group. The most notable feature of the program was the establishment of delegations in every district in the colony. The delegations comprised representatives from all the agencies that served the African population, and were in charge of overseeing the transformation of "noncivilized" African producers into modern peasants.[14]

The government's social program also included educating colonial officials about African social structure. During the 1940s and 1950s, Angola was the subject of several ethnographic expeditions conducted through the officially subsidized Center of Political and Economic Studies.[15] The colony was also host to privately funded ethnographic and anthropological research by foreign scholars, whose work provided Portuguese administrators insights into the social structure of African villages.[16] For example, in the Ovimbundu highlands, the authorities facilitated the research of foreign scholars such as the British anthropologist Adrian Edwards, and some officials themselves became involved in extensive official studies of Ovimbundu institutions. The research focused especially on the continuing role of sobas, sekulus, and Kimbandas in the lives of the population. Officials also implemented new regulations covering health, education, and religious practices among the population.[17]

Furthermore, the regime required all Portuguese *chefes* to learn the African language in their areas, to collect traditions, to write descriptions of local customs, and to make biographic registers of descendants of former ruling lineages and new leaders.[18] The regime used this information to get rid of sekulus and sobas who had served as collaborators, and replace them with Portuguese appointees who were supposed to be familiar with "traditional" African social structure.[19]

Social Policy and the Ovimbundu

Health

In the highlands, the authorities were most concerned about the role which the Protestant missionaries played in providing health services to the Ovimbundu and other Africans. They regarded the existence of a private, Protestant-controlled health system, geared specifically to Africans, as an obstacle to the government's plans to ensure the "material and spiritual interests of the natives and their protection from the influence of undesirable propaganda."[20] The immediate aim was to regulate Protestant medical work and develop a medical outreach program for the African population. Officials intended to replace the Protestant-managed health care system with a state-financed, Catholic-run health service for Africans.

Local Portuguese officials had reason to be concerned about the role foreign-born Protestants played in the provision of health services to the Ovimbundu and other African peoples in the highlands. By the middle of the 1940s Protestant missionaries had established and retained control of a number of public health facilities, including three hospitals, fourteen rural dispensaries, and two leprosy camps, offering a wide range of medical services to Africans. During the 1950s, the number of Protestant mission hospitals had increased to eight, along with two hundred clinics in the Ovimbundu highlands, in contrast to the few operated by Catholic nuns.[21] The Protestants supplied these services at a time when African emigration and mortality in Angola was causing a net decrease in the population,[22] and government expenditure on health and social services was minuscule.[23] Thus, unlike other African colonies, colonial authorities, who were making modest gains in expanding public health services and improving the demographic profile of their African subjects,[24] the Portuguese did very little in Angola before the 1950s.

Little reliable official information on the health profile of the Ovimbundu population is available in official records. In the late 1950s there were only 203 licensed Portuguese physicians and 1,150 auxiliary health care providers for a colony-wide population of more than five mil-

lion.[25] The medical service offered by these Portuguese medical professionals catered largely to the urban white and Afro-Portuguese population.

Research which the Protestants carried out at the Bunjie mission in
the highlands in the mid-1950s shed some light on what this meant for the
health of rural Ovimbundu. The study indicated a pattern of early marriages for women (16 to 17 years of age), a relatively high number of preg-
nancies (7 to 8 per woman), perhaps to offset an infant mortality rate that
stood at 500 to 600 per 1000 births for "uncivilized" women in the nearby
villages. This was double the rate of eighteenth-century Kongo.[26]

The health profile of Ovimbundu living in urban areas was little better. In Lobito, where 30,000 people (mostly Ovimbundu) lived in the African slum district, the infant mortality rate was 600 per thousand.[27] Such
rates were high even by the standards of other African colonies. Only Malawi
had infant mortality rates higher than 200 per thousand.[28] One reason for
the poor health profile of urban Ovimbundu had to do with the increase in
the number of poor white settlers who flocked to the coastal and highland
urban centers, and pushed the Ovimbundu to the outer margins where
they built slums far away from access to the limited public health services
that were available.[29]

Despite the limited resources at the period before the late 1950s,
local officials had attempted to provide health care for Africans, even trying
to recruit Portuguese doctors to replace foreign Protestant medical personnel. As early as 1939, officials in the Catholic Church appealed to Catholic
doctors to dedicate themselves to the work of "social medicine among the
Africans." They hoped to replace Protestant doctors with dedicated Catholic
professionals who, they believed, could maintain a high level of services.[30]
This appeal, like other government initiatives, largely went unheeded, because the government provided no financial subsidies for interested doctors.

Similarly, in 1949 Governor-General Captain Silva Carvalho established a category of African health care providers called "catechist-nurses"
to provide health care to the native population. But the Catholic missionaries who carried out their training were never able to send an adequate
number of trained workers to staff state health clinics in either urban or
rural areas, since very few of the Africans admitted to the program had the
academic background necessary to pass the course.[31] Thus, the number of
government-funded clinics offering care to Africans never met the demand,
in contrast to the Protestant programs which had trained many Ovimbundu
nurses and dispensers for work in the villages by the 1950s. Indeed, Protestant
medical personnel often decried the lack of government health services and

the absence of trained African personnel, which they believed handicapped the medical mission.[32]

The desire to demonstrate to their foreign critics that the government was capable of meeting the health needs of the African population (and preserve Portuguese hegemony) led to a marked anti-foreign bias in the health measures the government enforced. The most disastrous of these for the Ovimbundu were the ones which were aimed at replacing the Protestant health system with a government-run health service. Even before funds were forthcoming, the colonial government tightened standards for persons operating medical facilities in the colony and for the training of medical personnel. The government also required provincial and city agencies to exercise more control over medical practitioners, and to conduct regular inspections of private health facilities for Africans. Also, for the first time the government required that prospective African health care workers, especially nurses and anyone dispensing medical advice and medicine at the village level, must pass a government examination and obtain a diploma.[33] The authorities also placed a limit on the number of non-Portuguese doctors who could practice in private hospitals in the colony. Regulations also limited the amount of medicine that private hospitals could bring into the colony.[34] To replace the Protestant-run medical facilities that would be closed as a result of the new laws, the government promised to build and maintain health clinics for Africans. In the highlands, these measures drastically reversed the advances some Ovimbundu had made, due to the training they had received from the Protestants, and also cut the health services that Protestant-trained Ovimbundu were able to offer their fellow Ovimbundu and other Africans.

Hardening attitudes against things African and state labor policies also reduced the health services available to the population as the numbers of traditional practitioners declined drastically due to the demands of forced labor and health and worker-training legislation. Many young people who would have made up the next generation of traditional practitioners were either working as migrant laborers, or disdained the traditional knowledge. In addition, Ovimbundu men who became priests and men and women who became pastors, catechists, and deacons were prohibited from associating with relatives who followed traditional practices.[35] In addition, government regulations that imposed penalties on unlicensed practitioners made it difficult for the remaining Kimbandas to work openly.

Together, the earlier neglect and the later imposition of strict government regulations took a heavy toll on the health of the Ovimbundu. Old and new diseases ravaged both rural and urban populations. Records left by

Protestant medical personnel tell of villages overrun with disease. In some areas, entire families were exposed to tuberculosis, as contract laborers who had contracted the disease in the unhealthy fisheries and labor camps "passed it on to their wives and children who lived with them in the unsanitary, poorly ventilated, one-room huts."[36] The people also fell victim to diseases common to the region including smallpox, elephantiasis, leprosy, whooping cough, bilharzia, syphilis, and gonorrhea, according to reports by medical personnel.[37] Whooping cough, smallpox, and sexually transmitted diseases took their toll particularly among the Ovimbundu urban residents, who lived in overcrowded surroundings without potable water, sanitation, or health facilities.[38]

The lack of a sustained public health program for educating the population in proper nutrition and child care also had an impact. Malnutrition, a rare occurrence in the highlands in earlier periods, became commonplace. Testifying before a United Nations (UN) subcommittee in 1961, the missionary doctor Robert McGowan, who had worked for several years in the highlands, concluded his statement by stressing that the people were in poor health and that they were "in a chronic state of malnutrition."[39] In many areas, women could not find the time to forage for plants and insects to supplement their diet of corn as they had done in the past. Men, who had become full- and part-time migrant laborers, were unable to provide meat from wild animals, as hunting required time and extra income to cover the cost of the licenses that the government required for those wanting to hunt on what had become state lands. Despite the government's assertions to the contrary, New State corporatist policies were unable to deliver even minimally adequate health services to the population which the *bem-estar* policies advanced.[40]

Though some Portuguese census figures for the mid-1950s showed a demographic trend strong enough to promote fairly substantial population growth, the 1950 census showed a bad demographic regime.[41] Census data at a microlevel showed a correlation between increasing impoverishment, the poor health of villagers, and the declining population in the highlands.[42]

Religion and Education

The state's religious and educational policies also fell short of the goals of the *bem-estar* campaign. Again, a low level of government spending, the inroads that the Protestants had made, and the emphasis on the economy undermined the state's attempts at social engineering. Using the argument that the only way to make Africans "civilized" and willing to accept their status in the Portuguese empire was to promote the Catholic faith, the authorities pushed the Catholic Church to take over the religious and educational training of Africans.

In the highlands, local authorities, well aware of the significant advances the Protestant missionaries had made in the fields of religion and education, hoped that Catholic and government institutions would replace those the Protestants ran. They welcomed the emphasis on Catholic missionaries as agents of social change since they wanted the Catholic missionaries to make more headway. When the Republic fell in 1926, Catholic missionaries in the highlands operated ten missions staffed by forty-two French priests associated with the Holy Ghost Fathers.

Meanwhile, Protestant missionaries operated sixty-five mission stations and a large center and Church at Dondi, and far surpassed the assistance the Catholics offered.[43] By 1932, only four of the Catholic priests remaining in the region were Portuguese (the others were French and German), while the number of Protestant missionaries totalled eighty.[44]

The Catholic onslaught began in the 1930s, but really took shape in the 1940s after the signing of the 1940 Concordat. Local officials[45] pushed the Fathers Lecomte and Keiling, who were in charge of the expansion program, to open new mission stations even before there were enough missionaries to staff them.[46] In 1933, when some of the missionaries complained to their superior in France about the actions of local officials in the highlands, the Bishop in Luanda reminded the Holy Ghost Fathers' superior in France that missionaries in Angola should remember that "it is not for their work of evangelization that the state appreciates our missions . . . the interest is in . . . civilization and nationalization."[47]

After World War Two, as Angola witnessed a religious scramble between various European Catholic missionary societies eager to send missionaries to begin or expand their work,[48] the Ovimbundu highlands became a major center of Catholic activity. In addition to the Holy Ghost Fathers, there were Franciscan Sisters, the Sisters of St. Joseph of Cluny, the Benedictines of Tutzing, the "Doroteias," and the Sisters of the Most Holy Savior. During the 1950s, missionaries from these orders opened schools and health service centers along the rail-line from Nova Lisboa to the frontier with Northern Rhodesia (Zambia).[49]

The missionaries saw their subsidies from the state increase substantially after the 1940 Concordat, rising from 4,981,825 *escudos*—$304,000 U.S.) in 1940 to 7,075,800 *escudos* $423,000 U.S.) in 1945.[50] In 1944 the Diocese of Nova Lisboa (which included the provinces of Benguela and Huila) received a state subsidy of 1,870,000 *angolares* ($91,000 U.S.) to serve the population of 1,500,000 Africans, 26,114 whites, and 12,875 Afro-Portuguese in the region.[51] Financial assistance rose between 1950 and 1960, from just under 9,000,000 to 28,225,675 *escudos*.[52] In 1952, for example, each mission station received about 50,000 *angolares* (about $1400 U.S.).

The task of making Ovimbundu into Portuguese Catholics was formidable, since there were never enough Portuguese nuns and priests to serve the population, and those who came to the region preferred to work with the settlers. Despite this, the missionaries claimed that they were converting large numbers of Ovimbundu. In 1932, with 12 missionary stations and 30 priests in the highlands, the Catholics claimed a total of 225,000 Ovimbundu converts.[53] By 1944 the number of converts is said to have reached 319,629 Ovimbundu out of a population totalling 1,284,668,[54] even though the Catholics had trained only one African priest and one nun.[55] At that date they claimed to have settled at least 17,000 Ovimbundu in Christian Catholic villages in the former states of Huambo, Sambo, Cuima, Bailundo, and Quepeio, and they planned to use their state subsidy to establish more villages for converts. Their reports also claimed that they were housing at least 600 local male students in boarding schools, in addition to supporting thousands of students in village schools run by catechists.[56] Male students who successfully completed the boarding school program were encouraged to find wives among Christian female converts who received home economics training from the Cluny Sisters (these ran a few boarding schools including the Missão Feminina da Bela Vista for African girls by the 1950s).[57] As one Ovimbundu woman recalled, "the Catholic girls' education was all in Portuguese. They always spoke Portuguese and their matrons were Portuguese. After their training they continued to live in the cities."[58] In the decade between 1950 and 1960, the number of Ovimbundu Catholics increased from less than half a million to over one million. Furthermore, the number of Ovimbundu priests and nuns had grown to thirty-two, and the Catholics had trained hundreds of Ovimbundu catechist-teachers to serve the growing Ovimbundu Catholic population.[59]

The model program of the Catholics was a seminary for Africans in Caala which opened in 1943. African candidates selected for training here were part of the government-supported program to "civilize" the Ovimbundu and related peoples in the highlands. As a report of 1944 noted, "The native priest who graduates from this seminary will be an apostle of combined Christian education. He would not be a catechist . . . but a precious help in civilization which the Portuguese wish to give to her colonial children." The program called for the students to receive the best Portuguese, education so that they would turn into patriotic Portuguese, ready to defend Portugal's interests and help to attract support for Portuguese policies among the "natives."[60] One report on the achievements of students enrolled in the program praised their dedication and their willingness to study, and identify with, Portuguese heroes. The report even noted that students made up their own songs and poems in honor of their adopted Portuguese heroes.[61]

The idea that the Portuguese Catholics could be the instrument through which the dictatorship could implement its social design became enshrined in many education decrees issued by the government. One, dated February 6, 1950, objected that African children were taught almost exclusively by non-Portuguese Catholic and Protestant missionaries, a situation the authorities wanted changed. It urged administrative authorities to assist Portuguese-born Catholic missionaries, and stressed that they should be the ones chosen to educate the children of prominent sobas.[62] The law also required local government authorities to establish rudimentary schools in every village.[63]

To implement the program the government made special funds available to the Catholic Church specifically for African education. In 1951 the government allocated 12 million *escudos* ($336,000 U.S.) to the Catholic Church to build and run preparatory schools (*ensinos da adaptação*) throughout the colony,[64] and additional funds for building single-sex normal schools to train African teachers.[65]

The directives for the preparatory schools emphasized the education of children, as well as the need to develop programs aimed at African women who, officials believed, were particularly hostile to Western education. The legislation explicitly required all "noncivilized" African children aged six to fourteen to attend the preparatory schools for at least four years. Those who passed the exit examination were eligible to be admitted to government or privately run primary schools.[66] Africans attending primary schools were theoretically able to compete for the limited openings available in the few public high schools and technical training programs run by the Catholic Church and the government.[67] Most however, went on to the Colégio da Magistrate Teófilo Duarte—the government-run normal school for Africans. Here students received a three-year course modeled on the government curriculum. The subjects included the "three R's" and lessons on what the authorities considered essential elements of Portuguese geography, history, and culture. Graduates from teacher-training programs were expected to work with other African representatives—sobas, sekulus, African Catholic priests, catechists, and *assimilados*—to transmit Portuguese cultural values to the people. In 1958 the Colégio had a total enrollment of 225 African students.[68] The authorities warned all state and private agencies (particularly foreign missionaries) and settlers that they had to be good examples to Africans and help them to learn Portuguese values.

Distorted Visions or Dreams Deferred

The Failure of State Catholicism

In the highlands the state's *bem estar* program, under the direction of the Catholic Church, failed to live up to the ideal of making the Ovimbundu into black Portuguese. One problem was that the secular and religious authorities were more interested in responding to the needs of the growing settler population than in promoting the educational, social, and religious advancement of Africans. Indeed, the Catholic Church soon became a support center for impoverished Portuguese "bush" traders, who regarded the state-supported church as an institution from which to obtain free social services. As the British consul noted, with appropriate English contempt of the Portuguese, "the bush traders regard the missions as convenient hostels where they need not pay and suitable repositories for their mulatto bastards".[69] Moreover, few of the Catholic missions developed the kind of Catholic African community that could compete with the Protestant communities. For example, the Ovimbundu catechists and other converts who made up a significant part of the church membership were only marginally involved in the settler-controlled lay organizations such as Catholic Action.

Moreover, the hierarchical structure of the Church and the pervading racial ideology limited the number of Ovimbundu accepted into the priesthood, and therefore excluded Ovimbundu from church governance. Many Ovimbundu hoping to become priests had to settle for the inferior position of "catechist," a lay position reserved for "native converts."[70] Even those who became priests did not go back to the village but remained in the cities. As for the majority of the Ovimbundu converts to Catholicism, the most they could expect from the Church was permission to live in a Christian village run by a catechist.[71]

In fact, many disgruntled Ovimbundu catechists and teachers left teaching and religious work for more financially rewarding clerical work in the government and the private sector.[72] This was due to the dearth of leadership roles for Africans.[73]

Church-state collaboration failed dismally in education as well, as the educational program aimed at preparing Africans for assimilation into Portuguese society ran at cross purposes with the need for a cheap and controllable African labor force. Education was never a real priority of the dictatorship, and in 1960 only 117,768 people (or 7.7 percent of the entire school population in Angola) were in regular Catholic or public schools.[74] In this group, Africans were a small minority, and Ovimbundu a minority within a minority. Very few Africans went on to postprimary education. Indeed, in 1960, there were only 25 Ovimbundu in regular high schools in the Huambo province out of a total high school population of 5,784 students.[75] Moreover, the Catholic Church had not built many rudimentary (village) schools, and those that were operating sent few students on to government primary schools.

Even the government's own records detail the difficulties it faced in implementing its social agenda. Governor General Captain Silva Carvalho, voicing the concerns of the Catholic Church to the authorities in Lisbon, linked the slow rate of change to the contract labor system, noting that the demand for labor made "the work of the missionaries difficult and created a situation of suspicion" among Africans.[76]

Ovimbundu Catholic converts who lived in church villages and attended its schools blamed the missionaries, whose racist attitudes and treatment of the African people created an unbridgeable social gulf. Africans had little time to learn Christian teachings, the Portuguese language, or the rudiments of European civilization and culture. Many young converts were "forced to work in the gardens or as servants to the priests or on the farms of the missions" instead of attending classes.[77]

The Protestant Factor

The decision of the dictatorship to push its social program was motivated in large part by Salazar's concern in 1926 that various forces in Angola would undermine attempts to "civilize" the Africans and advance Portuguese claims. A major problem the government faced was regionalism and the various social distinctions and ethnic differences retained from the earlier period. In the Luanda region, for example, sustained opposition to New State social agenda came from Afro-Portuguese and assimilated Africans who capitalized on their African and Portuguese roots and urban expertise to create a more multi-ethnic environment than the homogenous Portuguese society that the government wanted. White Angolans and settlers who opposed the dictatorship also found ways of derailing government policies.[78]

Similarly, in the Bakongo areas to the north, a group of young *assimilados* frustrated the government's efforts to construct a new social order. By relying on the political arrangements the Kongo kings had worked out with the Portuguese in the nineteenth century, and by reenforcing ethnic links among themselves and with their cousins across the river in the Belgian Congo, they formed another strand of resistance. In contrast to government plans to build a Portuguese-dominated social order, they promoted their own dream of building a new Kongo monarchy and ethnic solidarity. These monarchist tendencies helped to inspire early Bakongo nationalism.[79]

In the highlands a different set of social conditions also conspired to frustrate the social agenda the government planned. In truth, by the 1960s, the Ovimbundu, the largest ethnic group in Angola, were the least affected by Portuguese assimilationist policies.

Yet the period from 1926 to 1960 was one of profound social transformation for all sectors of the Ovimbundu population. Much of the change, however, came not from official social engineering but as a result of the continuing social adaptations that the Ovimbundu had been making since the conquest. In many ways, the innovative social adaptations made by the different sectors of the Ovimbundu population prior to 1926 continued during the period of the New State. Ovimbundu Protestants, with the institutional support of North American and European Protestant missionaries, remained in the forefront of this social revolution, continuing to be in a better position than their Catholic counterparts.

During the period, the status of Ovimbundu Protestants as the model Ovimbundu grew; an increasing number of Ovimbundu became convinced that the Protestant missionary establishment and neither the Catholic Church nor the state was the conduit to assimilation into colonial society. The increasing role of Protestant missionaries in the social transformation of the Ovimbundu stemmed from the persisting contradictions between ideal and reality in the policies of the New State. Thus, even as the government threw its weight behind the Catholic missionary establishment, officials allowed the Protestants to expand their religious, educational, and social activities. By 1960 the Ovimbundu Protestant presence in the area was impressive. Protestants accounted for 365,000 people or about 30 percent of the Ovimbundu population,[80] and the religious, health, and educational institutions that the missionaries and Ovimbundu converts had begun had expanded greatly since 1926. The Protestants ran a complex network of institutions linking outlying Ovimbundu villages with mission stations. The largest station remained Dondi with its 9,000 acre complex. By 1934 the Currie Institute for boys at Dondi catered to 400 young men (the majority of them Ovimbundu) in postprimary classes, while the Means School for girls housed 200 to 300 females. The boys studied to become "teachers and ministers," while the girls followed a four-year course of "domestic science, hygiene, mother and baby craft, basketry, nursing, teaching, and evangelism."[81] Many of the graduates of these schools remained in the work of the church.[82] The number of ordained pastors and catechists grew from six pastors and several hundred catechists in the 1930s,[83] to 150 pastors and hundreds of catechists, deacons, and deaconesses who helped to run rural and urban missions by the late 1950s.[84] In the 1950s the Dondi Mission contained not only the Currie Institute for boys, the Means School for girls, but also the Sara Hurd Scott Memorial Hospital and Leprosarium, the Press and the Emmanuel Seminary.

As they had done during the early years of the colonial regime, Ovimbundu Protestants continued to shape the outlook of the Ovimbundu population more than their counterparts in the Catholic Church or the surviving non-Christian Ovimbundu leadership. One reason for this was the fact that the Protestant missionary structure remained flexible and egalitarian, which the hierarchically and racially organized Catholic Church could not. In the Protestant missions, unlike Catholic missions, trained Ovimbundu pastors, catechists, teachers, nurses, and others took the lead in opening new schools and founding Protestant villages; they held leadership positions in missions, churches, schools, seminaries, hospitals, and clinics. They also spearheaded the evangelization of Ovimbundu and other Africans in the region.

Another reason why the Protestant role in influencing Ovimbundu social structure was so great during the period was that the Ovimbundu Protestant community continued to keep and attract a cross section of preconquest leaders. During the period the leadership continued to include a significant number of Ovimbundu descended from preconquest ruling groups. Pastor Lumbo of Chissamba, for example, who was ordained in 1930, was actually a descendant of Chissamba's former rulers (who had welcomed the first missionaries in the 1880s), and he had grown up in the mission station.[85] Still others, like soba Katokola of Chissamba, and Chiwana of Chiuca, were children of the earliest converts from the ruling groups. Sekulu Wondumba, for example, who was from Bailundu, was "brought up in the royal village" and was familiar with "all the Umbundu customs and laws."[86] In the 1930s, Wondumba was in charge of patients at the Protestant hospital at Dondi. Sekulu Kalandula headed a prosperous village near to the mission station at Ocileso, while Sekulu Satumbela was a prominent leader at Ocileso.[87] Both Abraham Gulu (who was the pastor of

the church in Bailundu in 1930) and Elder Ngonga (one of the first graduates from the Dondi mission, secretary of the "native church," teacher, ordained minister and later supervisor of Dondi mission station) were sekulus
in their own right as well.[88] Sekulu Paulo was an elder in the church at
Dondi,[89] and another sekulu was a teacher in charge of the boys' school at
Lutumo.[90] Head nurse José Chimbungulu, a sekulu, ran the missionary
hospital at Camundongo in 1942.[91]

Ovimbundu of more humble origins, and even non-Ovimbundu,
continued to be well represented. Antonio Casela, for example, was the son
of a Luimbe ruler who had converted because of the work of an Ovimbundu
evangelist.[92] Some converts of humble origins, who had gained experience
in community work, "teaching, preaching and [providing] leadership," in
the villages were selected by their fellow Ovimbundu for preparation for
the ministry.[93] A former slave, Albert Katema Kanyanga, had been trained
as a teacher and was ordained as a pastor in 1937. At that time he ran a
mission in a center where there were twenty thousand non-Christians.
Rachael Chalulua, a runaway slave, was trained as a nurse.[94] Another leader
was Pastor Adolfo Chipaca who "was apprenticed as a witch-doctor
(Kimbanda)" before his conversion. In 1952 Pastor Chipaca had seventy-
five villages under his supervision.[95] Former prosperous Ovimbundu traders were also among the Protestant leaders.[96] In 1932 Jorge Chilulu, a former
caravan cook, became the first ordained minister of the Lutama mission in
the vicinity of Dondi, and in 1952 was in charge of seventy villages.[97]

Whatever their origins, Ovimbundu and neighboring Africans joined
the Protestants to benefit from the medical and educational services the
Protestants offered, and to avoid the humiliating experiences that non-
Protestant Ovimbundu faced in their daily dealings with secular authorities and even with some Catholic Church officials. Wondumba's experience as a Protestant, for example, was a far cry from the physical abuse that
members of the old elite suffered at the hands of local Portuguese administrators. The administrator of Bailundu in a official report of 1935 detailed
one of these incidents. He wrote that he applied to Chinjamba, "the son of
the *soba grande*, the representative of the highest native nobility, 100 lash-
ings with the palmatorio."[98] The outrageous physical brutality that Portuguese officials continued to mete out to members of the former ruling
groups was motivation enough for them to flock to the Protestants. Sekulus
Abraham Gulu and Elder Ngonga avoided this humiliation because of their
promptness in paying their people's taxes.[99]

The buffer that Protestantism provided between this segment of the
population and the state enabled Protestants to continue to play a crucial

role in further adapting Ovimbundu social institutions to the New State social order. This was owing to the opportunities for the development of new Ovimbundu leadership which the Protestant mission structure offered to pastors, catechists, and others. For example, the division of religious authority provided the basis of a new social organization among Protestant communities. Pastors, who were attached to several districts within each mission station area, served as both spiritual and secular guides to the people in the areas they supervised. At a lower level than the pastors, deacons, assisted by deaconesses (often their wives) also had religious authority over a select number of villages. Thus in 1952 the Dondi mission station region had eight ordained pastors, who, with catechists/teacher, elders (*akulu*), deacons, and deaconesses, supervised hundreds of Christian villages. The spiritual advisor—the *akulu* (elders) were in charge of the day-to-day spiritual guidance of members, while the catechist/teacher often served as the deacon.[100]

Overseeing all the various Protestant villages were the Ovimbundu who worked at the main mission stations and the North American and European missionaries. They made regular visits to Protestant villages to conduct religious services, offer medical services, and run special training sessions for adults. In addition, pastors, along with the catechists/teachers, *akulu*, deacons, and deaconesses, met annually at the native councils which the Protestant missionaries sponsored, and helped Africanize the liturgy and shape the standards of behavior and mores that the rest of the community followed and that Protestant non-Ovimbundu emulated. In 1931, for example, the authorities gave permission to the Protestant missionaries to establish the Council of Native Churches for Central Angola (*Onjango Yakulu*). This organization provided opportunities for Ovimbundu pastors and catechists to direct many religious, educational, and social activities of the church which foreign missionaries had formerly controlled.[101]

By the 1940s and 1950s, Ovimbundu pastors, deacons, and catechists supervised hundreds of native churches and Christian villages (131 new Protestant villages were set up in the no man's lands on the borders of Bié and Bailundo in one season—several weeks in the summer—alone).[102] The group imposed new standards of behavior on families living in the villages, set disciplinary procedures for members, examined catechumens, prepared people for church membership, and made decisions concerning church finances.

It was these Ovimbundu Protestants, not the American and European missionaries, who adopted rules for expelling "backsliders" from the churches and villages, and who imposed new behavior patterns on Christian households.[103] Their leadership roles were pronounced in the Protestant communities. As one Ocimbundu who experienced life in a Protestant village recalled, the *akulu* not only guided the community's spiritual progress but "they promoted meetings for learning new things such as agriculture, hygiene, child care, better housing." It was the catechists/teachers, however, graduates of Dondi, who brought the spiritual and technical expertise to the community, conducting worship services and teaching the people how to read and write, improve their agricultural output, and build better houses.[104]

Unlike the Ovimbundu Catholics who had to conform to an already established Catholic standard of behavior, Ovimbundu Protestants developed their own standards of behavior within an evolving social order influenced both by Protestant teachings and by Ovimbundu beliefs and customs. Protestant pastors, teachers, deacons, and deaconesses devised new ways of adapting Ovimbundu beliefs and customs to the demands of their new faith. The fact that the Ovimbundu were the trailblazers in establishing the villages and in converting non-Christian villages opened up many opportunities for adapting the old beliefs to the new realities.

One of the first parts of the older social norm that broke down in Protestant villages was the distinction between free born and slave. Even though some distinctions had already been undermined as a result of the long-distance trade, life as a Protestant provided many more opportunities for upward social mobility. The leveling process that came from Western education, especially at Means School for girls and the Currie Institute for boys, provided the impetus towards the full integration of those Ovimbundu and neighboring Africans from unfree backgrounds into the Protestant community. Thus, for example, Pastor Kanyanga, despite his slave ancestry, married the daughter of Chief Kanjundu, a second-generation Protestant. Former slave Rachael Chalulua, who completed a two-year course at Means School, was sent on to the Dondi hospital to study nursing, in order to "give her standing among her Ovimbundu associates."[105]

Ovimbundu Protestants who were part of the older elite made other adjustments. For example, they voluntarily agreed to give up their rights to own slaves held by their nonconverted kin, and adopted new attitudes towards neighbors such as the Luimbe who they had formerly raided and enslaved. The brother of Pastor Lumbo, when asked about the most difficult thing he faced as a Christian, replied that it was "to think of the Va Luimbe as people like ourselves." At ordination or at ceremonies in which they were formally admitted to the church, pastors, deacons, and even ordinary members had to be prepared to publicly denounce witchcraft, free their slaves (or at least give up their rights to slaves held by members of the kin), and agree to carry out the discipline of the church even against members of their own kin.[106]

Other distinctions also fell away. For example, kimbandas who converted were required to burn the tools of their trade in public. Some practices were harder to eradicate, and the Ovimbundu Protestant leadership made novel modifications. The custom of bride price was one example. When Paulo, a prominent Christian, insisted on giving away his daughter and refused to accept the traditional bride price, the women in the village, many of them Christians, scornfully rejected her company, accusing her of not being married because "no bride price was paid for you." They also predicted that she would be barren. She suffered more abuse when they refused to invite her to their weddings or include her in other customs. This led the Native Church to adopt the policy that allowed Christians to pay just a nominal fee. The local church also appointed a respected Christian couple to act as negotiators during the process. This became standard practice among Protestant Ovimbundu.[107]

Other customs were also amended. For example, a Christian who caused injury (bodily or otherwise) to someone no longer had to discharge his obligations to the injured man's kin by becoming a pawn or slave in his household. One Christian who had accidentally injured the eyes of another took care of his obligations by attending the victim in hospital and staying in his house until he recovered. The pressure to respect Ovimbundu legal tenets often came from non-Christian villagers whose support and respect the Christians hoped to retain. As one missionary commented, "Christians could not follow the literal interpretation of the Umbundu law, but some course must be found that would not be dishonorable in the eyes of non-Christian villagers who scrupulously regarded matters of justice according to the rulings of custom and native law."[108]

The rules which came to govern Ovimbundu behavior did not come down by fiat from the white missionaries as in the Catholic Church, but grew out of the adaptation of older Ovimbundu practices and prohibitions to those of American and European Protestantism. In this way, Ovimbundu Protestants were key to molding a system of beliefs and customs that ran contrary to the social order that New State officials were attempting to impose. The Protestant-influenced beliefs retained so much more of the older Ovimbundu beliefs and customs that they soon spread to Ovimbundu Catholics and non-Christians alike.

Another aspect of the evolving social order that in many ways conformed to the older pattern was the resemblacne between Ovimbundu Protestant villages and older villages in their origins and functioning. As in the preconquest period, many of the Protestant villages were offshoots of well-established non-Protestant and traditional ones. Some of them came into existence when enterprising members of the sekulu group moved off with their kin and supporters, while others appeared when the sekulu of a non-Christian village permitted the catechist ("katechista"—often kin to the sekulu) to establish a village. In such a case, the success of the Protestant village would depend on the goodwill of the non-Christian sekulu, who often lost people to the new village.[109] The catechist also performed many of the same functions as the non-Christian sekulu, serving as the representative of the people to the *chefe* (secular head) and the pastor (spiritual head), collecting taxes, sending out people to perform roadwork or contract labor, and providing policemen and soldiers to the *chefe*. Like the leaders of other villages, he also gave permission to villagers to open up new fields and establish new buildings and he settled disputes. This meant, as one missionary observed in 1942, that the catechists were the ones who determined "what changes in native laws and customs were necessary by the new Christian standards."[110] The precedents they set did far more to modify Ovimbundu customary law than government fiat.

Protestant villagers also adapted other Ovimbundu institutions. For example, they kept the custom of maintaining a public venue—the *onjanjo*—for village activities, but with some modifications. In Protestant villages the *onjango*, often the best maintained building in the village, became the center of the life of the Protestant community, serving as the chapel, the school, the court, and the recreation center. However, instead of being a male-dominated venue where young men heard fables intended to teach them how to be good husbands, hunters, smiths, or traders as in the precolonial period, the *onjango* was the location for the nightly worship services and the Sunday school. There, Protestant and non-Protestant villagers heard catechists use the standard Umbundu that they had learnt at Dondi. On weekdays, the *onjango* became the village school, where teachers taught the children in Portuguese. After the nightly worship services, the *onjango* became again the place where villagers met to resolve legal disputes, the center of celebrations, and the place for nightly revelries. Although the catechists allowed the traditional stories, folktales, and fables to be told as their counterparts in the non-Protestant villages did, Bible stories were added to give a Christian relevance. Moreover, instead of the beer drinking, dancing, and other activities that went on well into the night in the non-Protestant villages, catechists in the Protestant villages prohibited villagers from smoking, beer drinking, and unsupervised dancing. They did permit supervised folk dancing.[111] The fact that in Protestant villages the language used in church services was Umbundu and not Portuguese enhanced the distinctiveness of Ovimbundu Protestants, all of whom knew how to speak Umbundu, and many of whom read avidly the religious texts in Umbundu made available from the missionary press.

The relationship Protestant Ovimbundu had with their nonconverted kin and the ability of the latter to maintain preconquest customs despite religious and secular attacks also had much to do with the success the Protestants had in incorporating aspects of Ovimbundu beliefs into Protestantism. This was because Ovimbundu Protestants lived side by side with their nonconverted kin. In spite of the fact that by the fifties, in some Protestant communities in regions such as Andulu, a strict demarcation existed between Protestants, Catholics, and non-Christians, and that Ovimbundu Protestants were prohibited from marrying non-Christian or Catholic cousins, the other communities were also retaining aspects of the precolonial culture.[112] Jonas Savimbi recalled the words of his grandfather Sakaita, whose son Lott (Jonas' father) was an outstanding Protestant, explaining why he resisted conversion. He noted, "Me, I do not accept. I will treasure the tradition. I ought to protect the land." In the rituals to the ancestors which he performed daily, he repeated these words: "You who sleep, you who wish that I am faithful. If I am not punish me, but if I obey protect me."[113]

With some of the older generation so proud in resisting both the state and the missionaries, Ovimbundu Protestants could not help but be affected by the pride in the old order, belief systems, and rituals which their nonconverted kin retained. In Bailundu in the 1930s and 1940s, there were some sobas who were still being carried in hammocks, with bells that rang as the carriers jogged along, so that people could clear out of the path.[114] Moreover, many of these titleholders still conducted ceremonies associated with birth, death, initiation, and installation of leaders. On these occasions, even Protestants participated. Jonas Savimbi remembered that although he was a Protestant, his grandfather sent him to an initiation camp along with his nonconverted kin. There they learnt many of the legends, symbols, secrets, and rituals. As he recalled, when he returned to the Protestant school he did not reveal them to his classmates.[115] The Protestant missionaries Elizabeth Utting and Margaret Dawson left a description of the relationship between Protestant, Catholic, and non-Christian villages as they witnessed it in 1953. They wrote that the village of Chikala was home to a group of Protestant students but had, on one side, "the heathen section" and on the other side "relatives who have chosen the Roman Catholic Faith." They noted further that Christians and non-Christians alike were affected by the "witchcraft, moonlight dancing, drunken debauches and all evils of heathenism" which were still carried on in the villages.[116]

Moreover, there were still kimbandas who were in a unique position to maintain many of the beliefs and rituals, since many Ovimbundu turned to them for a wide range of services, particularly in view of the decline of the prestige of sobas and sekulus. As in the past, kimbandas proved adept at exploiting the insecurities which appeared as a result of both New State economic and political policies and the cultural inroads of the missionaries. In the face of the conversion of the descendants of the former ruling families, and the erosion of the prestige of sekulus and sobas because of the state's economic and political policies, kimbandas became the main bearers of many preconquest beliefs and rituals. Like the missionaries, they looked for new recruits, and may have made the initiation process even more forbidding, in order to instill fear and maintain the respect of the population. Indeed, the missionaries regarded them as the main stumbling blocks to the advancement of Christianity. One observer, writing in 1952, noted that the imitation camps of the kimbandas were "vile" and that their dress was "weird and grotesque. Their whirling dances, accompanied by drumming, strike terror in the heart. Their secrets are inviolable, and they can compel a man to join them. Death is the punishment for refusal."[117] Indeed, kimbandas instilled fear in converts who believed that their poison could bring instant death and disease. Protestant medical personnel knew that many of their fellow believers often sought medical and legal advice from the kimbandas before they coming to them or the *chefe*. But there was also a symbiotic relationship between kimbandas and the Protestant medical personnel, and the former did not hesitate to refer cases to the latter. They included in their divining basket an "ocindele thing" (a foreign object) which, when it appeared at the top of the basket, meant that the sick person needed "the white man's medicine".[118]

Indeed, some of the most devout Ovimbundu Protestants could be temporarily tested when medical crises arose and Western medicines and Christian teaching proved inadequate. The kimbandas were always ready to supply an alternative. The case of the Christian village of Songa is instructive. A convert from the Protestant Currie Institute had established Songa as a thriving Protestant village some time before 1941. By 1941, however, the catechist leader "fell into immoral ways, another graduate who lived there with his wife took to witchcraft, a third couple worried by the illness of their child undertook divining for a cure. The church collapsed."[119] Belief in witchcraft was especially hard to undermine even among devout Ovimbundu Protestants.

Nevertheless, the Ovimbundu Protestant community was different from the non-Christian groups, and its members formed a new clientele for the increasing numbers of teachers and nurses who were graduating from the Dondi and Means schools. By the 1940s and 1950s, Dondi and Means students who were not employed by the missionaries opened a number of independent schools in outlying villages and did well, in spite of the monopoly of the Catholic Church, which made these private schools technically illegal.[120] Eduardo Daniel Ekundi stimulated great pride in the generation of the thirties and forties when he opened a school called *Salva Terra* (Save the Country) in 1945 in Bié.[121] Local officials tolerated the schools although many of the teachers did not have the third grade education[122] that the state required.[123] Protestant-trained nurses and other health care workers often set up their own clinics as well, and carpenters, masons, and printers obtained government licenses and opened shops.[124]

Ovimbundu Protestants who traveled as contract and voluntary laborers throughout Angola and the neighboring countries recreated the days of the commodity trade, when entrepreneurial Ovimbundu strengthened Ovimbundu ethnic identity. As in the days of the commodity trade, when traders from the different Ovimbundu kingdoms helped spread Umbundu in the interior of central Africa, so Ovimbundu Protestants maintained the Protestant identity wherever they went, as the case of the Dondi graduate who in 1941 became a leader of the Ovimbundu working in Walvis Bay in South West Africa (modern Namibia) demonstrated.[125] Protestants who were sent as contract laborers to the fisheries in Porto Alexandre and Mossamedes between 1938 and 1943 initiated prayer and Bible study groups which eventually led to the establishment of Ovimbundu Protestant communities, with their own churches and schools, in the "native district" in both cites.[126] Despite the fact that the authorities were concerned about the role of the Protestants, they permitted Protestant pastors and catechists to follow Ovimbundu Protestant migrants throughout the colony. In the coastal labor camps, in inner urban areas, and in plantations in the sub-plateau regions, São Tomé, Principé, Luanda and other areas of the colony, Ovimbundu Protestants utilized the educational and social services of their pastors and teachers, which helped to strengthen regionalism and the ethnic distinctiveness of the group.[127]

They developed a sophisticated set of networks to assist their members. Thus in the fishing factories in Mossamedes and Porto Alexandre, where poor working conditions and persecution from Catholic priests and settlers were standard (one priest burnt the book of Psalms that some migrants were studying, accusing the author of being the "devil"), Protestant pastors encouraged their flock to obey the authorities. Constantinho da Cunha, the general manager of one factory, commented on the dedication of Protestant workers, noting that they "are different from the rest in their respect, humility and devotion to their work."[128]

Moreover, the authorities did not prevent Ovimbundu pastors and catechists from pioneering evangelical and educational work among the peoples of the Ganguelas (Luimbes in particular) and Chokwe regions to the east where they had formerly traded. Indeed, some in the government actually welcomed this "civilizing" work of Ovimbundu Protestants, because it cost the government nothing but assured a Portuguese presence in areas still being integrated into the colony. Already in 1932 there were six Ovimbundu church elders working among the Chokwe.[129] Some, like Fernando Chinyamo who was in charge of Protestant work in Cachingues in the Ganguelas, adopted a practice developed by the missionaries and dedicated half of his salary to help "a local man" to go to school.[130] Umbundu evangelical work among the Luimbe and Chokwe was so successful that by 1944 Enrique Gomes, an Ovimbundu pastor, was sent out to be in charge of the community,[131] and Luimbe and Chokwe students were attending school in the highlands along with the Ovimbundu.[132] The actions of these pious Ovimbundu Protestants built up a store of goodwill for the Ovimbundu which would prove vital in years when Ovimbundu Protestants in the region spearheaded the struggle against the colonial state.

Protestant Ovimbundu became a force in the region in other ways as well. Before the war when the settler population was still small, they comprised most of the population of Nova Lisboa, outnumbering settlers ten to one (forty thousand to four thousand) in 1943. They influenced consumer patterns and demands in the city and region, and in 1940 the local Portuguese agent of the Angolan bank in Novo Lisboa observed that "in the great centers the civilized black is a great consumer of imported articles, principally dresses and pants which are bought at the same price as paid by the Europeans."[133]

Those who had completed elementary school and had some additional postelementary training were concentrated in the *cantões* (administrative units within the city limits). Before the 1940s, when these positions were declared to be for white setters only, Ovimbundu Protestants worked as clerks, technicians, operators and craftsmen for the government, the railway, and other businesses in the city.[134] Some were also self-employed craftsmen.[135] Trained to be monogamous, they dedicated themselves to home and family and were regarded as model Christians.[136] In the 1930s some 15,991 Ovimbundu—the majority of them Protestant converts—passed the requirements set by the state (rudimentary education in Portuguese and a European lifestyle) to become *assimilados*.[137]

Although the growth in the number of Ovimbundu *assimilados* testified to the ability of the Protestant missionaries to meet New State goals of "civilizing" the African population, in reality gaining *assimilado* status did not guarantee integration into the Portuguese society. In contrast to the many illiterate, impoverished, and uncultured Portuguese settlers who were automatically accepted as "civilized," assimilated Africans were never accorded equal civil status with whites. In the city of Nova Lisboa, assimilated Africans were in effect disenfranchised by the 1950s, and in the city elections of 1960 almost no African voted, even though 532 Africans (out of 2,017 electors) had voted in 1947.[138]

Up to the 1950s, New State officials tolerated Ovimbundu Protestants. Although this had something to do with the fact that Ovimbundu Protestants were model colonial subjects, their position was in large part due to their connections with the foreign Protestants who provided them with the means to become assimilated, or at least to control the pace of westernization. They relied on the missionaries to plead their cases with *chefes* and other government officials, to register their births, to obtain death and marriage certificates, to fill out their assimilation papers, and to respond to other official demands. Many believed that the missionaries would protect them from the most pernicious actions of jealous settlers and the civil authorities.[139]

The Protestant missionaries were eager to maintain the support of their converts and protect their rights, but they were careful not to confront the government directly. To help their converts, they established the Pan-Angolan Evangelical Alliance in 1935.[140] The Alliance monitored developments in Angola and passed on relevant information about abuses and ill-treatment of the African population to the League of Nations, the International Labor Organization, and the Anti-Slavery and Aborigines Protection Society. This information provided the agencies with crucial evidence of Portuguese violations of African human rights and led to the condemnation of the Portuguese forced labor policy, with its substandard wages and disregard for the health and social needs of the African population.[141]

Missionaries assigned to the Protestant Alliance in Lisbon also pleaded with officials in the Overseas Office on behalf of African Protestants in Angola. In 1945 John Tucker, the Alliance coordinator, had an audience with the Colonial Minister, Marcelo Caetano, and tried to persuade him to change some of the more repressive aspects of colonial legislation. He argued that the laws did not advance Portuguese ideals and were particularly detrimental to the more forward-looking groups like the Ovimbundu who were "the Zulus of Central Africa, and their language a lingua franca for a wide area."[142]

Although suspicious and hostile to foreign Protestant missionaries, occasionally local officials capitalized on their work when they wished to curry favor in Lisbon by demonstrating to metropolitan authorities that Africans under their authority were becoming "civilized" and adopting Portuguese habits. For example, in 1943 at the time of a state visit by the President of the Republic, General Carmona, the Governor of Benguela requested the appearance of the two-hundred-voice Dondi choir, which had gained a reputation throughout the region for performing Christian and Portuguese nationalist songs. In his letter requesting the group to sing, the Governor noted that "the government is anxious that his Excellency the President should have an opportunity to see and hear the most advanced Africans in the country and Dondi young men and women are naturally indicated."[143] The missionaries readily complied with the request, believing that this would improve the standing of their charges in the eyes of the authorities and settlers.[144]

The growth of their educational and religious programs and the apparent ambivalence of the authorities in dealing with the missionaries before the Second World War led the latter to presume that the officials would leave them alone to turn out Ovimbundu ready to become obedient colonial subjects. Indeed, the missionaries came to see their role as helping to build a "strong African church [people] which can function within Portuguese norms."[145] The government, however, had no intention of allowing the Protestants to build a counter-state with democratic underpinnings that would undermine the corporatist ideology of the dictatorship.

Contrasting Visions: Ideals versus Reality

By the 1950s, the growth of the Protestant community organization with its elected leadership, shared Protestant Christian morality, familiarity with precolonial Ovimbundu beliefs and customs, and ability to speak Umbundu was a far cry from what New State planners had envisioned for the socialization of the Ovimbundu to Portuguese culture. Instead of Portuguese Catholic and secular authorities inculcating Portuguese culture and history into the Ovimbundu, Ovimbundu Protestants had instead put their own mark on modern Ovimbundu identity. Although this development resembled earlier adaptations that the Ovimbundu had made during the period of the long-distance trade, in the nineteenth century the unity the Ovimbundu from the various kingdoms had adopted in the trade proved fleeting and faded when caravan participants returned to kin, village, and kingdom.

Between 1926 and 1960, the new social mores that emerged among Ovimbundu Protestants reinforced many aspects of Ovimbundu culture by embedding them in a Protestant fabric. Having little in common with the Portuguese cultural heritage as groups such as the Kimbundus had, Ovimbundu Protestantism was a powerful social force in the rural regions of the southern and central parts of the colony. The fact that Ovimbundu Protestants remained such crucial players in the transformation of Ovimbundu culture made it more difficult for the Catholic missionaries to exert any influence. Indeed, the growth of Ovimbundu Protestant institutions played a crucial role in reinforcing and strengthening the social consciousness of both Protestant and non-Protestant Ovimbundu and in thwarting New State social engineering.

As the growth of this counter-social force took shape, especially after the Second World War, it exposed the contradictions in the social agenda of the New State and the Protestants. The state responded by closing some of the loopholes in the system. They began the attack by making it much more difficult for Ovimbundu Protestants to obtain *assimilado* status. New State policy on assimilation was spelled out in the 1954 Colonial Statute: according to this, prospective candidates were required to have a Catholic baptismal certificate, obtain a civil marriage license, secure a Portuguese sponsor, be employed in a "civilized" job, and live like a Portuguese. By 1958 the entire process cost $100 (U.S.), much of the money going as fees to Portuguese agents, who were familiar with the *processo*, and as bribes to keep the papers moving. The new procedures greatly reduced the numbers of Ovimbundu Protestants applying for "assimilated" status,[146] but had less effect on Catholic converts (who still made up only a small percentage of those Ovimbundu who had qualified for assimilated status, despite the increased social spending on them).[147]

A government census of "civilized" Angolans in preparation for the election of candidates for the National Assembly in the 1950s noted that only 48,985 "civilized" Angolans (mostly settlers), out of a population of 4,412,000 persons, made the electoral list.[148] Moreover, between 1950 and 1959 only 5,000 Africans in the entire colony qualified as *assimilados*,[149] and in 1960 only 0.8 percent (37,873) of Africans were listed as *assimilados* in the entire colony. In the district of Benguela where most of the Ovimbundu *assimilados* lived, the figure was even lower, as only 0.5 percent (2,391) were so listed.[150]

The government's failure to put an end to racial discrimination against *assimilados* who attempted to enjoy the same social and economic privileges as white Portuguese also impacted negatively on Ovimbundu Protestants. The growth in the number of settlers who came to the highlands and southern coastal cities also had much to do with the decrease in the status of Ovimbundu Protestant *assimilados*. In these areas, Ovimbundu Protestant *assimilados* faced residential discrimination, were unable to compete for places in government and privately run schools, and rarely had opportunities to socialize with whites and Afro-Portuguese in the private and public clubs, theatres, beaches, and other places that catered to the "civilized" population. Like the masses of Angola's "uncivilized" Africans, they resided in the slums (*muceques*), with none of the access to the public services which their taxes were supposed to provide. Yet they had to adopt the lifestyle of the settlers, pay to send their children to non-government Protestant schools, pay for licenses, and pay residence, and other taxes, while still enduring daily indignities such as carrying identity papers as proof of their urban residence.[151]

Fear of losing their jobs, of imprisonment, forced labor, or conscription into the military led many Ovimbundu Protestant *assimilados* to desert Protestant institutions and join the Catholics, a situation that threatened to weaken the still emerging modern Ovimbundu identity.[152] Some who formed discussion groups and ethnic organizations, or attempted to participate in activities that officials considered a threat to Portuguese nationalism, were accused of sedition.[153]

The pressure from state officials and settlers may explain why many Ovimbundu Protestants converts continued to look to traditional beliefs. A 1941 report from the Protestant villages near the Dondi station noted that of the 184 Ovimbundu men who were expelled from the church for "backsliding," most were guilty of participating in "divination." Interestingly, the expelled members were also wealthy men who headed polygamous households,[154] even though the church outlawed polygamy. Catholic missionaries reported similar occurrences among converts in 1944.[155] Others who found the social pressure burdensome simply succumbed to the social pressure from non-Christian relatives, left the community and churches, and returned to the non-Christian villages, blaming their misfortunes on the church. This backlash was particularly evident among descendants of the former ruling elite who had lost so much prestige and power in the decades since the conquest.[156]

A survey of the numerous folk tales and oral traditions recorded by missionaries and government ethnographers during the period shows that

Ovimbundu oral traditions were not disappearing, even among mission-ary-educated individuals.[157] In the 1944 annual report on the state of the Diocese of Nova Lisboa, Catholic Church authorities expressed concern over the pervasiveness of African practices. The report cautioned that the two most important customs which hindered the Christianization and im-provement of the people of Bailundo, in particular, were "circumcision and fetishes (witchcraft)." It expressed regret that even good Catholics preferred to consult with "feiticeiros" instead of priests, and bewailed the fact that the population lived "immoral, drunken and promiscuous lives" which la-bor migration made worse.[158]

Such reports became more numerous during the 1950s, and witch-craft, a common phenomenon in other parts of colonial Africa, figured prominently. Indeed, a 1952 report by the British consul in Angola noted the high incidence of witchcraft among the Ovimbundu population, ques-tioning the validity of missionary and official figures as to the number of real Christians among the population. He speculated instead that "witch-craft" was spreading on account of social insecurity and that no more than 20% of the population were Roman Catholics and 10% of the Protestants were real Christians".[159] A few years later, the British anthropologist, Adrian Edwards noted that in the villages of Bimbe where he carried out field-work, many of the men condemned to corvée labor were just as likely to have been convicted of witchcraft as to have defaulted on their tax.[160]

Protestant missionaries echoed these concerns, noting that "fetish-ism" was spreading among converts.[161] Indeed, "backsliders" were expelled from Christian villages and churches for "heathen practices" (consulting with the kimbandas), and for practicing polygamy, along with smoking, adul-tery, and drinking, as late as the 1950s.[162] In 1957, a missionary noted that one reason why there were many Ovimbundu "backsliders" was that many Christians "still have great fear of charms and witch doctors' medicines."[163]

The state's migrant labor program and the colonial laws that pre-vented nonassimilated Africans from adopting Portuguese ("Western") ways also explain why Ovimbundu Protestants remained tied to the precolonial Ovimbundu culture. For example, returning migrants and soldiers still brought back ocimbandas which they gave to sekulus, pastors, or catechists for their services at weddings, funerals, and initiation ceremonies.[164] Fur-thermore, many aspects of Ovimbundu customary laws regarding bride price and sexual division of labor, residence, inheritance, and land practices were kept alive in both the villages and the slums.[165] Protestant Ovimbundu adopted Western secular and religious customs and beliefs,[166] but like their nonconverted kin they had a knowledge of Umbundu and other Angolan languages, had Umbundu names, raised their children by Umbundu norms, and generally retained many of the customary practices found among their nonassimilated kinsmen.[167]

Ovimbundu Society: Despair or Hope?

It would be a mistake, however, to conclude that the retention of elements of Ovimbundu customs lessened the pernicious effects of the regime's economic and social policies. Since the aim of Salazar and his supporters was to create exploitable Portuguese-speaking subjects, and not to give Africans equal status with settlers in the colony, officials supported many aspects of the traditional culture, especially promoting "primitive" dress, dances, and customs that maintained the divide between "civilized" and "noncivilized."

A by-product of the government's policies was the growing number of demoralized and de-acculturated Ovimbundu who lived on the margins of both the African and European worlds. Among these were Ovimbundu women who became concubines (*mulheres*) of recently arrived settlers. Once these men were financially secure, they returned to Portugal to find brides, leaving the Angolan women and their offspring to fend for themselves. The women, unwilling to return to their villages, joined the growing number of "native" prostitutes so visible in every colonial city.[168]

As the 1950s drew to a close, New State policies were beginning to put the Ovimbundu on the defensive. Just as the policies of the marketing agencies and labor policies of the state had turned large segments of the Ovimbundu population into migrant laborers, the government's limited social agenda had undermined and in some cases destroyed both the traditional and Protestant institutions. Nowhere, however, had New State policies led to the dominance of Portuguese culture among the Ovimbundu. Instead, various Ovimbundu groups—*assimilados*, converts caught between African and European cultures, unassimilated "bush" Ovimbundu, and young Protestant and Catholic converts who tried desperately to adopt Portuguese norms—had in their own ways kept Ovimbundu culture and beliefs alive and given new life to the communities. This had occurred despite the laws which had effectively turned government-approved sobas and sekulus into timid colonial collaborators.[169] As the 1950s ended, most observers viewed the different groups of Ovimbundu as Africans who had accepted Portuguese propaganda about assimilation. Settlers believed them to be the most tractable of the colony's African population, and Africans in the other regions of the colony regarded them as uneducated migrant workers, servants, and slaves, or "primitives from the bush."[170] The events that erupted in the Bakongo and Kimbundu regions of the colony in March, 1961, spread anticolonial fervor throughout the colony. For the first time since the conquest, rural Africans, migrants, urban slum dwellers, soldiers, *assimilados*, nationalists, and others joined organizations and articulated ideologies that challenged the New State regime. For the various segments of the Ovimbundu population, 1961 also heralded a new beginning in their relationship to the state.

5

THE OVIMBUNDU AND THE LATE COLONIAL STATE: AUTHORITY VERSUS AUTONOMY, 1961–1974

Introduction

Several developments during the period from from 1961 to 1974 affected the Ovimbundu relationship with the state. These were the outbreak of the liberation struggle against the Salazar-Caetano regime in 1961, the founding of UNITA in 1966 by Jonas Savimbi and other exiles, the growth of an authoritarian Angolan state in response to the nationalist challenge, and the 1974 cease-fire between the liberation movements and the new Portuguese authorities who had gained power in Lisbon as a result of a coup against the dictatorship.

Although these developments all contributed to the growing tensions between some segments of Ovimbundu society and the state, two issues made this period profoundly different from the earlier times. The first was the willingness of Ovimbundu from the different social strata to expand their efforts to undermine the state, and the second was the role of Jonas Savimbi, the Ocimbundu who founded UNITA, and the rest of the leadership in mobilizing other Ovimbundu to join UNITA in its struggle against the state. For all Ovimbundu, the consequences of these developments were revolutionary. While at the beginning of the period, Ovimbundu anti-state activities were limited to the individual actions that foreign missionaries, sekulus, sobas, kimbandas, pastors, teachers, catechists, and others took against state exactions, by 1974 Savimbi and the UNITA leadership and membership articulated a modern nationalism heavily influenced by the ethnic, party, and regional background of their largely Ovimbundu and rural membership. This ethnic and rural bias so came to symbolize the movement that it created a profound gulf between the UNITA leadership and other Angolans. This development also spoke more to the political and personal choices of Savimbi and the UNITA leadership than of the larger concerns of the various segments of the Ovimbundu population.

The events which occurred between 1961 and 1974 also transformed the colonial state. Although on one level the developments exposed the failure of the earlier New State policies, on another the challenge reflected the contradictions between New State goals and Angolan realities. In 1961 by most visible measures the Angolan colonial regime had achieved many of the goals that Salazar had outlined during the early years of the New State. Forced labor, land alienation, forced cultivation, and heavy tax burdens on the African masses had become the norm in the colony. Yet these achievements had not brought about the main desire: complete economic exploitation of the African population.[1] The outbreak of the liberation war gave the Salazar-Caetano dictatorship the opportunity to invest enormous amounts of resources in the military and security, and opened the way for military and security personnel to assume a dominant role in the state. By 1974 the regime had achieved the goal of establishing an authoritarian colonial state in Angola, but was losing the fight to contain African and Afro-Portuguese resistance.

But the African/Afro-Portuguese opposition was far from united. Given the divergent histories of the indigenous populations in the colony, and the varying experiences of Africans and whites under the colonial regimes up to 1960, the contradictions between them increased rather than subsided. These contradictions manifested themselves in the growing regional, ethnic, class, and organizational distinctions between the various liberation movements.

The contradictions and differences first appeared in the northern Kikongo and Kimbundu-speaking regions. In early 1961, northern Kikongo-speaking producers led by the *União das Populações de Angola/Governo Revolucionária de Angola no Exilio* (UPA/GRAE; the name was later changed to *Frente Nacional de Liberação de Angola* the FNLA) with its headquarters in Kinshasa, (Zaire) rose up against German and Portuguese coffee plantation holders and government officials who had alienated their land and imposed severe labor and taxation demands on them. Holden Roberto and other leaders who instigated the rebellion were Angolan nationalists opposed to Portuguese rule and seeking an African-controlled state. They even went so far as to advocate the restoration of the Kongolese monarchy.

Kimbundu workers and peasants in Luanda and the Kasanje lowlands who rose up at the same time had similar grievances and pursued the same goals. In Luanda, the administrative reforms and settler expansion of the New State had resulted in urban discontent among the masses of African and Afro-Portuguese workers and Afro-Portuguese and Angolan-born white intellectuals. Similarly, in the region of Kasanje, state-imposed cotton growing schemes, forced labor, and increasing taxation had produced a large number of disgruntled African peasants. In early 1961 the anti-government forces coalesced under the umbrella of the Kimbundu and *assimilado*-led *Movimento Popular de Libertação de Angola* (MPLA) based in Congo-Brazzaville (Republic of the Congo). Although the movement encouraged and at times organized demonstrations, strikes, prison outbreaks, and rural uprisings in the hope of destabilizing the regime, the movement was confined to Luanda and the small urban neighboring centers along the railroad.

Although open anti-state agitation surfaced in the highlands only in the mid-1960s, the contradictions between state policies and the desires of society were also evident in the Ovimbundu region in the earlier period. This was seen in the retention of vestiges of the precolonial beliefs and practices and the emergence of home-grown Ovimbundu Protestant institutions, developments which were contradiction to state policy. As the challenge to authoritarian rule grew, however, the state moved to destroy these institutions. The undermining of their social anchors explains in part why, by 1966, Ovimbundu and other southerners formed their own regional, nationalist organization.

The contradiction between the New State regime and the different dynamics that had emerged in the colony was also evident in the growing friction between the state and some members of the white community. A growing number of the Catholic clergy, ex-military personnel, and Angolan-born whites opposed the policies that the state pursued in the wake of the uprisings, and some showed their resentment by supporting the nationalists. As the liberation war expanded throughout the 1960s and early 1970s, and the regime devoted more and more of its resources to put it down, dissatisfaction with the dictatorship reached the army. In April 1974, in Portugal, young officers who had served in the colonial wars toppled the Salazar-Caetano dictatorship and handed over the state to "the Angolan people" in November, 1975.

This did not signal the end of the contradictions, however: the coup leaders bequeathed to the nationalists a society disunited by regional and ethnic, class, and other contradictions which the authoritarian state had promoted.[2]

The aim here is to demonstrate how the military challenge from the Angolan nationalists led the authoritarian state to destroy the gains that the various groups of Ovimbundu had achieved up to 1960. The intention is also to show how this led to an increase in the regional and ethnic divisions which widened rather than narrowed the distance between the Ovimbundu and the state. This development disposed the various Ovimbundu groups that had emerged prior to 1960 to identify themselves as Ovimbundu and, by 1974, to be more inclined to affiliate themselves with UNITA, a regional "nationalist" movement, rather than to think of alligning themselves with the MPLA or FNLA.[3]

The Angolan Authoritarian Colonial State and the Anticolonial Movements

Although the ideal picture of modern mass nationalism posits the appearance of a unified anti-colonial movement undermining the colonial state, this scenario did not occur in Angola. Here, unlike other states in Africa, no colony-wide nationalist movement emerged to challenge the authoritarian colonial state. This was despite the fact that the state's policies—the economic exploitation of Africans and Afro-Portuguese, the promotion of settler rather than African interests, and the subordination of Angola's development to Portugal's—affected Africans and Afro-Portuguese throughout the colony. Instead, the ethnic and regional divisions the government had promoted in the years prior to 1961 dominated the anticolonial struggle.

Yet there is no work that explores this aspect of Angolan history, nor is there any study that links the actions of the authoritarian colonial state to the regional and ethnic consciousness (nationalism) that the Ovimbundu exhibited between 1961 and 1974. Indeed, studies of the liberation war only hint at the links between the authoritarian state and regional/ethnic consciousness as a manifestation of nationalism.[4]

Recent revisionist writings on the Mau-Mau uprising in Kenya,[5] and others which focus on the growing role of the state in the economic and political life of the colonies during the dying days of colonialism, however, suggest that Angola was not alone in the way the authoritarian state functioned in the regional and ethnic legacies it bequeathed to African nations.[6]

Some of the general and the more specialized works on the period of the anticolonial struggle in Angola do touch on the ethnic/regional dimensions of the liberation war.[7] Basil Davidson indirectly referred to these in his popular work on Angola, conceding that regional/ethnic differences between the Angolan nationalist movements hindered the effectiveness of the liberation wars against the Salazar dictatorship.[8] John Marcum's two-volume analysis also picked up on the subject, especially in his explorations of some of the ethnic and ideological dimensions which he argued weakened guerrilla efforts and made liberation politics more contentious.[9]

René Pélissier and F.W. Heimer focused more directly on the issue, suggesting that the nationalist struggle was a sign of the growing strength of the colonial regime, whose policies promoted class, racial, ethnic, and regional imbalances in the colony. For Heimer, however, the contradictions between the state and colonized Africans accelerated rather than slowed the pace of integration of African communities into Portuguese central society. Gervase Clarence-Smith agreed that the Salazar-Caetano dictatorship succeeded in extending authoritarian control through its economic and military policies, by investing enormous amounts of resources. He credited the fall of the state, however, to the disaffection of crucial elements of the metropolitan bourgeoisie, and not to Angolan nationalists, who could not overcome their regional and ethnic differences.[10] Other ethnographic and anthropological works provide more general views on the connections between the authoritarian colonial state and regional and ethnic politics in Angola from 1961 to 1974, but there is no work that focuses on the Ovimbundu.[11]

The Colonial Regime and the Anticolonial Challenge

In 1961 when the anti-colonial uprising occurred in the Kongo and Kimbundu regions, the colonial government sent in enormous army reinforcements, treating it as a regional, and not as a colony-wide, anticolonial movement. The strength of the reaction was understandable, as the Belgians had granted independence to Africans in neighboring Belgian Congo, and African nationalists in other colonies were calling for an end to European colonial rule. Between 1961 and 1975, as anticolonial activities spread throughout Angola, the Portuguese expanded the military, tightened security by repressive measures, and placed more controls over the population. As a result, Angola became an armed camp and the state became more authoritarian. Yet the regional and ethnic tendencies which had surfaced in 1961 did not abate.

The most significant policy response of the regime in Angola from 1961 to 1974 was its increased reliance on the army and security forces to defeat the nationalists and to implement its authoritarian policies.[12] The militarization of the state began soon after the 1961 uprisings, and the role of the military expanded as more Africans and Afro-Portuguese joined the anticolonial struggle against the dictatorship.[13]

The role that the army came to play in Angola after 1961 was something new, for after the New State regime took power in 1926, the military posts that were still functioning had given way to civilian authority, and soldiers had gone back to the barracks, except for African recruits who were used to round up forced laborers in some parts of the colony. Few of the Portuguese-born and other colonial soldiers who had been used in the earlier campaigns of conquest remained in Angola.[14] When the uprisings broke out in 1961, the Governor General called for massive military reinforcements to isolate Africans in the north and to end what was first regarded as nothing more than a serious breakdown of the social order in just a few areas. Before long, however, fear and suspicion among settlers and the subsequent spread of nationalist activities led to the spread of military operations to all corners of the colony.

The decision to turn to the military to keep order in the colony can be traced to the official belief that only a massive show of force in the coffee-growing regions of Kongo and Dembos could put the government back in control. Officials justified their actions at the time by pointing out some that two hundred to three hundred Portuguese men, women, and children had been brutally murdered or lost their lives in other ways as a result of the uprising, hundreds of coffee plantations had been destroyed, and hundreds of thousands of Africans and hundreds of Portuguese settlers had became refugees.[15] In retaliation for the deaths of the settlers and the destruction of their property,[16] the government drafted massive numbers of local and metropolitan troops as well as civilian combatants to put down the revolt and restore order.

Africans everywhere in Angola paid heavily, as the government attempted to quash this regional resistance to the state by heavy reliance on the military. Within less than a year the army, its units equipped with sophisticated NATO-supplied guns and bombers, put down the insurgency at a cost to the Africans of between 8,000 and 20,000 casualties and the displacement of 150,000 refugees.[17] The dictatorship's use of the army began a pattern of state-supported violence and intimidation against civilians, destruction of civilian property, foreign intervention, and refugee problems that became the hallmarks of the authoritarian state in Angola.

The military build-up and deployment did not lead to the elimination of anti-state activities among Africans and Afro-Portuguese population as the dictatorship had hoped. Instead, by the mid-1960s the regime faced liberation wars on three fronts—from the Kongo region, the Kimbundu area, and the central and eastern areas of the colony.

The key moment for the anticolonial movement in Angola was the independence of the Belgian Congo (Zaire/Democratic Republic of the Congo) in 1960 and Congo-Brazzaville (Republic of the Congo), since these states provided bases for a small number of anticolonial guerrillas from the Kongo and Kimbundu regions. As these early guerrillas made inroads (albeit small) through border raids with weapons from Russia and China, they provoked the state to respond and the settlers to overreact, thus creating worsening conditions in the colony which helped to radicalize moderate Africans. It was this situation which led to the full-blown anticolonial struggle and the involvement of segments of the Ovimbundu population. The 1964 independence of Northern Rhodesia (Zambia), which shared a frontier with Angola, proved crucial as well, for Zambia's President Kenneth Kaunda provided Angolan nationalists with sympathetic allies with whom to continue the struggle. By 1966, when UNITA appeared, the state faced a Bakongo-led UPA/GRAE/FNLA anticolonial movement with its headquarters in Kinshasa (Zaire), a Kimbundu and *assimilado*-led MPLA with its headquarters in Congo-Brazzaville; and an Ovimbundu–southern UNITA movement which opened bases in eastern Angola and Zambia. Although the three anticolonial movements were not united, from the state's point of view this did not count for much, because each movement was intent on undermining the state. From the point of view of anticolonial unity, Angolan nationalism, and Ovimbundu aspirations, however, the disunity proved disastrous. It magnified the ethnic, regional, and ideological differences between Africans and Afro-Portuguese in the colony and alienated the Ovimbundu from their fellow Angolans.[18]

With the expansion of the liberation war, the regime relied even more heavily on the military to keep the anti-colonial guerrillas from opening bases in the colony, to protect the settlers, and to prevent the resistance from spreading. To achieve its goals, the authorities also expanded the operations of the *Polícia Internacional e de Defesa do Estado* (PIDE), the metropolitan-based secret police and security arm of the dictatorship, whose agents had been operating in the colony since the late 1950s. Although PIDE was established in Angola to target settler and Afro-Portuguese intellectuals in Luanda, as the nationalist campaigns escalated in the 1960s, its agents moved against African peasants and workers.[19]

By 1974, high-ranking members of the army, PIDE directors, and top civilian members of the government formed a triumvirate ruling the colony, with PIDE directors and military officers influencing policy much more directly than the civilian authorities. Indeed, civilian bureaucrats increasingly played a subordinate role in the government.[20] The reliance on PIDE and the military to control the spread of African nationalism brought the government closer to its goal of establishing an autocratic colonial state in Angola.

Much of the state's growing autocracy resulted from the belief of the authorities in Lisbon that military and security operations were essential to achieve state corporatism and a larger Portugal made up of politically subordinated and economically exploited non-European populations. From 1961 to 1974, the military/security officials who controlled the state followed several strategies to deal with the growing nationalist opposition. In the first place, they sought to win a military victory against African nationalists by an all-out effort aimed at destroying nationalist bases as well as preventing new recruits from reaching training camps inside and outside Angola. Recalling some of the strategies that de Matos had adopted, the authorities moved to destroy the lingering vestiges of the precolonial civil institutions, but also the colonial ones that had emerged by 1960 and that they had allowed to operate. The aim was to achieve the full and rapid integration of loyal black Portuguese into the Portuguese Empire.[21] Again, as in the past, they gave a priority to white immigration and encouraged private investment in the industrial and plantation sectors.

Beginning in 1961, the government expanded the role of the armed forces and PIDE and redirected to these agencies ordinary and extraordinary funds from Portugal and the colony that had been slated for economic programs.[22] As a result, the colony experienced the greatest military build-up since the period of the conquest, along with increased security measures that included political repression, censorship, and other "anti-terrorist" activities.

The growing role of the military in Angola was evident by the mid-sixties. By that time, a little more than half of the Portuguese government budget went to support military operations against nationalists in the African colonies.[23] Moreover, with the strategic American bases in the Azores and the linking of the Angolan liberation war to the Soviet Union's Cold War strategies, Portugal was able to acquire American-supplied weapons that allowed its army in Angola to fight a technologically sophisticated war against the guerrillas.[24]

In 1971, when the Overseas Ministry shifted more of the financial burden for fighting the war to the individual territories, 9.6 percent of the

Angola's budget went to defense.[25] The administrative functions that the military and security agencies carried out in Angola enabled their agents to operate almost independently of earlier Overseas Ministry restrictions.[26]

During the period, army and security agents spread to every part of the colony. The armed forces included a total of 70,000 soldiers including 10,000 to 15,000 Africans. There were also 30,000 African, Portuguese, and Afro-Portuguese police and paramilitary personnel. By the beginning of the 1970s, the security forces also included 30,000 *flechas* (arrows), specially trained African local militia recruited by the secret police and posted in every African community in the colony to act as informers.[27] Furthermore, the white settler population (between 300,000 to 500,000 persons by 1974) formed a third force which periodically sent out mobs of civilian vigilantes against the 6,000,000 Africans in the colony. The government relied on this varied and formidable military, security, and militia force to fight the 10,000 or so nationalists, as well as to control the 6,000,000 Africans and Afro-Portuguese.[28]

The army and security forces used the latest military hardware, including chemical weapons, against the guerrilla bases and in the areas of the country where they suspected the African civilian population harbored or sympathized with the nationalists.[29] The authorities also relied on a wide network of informers who supplied information to the hundreds of PIDE agents who operated throughout the country. The information the informers provided led to the harassment, arrest, and imprisonment in Angola, in other Portuguese colonies, and in Portugal of thousands of African, Afro-Portuguese, and white dissidents on a variety of anti-government charges. Hundreds of these prisoners died from torture before the end of the war in 1974, while thousands more languished in colonial prisons for years.[30] By 1974 there was a total of 12,000 prisoners, many of them African nationalists in the infamous São Nicolau prison camp near Mossamedes.[31]

In addition to fighting guerrillas and intimidating the population, the military and PIDE carried out various counter-insurgency measures against the African people. The most notorious was the resettlement plan aimed at depriving the nationalists of recruits.[32] The success of the regime's counter-insurgency measures was revealed through 1974 as the authorities herded large numbers of Africans (who had formerly lived in areas far from guerrilla actions) into strategic villages. Those Africans not living in the so-called protected villages were surrounded daily by PIDE agents and informers.[33]

Throughout the colony, military personnel, security agents, and civilian officials incited mobs of armed settlers who harassed, injured, or murdered Africans and destroyed their property under the pretext that they were supporters of the nationalists.[34] Many of the vigilantes were poorer settlers who migrated to the colony after 1961 and who eventually became disillusioned by the protracted guerrilla war. When their efforts to gain control of the state failed, they gravitated to Southern Rhodesia (Zimbabwe) and South Africa.[35]

Directed Development: The Economic Alternative

Besides relying on security and military operations to maintain control in Angola, the state subordinated Angola's economy to pay for the militarization process and even more to underwrite the modernization that Portugal experienced during the 1960s.[36] In Angola, the economic reforms that the authorities implemented in 1961–62 in response to the uprisings in the north and again in 1968 spelled out the regime's goals. In line with the objectives that they had set down in the preceding period, state-directed economic development remained the priority for planners in the Overseas Ministry. The colonies, now called Overseas Territories, were to continue to play a major economic role in the development of the modern Portuguese Empire.

The expansion of American private investments in the petroleum and natural gas industries boosted Portugal's economic development. Portugal also received substantial financial support from the United States as part of U.S. efforts to retain Portugal as an ally during the Cold War. The signing of the Azores Agreement in December 1971 highlighted the alliance between the Nixon Administration and Portugal. The agreement provided Portugal with cash grants of $6 million, a Food for Peace loan of $30 million, and access to $400 million in export-import bank credits.[37]

Most commentaries on Angola's economy from 1961 to 1974 conclude that in both Portugal and Angola the economy grew at an impressive rate despite the war against guerrillas. In Clarence-Smith's words, the government's "crash programme of industrialization and economic growth" achieved spectacular results.[38] By 1971, 35.6 percent of Angola's budget went to economic development—in particular, to communications and transport. The impact of the economic transformation was seen in the new relationship between Angola and Portugal. In the first place, Angola became Portugal's largest single trading partner, supplying 36 percent of its imports and buying most of its exports by 1968.[39] The territory also shifted from exporting agricultural staples to Portugal to exporting minerals and petroleum. Moreover, Portuguese oligopolies participated in joint ventures with settler capital and foreign investors especially in petroleum exploration, petrochemicals, diamonds, and electrical energy.[40] By 1970, investments in the industrial sector stood at $1,120 million (U.S.), nearly five times the $268 million (U.S.) value of two decades earlier.[41] The new export sector was highly capitalized and generally had a low labor requirement, but the expanding diamond industry still required many unskilled laborers.

The plantation sector (in particular coffee, sugar, cotton, and sisal) also expanded. As part of the reform that Portugal undertook after the outbreak of hostilities in 1961, the headquarters of the various marketing agencies for cereal, cotton, and coffee were transferred from Lisbon to Angola to appease the Angolan-based white planters and merchants.[42] With fewer government restrictions, the plantation sector prospered. It controlled 60 percent of the cultivable land under use in Angola and employed over two hundred and fifty thousand African laborers in 1970.[43] The number of Ovimbundu employed as migrant laborers on the plantations continued to increase.

The reforms also increased state funding for education, research, labor, and urbanization for the settlers and some segments of the African and Afro-Portuguese population.[44] In addition, international agencies such as the Food and Agricultural Organization (FAO) gave Angola funds to undertake land surveying and hydraulic research, as well as to establish agencies to collect comprehensive agricultural statistics for the first time in the colony's history.[45] There was also some growth in the manufacturing sector and in the fishing industry. The acceleration of the pace of economic growth in the colony from the early 1960s on illustrated the success of the state's economic initiatives.

A major part of the economic program promoted and underwritten by the state focused on enhancing the settler sector in the central highlands. Through the *Junta Provincial de Povoamento de Angola* (Organization for the Settlement of Angola), the authorities set aside millions of dollars to establish in Angola planned rural resettlement communities for immigrants from Portugal, Madeira, and Cape Verde. The government also liberalized the immigration laws and allowed non-Portuguese white settlers—especially ex-soldiers—into Angola with the offer of land and credit. Many immigrants from Italy and other European countries took up the offer,[46] with the result that the white settler population in the colony increased from 175,000 in 1961 to 335,000 in the early 1970s; eventually the settler population swelled to more than half a million by 1975. These immigrants continued to swell the ranks of the urban population, especially in Benguela and in Nova Lisboa.[47]

Legislating Status: Africans and the Authoritarian State

The regime also devoted attention to economic and social issues that affected on the African population inside Angola. In 1961, the Overseas Office repealed the distasteful 1954 Native Law (*Estatuto dos Indígenas*) that identified Angola as a colony and Africans (natives) as second-class persons in the Portuguese Empire. The nationalist uprising made lawmakers realize that legislation that designated Africans and their culture as "uncivilized", and promoting legal barriers that made it impossible for Africans to become "civilized" undermined the legitimacy of the state in the eyes of Africans and of a world increasingly critical of Portuguese colonial policy.[48]

According to the legislation in force after 1961, the status of the African colonies changed from colonies to Overseas Territories: these were considered integral parts of Portugal. The repeal of the 1954 statute immediately allowed all Africans in the Territories to be full citizens of the empire. As Clarence-Smith has pointed out, however, the new laws were not so much a radical departure from the past as a return to the situation which had existed in the nineteenth century, when Africans in Portuguese colonies were regarded as citizens of Portugal. In reality, the reforms did not dramatically alter the status of the majority of the African population, because Africans were still divided into two groups. The smaller group comprised assimilated Africans subject to Portuguese civil law, while the larger group was made up of unassimilated Africans who were subject to customary (African) laws. Once an African chose his civil status, his descendants inherited it as well.[49]

The regime also implemented a series of administrative changes that affected the status of the African population in more general ways. The reforms changed the civil posts (*postos civeis*) to municipalities (*regedorias*), to conform with administrative divisions in Portugal. This change was meant to do away with the indirect rule system by further undermining the status of traditional authorities: it set up new procedures for nomination of Africans to government service. In the highlands, for example, men who had formerly been elected to the position of sekulu by specially designated village electors according to traditional custom and who had been approved by the state because of their ties to the preconquest elite lost out to men from ordinary lineages who were even more willing to support the state. Even though the move to appointive office for Africans had begun before 1961, the practice became more commonplace after the mid-sixties.[50]

In response to the political crisis, the government moved to reform taxation and labor practices in the colony and to give more attention to African rural development. Colonial representatives considered the changes a top priority. Critics in the Overseas Office blamed local officials for abusing the taxation system, which, they argued, was responsible for the rising African resentment against the colonial regime. In response, the authorities repealed the hut tax and replaced it with a general tax of about $10.00 (U.S.) which all males in the colony had to pay.[51] They also removed many of the detested aspects of the forced labor laws, such as defining legal work as an activity carried out under European or state direction.

The Ovimbundu Factor: Creating Collaborators

The attempts of Angolan officials to deal with the 1961 outbreak and the spread of anticolonial activities in the north also included colony-wide plans to isolate Africans who had not exhibited open anti-government sentiments. Officials targeted the Ovimbundu especially because they calculated that winning over this largest ethnic group in the country was essential to the success of counter-insurgency measures. The fact that the Ovimbundu had served in previous government campaigns against other Africans (in 1918, 5000 Bailundus had served as auxiliaries alongside regular troops in the military campaign in the south),[52] were largely rural, and exhibited strong regional, linguistic, and ethnic solidarity made them an excellent resource for the government. Officials believed that few Ovimbundu would be inclined to identify with the largely northern, urban and Western-educated Africans who were linked to the 1961 uprisings. Although in 1961 no one could predict where this thinking would lead, the realities of the war and the spread of anticolonial activities to the highlands eventually allowed the state to capitalize on the linguistic, ethnic, and regional tendencies that were already present. The state's promotion of Ovimbundu ethnic tendencies and regionalism contributed to the growth of modern Ovimbundu ethnic consciousness.[53]

The government's strategy for using the Ovimbundu as collaborators underwent several transformations between 1961 and 1974. In 1961, when the rebellion broke out in the north, the authorities, who had always relied on local troops from other parts of the colony to deal with anti-Portuguese activities, coerced large numbers of Ovimbundu who were working as contract laborers there into serving with regular troops against the Kongo insurgents.[54] At the same time the administration carried out sustained propaganda to gain Ovimbundu support.

One strategy the government adopted was radio broadcasts in Umbundu in rural and urban areas of the colony with large numbers of Ovimbundu listeners. The programs were designed to heighten "tribal" distrust between the Ovimbundu and Africans in the north (Kongo and Kimbundu), and they emphasized the differences (linguistic, ethnic, cultural, and regional) between the Ovimbundu and other Africans in Angola. Some of the reports put the government's gloss on the uprisings, by emphasizing that Ovimbundu migrants working in northern coffee plantations and urban centers were at the mercy of Kongo insurgents who had brutally murdered "loyal Bailundu" soldiers.[55] The authorities also distributed pamphlets and (censored) newspaper accounts[56] which warned the Ovimbundu that the Kimbundu and Kongo were planning to invade the central highlands and seize Ovimbundu land, women, and children. The propaganda reassured the Ovimbundu population that the authorities would protect them from their African enemies.[57]

As the war against the nationalists progressed, official propaganda continued to divide the Ovimbundu from the other Africans by publicly praising Ovimbundu soldiers for their contribution to the Portuguese war effort. The authorities also used both legal and illegal means to have a greater number of Ovimbundu soldiers fight alongside white troops and to recruit Ovimbundu as PIDE informers. These collaborators infiltrated guerrilla units operating on the colony's frontier with Zaire and Zambia and in the bases the nationalist had established inside the country.[58] Especially significant was the Portuguese decision to Africanize the military in the early 1970s (especially with the creation of the *flechas* and elite black commando forces) and to use the army as a way for Africans to achieve upward mobility. The strategy proved an overwhelming success. By the early 1970s, the Ovimbundu comprised the bulk of the 34,500 African conscripts in the Angolan army fighting against the nationalists, as well as most of the 60,000 man African militia force.[59] A great deal of the state's success stemmed from gaining the collaboration of the sobas and sekulus who continued to obey official policies whether this involved recruitment of men for the militia and army or the order to abandon old villages for government "strategic villages." One prominent Ocimbundu explained the complicity of the sobas and sekulus by noting that they obeyed the orders out of fear, and expalined the complicity by referring to a popular Ovimbundu truism which noted that "against force there is no resistance."[60]

Jonas Savimbi's relationship with the colonial government provides an excellent example of how complex the status of some educated Ovimbundu became. Savimbi began his career as an outstanding representative of the tightly knit Protestant Ovimbundu community that had emerged in Angola by the 1950s. His youthful influences included a proud and unrepentant traditionalist grandfather, who taught him the history of his people and sent him to initiation camp, a pious Protestant father, who had him educated at Protestant elementary schools and at Dondi and who wanted him to become a doctor, and a liberal Brazilian priest, Father Armando Codeiro, the headmaster at Silva Porto *Liceu* (high school), who provided him with monetary and intellectual support. The books Codeiro loaned the young Savimbi on Brazilian resistance to the Portuguese went a long way towards radicalizing Savimbi.[61] Yet Savimbi secretly cooperated with the Portuguese colonial government in its drive to destroy the MPLA. Thus, although a leader of the anticolonial resistance, Savimbi's collaboration with the regime stamped him as an opportunist who would betray the anticolonial cause. His collaboration with the regime severely undermined his status in anticolonial circles, and contributed greatly to the distrust that the MPLA leadership harbored about UNITA as a genuine nationalist movement.[62] Many less famous Ovimbundu also worked in different capacities for the state, serving as its agents and clerks in the courts and other facilities.[63]

The military and security relations between the state and Ovimbundu collaborators, together with the success of the state in implementing its military and security policies on the larger Ovimbundu population, frustrated the efforts of the MPLA, for example, to recruit significant numbers of Ovimbundu as members. The government thus succeeded in driving a wedge between the Ovimbundu and other Angolan nationalists by exploiting the ethnic, regional, and ideological differences which their own policies had created. Savimbi, reflecting on how this affected relations between people from Luanda and people from the south, recalled that when the Luandans referred to southerners "they call us people of 'Bailundo,'" which he noted was a pejorative term, referring to an "inferior". These prejudices, which became pronounced only from the 1960s, helped undermine anticolonial unity and prejudiced Angola nationalism.[64]

The Ovimbundu Factor: Economic Agents or Unwilling Migrants

The success of the government's economic policies which further undermined the economic advances the Ovimbundu had made during the earlier period; they also undermined any efforts to get the masses of the population to support the anticolonial struggle. Between 1961 and 1974, as before, the government's drive towards economic modernization relied for success on a steady supply of cheap labor. Security measures also figured prominently in the government's calculations. In the end, the migrant labor system and the government's wartime campaigns against African civilians destroyed the village economy and forced the Ovimbundu to work for the settlers and the state or serve in the army.

The effort to use the Ovimbundu as cheap labor succeeded because the vast majority of the population had few ways in which to resist the regime. In this respect they were unlike the Kongos in the north, many of whom could escape across the border and join the refugee Angolan communities in Zaire. They also had few opportunities to join the underground African and mulatto-dominated opposition movements that operated in Luanda and Benguela and attracted a growing number of Kimbundu.

In the rural areas of the highlands where the majority of Ovimbundu lived, state officials relied on Ovimbundu men and women to perform unskilled work in the various public, plantation, and manufacturing establishments throughout the territory. The number of Ovimbundu migrant laborers inside and outside Angola increased in the late sixties and early seventies despite the war. In 1961 there were some 78,000 Ovimbundu migrants in the north,[65] and by 1965, about 100,000 Ovimbundu males, one quarter of the able-bodied men, worked as migrant laborers on the northern coffee plantations. Another 75,000 worked in other plantations in the territory.[66] Colonial officials also recruited about 35,000 Ovimbundu to work in the mines of Namibia, South Africa, and Zambia.[67]

Cheap Ovimbundu labor was critical to the state's program of expanding the manufacturing, industrial, and plantation sectors. As Portuguese settlers and foreigners opened businesses and plantations in all parts of the colony, their need for cheap labor increased. This was especially true in Luanda, where white employers, who feared Kimbundu employees would sabotage operations, turned to Ovimbundu immigrants.[68] State agencies relied heavily on unskilled Ovimbundu laborers for public works projects. By 1970, Ovimbundu employees made up 10 percent of the nonwhite population of Luanda. They accounted for the majority of blacks in the other major cities of Nova Lisboa, Lobito, and Benguela.[69] Their greatest urban concentration was Nova Lisboa. In 1974, between 15,000 and 20,000 Africans (mostly Ovimbundu) worked in factories in Nova Lisboa and on the European farms which encircled the city. In addition, many of the 300,000 Ovimbundu who lived on the *olosinges* (shanty towns) in the city's outskirts performed the menial labor for the municipality and for white-owned shops and restuarants.[70] Finally, Ovimbundu still comprised the majority of the contract laborers in settler-run businesses including fishing and other operations, from Benguela to the border with South West Africa.

The Ovimbundu Factor: Autonomy Undermined or Nationalism Created

In addition to their military and economic objectives, the authorities also implemented a social program that undermined the gains that Protestants and other forward-looking Ovimbundu had made to 1960. The program affected the health, educational, religious, and social institutions that had allowed Ovimbundu Protestants to provide crucial educational, health, and other social services to the rural population in the highlands and to Ovimbundu migrants in other parts of the colony. As the anticolonial movement spread, however, officials and settlers regarded these institutions as a threat to the state and moved to undermine them.

The anti-Protestant campaign had its roots in the late 1950s, when local officials used intelligence surveys to discover potential troublemakers, especially young catechists and Protestant students and pastors. Officials first moved to end any potential political mobilization by the Ovimbundu after the independence of the Gold Coast (Ghana) in 1957, for they believed that Africans in Angola might agitate for independence from Portugal. Some of these young people were avid readers of a Lobito newspaper called *Olupito*, as well as the Benguela daily, *O Jornal de Benguela* (*Journal of Benguela*) and *O Intransigente* (*The Intransigent*). Security agents carefully watched and targeted for arrest these urban Ovimbundu Protestants (along with some Catholics) in Lobito who attempted to contact sailors and visitors from Ghana and other countries in West Africa.[71] Aaron Kunga, a member of a group that security agents arrested in Benguela in 1958, died while in government custody.[72]

In 1960 the government also increased its surveillance of the Ovimbundu living along the railroad near the frontier with Katanga (Shaba Province) as independence loomed in the neighboring Belgian Congo. The civil war there, which erupted in 1960 and put at risk thousands of white settlers, alarmed Angolan rural and urban settlers alike. The sight of thousands of Belgian settlers fleeing the bloodshed and ethnic conflict in Katanga by way of the Benguela Railway was a chilling forewarning that Angola could explode in the same way if the government did not stamp out nationalist sentiments.[73]

In this case, official and settler unease was well founded. Unknown to the authorities the Ocimbundu Noé Adolfo Kapiñala (who later became a member of the Central Committee of UNITA) and some friends had established a cell in Lobito. This cell gave information to crewmen on ships bound for Matadi about atrocities and massacres that the Portuguese government was carrying out at the infamous Ambaka prison in Benguela and called for international exposure.[74]

When fighting in northern Angola flared up early in 1961, *chefes* and agents of PIDE aggressively attacked Protestants in the highlands and elsewhere, to stem the spread of anti-Portuguese activities. Also, settler vigilante groups arrested, killed, or threatened any individual or organization they suspected of involvement in nationalist activities, or who harbored Africans who expressed anti-Portuguese or anti-settler sentiments.[75]

Foreign Protestant missionaries initially bore the brunt of the official reaction, since the authorities believed that they had incited the uprising. A number of British Baptist and American Methodist missionaries were expelled from Angola in 1961. During the 1960s and up to 1974, officials tightened the restrictions against all Protestant missionaries—routinely denying them entrance visas to Angola, despite the appeals which their Boards made to the Office of Overseas Territories and to the Minister of Foreign Affairs.[76]

The real campaign against the Protestant missionaries spread to the highlands after Jonas Savimbi and a few other Ovimbundu became spokesmen for the MPLA and FNLA in 1964. When Jonas Savimbi and other southerners announced the formation of UNITA in 1966, officials accused the foreign Protestant missionaries of encouraging the Ovimbundu to push for independence against Portugal. PIDE agents and the army mounted a campaign to destroy the Protestant institutions that had provided a semblance of economic and cultural development for the Ovimbundu. The authorities rightly believed that these institutions were at the root of the emerging nationalist sentiments among the Ovimbundu.

They first attacked those Protestants (pastors, teachers, nurses, students) who lived in the urban centers, along with those who had the closest contacts with the missionaries. In 1964, for example, PIDE agents infiltrated the cell that the Ocimbundu Kapiñala had established in Lobito and discovered explosives, forcing Kapiñala to flee to Zaire.[77] Moreover, in the villages and the areas surrounding European settlements in the highlands, *chefes* tried to restrict contacts between the missionaries and the population, by insisting that Protestant missionaries could meet no more than three Ovimbundu on any one occasion. Their systematic attempts to destroy, weaken, and eventually take over the health and educational institutions the Protestant missionaries had built resulted in a severe decline in the services offered by them to the local population. The government also severely curtailed the freedom of religion that they had enjoyed. Officials restricted the topics they could discuss in churches and schools,[78] and censored all publications, including locally printed Bibles and Biblical tracts that the missionaries and pastors were accustomed to distribute to their congregations.

By the late 1960s, the campaign showed some results, as very few new foreign Protestant missionaries entered Angola, and those who remained were not directly involved in the programs that served Ovimbundu Protestants. The total number of Protestant missionaries in Angola had dropped from 256 persons to 11;[79] it stood at 35 by 1972.

Officials also moved to undermine the social and economic standing of Ovimbundu Protestants. Attacks began in 1961 at the first news of the uprising, as the authorities and the settlers believed that Protestants in the highlands were involved. *Chefes* called for military reinforcements and allowed PIDE to enlarge its operations in the area, although there was no evidence of Ovimbundu involvement in the uprisings in the north and there was no unrest in the highlands.[80] Seven months after the outbreak, PIDE agents and soldiers had arrested and detained between 250 and 300 Ovimbundu Protestant teachers, pastors, village elders, health workers, and church members.[81] They were charged with various offenses against the state; among the most serious was that the Protestants were circulating plans for a rebellion against the state and for the murder of settlers.[82] By November 1961, 157 of those arrested were still in prison, 42 had been sent on contract labor, and another 15 had died in suspicious circumstances, apparently at the hands of soldiers and PIDE agents.[83] The authorities also began the intimidation of educated Ovimbundu by confiscating their radios, harassing the population, and recruiting informers.[84]

As the anticolonial struggle expanded, the official backlash against Ovimbundu Protestants in the central highlands increased. Despite the fact that forced labor had been abolished by the 1961 reforms, state representatives in the highlands sent off to corvée labor hundreds of innocent

Ovimbundu Protestants who had been accused of various crimes against the state.[85] The authorities attempted to stop Protestants from publicly demonstrating against the state, by conscripting into the army Ovimbundu Protestants who had completed their first cycle of high school. The men had to serve four years or more in the military. One report of 1965 reflecting the trend noted that the Protestant seminary at Bela Vista had lost 20 percent of its students to the army in the first two weeks of the school year.[86]

As the war against the nationalists intensified, state authorities continued to single out and harass educated Ovimbundu Protestants; they coopted many former conscripts into the state bureaucracy after their discharge, this being their only refuge from harassment by PIDE agents. With the official formation of UNITA in 1966, the anti-Ovimbundu campaign reached fever pitch. Local statutes prohibited pastors from holding communion services unless a government agent was present, and required them to obtain travel permission months in advance in order to visit pastorates in the highlands or attend annual church gatherings.[87]

The authorities also ruled that it was illegal for pastors and other church officials to visit Ovimbundu living in Christian villages without having an official identity card. Since *chefes* refused to issue passes to Protestants, their villages lost cohesion, unable to carry out the community work that had kept them together and given them a separate identity from Catholics and nonconverts. When a pastor or other Protestant spokesman obtained permission to do pastoral work, an army or PIDE agent accompanied him. By the early 1970s, these policies had resulted in the co-optation of some Protestant Ovimbundu who avoided persecution by collaborating in the army and the colonial bureaucracy, but lacked the autonomy as selfsufficient farmers and workers that they had previously enjoyed. Their departure led to the decline of Protestant work in the highlands, as buildings were left in disrepair or abandoned. The schools, clinics, and training centers that remained open were often run by a small corps of dedicated but inexperienced Ovimbundu.[88]

Settler vigilantes also waged their own private war against Protestants, destroying many of their Christian schools and homes as well as traditional villages.[89] Anti-Ovimbundu campaigns by settler vigilantes began after the uprising in the north, when PIDE agents armed settler vigilante groups with the encouragement of the civilian authorities.[90] Vengeful settlers turned against the Ovimbundu early in 1961 because of the rumors that thousands of their fellow Portuguese had been murdered by Africans in the north. The attacks spread and were transformed into an all-out anti-

Ovimbundu campaign as settler anger, suspicion, and insecurity grew with increasing nationalist activity. The Ovimbundu became the target of racist, vengeful, and nervous whites for what the whites perceived as the ingratitude of the Africans. At Easter 1962, a group of hysterical settlers armed with guns and knives broke into a Good Friday service conducted by an Ovimbundu Protestant minister and "hacked, killed and wreaked vengeance" on the congregation.[91]

Other attacks by settlers led to the imprisonment, death, or exile of many other Ovimbundu Protestants.[92] In some cases setters also moved against Ovimbundu who had joined the government, and who were perhaps more zealous in applying the law against settlers than the typical settler bureaucrat. Pastor Marcos Fortuna, who served as an agent of the municipal tribunal between 1967 and 1972, and whose special duty was to investigate incidents of enslavement of Africans by settlers, was nearly killed by a crowd of angry settlers when he attempted to crack down on the slavery which some settlers still practiced. He recalled that when he arrested a settler for burning the house of an African in Cubal, a crowd of whites numbering in the hundreds surrounded him and demanded that he release his prisoner or face death. He only escaped after a telephone call from the local police commander to the governor brought an order from the latter to send the police to protect Fortuna. He, his wife, and children escaped from Cubal under police protection.[93]

Angry settlers also burnt or destroyed a significant amount of Protestant property.[94] The official and unofficial attacks against Protestant institutions and persons resulted in a stampede by some to join the ranks of the government, in the hopes of its diverting attention from them. Many also joined because they saw the army as a newly opened channel of social mobility. Among them were many nurses, teachers, and high school graduates who found employment and opportunities for further training in the Catholic and state schools, clinics, hospitals, and other state agencies. Indeed, settler terrorism initially forced many Ovimbundu Protestants to come to terms with the regime.

The war also pushed many Ovimbundu peasants away from the villages to the cities in the highlands and to the coast, bringing them more directly under state control. Nova Lisboa was a major center for Ovimbundu migrants from the village. Rural villagers were among the three hundred thousand Ovimbundu who lived in the surburban shanties surrounding the city and who provided the labor to clean the streets and office buildings and dig the graves. Others did menial work in the three thousand and more small settler-run businesses in the city. For others, however, prostitution houses serving the many soldiers and white males in the city became their lot.[95]

A few of the more educated urban Protestant Ovimbundu attempted to assimilate into the settler world. An example of what such a transition entailed comes from Aarão Cornelio, a Protestant attending high school in Nova Lisboa in 1961. He, like other educated Protestants and Catholics who joined the world of assimilated Africans in the colony during the period of the liberation war, spent two years at the noncommissioned officer training school in Nova Lisboa before serving in the army.[96] On his discharge, he joined the civil service as a clerk in a local state agency in Huambo.[97] Individuals like Cornelio welcomed the prospects of becoming black Portuguese with the formal abolition of the law which distinguished "civilized" from "noncivilized." A few who found this option distasteful, and who, could escaped from the colony.[98]

In the highlands, Ovimbundu Protestants were not alone in facing persecution, for the authorities and settlers also harassed Ovimbundu Catholic priests, converts, and foreign Catholic missionaries whose actions they regarded as detrimental to the goals of the state. The first attempts to rein in independent-thinking black and white Catholics occurred in the late 1950s when the Catholic hierarchy, under pressure from the civil authorities, dismissed a number of Ovimbundu seminarians from the seminary at Nova Lisboa because they had formed an organization called the *Juventude Cristão de Angola* (Angolan Christian Youth). The aim of the organization was to provide institutional support for seminarians wishing to undertake volunteer work among the Ovimbundu Catholics in Nova Lisboa. The plan also included spreading anti-Salazar propaganda among the Ovimbundu in villages near Nova Lisboa.[99]

With the outbreak of the war in 1961, the expelled seminarians and other Ovimbundu Catholics critical of the state were driven underground, imprisoned, or sent to forced labor or the military like their Protestant counterparts.[100] By 1964, officials had expelled sixteen Roman Catholic priests and imprisoned others.[101]

PIDE agents concentrated on a group of dissident metropolitan Portuguese priests who had been accused of subversive activities and exiled to Angola. Some of the priests had worked in central Angola and had set up and helped to manage an anti-state institution called the *Instituto Superior Católico de Nova Lisboa* (Higher Catholic Institute of Nova Lisboa). PIDE agents believed that the priests were using the institute to continue their subversive activities against the state, and in 1968–69 they expelled the priests associated with the institute and closed its offices.[102]

Despite the actions taken against the minority of Catholic priests engaged in anti-government activities, an underground network of foreign, Portuguese, and Angolan priests continued to work in the colony. Local officials in the highlands warned the Ovimbundu and settlers who sided with the nationalists that they would take measures necessary to preserve the hegemony of the state.[103]

The Counter-Insurgency Campaigns

The government's counter-insurgency campaigns to encourage Africans to close ranks against internal and external enemies had the effect of co-opting some Ovimbundu farmers, both Christian and non-Christians, and alienating others.[104] The campaigns which began in the late 1960s and early 1970s had of two aspects: resettlement schemes and rural extension projects. The resettlement schemes were the most notorious, as local military and security officials implemented them in central Angola out of panic following dramatic nationalist successes against the Portuguese army in eastern Angola in 1967.[105] When guerrillas began penetrating into the district of Bié, the resettlement program came to include large numbers of Ovimbundu subsistence/cash-crop producers. These became fodder for the army and fuel for the economy.

Fearful of armed angry settlers and of a police, army, and security network with arbitrary power, hundreds of thousands of Ovimbundu producers had no alternative but to comply with official orders to move into "protected" villages far away from their farms. Others villages that the Portuguese feared were subject to guerrilla infiltration were designated "strategic" villages and put under security surveillance.[106] The rural extension projects and resettlement programs were intended to reduce opposition to the government's anti-nationalist campaigns. The campaigns were supposed to offer the Ovimbundu population social and educational benefits that would allow them to assimilate, and were also meant to silence critics of the regime who accused the administration of disregarding the interests of the Africans in Angola.[107]

Andulu, a preconquest kingdom located in the district of Bié, was the resettlement program's centerpiece. By 1973, the project involved about fifty-five teams of extension workers giving training to more than a half a million Ovimbundu farmers.[108] The program also promised some educational benefits as schools were built in the villages and elsewhere. Overall, however, although government agents promised that the project would modernize Ovimbundu agriculture, the war diverted too much of the financial and manpower resources, and the project only succeeded in eroding further the social fabric of Ovimbundu villagers. Disgust with their life in the strategic villages together with the strain on their social fabric that these villages had created, sowed the seeds of growing anti-government sentiments among this segment of the Ovimbundu population as well. The government achieved its authoritarian goals at the cost of growing Ovimbundu alienation.

Exploitation, Disaffection, and Discontent: Migrants and Peasants

The wide array of wartime measures against the nationalists accelerated the pace of economic development, imposed draconian security measures to suppress opposition, quieted settler fears by acquiescing to their demands for cheap labor and allowing them to brutalize innocent African civilians, and repressed rising nationalist sentiments.

The government confronted two problems as it imposed its authoritarian policies on the Ovimbundu. The first was the collapse of the education and welfare system that Ovimbundu Protestants had built under the guidance of the foreign missionaries. This was because fewer and fewer of the graduates from the Protestant schools returned to work in the older villages or founded new ones, for fear of government and settler reprisals. The second was the growing political consciousness of the masses of non-Christian Ovimbundu and their disaffection with the state. By the early 1970s, disaffection with the state had spread among all segments of the Ovimbundu population.

Dragooned Ovimbundu workers, who made up the backbone of the laboring population in the territory during the years of the anticolonial struggle, also resented the demands made on them. Government and private reliance on Ovimbundu workers increased during the period with the result that labor migrancy among the group grew rather than declined. In 1967 the provinces of Bié and Bailundu, in which a majority of the African population was Ovimbundu, provided 74 percent of the contract labor for the entire colony.[109] To facilitate worker migration from the highlands, the government passed legislation that allowed wives and "as many children as were able to work," to accompany male migrants to the plantations.[110] In addition, illegal recruiting of underaged children expanded dramatically in the 1960s.[111] As usual when confronted with these abuses, authorities defended existing practices by arguing that the migrants were voluntary laborers, although the system was "basically the same old contract labor."[112] The situation was now much worse, however, because families and juvenile recruits were treated the same as single male adults.

Apart from the institutionalization of migrancy among the Ovimbundu, the expansion of the settler-controlled sector led to a dramatic drop in the economic and social standing of Ovimbundu workers. Foreign and Portuguese investments which expanded from 1961 to 1974 did not bring higher wages or improve health and working conditions for the thousands of Ovimbundu laborers in plantations, and in the fishing and commercial sectors. In 1965, 95 percent of the 105,925 salaried rural workers earned less than three cents (U.S.) per day or two *escudos* and fifty *centavos* a month, much less than the lowest-paid white worker.[113] With the war lowering the value of the escudo, by 1970 the wages of Ovimbundu workers were even lower, and still trailed those of their white counterparts. A comparison of the 1974 wages of white and African workers showed the glaring disparities. An Ovimbundu contract laborer working on the same coffee plantation and doing work similar to that of a Portuguese worker received 200 *escudos* or $2.00 (U.S.) per month, less than 5 percent of the wages of his Portuguese counterpart who made 2,300 *escudos* or $23.00 (U.S.) per month. [114]

Painful realities still confronted Ovimbundu laborers from 1961 to 1974. Many of them were forced to take out labor contracts and become migrants because of cost of living increases. Between 1969 and 1973 the government's wartime policies led to a 79 percent cost of living increase,[115] in part because of the yearly 300 *escudos* taken in taxes covered taxes as the 1961 reforms stipulated.

Resentment against government policies was high among Ovimbundu herded into the "protected" villages, as well as among those who remained in the their old villages but who were still subjected to security measures. The situation demonstrated the problems officials faced in attempting to impose an authoritarian state in Angola, given the regional and ethnic realities. Villagers resented government orders which forcibly integrated the men into a people's militia to defend the villages. In most villages, up to 95 percent of the males served in the militia that was supposed to protect the population against the nationalist guerrillas.[116]

One of the most explosive policy initiatives in the rural area was land alienation. In some regions of the highlands, officials made it easier for whites to purchase Ovimbundu land. The land issue was the result of the two opposing tendencies in the government's approach to African agriculture. On the one hand was the idea that the state and settlers would benefit if African peasant farming was encouraged but kept subordinate to settler farming demands, and on the other was the belief in settler agriculture. In the 1960s and early 1970s, because of security concerns, officials abandoned the idea of supporting African peasant farming. Instead they favored settler agriculture because of pressure from land speculators who wanted Ovimbundu land, most of which had not been alienated up to 1961.

The official change in the land policies of the administration had far-reaching effects on the amount of good farming land available to the Ovimbundu. The land issue ignited Ovimbundu resentment as no other issue had done in the past. It created an additional and crucial wedge between rural Ovimbundu and the state.

The first Ovimbundu to lose out to the speculators were the modernizing farmers, whose fallow fields were taken over by land-grabbing whites. Because the laws continued to favor the settlers, when the settlers claimed land that Ovimbundu farmers worked, local officials invariably sided with them.[117] Eventually, land alienation touched other segments of the Ovimbundu population. The results of all this were evident in the Huambo district, where between 1968 and 1970 the amount of land which settlers owned more than doubled, increasing from 249,039 to 526,270 hectares. On the other hand, the amount of land Africans farmed fell by 36.9 percent.[118] Moreover, 150,000 Ovimbundu in the district, or 23 percent of the rural population, had no land to farm.[119]

The impact of increasing land alienation was also evident in Bié, a province where the government's resettlement program and strategic villages were located. Ovimbundu farmers participating in the program were forced to give up their large fertile plots for small, less fertile ones. Furthermore, despite the gallant efforts of the agricultural agents who worked hard to help some of the farmers diversify and practice better land management, the decline in land fertility and productivity continued. As with past attempts at creating an Ovimbundu Kulak class, the efforts failed, as the resettlement schemes simply led to increased soil depletion.[120]

In the end, anti-Protestant policies, labor recruiting, falling agricultural productivity, and land alienation all had their impact on Ovimbundu peasant agriculture. They weakened civil society by reversing the trend towards diversification and innovation that some Ovimbundu farmers had spearheaded earlier, and thus exposed the group to more direct exploitation by the state and the settlers. From the mid-sixties onward, fewer and fewer Ovimbundu relied on subsistence and/or cash-crop farming for a livelihood. Already in 1965 only 49 percent of the Ovimbundu population were listed as producers consuming two-thirds of the maize they harvested.[121]

By the early 1970s, the economic and social situation of the rural population had reached crisis proportions. The work of João Morais and Herman Pössinger, who undertook state-sponsored studies for the Angolan Agricultural Research Mission (*Missão de Inquéritos Agrícolas de Angola*) which surveyed African farming in the Huambo district, presents a picture of rural decay unknown in the previous periods. The authors noted that the number of Ovimbundu working their own farms hovered at only 57.7 percent by 1970–71 and that wage laborers had increased from 5.1 percent of the Ovimbundu population in the early 1960s to 30.95 percent by 1970–71.[122] Furthermore, farm yields were the lowest recorded—385.6 kilograms per hectare, compared to 600 kilograms and higher in the earlier periods.[123]

African farmers in some of the strategic villages where guerrillas were infiltrating were hit worse since officials prohibited farming there altogether. In many strategic villages the Ovimbundu were in effect slaves to the state. *Chefes* required them to work for the state in return for the twice-weekly ration of two canisters of maize that they received to feed their families.[124]

Official policies and settler actions had a disastrous impact on the social life of the Ovimbundu as well. Migrancy, urbanization, and resettlement programs destroyed many families as the kin structure collapsed under the strain of the dislocation.

Women, who had been protected from state exactions during the previous period, felt the full impact of state policies as they shouldered the increased labor obligations. Few found time to meet their own subsistence needs and other kin obligations—preparing food and drink for redistribution—as state labor requirements increased. Behavior changed. Women and girls who migrated to the urban centers and plantations with their husbands or other kin often turned to prostitution (which had already become a problem in the urban centers in the highlands and coastal cities in the 1950s). Female prostitution increased as Portuguese prostitutes came with other settlers to the temperate highlands and opened brothels that serviced soldiers and settlers alike. The Portuguese women who operated these brothels employed young Ovimbundu and Afro-Portuguese females whose white fathers had abandoned them to their African mothers.[125]

The increase in prostitution contributed to the higher incidence of venereal diseases, and the general public health crisis that medical authorities noted had become a major problem among the black urban population. Government policies driving away the foreign missionaries who had provided most of the health and social services for the Ovimbundu may actually have led to a serious deterioration in the health of the people.[126] The clinics and health centers where trained Ovimbundu had met the medical needs of many people in both the rural and urban areas no longer operated by the early 1970s. Many of the health providers were in exile, in hiding, imprisoned, or were working in some other area of the colony. In 1970 the 10,000–acre Dondi missionary station comprising the Currie Institute, Means School, seminary, and hospital had a staff of only nine trained foreign missionaries and a skeletal Ovimbundu staff, compared to the twenty-four missionaries and numerous Ovimbundu who had assisted them in operating the complex in 1961.[127]

Although the war against the three anticolonial movements had allowed the government to achieve its goal of establishing an authoritarian state, and of destroying the lingering vestiges of the precolonial civil institutions and the Protestant structures that had emerged, the very success had created its own crisis. With a government and settler class opposed to their interests, the Ovimbundu became more disposed to ally with other Angolans or to look for help outside Angola in order to confront the situation.

Among those who led the way were the Protestant pastors and Catholic catechists and priests, primary and secondary school graduates, nurses, and others who foresaw a dim future in a settler-controlled Angola and who sought links to the anticolonial movements. Although by the late 1950s some of them had taken the first tentative steps, between 1961 and 1974 their influence would grow, and more of their fellow Ovimbundu became more disposed to follow their lead and develop a new level of political consciousness.[128]

However, when they first came into national and international prominence with the founding of UNITA in 1966, theirs was a fractured consciousness, linked with ethnicity, regionalism, and opportunism.[129] Few Angolan observers were inclined to see them as anything but junior partners of the more sophisticated and Westernized Kongo and Kimbundu anticolonialists who, despite their class, color, and regional divisions, were at the forefront of the anticolonial campaign against the Portuguese.[130]

6

THE ANTICOLONIAL STRUGGLE AND THE ROOTS OF OVIMBUNDU NATIONALISM, 1961–1974

Introduction

During the late fifties and early sixties, a small cadre of educated Ovimbundu and other southerners organized to challenge the state. The group comprised a few university graduates, seminary and high school students, Protestant pastors, and others who were in exile in Europe, Leopoldville (Kinshasa) and Congo Brazzaville. Although the security dragnet, and the terrorist campaign PIDE agents waged and settler vigilantism kept the majority of the Ovimbundu inside the colony from participating in anti-state activities, some railway and port workers as well as students also engaged in anti-state activities. Up to the mid-sixties, however, the majority of Ovimbundu and other southerners did not challenge the regime.

This situation changed in 1966 when some of the exiled Ovimbundu who had joined the FNLA along with some fellow southerners and a few Cabindans and Kongo fled the movement and formed UNITA.[1] Between 1966 and 1974, Jonas Savimbi, the Ocimbundu who led the revolt, used UNITA to mobilize Ovimbundu and other southerners to join the anticolonial struggle. Savimbi's appeal to the rural southern population, as opposed to what he and the UNITA leadership argued was the assimilationist, northern, and urban orientation of the MPLA, and the royalist and ethnic arrogance of the FNLA, soon made UNITA a force in the anticolonial struggle. By 1974 the movement had become an instrument of rural sentiment and pride for the Ovimbundu, and its leader Savimbi had become the main architect of a recast Ovimbundu opposition to the state. Under Savimbi's leadership, UNITA provided a forum in Angola's nationalist politics for a significant percentage of the Ovimbundu and other peoples from the south to demonstrate their opposition to the state.

Although the Ovimbundu who formed UNITA talked of fighting to redress regional and ethnic under-representation in the anticolonial movements, by 1974 the regional and ethnic orientation of UNITA's leaders led to fundamental rifts between UNITA and the MPLA. This weakened the nationalist cause in Angola, and instead of bringing Ovimbundu and southerners more in line with the aspirations of the MPLA and FNLA, UNITA became a forum for rural, regionalist, and ethnic sentiments. The movement thus diverged more and more from the urban, internationalist, and nationalist positions which the MPLA, the most important liberation movement, espoused. This put the two movements on a collision course.

The Anticolonial Struggle: The Northern Roots

The outbreak of anti-state agitation in the Kimbundu and Kongo regions of Angola in 1961 was the trigger which fomented a colony-wide anticolonial rebellion in Angola by the early 1970s. The 1961 uprising was rooted in the simmering tensions between the demands of an expanding colonial state and the leaders of the Afro-Portuguese, assimilated and non assimilated Kimbundu, and Kongo monarchists. In Luanda, anti-state agitation originated among a small, urban, Catholic, Portuguese educated group of assimilated Africans and Afro-Portuguese who were denied a share of power when the Republican government intensified state control in Angola in 1910. The group was also the first to challenge the dictatorship after the establishment of the New State. Although their earliest anti-Portuguese propaganda dates from the mid-nineteenth century,[2] it was in the 1920s, in the heyday of the Pan-African movement, that they established formal organizations.[3] Like other Pan-Africanists at the time, the group pushed for greater self-determination for Africans in Portuguese colonies. With the appearance of the New State regime, however, anti-state agitation went underground until after the Second World War.

During the 1940s, ferment again surfaced among Luanda's Afro-Portuguese community, *assimilados* with deep urban roots, and recent

Kimbundu immigrants who lived in the urban slums. This postwar development was a product of the growing political consciousness of some members of Luanda's Afro-Portuguese and African community who were committed to confronting the state after returning from studies in Portugal. The growing activism also reflected rising cultural and intellectual currents in Angola's urban centers.[4]

Afro-Portuguese literary figures such as Viriato da Cruz, António de Oliveira, Mario António, and others were well known critics of the government. Viriato da Cruz, for example, was a leading figure in one of the many cultural nationalist movements that the authorities considered dangerous.[5] By 1956, general dissatisfaction over the situation in the colony had led to the formation of several *assimilado* and Afro-Portuguese clandestine organizations whose members met in the homes of leading Afro-Portuguese families. In time the cultural nationalists merged with other antigovernment organizations including the Angolan Communist party (*Partido Communista de Angola*), the Party for the Struggle for Africans in Angola (*Partido da Luta dos Africanos de Angola*), and the Movement for the Independence of Angola (*Movimento para a Independência de Angola*) to create the MPLA.[6]

In 1959, the efforts of MPLA militants to expand the movement and challenge the dictatorship were countered by the authorities with mass arrests. Those who escaped became political exiles in neighboring Leopoldville (Kinshasa) Brazzaville, and Europe.[7] With their underground networks among African slum-dwellers in Luanda and peasants in the Mbundu cotton growing region of Kasanje, the MPLA claimed credit for helping to coordinate the February 1961 uprisings in Luanda and Kasanje that initiated the all-out struggle against the state and which led to the growth of modern African nationalism in Angola.

State/society tensions were also present in the Kongo region. Although the more radical members of the Kongo nobility regarded Dom Pedro VII (the last Kongolese king whose nomination was approved by the Portuguese, and who served from 1923 to 1955) as a Portuguese lackey, by continuance of the rituals and customs of Kongo sovereignty which the indirect rule system afforded him, he too contributed to another strain of modern African nationalism.[8] Kongo exiles in Leopoldville drew on these monarchist sentiments to agitate for an independent Kongo kingdom. In 1958 Eduardo Pinnock, with Manuel Barros Necaca and his Kongo monarchists, founded the *União das Populações do Norte de Angola* (UPNA). Under prodding from George Padmore and Kwame Nkrumah, the group changed its name to the UPA—to deflect attention from its ethnic and regional base, and promoted itself as an Angolan nationalist movement. In 1961 the movement became known as the *Frente Nacional de Libertação de Angola* (FNLA) and came under the leadership of Holden Roberto. In 1962 the FNLA also became known GRAE (Revolutionary Angolan Government in Exile. Roberto did more to advance himself as a businessman and to encourage claims of Kongo regional and ethnic separateness than to promote Angolan nationalism.[9]

The Anticolonial Struggle: The Southern Roots

The Ovimbundu path to nationalism took a different route. Until the appearance of UNITA in 1966, no organized group of Ovimbundu had challenged the colonial state.[10] This was the case despite the fact that all segments of the Ovimbundu population that faced increasing hardships in the postwar period as a result of the authoritarian policies of the dictatorship.[11]

Although some of the early developments which laid the groundwork for the anticolonial struggle in the Ovimbundu region paralleled those taking place in the Kimbundu and Kongo regions, the Ovimbundu experiences differed from those in other regions of the colony in some fundamental ways. One major difference was the fact that the Ovimbundu Protestants who led the struggle were the children of educated Ovimbundu, who exercised a level of responsibility in their community that their Catholic, Methodist, and Baptist counterparts in the north did not. These were the Ovimbundu who pioneered and directed the Protestant schools, clinics, churches, hospitals, and other institutions that existed in the central and southern parts of the colony. Their affiliation with the Congregationalist missionaries, with their more decentralized missionary operations, allowed the group to exercise a level of institutional control that was absent from Ovimbundu, Kongo and Kimbundu villages where Catholic personnel carried out religious and educational activities. Kongo Baptists and Kimbundu Methodists who became active in the anticolonial struggle also lacked the rural links of their Ovimbundu counterparts. Many Ovimbundu Protestants were able to maintain stronger ties with the masses of their fellow Ovimbundu than members of the Kimbundu and Kongo elite could with their fellow Kimbundu and Kongo. Another difference between the Ovimbundu Protestants whose members joined the anticolonial struggle and their counterparts in the north, in particular those in the Kimbundu region, was their ability to speak Umbundu, the language of the masses of Ovimbundu. Unlike many Kimbundu nationalists who only knew Portuguese, all Ovimbundu Protestants knew both Umbundu and Portuguese. Many were also familiar with other African languages spoken in neighboring regions.

Perhaps because the pre–World War II generation of Ovimbundu Protestants spent most of their time building and managing the Protestant institutions, they were largely apolitical. The first signs of anti-state sentiments among the Ovimbundu appeared in the late 1950s among second and third generation Protestants and a few Ovimbundu Catholics. In fact, the social revolution that the older generation of Protestant Ovimbundu had led in the period before the war did much to prepare the way for the growing political awareness of young Protestant Ovimbundu students and workers who became active in the anticolonial cause.

The teaching that the older generation of Ovimbundu Protestants provided in village preparatory schools and the mission boarding schools at Dondi and Means, as well as in the Protestant villages where the deacons and deaconess instituted the new social values, did much to heighten ethnic and political consciousness among young Ovimbundu. Members of the younger generation of Ovimbundu Protestants benefited immensely from the educational advances, and from the organizational experience of their parents in the schools, churches, and other institutions that they helped to found and operate. Their use of Umbundu was particularly significant. Although the law required assimilated Africans to be fluent in Portuguese, older Protestants used Umbundu as the language of communication at home, in preaching and singing both religious and secular songs, and in many informal social activities. Their continuing use of Umbundu in formal and informal settings allowed them to maintain a deep sense of pride and solidarity with fellow Ovimbundu. Many Protestant Ovimbundu parents who continued the Ovimbundu habit of teaching the young through fables and history used Umbundu to teach values and pass on histories of the old Ovimbundu kingdoms to their children. Many of these histories highlighted the exploits of their own forebears who had resisted the Portuguese. Pastor Fortuna, for example, recalled Ovimbundu pride in the war of Kandumbu which took place in 1912.[12]

Despite their ability to forge new institutions and to hold on to many aspects of the precolonial culture, the older generation of Ovimbundu Protestants had bought into the Portuguese ideology of assimilation. One result was that although they continued to speak Umbundu, increasingly the language in church, work, and school was Portuguese. For example, up to the early 1960s at debates in the Council of Churches of Central Angola, at which pastors, deacons and deaconesses, teachers, nurses, and other Protestant

leaders made church policy, the language in use was predominantly Portuguese.[13] Although they exhibited deep pride in Ovimbundu culture, they
took the assimilationist route that the Portuguese offered. Their devout
faith, dignity, and belief in their personal worth convinced them that assimilation was the best way to safeguard the religious and other institutions
that they had helped build and manage.[14]

By the 1950s, however, the linguistic and cultural legacy the older
generation had passed on to their children plus the contradiction in their
own lives began to radicalize many of their offspring and even members of
their own generation. The roots of this transformation lay in the stories
that the older generation told their children, recalling the heady days of
Ovimbundu commercial successes; these, together with their pride in their
language and the closeness of their family life helped the younger generation to identify with their proud past. At the same time, the older generation's
apparent willingness to accept the partial assimilation into a Portuguese
culture which denied them full equality with white Portuguese disgusted
and alienated many young Ovimbundu Protestants.[15] Some of them showed
their resentment by popularizing old songs which ridiculed the Portuguese.
A popular refrain of the 1950s (which reappeared with new words during
the anticolonial struggle) used the theme of exploitation of the porter by
the *pombeiro* to ridicule the Portuguese treatment of Africans. The song
went, "You eat well, oh *pombeiro*, you do not give to the porter who carries
your load for you."[16]

The generation that came to maturity in the post–World War II period was better prepared than their parents to challenge the colonial status
quo. For example, César Pedro Kaliengue, who was a classmate of Jonas
Savimbi when he entered the Dondi mission in 1951, and who became an
early supporter of UNITA, wrote that when be began work as a assistant
conductor for the Benguela Railway in 1952, he promised himself not to
forget the stories about the kingdom of Viye, the famous sobas, and his
own father's suffering which the old man related every night while "sitting
around the fire, at the side of our house."[17]

Jonas Savimbi, who also remembered his interactions with his father,
noted that what to him stood out were the contradictions. Lott Savimbi,
one of the few Ovimbundu station managers for the Benguela Railway, the
devout Christian who built a series of Protestant villages at different points
along the railroad, lived as a European but was closer to the ordinary villagers than the missionaries or his Portuguese fellow workers. Savimbi wrote
that "the life of my father . . . was a permanent contradiction, he lived with
the Portuguese, had a high salary compared with village people, a much

larger house, and we had western habits, however, the Portuguese were strangers, they came to dominate us."[18]

Like Lott Savimbi, the thousands of older assimilated Ovimbundu Protestants who lived in the cities and maintained ties with their rural villages bases reinforced a larger Ovimbundu identity. They helped maintain a level of ethnic cohesiveness and distinctiveness which separated them from the more thoroughly assimilated urban Kimbundu or and from the Kongo monarchists in northern Angola.[19]

The younger generation of Ovimbundu Protestants, coming to adulthood in the late 1950s and 1960s, was different from the older generation in other ways. Many were much more impatient with the contradictions that they saw around them. Young railway workers like César Kaliengue (who was sixteen when he began to work for the railway) often argued and had physical altercations with his white fellow workers. Young workers berated the Portuguese in more subtle ways as well. In one anecdote that was circulated among Ovimbundu workers on the Benguela Railway when Kalingue worked there in the 1950s, the local beer, representing the African, says to the wine, representing the white settler, "Yes, I am poor and not appreciated. But what is certain is that I am a local product and I always exist in my land without having to travel by boat or dependent on the Metropole."[20] Although the supervisor dismissed this as a childish pastime, these early activities reflected a political activism which separated the generation of the 1950s and 1960s from the older one.

The experiences of the younger generation of Ovimbundu Protestants were different from those of their parents and grandparents in other ways. Instead of separating them from the rest of the peoples in Angola, the ability to speak Umbundu allowed them to move freely between village and missionary school, migrant labor camp and urban slum dwelling. Umbundu allowed them to reinforce a Pan-Ovimbundu ethnic identity that was lacking in their parents and grandparents. Prior to 1961, young Christians used Umbundu only in conversation with the older generation. After 1961, however, young educated Protestants and Catholic Ovimbundu demonstrated their growing consciousness and solidarity by the widespread use of Umbundu. Thus, while accepting the Protestant institutions that the older generation had established, they reinforced a modern Ovimbundu ethnic identity at the same time as questioning their status as Portuguese colonial subjects.[21] This ethnic/nationalist outlook would comprise the salient element in the modern political culture of the Ovimbundu.

When workers and peasants in the north, encouraged by the political work of MPLA and FNLA activists, revolted at the beginning of 1961, most observers, familiar with the sight of masses of Ovimbundu contract workers and uneducated rural people, did not believe that they were capable of organizing similar anticolonial activities. In the Benguela region, officials and settlers attempted to preempt Ovimbundu political organizing by brutally cracking down on the few Ovimbundu Protestants and Catholic catechists they suspected of planning anti-state activities. Officials also targeted foreign missionaries, especially American, Canadian, and British Protestants, who they believed, were the main instigators of anticolonial sentiments in the region. Official action was based more on paranoia than on the conviction of an impending Ovimbundu uprising, since the officials viewed the masses as compliant laborers who were politically unsophisticated and easy to control.[22]

Port and railway workers, skilled artisans who lived and worked in the urban centers on the coast and the interior, and students were the first Ovimbundu to organize anti-state activities which directly influenced the growth of modern Ovimbundu nationalism.[23] This was largely because of their access to African and international radio, journals, and newspapers which exposed them to the decolonization process taking place in Africa.[24] Although PIDE agents moved swiftly to prevent the entry of foreign journals and newspapers after the independence of Ghana in 1957 and Guinea Conakry in 1958, many Ovimbundu port and railway workers obtained the banned publications.

The period between 1959 and 1962 witnessed a steady increase in Ovimbundu political organizing. As one missionary who worked in the Ovimbundu region recalled, during that period "several rolled up packages . . . of handwritten documents which cited cases of human rights abuses and were comprised of rhetorical arguments making plain the oppression of the people" were left at his doorstep at night. The bearers of the documents made sure to leave them unsigned. The missionary believed at the time that the people behind the manuscripts wanted them to be delivered to the United Nations.[25] The Ovimbundu activists made sure to hide their tracks because of PIDE ativities. Agents from PIDE suspected that some of the port workers were making secret contact with Ghanaian sailors who were passing on nationalist propaganda. Even before 1960, PIDE agents harassed and imprisoned several of these Ovimbundu port and railway workers and their families.[26]

With the independence of the Belgian Congo, Ovimbundu workers on the Benguela Railway also became a conduit of nationalist ideas. They foiled official attempts aimed at limiting African access to outside information, and devoured the anticolonial and anti-Portuguese propaganda beamed from Moscow and Ghana. They also had access to newspapers and journals that foreign passengers brought from the West.[27] Some of them took the radical step of sending petitions to the Portuguese governor, asking him to open up skilled positions (as machinists) to Africans and Afro-Portuguese. By early in 1960 these young workers had formed an *Associação Africana do Sul de Angola* (African Association of the South of Angola) under the presidency of António Burity da Silva. This organization was soon crushed by PIDE, however, which recruited Da Silva as an informant.[28]

Young Ovimbundu priests also became more vocal and began to declare their resentment of the racism in the Angolan Catholic church. Their growing radicalism was in large part owing to the progressive policy of Pope John XXIII, who did much to promote racial inclusion in the Catholic Church hierarchy by consecrating the Tanzanian Cardinal Mugambua.[29]

Students at the Protestant Dondi Mission also demonstrated a growing political awareness between 1959 and 1962. Their most significant anti-state action occurred in November, 1960, when many of them refused to the join government-sponsored public meetings held by the authorities to deflect foreign criticism of Portuguese colonial policies. Those in high school particularly resented the tight security measures which brought agents and informers into schools and churches. They also scoffed at the official attempts to force them to support the state by making them sing patriotic Portuguese songs and listen to administrators (and the African collaborator António Burity Da Silva) deliver speeches glorifying the benefits of Portuguese rule at government-sponsored rallies.[30]

The authorities initially failed in their efforts to stamp out organized Ovimbundu activists, despite banning several of the small cultural and sporting groups Protestant Ovimbundu had formed.[31] By October 1960, a group of about sixty young people associated with the Protestant-run Dondi Institute in Bié created an organization called the *Grupo Avante de Bié* (Bié Progressive Group) to coordinate anti-state activities. The immediate reason for the students' action was resentment of the Portuguese dismissal of some of their colleagues who had refused to participate in the state-sponsored public demonstrations.[32]

The young members who formed the *Grupo* lacked the organizational experience and the international connections of their northern compatriots, but did share with them a common Protestant, mission-educated background. With none of the financial resources available to the northerners, Júlio Cacunda, the son of Pastor Vanhale Cacunda who served in the Elende region, was the organization's secret recruiter. He scouted the colony, and between January and March, 1960, he succeeded in establishing cells in

Luanda, Benguela, Lobito, Bié, and Mossamedes. He was particularly active around the mission station in Elende, which was also a recruiting center for a good number of Lobito port workers. His efforts even attracted a few active-duty Ovimbundu soldiers, who reportedly promised to secure guns for a planned revolt.[33] Julio's political activities soon led to his death and the imprisonment and death of his father.[34]

The actions of the port and railway workers, students, and others marked the first phase of modern Ovimbundu political organizing, and also represented the appearance of southern Angolan interethnic political cooperation.[35] The appearance of the *Grupo* marked a significant break from the past. Although the majority of the supporters of the *Grupo* were Ovimbundu, there were also Chokwe, Guanhama (Ovambo), Ngangela, and others were also represented. For example, two important members of the *Grupo*, Moises Chingolola and Chicote, were Guanhamas from the region to the south of the highlands.[36]

The *Grupo's* activities were seriously compromised, however, when the uprisings in the north broke out in the spring of 1961. The authorities moved aggressively to destroy the organization inside Angola arresting, imprisoning, or murdering several members of the group. At the same time, more than twenty teachers and nurses at the Bailundu mission, who had sent a letter to the United Nations asking them to investigate Portuguese abuses, were arrested and sent to the concentration camp of Menongue in the east.[37]

Despite this, the treatment of assimilated Ovimbundu during the crisis contributed to a heightened political consciousness among in the older generation as its members openly confronted racism and bias. For example, in 1961–62, teachers, nurses, and others who went to the administrator in Cuima (now Ukuma) to receive arms for self-protection in response to a general invitation were denied arms, while white and mulatto merchants were given them. Many Ovimbundu teachers, nurses, railwaymen, students, and others were also imprisoned, beaten, and harassed by whites during the crisis. It was in response to this kind of blatant discrimination that many older Ovimbundu began to take the first tentative steps towards asserting an Ovimbundu cultural and linguistic identity. In 1963, for example, the language of debate at the annual meeting of the Council of Churches was Umbundu instead of Portuguese, a direct challenge to the agents of the secret police who attended the meeting. More and more members of this group engaged in discussions concerning their grievances against the colonial government. Some Ovimbundu continued placing the bundles of papers on missionary doorsteps, specifically requesting that the papers be forwarded to the United Nations, while at the same time prodding reluctant missionaries to speak out publicly on their behalf.[38]

Ovimbundu activists engaged in many other covert activities. For example, César Pedro Kaliengue, Oseas Chinhama, Jerimias Kusyia, and Nóe Kapiñala, all of whom resided in the African barrio of Canata in Lobito, held extensive political discussions in the barbershop of Isaías Kawema, passing news by word of mouth about the independence of other African countries, under the watchful eye of PIDE and its African informants. One piece of news which circulated among the group was the advice which the young Ocimbundu Savimbi, who had left for Portugal in 1958, was supposed to have uttered. It called on each Ocimbundu "to learn the most where they worked so that tomorrow we can walk with heads high in front of our children and grand-children."[39]

Exile Politics: The Ovimbundu Perspective

From the late 1950s. Savimbi, Liahuka, and the many Ovimbundu workers, students, and peasants who left Angola to study abroad, or who fled to neighboring Zambia, Zaire, Brazzaville, Europe and America after 1961, carried with them the nascent political consciousness which they had secretly harbored inside Angola. Although there were a few Catholics, most of those in exile were the Protestant, mission-educated Ovimbundu including pastors, teachers, nurses, and workers. Ovimbundu Jeremias Chitunda, Samuel Epalanga, and Ernesto Mulato arrived in Leopoldville (Kinshasa) in 1961, and others like Nicolau Chiuka Biangu, Rev. Marcolino Nahane, and Samuel Martinho Epalanga who came in later became associated with Kongo and Cabinda nationalists affiliated with the FNLA. Other Ovimbundu, such as Dr. Jose Liahuca, established a southern presence in Congo-Brazzaville by 1964. In Leopoldville, the Ovimbundu made contacts with Kongo exiles José N'dele, Miguel N'Zau Puna, and António (Tony) da Costa Fernandez, all of whom later became involved in UNITA.[40] In 1968, 125 Ovimbundu who had been contract workers in the north and had fled the fighting in 1961, still formed part of this exile community.[41]

Eastern Zaire and western Zambia, which had long been refugee areas for a large number of eastern and central Angolans, also attracted a significant number of Ovimbundu refugees who fled by means of the Benguela Railway in the wake of the 1961 uprisings. Here, the majority of the Angolan exiles were economic refugees and were no more inclined to affiliate with the growing nationalist movements than were the masses of

Africans inside Angola, or the majority of refugees from the Kongo and Kimbundu regions living in exile.[42]

The impetus to continue with the nascent political activities came from the Ovimbundu and other southern students and religious leaders who were outside of Angola. Among them were José Liahuca, Jonas Savimbi, Jorge Valentim, Daniel Chipenda, and José Belo Chipenda in Europe, Jeremias Kalandula Chitunda in the United States, and numerous pastors and other leaders in Leopoldville, Zambia, and Congo-Brazzaville.

The two most important Ovimbundu were Jonas Savimbi who joined the FNLA, and Daniel Chipenda who became a major player in the MPLA.[43] Before long, they became the representatives of southern nationalism in the MPLA and FNLA, as the leaders of both movements worked to build alliances with all Angolans.[44] Savimbi, however, would move quickly to articulate his own brand of Angolan nationalism.[45]

The young southerners who linked up with the MPLA and FNLA faced some major hurdles connected with their youth, inexperience, and their desire to be at the head of their own movement. The differences in experience and status between Agostinho Neto and Holden Roberto on the one hand, and the southerners on the other, were troublesome. An *assimilado* doctor and the leader of the MPLA, Agostinho Neto was a veteran of the anticolonial struggle in the Luanda area since the 1940s, and had written biting commentaries condemning Portuguese exploitation in Angola.[46] His support came not only from the Portuguese Communist Party but from other organizations in Europe and the Americas. Roberto, a Kongo aristocrat and the leader of the FNLA, also commanded significant respect in Africa and abroad. Kwame Nkrumah, Kenneth Kaunda, and other African nationalists recognized Neto and Roberto as the two major forces in the anticolonial struggle in Angola.[47]

In contrast, the Ovimbundu and other Angolan southerners lacked the national and international stature of the two northern leaders. The early experiences of Jonas Savimbi and Daniel Chipenda illustrate the problems that this presented for the anticolonial struggle in the early 1960s. Savimbi was twenty-four years old when he arrived in Portugal in 1958, with plans to complete high school and to study medicine. As was one of the few Ovimbundu students in Portugal, he was eager to be associated with the anticolonial struggle, and by April 1959, he had already had his first meeting with Neto, who was recruiting members for the movement. He also became active in the student organizations in Lisbon, being nominated as a representative of the General Union of Angolan Students in Portugal. By December 1959, however, with PIDE on his tracks, Savimbi fled from Portugal to Lausanne, Switzerland, where he obtained more information about the MPLA. He also met Holden Roberto and his supporters there, prior to the 1961 uprising.[48]

When the uprising broke out in northern Angola, Savimbi did not publicly support violent action against the state.[49] His reluctance was in part due to his own personal ambition and his desire to protect his regional base. He suspected that some in the MPLA leadership expected young southerners like himself to help expand their base beyond the urban and Kimbundu regions, but did not intend for them to play a leading role in party organization. Savimbi did not immediately break with the movement, but waited for the right occasion to organize his own version of anticolonial resistance.[50]

It was in Brazzaville and Kinshasa, where the southern presence was stronger, that Savimbi emerged as the spokesman for the southerners and a for few disgruntled Cabindans and Kongos who were jostling to claim a place in the MPLA and FNLA movements. Part of their concern stemmed from their own youth and inexperience, which made them suspicious of the efforts that the experienced and internationally recognized Neto and Roberto made to recruit them into the existing movements.[51] The Ovimbundu members, in particular, who believed that the leaders of MPLA regarded "Bailundus" as collaborators and traitors, were reluctant to commit themselves fully to the northern movements.[52] Moreover, their unfamiliarity with the ideological currents (Marxist, Pan-Africanist and socialist) which were becoming central to African nationalism, left them more open to external manipulation.[53] To gain legitimacy within the anticolonial struggle, they pushed to protect southern interests and worked to secure parity for party positions for their members within the movements.

In April, 1962, Savimbi accepted the position of Secretary General of the UPA (FNLA/GRAE), and joined another Ocimbundu, José Kanjundo, as the two highest ranking southerners in this movement. Savimbi regarded his appointment as a first step towards fulfilling his ambition of becoming the leading spokesman for southern and, in particular, Ovimbundu in the anticolonial struggle. By May 1963, his position in the FNLA allowed him to chair the African Liberation Movement Committee of the newly created Organization of African Unity.[54] He tried to influence FNLA policy by pressing the leadership to commit troops to fight inside Angola with the peasantry, a move that both the FNLA and MPLA were reluctant to undertake at that time.[55]

During his two years in the FNLA, Savimbi grew increasingly dissatisfied with the politics of Holden Roberto, and worked to develop his own independent contacts in Europe and Africa. The goal was to develop a dominant position in the exile community by claiming to lead the southerners. Before long, Savimbi had built an "Opposition Group" within the FNLA. This group included Jorge Isaac Sangumba, Smart Chata, Nicolau Buangu, the Rev. Marcolino Nahana, and Jeremias Kussuia Chinhundu. Student *émigrés* from the north such as António Fernandes, Miguel N'Zua Puna, and Ernesto Mulato, who wanted to restructure the UPA/FNLA and challenge the leadership of Holden Roberto, also joined the group.[56]

In July 1964, the group, which included 186 soldiers, left the FNLA.[57] Savimbi, who was in Cairo to attend the OAU meeting, had the full support of the frustrated Ovimbundu exile leadership when he read his resignation address to the assembly. He, along with the Ovimbundu exile leadership, was convinced that they would never have access to the Ovimbundu community because of Holden Roberto's refusal to open up an eastern front, and believed that money which should have been used for that purpose was being diverted elsewhere.[58] At the time, Savimbi explained the group's position by noting the need for a "new revolutionary strategy in Angola," for the formation of a United Front of all Angolan nationalists, and the "integration of all leaders and intellectuals inside the country."[59] He also expressed his displeasure and concern over what he described as Holden Roberto's network of Kongo acquaintances, whom he accused of misusing the organization's funds.

Savimbi's move caught most supporters of the anticolonial struggle by surprise and left them suspicious. In Geneva, the Director of the Program to Combat Racism, whose organization had provided grants to the MPLA and UPA/FNLA, hesitated to continue funding the movements because of concern of the possibility of having to give grants to three movements.[60] Other skeptics denounced and derided Savimbi and his followers for promoting ethnic divisiveness and Maoist ideology.[61]

Undaunted by the criticism, and with the goal of establishing his own southern front, Savimbi refused to join the MPLA, whose leaders had offered him the post of Secretary of Foreign Affairs of the movement.[62] The MPLA leadership interpreted Savimbi's refusal as illustrative of the uncompromising and narrow ethnic-based politics of the southern (Ovimbundu) nationalists.[63] By December the southerners published their manifesto, *Amangola* (Friends of Angola), in which they called for all Angolan exiles to return home and train the people for armed struggle. Even so, UNITA did not have the support of many other Angolans, who joined with the MPLA in regarding the UNITA leaders as opportunists with no strong ideological commitment to genuine Angolan nationalism.[64]

In fact some high-profile southerners ignored Savimbi's regionalist strategy, as the early political experience of Daniel Chipenda, an Ocimbundu who became the highest southern official in the MPLA, illustrates. Chipenda was among the few Ovimbundu who stressed their urban (Lobito) roots as opposed to their rural ethnic background.[65] Unlike Savimbi, who rejected MPLA overtures, by 1963 Chipenda was vice-president of the Policy Committee of the National Council of the MPLA,[66] becoming the movement's highest-ranking Ocimbundu by the late 1960s. In addition, he was the overall military organizer of the eastern front.

Savimbi's split from the FNLA, his refusal to join the MPLA, and the MPLA's recruitment of other southerners laid bare the complex interplay of personal ambition and regional factors that created turmoil in the anticolonial forces in the early 1960s. By the mid-to-late 1960s, strategic anti-Portuguese calculations and the realities of lack of political resources also plagued the anticolonial struggle. This at times resulted in collaboration with the colonial regime,[67] or a reluctance to confront the Portuguese authorities, both of which contributed to the fractured nationalism that emerged by 1974.[68]

UNITA and Exile Politics to 1970

Despite their criticism of the links that the FNLA and MPLA leadership had with governments and support groups in Africa, the United States, Western Europe, and the Communist bloc, UNITA's leaders looked to these very agencies and governments for recognition and for military, logistical, and financial assistance. Immediately after the announcement of the movement's founding, UNITA sent emissaries to seek support from African, European, American, and Asian governments and individuals. By February 1965, Savimbi and eleven other Angolans were in the People's Republic of China looking for financial and military training. The group also visited North Vietnam and North Korea seeking assistance.[69]

UNITA's representatives in Western Europe also worked to spread the movement's ideas. José N'dele, a Kongo, and Francisco Talanga unofficially represented UNITA in Switzerland, while the movement also established an office in Britain. Jorge Sangumba and Jorge Alcires Valentim campaigned on UNITA's behalf in England, America, and Africa, making presentations before the Organization of African Unity, the United Nations, nongovernmental organizations, universities, and churches.[70]

Several events which Savimbi and the other eleven Angolans staged in Angola a few months after their return from military training in China helped the movement gain some international credibility. One of these was the meeting of the first Congress of UNITA which took place at Muangai in the eastern Angolan province of Mexico on March 13, 1966, and another was Savimbi's trek into eastern Angola in December 1966, with a group of sixty ill-equipped guerrillas. Most of the group were non-Ovimbundu southerners.[71] On December 4, 1966, one segment of the group established UNITA's first base inside Angola and launched the first attack against the Portuguese at Cassamba, two hundred miles inside Angola. A second attack, launched by two of the Chinese trained eleven and a contingent of Chokwe peasants on Christmas Day against Teixeira de Sousa, an Angolan border town along the Benguela Railway in Mexico Province, left several Portuguese dead, including the local PIDE chief.[72]

Although the movement attacked a few other targets in 1967, Savimbi had left Angola for a fund-raising trip to Egypt and an inspirational meeting with Mao. On his return to Zambia in the middle of 1967, he was arrested, and was deported to Egypt after the intervention of Nasser. He returned surreptitiously to eastern Angola in 1968 to revive the liberation struggle against the Portuguese. From 1968 to 1974, he remained at the head of the UNITA guerrilla forces operating in eastern Angola.

MPLA supporters were among the most severe critics of UNITA, quickly dismissing the new movement as a creation of the Portuguese, and accusing the southerners of catering to ethnicity and regionalism.[73] To combat this perception, Savimbi launched a propaganda campaign designed to shore up UNITA's image in Africa and abroad, promising to build the membership from among the forgotten southerners, and vowing to continue launching attacks inside Angola against Portuguese positions.[74] Capitalizing on the publicity that the December guerrilla attack on the Portuguese military base had generated, Savimbi marketed UNITA as a legitimate nationalist group, and also portrayed himself as the main ideological spokesman of UNITA. He argued at the time that UNITA represented an alternative to the urban bias of the MPLA and the ethnic foundations of the Kongo-backed FNLA. Recognizing one way to gain international credibility and widen the support base of the movement inside Angola, he pointed out that rural cultivators and migrants inside the colony would make up the bulk of UNITA's membership.[75]

Despite the publicity brought by the December attacks, UNITA's leaders experienced many setbacks in their attempts to acquire funding and legitimacy abroad. The main reason was the skepticism of anticolonial organizations and governments which regarded the MPLA and FNLA as the legitimate nationalist movements.

Gaining support from the heads of newly independent African states proved a formidable challenge. The dilemma was evident in Savimbi's relationship with Kenneth Kaunda, who became president of Zambia, Angola's western neighbor, in 1964. Savimbi, knowing that Kaunda supported the MPLA and allowed Zambia to be a base for the training and recruitment of guerrillas, hoped to get recruits from among the thousands of Ovimbundu and other southern Angolan refugees in Zambia's Western Province. Kaunda, however, already supporting MPLA and ZIPLA guerrillas who were fighting the Smith regime in southern Rhodesia, and wary of Portuguese counterattacks, placed many restrictions on UNITA's operations.[76]

Kaunda's reluctance to support Savimbi stemmed in large part from landlocked but copper-rich Zambia's economic dependence on the Benguela Railway that passed through the central highlands, providing an alternative to lines running through Mozambique or South Africa. Kaunda realized that supporting UNITA guerrillas could spell political disaster at home. Thus in July 1967, when Savimbi failed to live up to the terms Kaunda had laid down for UNITA, Kaunda did not hesitate to arrest him, and he would have been turned over to the Portuguese had not a telegram to President Kaunda from Egypt's President Gamal Abdel Nasser resulted in Savimbi's deportation to Cairo.[77] Additionally, Zambia's diplomatic commitments to the Organization of African Unity which had recognized both the MPLA and the FNLA-GRAE in 1965, also limited any outright Zambian support for UNITA. Thus, although there was an UNITA office at the Liberation Center in downtown Lusaka, Zambia did little to support the movement until the OAU's Liberation Committee recognized UNITA as a legitimate liberation movement.[78]

Egypt's Nasser was initially UNITA's biggest financial supporter, allowing it to open an office in Cairo in 1965. His successor, Anwar Sadat also supported UNITA, and the movement maintained its Cairo office until 1974. Some help also came from sources in Senegal, Sudan, and a few other groups that made it possible for the UNITA's representatives to appear at the annual meetings of the Organization of African Unity. No other African country was forthcoming with material or military assistance, as the Organization of African Unity Liberation Committee's official recognition of the MPLA and FNLA as legitimate liberation movements in 1965 held back official support for and recognition of UNITA. Indeed, as late as 1974 the movement still had only two representatives abroad, one in Cairo and the other in London.[79] Tanzania was used as a training base and entrance point in Africa for its first group of fighters, only because of the skillful diplomacy of Sam Nujoma of SWAPO who allowed the UNITA fighters to train alongside SWAPO guerrillas at their training base in Tanzania.[80] As late as 1969 African states continued to deny UNITA, along with the Pan-African Movement (South Africa) and Robert Mugabe's ZANU, official recognition as liberation movements.

UNITA's international and African support thus remained narrow, as the only groups or governments willing to offer openly humanitarian support were missionary organizations and Egypt.[81] Although China's Mao Zedong and Zhou Enlai trained the first eleven guerrillas, including Savimbi, and the movement's leaders acknowledged the ideological debt they owed the Chinese, military and logistical support were never forthcoming from China. The most important international support for the movement came not from governments and liberation support committees, but from the free publicity from Western journalists. Their reports on the attacks Savimbi and his men launched against the Portuguese, and descriptions of Savimbi and his fighters' involvement with the rural population in eastern Angola did much to legitimize the movement and broaden its support base both in Africa and abroad.[82]

In fact, although Savimbi had accused the FNLA and MPLA of "tribalist" tendencies and regionalism which, he argued, prevented colony-wide opposition to the state, he himself exploited these very tendencies to transform the small group of southern Angolans and alienated northerners who had broken away from the MPLA and FNLA into a liberation movement. Crucial to his success was his reliance on Umbundu ethnic loyalty, expressed through language and customs, and his opportunism in portraying UNITA as a multi-ethnic movement with long historic ties (through long-distance trading and migrant labor) to other parts of Angola and to Zambia, South Africa, and Katanga. Savimbi also worked on his image as a nationalist leader, capitalizing on his facility with several of Angola's languages, and showing his dedication to the anticolonial struggle by fighting in Angola alongside his men. His role in UNITA contrasted sharply with the urbanity and military inexperience of Agostinho Neto and Holden Roberto. Moreover, by transforming UNITA into a full-fledged hierarchical organization with its own flag and symbol (the cockerel), its Central Committee, its youth and women's committees, and its party Congresses, Savimbi equipped UNITA with all the prerequisites of a nationalist movement.

By the late 1960s, Savimbi was articulating an ideology which relied heavily on the socialist teachings of China's Mao Zedong. Taking his lead from Mao's *Red Book*, he urged a political program aimed at winning over the countryside and peasants and developing a self-reliant guerrilla force. He also condemned tribalism, arguing that it was not sufficiently strong in Angola to prevent unity. His aim was to project UNITA as a reformist and flexible movement whose leaders were ready to work together with the colonial authorities. He argued that if UNITA put sufficient pressure on the state, the Angolan authorities would be forced to negotiate.[83]

Savimbi and the UNITA leadership also pointed to their guerrillas' sabotage operations against Portuguese outposts, to legitimize their assertion that UNITA was a genuine liberation movement representing the southern and rural populations of Angola. Their strategy of attracting free publicity sometimes paid off. For example, when UNITA guerrillas released some captured settlers to the International Red Cross in 1970, the movement's image greatly improved. To some Western governments and organizations who were becoming alarmed at MPLA's Marxist ties, UNITA's rhetorical message of peasant development presented a positive alternative.[84]

Although up to 1970 Savimbi and the UNITA leadership had been unable to convince most African and Western governments and groups that they represented a major segment of the Angolan population,[85] they were successful in building bridges with Protestant organizations in North America. From 1961 until the late 1960s, these organizations had secretly channeled monetary support to FNLA and MPLA, but had made no donations to UNITA. Savimbi and the UNITA leadership lobbied tirelessly for Protestant support. They viewed such backing as crucial for enhancing their status, since the National Council of Churches in New York had become a powerful progressive force behind many well-publicized efforts which put pressure on the Portuguese to change their policies in Angola. The organization supported various boycotts against Portuguese coffee, wines, sardines and other products, and Portuguese banks. In 1970, for example, the Ohio Conference of the United Church of Christ passed a resolution boycotting Gulf Oil, whose subsidiary, Cabinda Gulf Oil, they accused of contributing 50 percent towards the Angolan defense expenditure.[86] At the same time, Gulf Oil Canada was the subject of boycott campaigns conducted by the Toronto Committee for the Liberation of Portuguese Africa. Former missionaries and their congregations in the United States and Canada lent their full support to the boycotts and often funded the travel of the MPLA and FNLA leaders.[87]

In 1973, UNITA's credentials as a genuine liberation movement improved dramatically when the leadership and members of the Congregational Churches of Canada and the United States went on record as supporting the movement. The UNITA leaders received $37,000 (U.S.) in badly-needed funds from the National Council of Churches, which compared well with the $60,000 and $78,000 (U.S.) which the FNLA and MPLA received during the same period.[88] UNITA also received $7,000 (U.S.) in aid from the African Liberation Support Committee, an Afro-American activist group.[89] The fact that several Afro-Americans joined UNITA, fighting alongside the Africans or serving as teachers and medical helpers during the early 1970s, also bolstered the organization's claims of being Pan-Africanist in its orientation.[90] UNITA also received contributions from private agencies in a number of European countries. The greatest triumph, however, came in November 1974 after the Portuguese coup, when the African Liberation Committee of the Organization of African Unity officially recognized UNITA. This made it possible for the movement to receive the additional financial and logistical help that it badly needed.[91]

UNITA inside Angola

UNITA's success in attracting international support and raising its profile as a legitimate nationalist movement after 1970 was due partly to its activities inside Angola, despite the near collapse of the movement following the December 1966 attacks. Two developments allowed UNITA to strengthen its presence in Angola. The first was the support the movement generated among the small cadre of educated Ovimbundu who had gone underground in the wake of the 1961 uprisings. The second was Savimbi's ability to sustain a guerrilla war against the state, and at the same time develop a base that allowed UNITA to recreate some of the Protestant structures that had proved so successful in breaking down differences between the Ovimbundu and other southerners.

The first Ovimbundu inside the colony to view UNITA as an anti-state Ovimbundu organization were railway workers, clerks, nurses, pastors, teachers, civil servants serving in lower ranks of the administration, and students who had gone underground and who were anxious to continue the political activities they had started in the late fifties. Activists like César Kaliengue, Samuel Piedoso Chingunji, David Jonatão Chingunji, and Augusta Sakuanda were in contact with Savimbi early in 1967 following the December 1966 attack, and envisioned a general Ovimbundu uprising against the state. They developed detailed plans to infiltrate "the academic high school . . . mobilize the students of both sexes, penetrate the seminary of Christ the King and mobilize the seminarians, and if possible, some African priests, mobilize the workers of the Benguela Railway, of CUCA [the brewery], public functionaries, etc." The plans also included opening up networks in Nova Lisboa (now Huambo) to prepare for the appearance of UNITA.[92] By 1970, some of these Ovimbundu had opened UNITA cells in the cities of Benguela, Lobito, and Lubango, in Nova Lisboa, and in Luso, the capital of Moxico province.

In Silva Porto, capital of Bié where Savimbi's father had been stationed, and where he had opened a series of Protestant villages along the railroad, the people were sympathetic to UNITA's cause. UNITA sent Amelia Edith Eyiuva Epalanga of Silva Porto to organize the personnel of the Protestant missions, despite the constant surveillance by PIDE officials and the threat of being exposed by Ovimbundu informers.[93] Nova Lisboa, where many Ovimbundu Protestants worked and studied, became the hub of anti-state and pro-UNITA clandestine activities. In the African areas of the city, a network of UNITA safe houses functioned, offering protection to the few intrepid UNITA guerrillas who reached the highlands. Both Savimbi and Miguel N'Zau Puna, the secretary general of the movement, managed secret visits to the highlands in 1969, although Savimbi's critics charged that his visit could not have been possible without official knowledge.[94] UNITA's Ovimbundu sympathizers even surfaced in Luanda in 1969, and some Ovimbundu managed to evade state and settler vigilance and attended UNITA congresses held in liberated zones.

Many of the activities which led to increased support for UNITA inside Angola, especially in the urban centers, stemmed from the new direction that the movement took after Savimbi's return to Angola in 1968, following his expulsion from Zambia and his trip to Egypt and China. Savimbi and the UNITA leadership adopted two strategies to advance UNITA's cause inside Angola. First, they shifted their emphasis, from sending small groups of UNITA guerrillas to strike border villages, to a broadly based guerrilla war, where combatants went out among the people and cultivated the local chiefs. Some of the guerrillas later recalled that this strategy came straight from Mao's dictum which called for revolutionaries to "go to the people, live with them, build on what they have so that they could support you."[95] Second, UNITA established its own network of villages in liberated rural areas and a government in exile.

UNITA's strategy was unsuccessful in the Ovimbundu strongholds and in the urban centers, as PIDE security made it difficult for the guerrillas to reach UNITA sympathizers there. In fact, many of UNITA's organizers were killed, deported, imprisoned, or recruited as informers. In 1970, for example, some twenty-five UNITA operatives were deported to the infamous Tarrafal prison on the Island of Tiago in Cape Verde, while others were sent to prisons in Luanda and Mossamedes on the strength of information PIDE received from Ovimbundu informers.[96] Ovimbundu from the central highlands and other southerners, however, provided crucial information to UNITA about the operations of PIDE and the Portuguese forces.

UNITA was more succesful in its attempts to draw Ovimbundu inside the colony to its bases in the bush. UNITA's attempts to build an organizational structure enabled Ovimbundu Protestant structures to be reborn outside the highlands as Ovimbundu Protestants came to play a prominent role in the movement. For example, at the first UNITA Congress at the Chokwe village of Muangai, Protestant Ovimbundu were among the sixty participants, including sekulus, sobas, teachers, pastors, and deaconesses. During the several days of the conference, the level of fraternizing among the Ovimbundu members gave the appearance of an Ovimbundu Protestant reunion, as participants took the opportunity to renew ties with kinsmen and friends who had fled Angola. Many recalled the earlier proto-nationalist sentiments that the *Juventude Cristão de Angola* had promoted, and committed themselves anew to fight against the Portuguese colonial state.[97]

UNITA came to rely on the expertise of Ovimbundu Protestants and other southerners who reached the movement's bases in eastern Angola offered. These Protestants played a central role in broadening UNITA's support among some segments of the non-Ovimbundu populations in Moxico province. Ovimbundu nurses, teachers, clerks, pastors, and railway workers who had managed Protestant-run health, educational, and other services found themselves setting up and managing schools, clinics, health, churches, and other centers which appeared in the liberated zones that came to be identified with UNITA.

Like the "strategic hamlets" that the Portuguese had set up in eastern Angola, and the camouflaged camps from which the MPLA operated, the villages associated with UNITA helped to give the movement an aura of legitimacy.[98] Although the movement attracted a variety of southerners, including Ngangela, Lunda, Moxico, Luena, Guanhama, all peoples with whom the Ovimbundu had historic ties,[99] and non-Ovimbundu southerners made up the core of the movement's early leadership and guerrillas, the Ovimbundu Protestant presence was crucial.[100]

The fact that the UNITA leadership could rely on this network of Ovimbundu Protestants for leadership expertise was a crucial factor in transforming UNITA into a viable liberation movement. Protestant Ovimbundu, along with a few Catholics, were the force behind the establishment and operation of scores of Protestant-style villages which sprang up alongside traditional Chokwe, Ngangela, Ovimbundu, and Lunda villages in the areas of eastern Angola where the movement was operating.[101]

In many ways, the "liberated villages" recreated in eastern Angola the Protestant educational, health, agricultural, and social service network that had worked so well in the highlands.[102] The favorable comments on the "well-run and organized" camps and the discipline of UNITA's guerrillas by Austrian journalist Fritz Sitte and *Washington Post* journalist Leon Dash spoke to the penetration of Ovimbundu Protestant structures in the organization that UNITA was building in the non-Ovimbundu regions in which it operated.[103] Kwadwo Akpan, an Afro-American who attended UNITA's Third Congress at a site eighteen days march from the Zambia border, recorded that the villages he visited each an "ngungu [njango] used . . . as a central point for the community to meet." He also commented on the boarding schools run for girls from the local villages and the many clinics which the movement had established. The staff of most of the schools and clinics had been trained in Ovimbundu Protestant institutions.[104]

The ethnic and social ties between the Ovimbundu inside Angola and those in UNITA also explain both why the movement became the vehicle for the growth of modern Ovimbundu nationalism and also the inconsistencies in its political ideology. The deep roots of Jonas Savimbi, George Sangumba, and other Ovimbundu in the UNITA leadership in the precolonial ruling lineages, their Protestant background, and the politics of African decolonization guaranteed that modern Ovimbundu political ideology would be both traditionalist and forward-looking. Within UNITA, ideas, structures, and customs associated with former kingdoms, sekulus, sobas, and American Congregationalist puritanical ethics coexisted with Maoist ideology, a cult of personality, and western concepts of democracy and free enterprise.

Throughout the early seventies, UNITA continued to attract an increasing number of Ovimbundu into its guerrilla ranks, while it provided opportunities for others to go overseas to further their training. The majority of Ovimbundu who joined the movement, however, worked in the liberated villages as teachers, nurses, pastors, and agricultural aides.[105] Thus, despite the preponderance of non-Ovimbundu in the movement in the first few years, the Ovimbundu presence grew steadily, and Ovimbundu members clearly identified with Savimbi as an Ocimbundu and regarded UNITA as an Ovimbundu nationalist organization. Many Ovimbundu Protestants saw in UNITA their opportunity to influence Angola's decolonization.[106]

Meanwhile the masses of Ovimbundu and other southerners who remained in the government controlled areas, and who were increasingly resisting the state's attempts to place them into so-called protected villages were also developing pro-UNITA sympathies. Indeed, the disaffection within eastern Angola was so widespread by 1970 that MPLA and UNITA guerrillas actively recruited supporters in Luso and the surrounding regions, where the resettlement villages were located.

UNITA and the Colonial Regime

Despite the advances which UNITA made in eastern Angola and the pride many Ovimbundu and other southerners had in the movement, it never became a serious threat to the colonial regime. Indeed, until 1974, colonial officials involved in suppressing anti-state activities concentrated on weakening the FNLA and MPLA, and at times relied on UNITA in order to achieve their goals. To both Portuguese officials and the UNITA leadership, eradicating the MPLA, in particular, meant weakening the support base the movement had among a significant percentage of the Angolan refugee populations in neighboring countries. Moreover, a weakened MPLA damaged that movements's popular image inside Angola, and the support it received from progressive forces in Africa, Europe, and America.[107]

With the MPLA as the common enemy, the Portuguese and UNITA officials secretly collaborated in driving the movement out of its bases in eastern Angola.[108] In a dispatch later made public in 1974 but referring to earlier events, Savimbi spelled out details concerning military supplies he was receiving from the authorities. In the dispatch, he asked the government to stipulate where exactly in Moxico his guerrillas could operate without threat of attack from government troops.[109] These revelations clearly suggest that at the time one of Savimbi's strategies was to weaken MPLA, to prepare the way for compromise with Portuguese state officials. UNITA's activities in Moxico did more to thwart the MPLA goals in the region than to advance Ovimbundu ethnic solidarity or southern nationalism.[110]

Savimbi's collaboration with the Portuguese was not inconsistent with the accomodationist position that many Protestant Ovimbundu had taken in their dealings with the colonial state. Throughout the 1960s, PIDE agents, government authorities in Luanda, agents of the colonial army, and the

Department of Military Intelligence recruited a number of Ovimbundu to work as informers and spies. In fact many of the *flechas* (the specially trained African units in the colonial army) were Ovimbundu. In the early seventies when the numbers of southern and Ovimbundu recruits in the Angolan army increased, the *flechas* inflicted heavy losses on MPLA guerrillas.

Ovimbundu who had retained their membership in MPLA did not escape suspicion. In 1973 when factionalism and ideological tensions nearly destroyed the MPLA, Chipenda, the highest ranking Ocimbundu, became involved with a faction (*Revolta do Leste*) which had supporters in eastern Angola where the MPLA had bases. He was publicly accused of heading a plot to assassinate Agostinho Neto, with the complicity of the "Ovimbundu tribe" within the organization, and to take over the presidency of the party. In a party document, MPLA leader Neto accused Chipenda of having for years provided arms to UNITA for "tribal reasons."[111]

Portuguese security and military officials kept UNITA's small guerrilla bands pinned down in the lightly populated backlands of Moxico province and forestalled any political activities in the heavily populated Ovimbundu central highlands.[112] Until 1974 the state's large and well-equipped army, secret police, African informers, paramilitary forces, and settler vigilantes effectively restricted guerrilla operations in the highlands.[113]

By that time, the government had built up a formidable military and security presence in Angola. After nearly fifteen years of the liberation war, the regular army numbered 70,000 men, with many of them trained in counter-insurgency methods. The government forces were also equipped with American-made and NATO-supplied napalm and herbicides that represented part of the Portugal's payment from the United States for the use of its bases in the Azores.[114] These measures enabled the government to protect the 350,000 white settlers in the colony and insulate the vast majority of Angola's 6,000,000 people from the nationalist guerrillas. Many officials in Angola believed that the sacrifice of the 11,000 soldiers who had died in action against the nationalist guerrillas and the 30,000 wounded or disabled (the majority Africans) up to 1974 was worth it, since it had saved Angola from the fate of other colonial powers. None of them envisioned giving up the authoritarian state they had built.[115]

They based their optimism on the colony's heady economic transformation. By 1974 petroleum had become the leading export, followed by coffee, with some 5.2 million sacks being exported in the early 1970s. The economic boom was also evident in other sectors. Increased industrial output, including iron ore production that reached an all-time high in the early 1970s, made the state appear almost invincible.[116]

The boom also spilled over into the highlands where manufacturing, urban spread, development of infrastructure, and industrial growth gave inland urban centers like Nova Lisboa all the appearance of their Western counterparts. One exile Angolan who returned to the city in 1974 recalled that "the stores were just like those I saw in Rochester, N.Y. and New York City."[117] Despite being listed officially as a European city, more than 75 percent of the population of the city were Ovimbundu, and it served as a magnet for the over 300,000 Ovimbundu in the region.

It was this ability to strengthen the authoritarian state, achieve tremendous economic leaps, and yet keep the guerrillas of the liberation movements at bay that made the late colonial state appear so formidable. The economic boom meant that many Ovimbundu who would otherwise have been attracted to UNITA found accommodation the best method of survival. This situation explains why UNITA's efforts to recruit urban Ovimbundu largely failed. Although most Ovimbundu had of heard of Savimbi and UNITA, the movement's isolation in eastern Angola led many Ovimbundu to invest the movement and leadership with largely mythical qualities quite unrelated to the realities of the movement.[118] Besides this, the imprisonment, killing, and intimidating of suspected UNITA supporters in the highlands, the setting up of "protected villages," and the suppression of news about the liberation movement proved effective in preventing Ovimbundu ethnic loyalties to Savimbi and UNITA from surfacing.[119] The location of the central highlands, some five hundred miles from the eastern frontier where UNITA's guerrillas had their base, also helped to keep the majority of the population well-insulated from guerrilla influence.[120] The few deeply committed Ovimbundu who succeeded in making secret contacts with UNITA's guerrillas and leaders were no match for the security forces.[121]

Contradictions Unleashed: The Lisbon Coup

Had the military and economic success in the colony resulted in the political appeasement of critics of the regime in Portugal, the colonial state would have continued to shape the terms of its relationship with UNITA and the Ovimbundu. But fourteen years of nationalist agitation in its colonies, especially the much more coherent and successful campaigns which nationalists in Mozambique waged against the regime, forced the dictatorship in Portugal to confront grave domestic and international consequences. By the 1970s, the metropolitan government was disintegrating as a result of resistance to prolonged military service in the army, social unrest, and dissatisfaction with the way the regime was handling the war. Internationally, Portugal had become a pariah, battling criticism and condemnation of its colonial policies in the United Nations, and in capitals in both East and West, state and private support for the liberation movements included military support for the movements and popular boycotts of Portuguese wines and other exports. In America, stockholder action against Gulf Oil's operations in Angola threatened to sever the lifeline of the economic transformation.[122]

In Portugal the pressure came from a wide range of groups. Critics included lower-ranking officers in the Portuguese army, conservative supporters of the settlers who believed that the Angolan regime was soft on the nationalists, some elements of the Catholic hierarchy, and some collaborating Afro-Portuguese and assimilated Africans.[123] They were all dissatisfied with the authoritarian system of government in Portugal and the colonies since the establishment of the New State in 1926.

The most outspoken groups were the liberals, socialists, and Marxists among unionized workers, alienated intellectuals, and members of the armed forces. Officers who had participated in the colonial campaigns resented paying for the colonial agenda of a government which supported political repression at home as well as in the colonies.

On April 25, 1974, the *Movimento das Forças Armadas* (Armed Forces Movement), a group of young, Marxist-oriented officers, staged a successful coup after the dismissals of General António de Spínola and General Francisco da Costa Gomes, two popular officers and outspoken critics of the Salazar-Caetano regime. Although General Spínola had no intention of giving the colonies independence, believing at the time that "without the African territories the country . . . will be reduced to a voiceless corner of a gigantic Europe," young radical officers lost no time in disengaging from the Angolan colonial state and transferring it to the "Angolan people." The prospect of independence, however, only opened up another chapter in the contest between the Ovimbundu and the state, as Savimbi and the UNITA leadership capitalized on the opportunity to present themselves as the legitimate representatives of all Ovimbundu and southerners.

UNITA, the Ovimbundu and the 25th April Coup

As the events in Portugal gave rise to political chaos in Portugal and its colonies, UNITA's status in an independent Angola began to occupy the regime in Angola and many governments in the West who had supported

Portugal over the years. Despite the fact that few knew or trusted Savimbi and the UNITA organization, most of the decision makers in the post-coup era realized that it was impossible to think about independence without a UNITA input. They based this calculation on the belief that the two million Ovimbundu who made up the largest ethnic bloc in Angola were the natural constituents of UNITA, and would likely control the largest bloc of votes in a future independent Angola.

The coup thus brought unexpected benefits to UNITA, since it opened opportunities to propel a movement with little prior international backing into the center of Angolan politics and the international political limelight. From the instant the coup occurred, Savimbi positioned UNITA in such a way as to capitalize on its Ovimbundu ties, and also to envelop the movement with Western, democratic, and anti-Communist values, in fundamental opposition to the stronger and more Marxist MPLA with its ties to the Portuguese Communist Party, and the FNLA with its CIA links and narrower Kongo ethnic association.[124] The international baptism of the movement by democratic governments in Africa and abroad, and by foreign journalists and political analysts began in just after the coup. Many governments and anti-Communist Cold War warriors in the West were fearful of the MPLA's Communist connections, and used UNITA for their own purposes.[125]

Savimbi's and UNITA's changing profile in the West was not immediately guaranteed, and for some time after the April coup UNITA's status as the alternative to the MPLA remained questionable. The most serious setback for UNITA occurred when news of Savimbi's collaboration with the Portuguese government began to appear in the Western press in the wake of the coup. The leadership had to answer criticism from the MPLA and other detractors, although the news made little difference among the Ovimbundu and UNITA's supporters inside Angola.[126]

UNITA's military situation also left much to be desired; in contrast to the much larger MPLA and FNLA forces. The movement's guerrillas could barely muster a force of one thousand men and women who operated in eastern Angola, and its population of about five thousand peasants in the liberated zone was a far cry from what the organizers had hoped for when they established the movement.[127]

But it was the intention of the young radicals in Portugal to end Portugal's status as a colonial power immediately that shaped the way Savimbi and the UNITA leadership responded to the situation. Following the coup the new Portuguese leaders dismissed the last head of the Angolan government, Governor General Santos e Castro, and sent their own representative to Angola. He was General Costa Gomes, who had been reinstated in the military. In May 1974, he announced in Luanda that if the nationalists stopped fighting, the Portuguese would recognize them as political parties.[128] Additionally, General António de Spínola, now head of the Portuguese state, stated that the government was ready to recognize the "rights of the people of Portuguese Overseas Territories to self-determination, including the immediate recognition of their right to independence." He also stressed Portugal's willingness to "initiate the transference of power to the native populations of those territories, namely Guinea, Angola and Mozambique."[129] A few weeks later Vice-Admiral Rosa Coutinho (the "Red Admiral") replaced General Costa Gomes as head of a transition government. The decision to grant independence to Angola led immediately to a scramble by the nationalist movements and various social and political groups including settlers, former state functionaries, Afro-Portuguese elements, and security personnel to position themselves to fight for power by controlling the postcolonial state. Representatives of the contending factions floated several suggestions detailing the type of government that the future independent Angola should have. If the settlers had their way, they would have imposed a unilateral declaration of independence along the lines of that of the white Rhodesians.[130] The leaders of the three Angolan nationalist movements, Agostinho Neto of the MPLA, Holden Roberto of the FNLA, and Jonas Savimbi of UNITA, also presented various proposals to the new administration in Lisbon.[131] Newly formed political coalitions in Angola also announced their own plans for controlling the state.

Eager to present itself as a serious contender for the state, and conscious of the perception that UNITA was an accomodationist Ovimbundu movement, Savimbi and the leadership moved immediately to improve the movement's image in Angola and abroad and to push for a coalition government. The international media, which were responding to popular and official demands for assessments of who would control the state in a postindependence Angola, became the first of UNITA's targets. The strategy here was to highlight the movement's achievements and present it as a serious political force that could oversee the transition to independence. In broadcasts and written declarations, Savimbi reminded people that UNITA's guerrillas had struggled in eastern Angola since 1966, in contrast to the MPLA which had only a few guerrillas in the Dembos region and the FNLA whose guerrillas were all in Zaire. To refute the accusation that the movement had collaborated with the government, UNITA countered with evidence showing that their supporters had not been spared political torture, repression, and imprisonment. They, like their MPLA counterparts, could recount their tortures in the infamous political prisons run by the Portuguese in Cape Verde and Mossamedes.[132] Finally, UNITA spokesmen always made sure to identify UNITA as the representative of Angola's two million Ovimbundu and several hundred thousand other southerners.

Besides publicly defending the actions of the leadership, Savimbi organized delegations to the United States, Canada, African states, and several European countries. These diplomatic missions were designed to position the UNITA leadership to play a leading role in the negotiations leading to independence. For example, Maria Chela and the Rev. Frederico Mussili, both well known in Canada at the time, pleaded the movement's credentials to church audiences there.[133]

In June, UNITA became the first movement to sign a truce with the Portuguese, and by December Savimbi had signed bilateral agreements with both Holden Roberto and Agostinho Neto in an attempt to reconcile differences and establish rules for joint negotiations with the Portuguese regarding a transitional government. By December, UNITA's efforts to prepare for a transitional coalition government bore fruit when the Portuguese and the three liberation movements agreed to an early January meeting to discuss details.[134]

The only serious threat to the Savimbi's efforts to position UNITA as the representative of the Ovimbundu and southern Angolans, with Savimbi as the leader came from Daniel Chipenda, the only high-ranking Ocimbundu in the MPLA. Chipenda, however, had his own problems in the MPLA, where he was battling with Agostinho Neto for leadership of the movement. The fact that many MPLA leaders believed that many of their Ovimbundu members were spies placed their by PIDE to foment discontent in the movement, and[135] that they would close ranks behind a fellow Ocimbundu instead of showing loyalty to the party during the crisis, weakened Chipenda's status in the movement. On the other hand, the MPLA found Chipenda more useful inside the movement than outside, since internal disunity was threatening to destroy the organization as a viable nationalist group. He reluctantly accepted the vice-presidency to prevent the MPLA's imminent collapse.[136] When his supporters in eastern Angola were implicated in an uprising against the main body of the MPLA, although he retained his official military position, he lost credibility. In 1974 Chipenda became the leader of one of the three factions contending for control of the MPLA,[137] but failed to rally any popular Ovimbundu support during the period immediately after the coup. He thus left the field clear for Savimbi and UNITA.

As the Portuguese coup opened the way for a transfer of the state to the Angolan anticolonialists, Savimbi and the UNITA leadership confronted the reality of actually participating in running the state. But 1974–75 was not 1966, and as Savimbi and the UNITA leadership prepared to contest control of the state with the MPLA and FNLA, they failed to come to terms with many of the unprincipled acts, confusions of roles (political leaders, church representatives, or UNITA representatives), shifting alliances, and propaganda ploys that they had adopted or perpetrated during the heady days of the guerrilla war. This legacy of the anticolonial struggle proved disastrous for the growth of Angolan nationalism and the consolidation of the postcolonial Angolan state. The fact that, even as the colonial state was collapsing, Angola became one of the locations where America and Russia fought out the Cold War also helped to undermine Angolan nationalism and consolidation. These issues continued to shape the Ovimbundu relationship with the postcolonial state from 1974–75 to 1997.

7

THE OVIMBUNDU AND THE POSTCOLONIAL STATE, 1974–1992

Introduction

Several developments widened the gulf between the Ovimbundu population and the state in the period from 1974 to 1992. Some had to do with the differing ethnic, regional, urban-rural, and other legacies that Portuguese colonialism had bequeathed to Angolans, others were linked to the geopolitics of the Cold War, while still others arose from the personal ambitions of the anticolonial leaders. Personality conflicts, competing ideologies, the politics of the Cold War, and differing political and military strategies of the MPLA and UNITA leaderships (high politics) all mediated the relationship between the Ovimbundu and the rest of the rural population and the postcolonial state from 1975 to 1992. As a result, this chapter devotes a great deal of attention to these issues. It takes the position that the localism of the Ovimbundu and other rural populations informed in fundamental ways the activities of Jonas Savimbi and the Unita leadership in their efforts to control the postcolonial state. Localism also thwarted the efforrts of the MPLA leadership in establishing its own version of the state.[1]

Although during the period of the anticolonial struggle the three Angolan movements were identified with specific ethnic groups and each articulated its own version of nationalist ideology, their central aim was to bring an end to Portuguese colonial rule in Angola. After the 1974 coup, the UNITA leaders, like their counterparts in the MPLA and FNLA, positioned themselves to contest for control of the state. Without a strong popular base inside Angola, the leadership hoped that an appeal to ethnicity and regionalism would provide an expedient and guaranteed route toward gaining a foothold inside Angola and a first step to developing a national platform. Between May 1974 and November 1975 this rush to secure a regional base pitted the two northern guerrilla armies and their supporters—the Kimbundu/Afro-Portuguese dominated MPLA and the Kongo-dominated FNLA—against each other. When UNITA joined the conflict and allied itself with the FNLA, the ethnic/urban/regional divisions that would dominate the Ovimbundu relationship with the postcolonial state for the next eighteen years took root.

The expansion of the Cold War in Southern Africa was another development which affected the Ovimbundu relationship with the postcolonial state. The most significant impact was the intensification and prolongation of the military contest between the anticolonial leaders, as between 1976 to 1992 the MPLA leadership strengthened their ties with the Soviet Union and Cuba, and UNITA relied increasingly on South Africa and the United States and its allies. These alliances forced the Angolan nationalists to adopt sharper ideological positions to conform to the existing ideological distinctions between East and West. By 1992, MPLA's socialist ties had helped its leadership to consolidate control over the postcolonial state and to define Angolan nationalism. On the other hand, Savimbi's strategy of exploiting Cold War tensions placed UNITA opposite to the MPLA on the ideological scale. Moreover, Savimbi's cultivation of local ethnic and regional ties made UNITA a formidable opposition to the MPLA state. Neither of these developments, however, brought the different segments of the Ovimbundu population closer to the state, as Savimbi and UNITA remained the mediator between the Ovimbundu and the MPLA-controlled postcolonial state.

Savimbi's tendency to place his own reputation and status above the Ovimbundu quest for representation in the state also helps to explain the continuing distance between the Ovimbundu and the state. The roots of this went back to the anticolonial struggle when Savimbi began his collusion with the Portuguese army to thwart the MPLA goals in eastern Angola. During the period from 1974 to 1992, Savimbi continued to rank his own ambition above that of the Ovimbundu and other Angolans who joined UNITA. To fulfill his goal of representing the Ovimbundu and other southerners in the state, he accepted and later defended his alliance with the Apartheid regime in South Africa, irrespective of the global distate for South Africa. He also received support from and defended conservative forces in America and Africa—actions that again helped to put a distance between the Ovimbundu whom he represented and the MPLA party which controlled the postcolonial Angolan state.

Savimbi's continued dependence on the Protestant leadership that had given him support during the anticolonial struggle also worked to alienate the Ovimbundu from the postcolonial Angolan state. As more and more Ovimbundu Protestant leaders and the Ovimbundu population as a whole came to support and rely on Savimbi and UNITA, he was able to co-opt Protestant churches and other Ovimbundu organizations. This relationship between UNITA and the Protestant leadership led many Ovimbundu to defend UNITA's actions, thus allowing Savimbi to continue to put his own legitimacy and status above considerations of the future of the Ovimbundu in an Angolan nation. All of these developments in the period from 1974 to 1992 served to alienate the Ovimbundu even further from the state, and increased rather than eliminated the tensions between them.

The Road to Civil War

The civil war broke out in 1975 because Holden Roberto, Agostinho Neto, and Jonas Savimbi all believed that their own movements had legitimate claims to the postcolonial Angolan state. Thus, although taking tentative steps in 1974 to agree on a common platform to put a government of national unity in place after the Portuguese left, the leaders also moved to undermine each other.

Jonas Savimbi, recognizing the military weakness of UNITA, had staked out the movement's position soon after the 1974 coup and pushed for UNITA's participation in a coalition of the three movements "to form a new government in Angola." In contrast, Agostinho Neto, claiming history on his side, swore early in 1975 that the MPLA "will not abdicate its historic right towards the Angolan people."[2] On the sidelines, the people waited. An old peasant in Luso who witnessed the turn of events in the summer of 1975 as MPLA and UNITA guerrillas and partisans situated themselves to take over key state institions, used an apt analogy to characterize the estrangement between the two movements and the masses. He observed, "the elephant and the hippapotamus will be fighting tonight, and they will trample on the grass and shrubs."[3]

The civil war which came to a pause in 1992 witnessed the interplay of internal and external forces that heightened regional and ethnic differences on a scale unimagined during the period of the liberation struggle. The intervention of the Soviet Union and its allies on the side of the MPLA, and the United States on the side of FNLA and then of UNITA, at times made the Angolan partisans appear more as proxies for the Cold War between the Communist East and the Western democracies than as Angolan nationalists. As the Cold War ended in the late 1980s, the MPLA and UNITA, who had fought sixteen years of bloody war, signed a cease fire on May 1, 1991. For the first time since 1975, the Angolan people had an opportunity to take stock of their situation. For them, the ruin and destruction of the war had no parallel in their history prior to 1975. Moreover, the vast majority of Ovimbundu and not a few other Angolans were as alienated from the vestiges of the colonial state structure and the postcolonial state institutions that had evolved as a consequence of the civil war as they had been from the colonial regime. Many Angolans in the MPLA-controlled regions had come to resent the Marxist-Leninist regime that had replaced the colonial state, while the people who lived in the string of fortified encampments that developed in UNITA-controlled areas confronted a cult of personality with elements of precolonial justice that Jonas Savimbi exercised when expedient.

In 1992, United Nations–supervised elections gave Angolans throughout the country the opportunity to live under a democratic state through the ballot box. This event was the first real attempt to dismantle the authoritarian institutions that had alienated the majority of Angola's population from the state since the Portuguese conquest.

The positions which the leaders of the Angolan liberation movements took, and the impact this had on the majority of Angolans bore many similarities to the problems in other regions of Africa where nationalists competed for control over the postcolonial state. Basil Davidson has studied postcolonial Africa's dismal record of political disintegration and has placed the blame squarely upon independence leaders. He has accused them of uncritically accepting democratic political models based on those of European nation-states, and simultaneously and contradictorily leaving in place repressive colonial laws and undemocratic and authoritarian institutions in order to preserve their own power. For Davidson, the foreign system which kept the Western-educated leadership in power was at the root of Africa's political crisis, leading to the leadership's alienation from the African masses and the culture and history which they share.[4] Thus, the policies followed by nationalist rulers in the postindependence period deprived all but a small segment of the population from benefiting from African control over the state.

Long an admirer of the MPLA, Davidson nevertheless criticized its leadership for its "failed Stalinist policies." He reserved his harshest criticism for the UNITA leadership, however, accusing the movement of being a creation of South Africa and its "Western friends." He argued that UNITA's actions thwarted the MPLA's drive to transform Angolan society after independence, and led to violence and impoverishment on an unprecedented scale.[5]

Davidson's criticisms aside, the civil war and the related problems that have plagued Angola since independence again revealed the underlying conflicts between the authoritarianism of the state and the tendencies of rural African communities to retain their local autonomy. These have been constants in Angola's history for the past century. The tension was present in 1974 in the form of heightened regional and ethnic consciousness, and was exploited by politicians both in the West and in the Soviet Union as part of their global geopolitical strategy. The view that up to 1992 the Angolan civil war between the MPLA and UNITA was an example of Soviet-Cuban backed leaders and opportunist CIA-Apartheid puppets acting as proxies in the politics of the Cold War, a view which still dominates the literature of postindependence Angola, misses the more dynamic domestic perspective.[6] The war was a theater where both external and internal factors came to bear on the postcolonial state. The contending parties, each intent on controlling the state, resorted to the politics of ethnicity, adopted socialist and democratic ideologies and models, and relied on the politics of personality and demagoguery, none of which resolved the tensions between the state and society. The Ovimbundu relationship to the state from 1974–75 to 1992 provides a classic study of the complexities and challenges of nationalism in the late twentieth century.[7]

MPLA Ascendancy

In the spring of 1974, as the authoritarian and repressive dictatorship gave way to a more open and competitive political system in Portugal, Angola slid towards political and social chaos, war, and destruction. The central issue the liberation movements confronted was how the state was to be reconstructed and what the people's relationship to it would be. At the time, each nationalist movement and settler representatives had its own blueprint for a postindependence Angolan government. None of the discussions, however, focused on how to deal with the political and social legacy and the divisions that had surfaced among Angola's population as a result of the liberation struggle. Of these, the most crucial were the ethnic and regional divisions of the liberation movements and the African populations in the country, the urban-rural divide, the ideological divisions and the racist attitudes among the majority of the Portuguese settlers, and the political inexperience of both Africans and whites.

The prospect of the Angolan nationalists managing the corporate government that the dictatorship had established also presented formidable problems. Unlike their counterparts in other regions of Africa, where African traditional authorities wielded local power or where members of the educated elite had participated at some level in the government, none of the Angolan nationalists had ever held a responsible position in government, and only a handful had any civil service experience. In addition, most of the nationalist leadership lacked the educational and management expertise to run a state.

In hindsight, a system of power sharing would have been the most fruitful option for the nationalist contenders and those settlers willing to live under an African-controlled government in an independent Angola. However, the massive intervention of the Soviet Union and the United States in the Angolan crisis, the actions of the post-coup decision makers in Portugal, and the continuing ethnic and ideological divisions among the liberation movements all conspired to thwart any move towards power sharing.

The ethnic, ideological, regional, and other differences between the leadership of the MPLA, UNITA, FNLA, and settlers surfaced soon after the coup. At one end were more than 500,000 right-wing settlers who worked to destroy the MPLA because of its pro-Marxist ties, co-opt the FNLA and UNITA leadership, and install Rhodesian-style minority government in Angola.[8] At the other end was the MPLA leadership, whose anti-imperialist message promoted *poder popular* ("people's power") under MPLA guidance. Somewhere in between were UNITA, the FNLA and smaller groups that sprang up in the wake of the coup. Savimbi, for example, had for UNITA's slogan "Liberty, Negritude, and Socialism," and promised a state in which Angolans would be able to practice their culture and be proud of their Angolan, rather than Portuguese, heritage, while the FNLA advocates promoted their version of capitalist development.[9]

In the days immediately following the coup, the MPLA leadership reiterated its position of 1972, when Agostinho Neto had asserted that "the Angolan people must have the riches of our country . . . we don't intend to allow either Angolans or foreigners to exploit others in the country."[10] Although critical of Savimbi and Roberto, on January 15, 1975, Neto joined them in signing the Alvor Agreement, which committed the nationalists to work towards a transition government under a Portuguese high commissioner. The Agreement set 11 November 1975 as the day when the Portuguese would hand over the Angolan state to the "people of Angola." By including a clause that called on the liberation movements to allow democratic elections, so that the various populations in Angola could nominate candidates to run the state on behalf of the "people of Angola," the agreement opened a way to overturn the authoritarian institutions that the dictatorship had established.[11]

Despite signing the Alvor Agreement, the MPLA leadership also publicly supported the idea of a strong unitary state under the control of a single party, with a well-organized military and security apparatus, state ownership of the means of production, and a social agenda which would transform colonial subjects into Angolan nationals.[12] Acknowledging that their plans would only advance if they "neutralize FNLA as well as UNITA before independence," the MPLA set about to take over the state. Neto and the MPLA leadership first targeted the FNLA, with its large troop strength, its strategic presence in the Kimbundu region, and strong backing from African and Western governments, as the main opposition.[13] But they also feared UNITA, believing that despite its weak military showing and Savimbi's questionable nationalism, he could deliver to UNITA "the large Ovimbundu ethnic group."[14] Undoubtedly the MPLA leadership understood that open elections would reveal that ethnicity counted for more than ideology or Cold War status.

The MPLA had many opportunities to solidify its position in Angola in the months following the Lisbon coup, because civil, security, and military activities had almost come to a halt. The cease-fires that the new Portuguese government signed with the leadership of the three movements in June 1974 worked to the MPLA's advantage. Not only did peace relieve members from guerrilla duties, it also allowed the MPLA to spend more time undertaking political work in the urban centers.

In Luanda its underground network quickly surfaced and mobilized supporters. Much the same development occurred in other major cities, including Benguela, Lobito, Mossamedes, Lubango, and Nova Lisboa. MPLA leaders also stationed guerrillas in the cities and consolidated its military positions in Moxico, the Dembos, Cabinda, and other regions where they had established guerrilla bases.

During the months leading up to independence, MPLA also expanded its political broadcasts from the radio station *Angola Combatente* which broadcast from Congo-Brazzaville and which had brought its anticolonial message to Africans and Afro-Portuguese during the period of the liberation war. The post-coup broadcasts popularized the integrity of Angolan nationalism and replaced colonial slogans (such as "Angola *nossa*, Angola é Portugal," "Our Angola, Angola is Portugal," which linked Angola's destiny with Portugal's) with new ones that stressed Angola's territorial integrity, nationalism, and loyalty to the MPLA. Some of the most popular and effective were "from Cabinda to Cunene," "from the sea to the east," "one people one nation," "MPLA is the people and the people are MPLA," and *poder popular* (people's power).[15] This type of campaigning proved extremely successful in motivating significant numbers of disadvantaged Kimbundu and frustrated *assimilado* and Afro-Portuguese in Luanda to affiliate with the MPLA. In fact, some of Luanda's young people quickly took "people's power" to mean that they "just come to your door and take everything they want".[16] These popular campaigns allowed many members of the oppressed Kimbundu population to challenge the state for the first time since the establishment of the dictatorship. Outside of the Kimbundu areas, however, the campaigns were less successful.

The MPLA's efforts at mobilizing the population in the capital paid off, not only because of the support of the urban Kimbundu and Afro-Portuguese, but also because the young officers who dominated the *Movimento das Forças Armadas* and had staged the coup wanted the MPLA to take over the state. This explains why the Portuguese army in Luanda did little to ensure that the unity transition government called for by the Alvor Agreement carried out its functions in Luanda. In large part this was because the new Portuguese leadership regarded the Portuguese-speaking Kimbundu and Afro-Portuguese leadership of the MPLA as fellow Portuguese, a camaraderie they did not feel for the French, Kikongo, amd Umbundu-speaking representatives of the FNLA and UNITA.

The pro-MPLA position of the new authorities in Lisbon became public in July 1974 when they nominated Admiral Rosa Coutinho, the "Red Admiral," to serve as high commissioner of Angola.[17] Before he took up his post, Coutinho let it be known that the MPLA was the only true revolutionary movement and that he would turn the state over to Agostinho Neto, the Luanda *assimilados*, and the Afro-Portuguese.[18] During the six months he held office he adopted a hands-off policy when military confrontation between partisans of MPLA and the FNLA seemed imminent.[19] It was this hands-off policy that allowed the MPLA to build up its military strength in Luanda. In fact, the MPLA was able to neutralize the Portuguese army still stationed in the colony, and rout the FNLA out of its strongholds in and around the capital Luanda mainly because of its ties to radical elements in the Lisbon government.[20]

The close ties that members of the new government had to the Portuguese Communist Party also guaranteed MPLA access to more committed support from the Soviet Union and Cuba.[21] Coutinho personally negotiated with Cuban officials to provide military and logistic help, so that the MPLA leadership could gain a military victory against UNITA and FNLA.[22] The Soviet Union made some tentative approaches to the MPLA as early as March 1974 by offering technical and logistical advice. By late spring, Soviet and Cuban advisors and arms appeared in Luanda. Yugoslavia and other Eastern bloc allies soon joined in.[23] It was early in 1975, however, that the MPLA leadership achieved a decisive military advantage over the other two movements when the Soviet Union, as part of its "global hegemonic strategy" in southern Africa, threw its weight behind Agostinho Neto.[24] By April 1975, Cuba sent the first two hundred military advisers to Angola. By November 5 the MPLA had between between a thousand and four thousand Cuban troops supporting its cause.

As military intervention by the superpowers became a reality, fighting between the MPLA and FNLA escalated, costing over five hundred lives in Luanda in early August. During the same period, the MPLA also succeeded in driving the FNLA forces from their Luanda strongholds. Indeed, talks broke down at the same time between Lopo do Nascimento and José N'dele, the MPLA and UNITA prime ministers in the provisional government, and the MPLA eventually turned UNITA and FNLA representatives out of Luanda.[25] The new equipment and training that Cuba and Russia provided allowed the MPLA to control all the roads leading out of Luanda. Thus, well before independence the MPLA leadership had consolidated its position in the capital, legitimizing its claim as the successor to the Portuguese state and the embodiment of Angolan nationalism. Its actions assured that the Alvor Agreement remained a dead letter.

The MPLA's victory in the capital led over a hundred thousand Kongo and Ovimbundu residents to flee Luanda, many of them pleading with Portuguese officials to provide them with armed escorts to their homelands. At the same time, thousands of Portuguese settlers and government officials also fled Luanda, many leaving by sea or air for Portugal or Brazil. The final victory of the MPLA came in September, when the remaining UNITA representatives left Luanda for Benguela and the central Angolan towns with some ten thousand supporters. As a result the provisional government collapsed and the MPLA was left in control of the state institutions in the capital.[26] Fighting also broke out in Nova Lisboa and other cities where MPLA supporters also attempted to take control over the machinery of state.

While consolidating its position inside Angola, the MPLA movement also mounted an international campaign, sending representatives to tour the capitals of African and Western countries to present its case. During those heady months, public sympathy for the MPLA escalated among activist groups and organizations, who accepted the MPLA's claim to be the rightful movement to inherit the postcolonial state. Even those governments which officially took a wait-and-see attitude essentially accepted the MPLA, but many other governments came out firmly and publicly behind the movement.[27]

In Africa, representatives of the Organization of African Unity (OAU) were reluctant to criticize the MPLA, and worked to avoid a repetition of the bloodletting that had occurred in the Belgian Congo more than a decade earlier. The representatives overlooked MPLA's intransigence and the authoritarian tendencies of its leadership.[28]

When Angola's independence came on November 11, 1975, the MPLA had succeeded in militarily overcoming Roberto's FNLA and outmaneuvering Savimbi. Neto and his Afro-Portuguese/Kimbundu supporters accepted the responsibility of rule from High Commissioner Leonel Cardoso, as four hundred years of Portuguese rule in Luanda came to an end. The victorious MPLA leaders raised the red, yellow, and black flag of the newly proclaimed People's Republic of Angola. In the background stood Cuban, Soviet, and Eastern European military advisors and technocrats, and thousands of members of militia, women's units, and guerrilla groups who would soon be called on to defend the new government against the anticipated onslaught from the FNLA-UNITA and their foreign supporters.[29]

The MPLA achieved full entry into African statehood on November 27, when Nigeria, at the time one of the most influential members of the OAU, and whose government had gone on record three days before the country's independence as condemning Soviet and Cuban intervention, changed its position and recognized the MPLA government.[30] By forestalling elections, the MPLA succeeded in depriving Savimbi of the opportunity of using his Ovimbundu ethnic bloc as an electoral force. They thus frustrated his goal of representing the Ovimbundu in the postcolonial state.[31]

UNITA, the Ovimbundu, and the Road to Civil War

In the aftermath of the coup, Savimbi and the UNITA leadership, like their MPLA counterparts, also attempted to take advantage of the rapidly changing situation to improve UNITA's image outside Angola and consolidate its position in Angola. In meetings with Portuguese military officials, with Presidents Nyerere, Kaunda, and Kenyatta of Tanzania, Zambia, and Kenya respectively, as well as Senegalese and Moroccan leaders, UNITA agreed to collaborate with the MPLA and FNLA. At these well-publicized meetings Savimbi presented UNITA as a centrist and multi-ethnic movement, contrasting it with what he stressed was the anti-Western position of the MPLA and the narrow ethnic aims of the FNLA. Savimbi argued that UNITA was the organization best equipped to head a transitional government.[32]

The first positive result came in May, when the Organization of African Unity (OAU) recognized UNITA as a legitimate liberation movement. Then, on June 14, when the new Portuguese leaders announced that they were suspending military action against the nationalists, Savimbi signed a cease-fire with Portuguese military commanders, and became the first nationalist leader to seek a peaceful transition to independence.[33] After this, several Western governments endorsed UNITA as a genuine nationalist movement.

Savimbi's strategy inside Angola focused on bringing recruits into the movement and building up the movement's military standing by the seeking financial and military support of settlers apprehensive about the MPLA's growing strength. By November 1974, UNITA's metamorphosis into a genuine nationalist movement, with the support of a significant segment of Angola's population, was almost complete. A *New York Times* reporter observed that UNITA had a realistic chance "to become a political force," and linked this to the movement's support by the Ovimbundu who comprised 38 percent of Angola's six million population and were the largest ethnic group.[34] As representatives from various Western countries officially recognized UNITA, Savimbi and the UNITA leadership began to plan for the time when they would run the government. Although militarily they were no match for the MPLA and FNLA, they pinned their hopes on elections, believing that they could rely on the support of the Ovimbundu and draw sufficient support from the FNLA and settlers to derail the MPLA.[35]

On January 15, 1975, when Savimbi headed the UNITA delegation to sign the Alvor Agreement that committed the three nationalist leaders to a transition government, the movement's status reached an all-time high. In fact, the language of the agreement led many Ovimbundu to believe that the coalition government would guarantee representative government. They could point to Article 8 of the Alvor Agreement and note that the Portuguese government pledged to transfer to Angolans "organs of sovereignty" and all the power the colonial state had held and exercised. In addition, the agreement called on the leaders to "settle in their rightful regions and localities," thus acknowledging ethnic regional divisions as well as Angolan national unity.[36]

Since one of his priorities was to increase the movement's membership, Savimbi focused particularly on bringing Ovimbundu migrant laborers and rural producers into the movement. Thus just as Holden Roberto put his hopes in the FNLA fighting forces, and Neto turned to his Communist allies, Savimbi planned to win contested elections with Ovimbundu backing, counting on the fact that the group would vote as an ethnic bloc for UNITA-sponsored candidates. Even before the public campaign to win Ovimbundu support began, UNITA was the movement of choice for the small number of educated Ovimbundu inside Angola. Many joined UNITA's ranks and soon oversaw a burgeoning political machinery in regions of the south with large Ovimbundu populations. Hundreds of thousands of uneducated rural cultivators and workers welcomed UNITA's representatives to villages in which Savimbi's exploits were already legendary. Rumor had it that he could fly, make himself disappear, and had outsmarted the Portuguese with his incredible powers.[37]

It was during the months following the signing of the cease-fire that Savimbi became the de facto leader of the Ovimbundu masses and the dominant force in Ovimbundu nationalism. No other leader challenged Savimbi's position, because Daniel Chipenda, the only potential competitor for Ovimbundu allegiance, was still a member of the MPLA and did not have a wide base of support among his fellow Ovimbundu. Savimbi was able not only to fulfill the dream he had had since 1966 of getting a significant number of the Ovimbundu people to support UNITA, but he also attracted other Africans from the rural regions of the south, as well as those Afro-Portuguese who had been raised with their African mothers in the towns and villages of the region.[38] Many of the settlers in the south, fearful of an uncertain future under a pro-Russian MPLA or a Kongo-led FNLA, also looked to Savimbi. Hoping to capitalize on their suspicions of the Communist-led government in Portugal which had abandoned them and promoted the MPLA, Savimbi encouraged them to join UNITA. He portrayed the movement as a populist, multi-racial political party which represented all Angolans.[39]

Savimbi, whose Machiavellian approach to nationalist politics has earned him the reputation as a superb politician with the qualities of "warlord, paramount chief, demagogue and statesman," was the main architect of UNITA's success.[40] His pragmatic, opportunistic attitude enabled him to push UNITA's cause at the national and international level, while his charisma and linguistic ability (many rural southerners were impressed by his mastery of most of the local languages as well as his tolerance and respect for local customs) gained him immense support in central and southern Angola.[41] UNITA's message attracted white settlers, international skeptics, and important segments of Angola's African population.

Savimbi and the UNITA leadership took advantage of the fast-changing situation after the coup, and by late summer UNITA's guerrillas were operating inside Angola in areas with large Ovimbundu constituencies, including Benguela, Lobito, Nova Lisboa and Silva Porto.[42] Savimbi expanded UNITA's membership with thousands of Ovimbundu who were sent for military training at the movement's central base at Massivi, while a number of seasoned guerrillas were sent to countries like Tanzania for officer training. He also stockpiled weapons that the movement had purchased from friendly governments and arms dealers.[43] As early as June 1974, after he signed the cease-fire, Savimbi set up his headquarters in Nova Lisboa at the estate of a former Portuguese industrialist. From there, he began to create a local party apparatus from almost nothing, and was soon directing his own transitional government, initiating diplomatic ties with a number of African and European governments. Before the Alvor Agreement, UNITA had become an umbrella for southern Angolans of many different political persuasions and a variety of ethnic, racial, and religious backgrounds.[44] As UNITA's popularity increased, Savimbi's detractors broadened their criticism of his tactics, especially faulting him for relying on white settler support.[45]

Moreover, his appeal to the Ovimbundu also strengthened the belief that UNITA was not a nationalist movement as its propaganda asserted, but an ethnic Ovimbundu organization. Indeed, Savimbi's pro-Ovimbundu campaign strategy kept many non-Ovimbundu southerners from making a commitment to UNITA. Many of them were aware that at the various public forums he held in the highlands, Savimbi openly appealed to Ovimbundu loyalty, outlining a future Angola where an ethnically plural society would be both Ovimbundu and Angolan.[46]

Although failing to attract firm support among large segments of the non-Ovimbundu population, Savimbi's message resonated through a broad spectrum of the Ovimbundu population. Soldiers, workers, students, clerks, to Protestants, Catholics, peasants, migrant laborers, and sobas and sekulus in the rural villages and plantations heeded his call. Young people barely in their early teens took out UNITA cards and signed up for military training, the numbers exceeding anything the leaders had expected.[47] By November 1974, UNITA had thousands of new Ovimbundu members, many of them brought through the efforts of settlers and former bureaucrats who had joined the movement and provided badly needed organizational expertise. When Savimbi signed the Alvor Agreement in January 1975, UNITA supporters were seasoned political campaigners, distributing hundreds of thousands of pamphlets in Benguela, Nova Lisboa, and the smaller urban centers in the highlands. They also sent campaign literature to strategic villages, barracks, prisons, and plantations where Ovimbundu communities were located, and opened and directed youth, military, communications, and other cells on behalf of the movement.[48]

Some of these new Ovimbundu recruits became part of the UNITA contingent that made up the quadripartite transitional government which was inaugurated in Luanda on January 31, 1975. Men like Almerinda Jaka Jamba, Jorge Valentim, Jermias Kalundula Chitunda and others joined their Cabindan and Guanhamas counterparts Fernando Wilson dos Santos, Miguel N'Zau Puna, and Benicio Chissalucombe to occupy the various portfolios UNITA shared with the MPLA and FNLA in the short-lived transitional government. These included the Ministries of Labor, Education and Culture, and Natural Resources, and Secretaries of State in various departments.[49] At this juncture the tensions which had kept educated Ovimbundu apart from the state faded, as they occupied some of the posts reserved for southerners in the transition government.[50]

Many Ovimbundu recruits became state functionaries, while the movement sent others to study in other African countries, Europe, and North and South America.[51] Other Ovimbundu expanded UNITA's military forces, as the UNITA leadership not only met but exceeded their obligation of supplying eight thousand soldiers for the mixed Portuguese-UNITA-MPLA-FNLA transitional force that was to replace the colonial army and the guerrilla forces. Some estimates put UNITA's forces in the months before independence at between fifteen thousand and sixteen thousand men and women.[52]

Convinced that with Ovimbundu, settler, and southern support the movement would win elections and gain control of the state in an independent Angola, Savimbi and the UNITA leadership seemed oblivious to the political crisis that was engulfing the country. Only when civil war seemed inevitable would some in the UNITA leadership raise the issue of delaying independence until Angolans could learn to live together.[53]

Savimbi's calculation that UNITA could capture the state in open elections was not mere speculation. An OAU delegation visiting Angola in April and May predicted that UNITA would win 60 percent of the votes if elections were held then. Thus in 1975, as the Portuguese were disengaging from the Angolan state, UNITA's forces worked with the transitional military

team to keep the peace in Luanda, despite growing tensions between partisans of the MPLA and FNLA. When, in September 1975, fighting raged
in Luanda, and Zairian troops, and Cuban, Portuguese, and South African
advisors were already in Angola, each to ensure that their liberation movement would gain the upper hand,[54] UNITA's leaders still acted as though
there were a chance for them to capture the state through contested elections. The movement's supporters in the urban and rural centers of the
south continued to campaign, attracting large crowds of Ovimbundu and
settlers, and seemingly ignoring the mounting chaos in the north.[55]

As the crisis worsened, the leadership found it difficult to expand the
movement's support base outside Angola. Unlike the MPLA, whose leaders could look to their Communist and socialist allies, or the FNLA whose
leader Roberto could rely on Zaire's Mobutu and on American assistance,
UNITA lacked strong backing from foreign governments. Moreover,
Savimbi's ties to the colonial army came under intense scrutiny in the crucial months leading up to independence. Thus while FNLA as well as MPLA
forces were securing strategic areas vital to their survival, Savimbi and
UNITA became more isolated. Their isolation was also due to their past
history of ties to the dictatorship and conservative settler elements in Angola.
In Europe and North America, they looked for new allies willing to regard
them as a stabilizing force in Angola. Former Congregationalist missionaries provided the means for UNITA representatives such as Maria Chela
and Rev. Frederico Mussili to argue Savimbi's case and ask for humanitarian support before congregations in Canada and the United States, in England, and at the World Council of Churches in Geneva.[56]

During the spring and early fall of 1975, UNITA's military weakness
and lack of popular support in Luanda paralyzed its representatives. The
movement could not compete with the MPLA whose guerrillas had captured key positions in Luanda from rebel forces loyal to Daniel Chipenda,
and moved to neutralize the FNLA presence in the capital. In the face of
the MPLA's victories, and continuing clashes between MPLA and FNLA
forces, UNITA's guerrilla detachment and representatives withdrew from
Luanda to Benguela and other central Angolan towns.[57]

UNITA and the Ovimbundu became even more regionalized when
the FNLA launched a campaign to control the Kongo-speaking area, leading to the expulsion of more than sixty thousand migrants and urban workers
from coffee fields and other localities in Carmona.[58] They joined the more
than ten thousand other Ovimbundu forced out of Luanda on the long,
dangerous, and arduous trek to the central Angolan region. The campaigns
of both the MPLA and the FNLA to clear their regions of the Ovimbundu

outsiders exposed the ethnic nature of the two northern movements, a condition that the anticolonial struggle had been unable to erase.

With his plans for taking over the state through elections derailed, and ethnicity apparently surfacing as an important factor in decolonization, Savimbi openly promoted Ovimbundu ethnic consciousness while still attempting to keep non-Ovimbundu people involved. He was able to rally the thousands of refugee Ovimbundu migrant laborers who arrived in the central highlands and who were ready to move against the northerners.[59] But Savimbi was not alone in exploiting ethnic sentiments, and for a while ethnic and regional nationalism supplanted the facade of national unity and democratic decolonization among the leaders of all three movements.

The State Contested: Angolans and the Politics of Nationhood

Savimbi and UNITA's most controversial move, however, was the decision to join the FNLA and CIA-supported mercenaries and troops from South Africa to contest the MPLA's claims to the state.[60] Although this relationship was decisive in salvaging the movement as a major factor in Angola's decolonization, Savimbi's MPLA rivals used it to question once again his position as a genuine Angolan anticolonialist. It also placed Angola in the middle of the Cold War.

Savimbi's continued military weakness allowed America to expand the Cold War geopolitical frontier, and orchestrated South Africa's presence deep in Angola. While Savimbi may have regarded the South African–CIA assistance as essential for his survival as a contender in postcolonial Angolan politics, his move compromised the Ovimbundu relationship with the postcolonial Angolan state. Years later, the unholy alliance would haunt the UNITA leadership.[61]

What Savimbi seemed to have totally disregarded at the time was that the events that would bring him into the South African orbit and send South African troops to Angolan soil were an outgrowth of the South African role as the bastion of white rule in Southern Africa. With the sudden collapse of white-ruled Portuguese Angola, and the reality of Marxist regimes emerging in both Mozambique and Angola, southern Africa became the center of Cold War politics and South Africa became its center of gravity. The plan to use Savimbi to stop the spread of Marxism that America and South Africa believed would occur with an MPLA victory was hastily conceived in the CIA headquarters in Washington, and in the headquarters of the South Africa Defense Force (SADF) in Pretoria, in the spring of 1974 following the coup in Portugal. Although this was the case, Savimbi willingly joined the game to ensure UNITA's military and political survival.

The original CIA/South Africa's plans did not involve Savimbi, but the FNLA, whose leader Holden Roberto had family ties with, and was supported by, the Mobuto regime in Zaire. In the wake of the Portuguese coup, officials of the Republican administration in the United States, convinced that the Russians were planning to expand their influence to southern Africa, increased their backing of the FNLA. Shortly afterwards, the South African government offered to a demoralized FNLA leadership and a militarily weak UNITA the prospect of gaining control over the Angolan state.[62] The decision to become involved in Angola had nothing to do with any desire by the United States government and its South African partner to help Angolans resolve their political differences. The move to support UNITA was a signal to the Soviet Union that the United States would "face them off" in Angola. The CIA was authorized to advance $300,000 in arms to UNITA's Jonas Savimbi, adding to the secret funds that had been channeled for some time to the FNLA's Holden Roberto. The Americans had the full support of Zaire's Mobutu and Zambia's Kaunda, both of whom feared a Marxist regime on their borders.[63] CIA support began reaching Savimbi by June 1975, and Mobutu had allowed fifteen hundred Zaïrian troops to join Roberto's guerrillas pushing into Luanda in March 1975.[64]

After the Lisbon coup, the regime in South Africa had every reason to seek African clients. With the imminent withdrawal of Portugal from its southern African colonies, Prime Minister Vorster of South Africa had to try and ensure that the buffer states of Angola and Mozambique did not come under the control of radicalized anti-Apartheid African regimes. South Africa and the CIA sought out UNITA, believing that Savimbi would make a more pliable client than the avowedly Marxist ZANU guerrillas fighting against the Smith regime in Rhodesia, or Agostinho Neto and Samora Machel, whose Marxist rhetoric and distaste for the apartheid system were no secret.[65] They may have hoped that if a militarily strengthened Savimbi could weaken MPLA sufficiently, then Neto would be willing to compromise.

Savimbi's willingness to accept South African assistance strengthened the distrust of many in international "progressive" circles who believed that he did not truly represent the rural strain of Angolan nationalism.[66] Thus, at a time when the MPLA was proclaiming that it was the legitimate voice of the popular masses in Angola by seeking help from the Soviet Union and Cuba, UNITA and the FNLA's collaboration with South Africa marked Savimbi, and those who supported him, as neocolonial agents. The fact that this was a hastily put together alliance, after the South Africans had failed to recruit the disaffected MPLA leader Daniel Chipenda in March 1975, confirmed for many the suspicion that Savimbi was an unprincipled opportunist.[67]

At the time, Savimbi defended the relationship, noting that, "If you are a drowning man in a crocodile-infested river and you've just gone under for the third time, you don't question who is pulling you to the bank until you're safely on it."[68] By linking his inexperienced troops with the South Africans and the mercenaries that CIA money helped attract, Savimbi demonstrated his ability for political survival despite international criticism. Years later, he defended his South African connection by pointing out that although he was against apartheid, "We would receive help from wherever it came; that does not represent for us abdication of principles."[69]

The war for control of Angola began between August and October 1975 when Zairian commandos and paratroopers entered northern Angola in support of FNLA guerrillas fighting to limit the MPLA's advances in Luanda. At the same time a thousand SADF troops invaded Angola and occupied the Cunene region bordering Namibia.[70] The real test came on October 23, when a fifteen-hundred-man South African force fanned out from the Cunene, and with strategic air cover from the South African Air Force, quickly moved north. At the same time, thousands of recently trained UNITA soldiers and hundreds of foreign mercenaries marched to Luanda. By November, lightning success had been achieved along the Benguela-Lobito coast, and by mid-December the South African forces and UNITA reinforcements were poised at 180 miles south of Luanda.[71]

Despite the rapid advances the FNLA and combined UNITA-SADF forces made, the political fallout from the South African invasion soon immobilized the advance. In the weeks following the invasion, Savimbi found himself embroiled in a propaganda war. The same Western press that had promoted him and UNITA as representing the best hope for an independent Angola now relentlessly exposed his South African and CIA connections.

While Savimbi's status was under attack, the MPLA's stature as the legitimate government of independent Angola soared and Neto was able to welcome Soviet military advisers and Cuban troops without widespread condemnation from African and other governments. Socialist Yugoslavia, Hungary, Algeria, Mali, and Guinea-Conakry were the first countries to recognize the MPLA government when they allowed Cuba and the Soviet Union to use their air space to airlift men and equipment to the MPLA. Socialist governments guaranteed the MPLA access to military hardware and technical training and expertise. News of the South African invasion pushed countries which had withheld support from the MPLA to back it in order to derail the UNITA-backed South African–CIA plans. Thus, Tanzania's government seized Chinese arms that had been sent for the training of UNITA forces.

In was in this atmosphere that Savimbi and Roberto celebrated with twenty thousand supporters the establishment of the short-lived Democratic People's Republic of Angola, disregarding the skirmishes among the very troops who were in Nova Lisboa (renamed Huambo) for the event.[72] Less than three weeks after the establishment of the two independent Angolan republics, they were at war. This, however, was not just a civil war between the MPLA which had inherited the colonial state and the UNITA/FNLA leaders who wanted to wrest it from their rivals, but was an outgrowth of the Cold War between the United States and the Soviet Union. The war became both a civil war between Angolan nationalists and a proxy war between Cold War enemies.[73]

In the short run, the MPLA came out victorious on both the diplomatic front and the battlefield. With massive assistance from the Soviet Union and its Communist allies, it led a counterattack against the FNLA-mercenary units and the South African and UNITA armies. During the first week of December 1975, MPLA-Cuban troops succeeded in retaking Ambriz in the north and Luso in the east. By early January, 1976, they had taken over the last northern FNLA outpost at Santo Antonio do Zaire.[74]

The MPLA-Cuban forces also proved victorious in the south, where the South African–UNITA forces had placed a cordon around Luanda. With massive Soviet airlift of materials from December 1975 through January 1976, the MPLA forces moved south. By the third week of January, UNITA-SADF positions in Novo Redondo, Benguela, Lobito, and other areas to the south were under massive air, sea, and land attack. This offensive and the diplomatic turnaround resulting from the worldwide press condemnation of South Africa's invasion frayed the shaky alliance between the South Africans, UNITA, FNLA, and the governments in Lusaka and Kinshasa which had secretly supported the invasion. South African policymakers and military leaders quickly reassessed their Angolan adventure. On January 24, 1976, Defense Minister Pieter Botha announced the country's retreat from the outskirts of Luanda, but left more than five thousand troops in the narrow strip bordering Namibia.[75]

In the United States, a popular outcry forced the government to reassess CIA involvement in Angola and to cut off the secret funds that the CIA had been funneling to the FNLA and UNITA. The greatest blow to

Savimbi's hopes came in January 1976 when the United States Congress passed the Clark Amendment that stopped the CIA from secretly aiding the Angolan combatants.[76] As a result, the MPLA-Cuban alliance pressed its attack against Huambo, where UNITA had its headquarters. On November 7, when Fidel Castro launched Operation Carlota, the air-bridge between Cuba and Angola became firmly established. Cuban troop strength reached 12,000 by January 1976,[77] peaking at between 35,000 and 45,000 soldiers by 1986.[78]

In the wake of the MPLA/Cuban advance, Savimbi, his guerrillas, and thousands of supporters retreated east to Luso and then to Gago Coutinho. When Gago Coutinho was bombed a month later on March 13, he and his thousand-strong contingent retreated to the Cuanza. There in May he gave a speech in which he vowed that Angola would have "no peace nor economic development."[79]

Thus the prospect of a long civil war became a reality, and the issues that had separated the Ovimbundu from the state were no nearer being resolved than they had been during the colonial period. Diplomatically isolated and militarily outmanned, the group trudged east in a "long march" that took them 3,000 kilometers at the cost of all but 79 survivors. They settled at Culei, a region about 150 kilometers southeast of Huambo province, and appropriately called "the end of the world" (*o fim do mundo*). There Savimbi and the survivors evaded MPLA-Cuban military attacks, rebuilt their guerrilla army, and remained hidden from international scrutiny until 1977.[80]

The war against UNITA and the South Africans switched the diplomatic tide in favor of the MPLA. By the end of February the OAU formally recognized the MPLA government. With the exception of the United States of America, most other governments recognized the movement, and the MPLA and its leadership took steps to consolidate its position over the state.[81]

The MPLA-PT: Constructing the Postcolonial State

Although the victorious MPLA had gained control over the country, its hold was still tenuous. The new government was still threatened by fratricidal wars, major social dislocations, and economic disaster. The most pressing concern of the authorities was the crisis in the bureaucracy caused by the disorderly departure of more than three hundred thousand Portuguese settlers who had dominated the state and the economy. Another issue was how to cater to the large refugee African populations which filled all the urban centers. Faced with this situation, the government consolidated its control by strengthening the authoritarian institutions of the state rather than addressing the issue of local autonomy. The prospect of success, however, rested on the willingness of the MLA to allow representative government or on its ability to defeat a resurgent UNITA. The MPLA leadership, however, never envisioned establishing representative institutions, and was unable to defeat UNITA.

The MPLA leadership transformed their movement into a national party by moving to expand from its primarily urban, intellectual, mulatto, and Kimbundu base. To the movement's strategists, this transformation was essential for the social revolution which they had begun in the villages of the "liberated zone" during the fight against the Portuguese. They regarded this as the first step in the emergence of the *homem novo*, the modern Angolan citizen.[82]

At its First Congress held in December 1977, the Central Committee of the MPLA voted to transform the movement into a "Marxist-Leninist party of militants," comprising "workers, peasants and revolutionary intellectuals." The movement, now called the MPLA-*Partido dos Trabalhadores* (the MPLA-PT), was confirmed in a new constitution and given a leading role in the government. Its prime responsibility was to exercise a "democratic revolutionary dictatorship" that would make Angola a socialist state.[83] In 1980, the party approved the establishment of a parliament, with those involved in the popular assemblies being eligible for election.

The party structure was arranged hierarchically from the central ministries down through provincial levels, represented by party secretaries and provincial heads, through municipal commissioners to the party cells. The armed civil defence force and secret service also became part of the party organization.

By 1990, the MPLA-PT government in many ways resembled the colonial state that it had replaced. The major agencies of the government, including the army (FAPLA—The People's Armed Forces for the Liberation of Angola), the secret service (DISA), and provincial and municipal agencies, in many respects resembled the colonial army, PIDE, and the provincial divisions and postos of the previous regime. In addition local party apparatus including the women's group (OMA), the trade union organization (UNTA), the youth arm of the party (JMPLA), and the children's organization, enabled the government to control the urban population, as PIDE and the network of informers had done during the colonial period. Like the colonial state, the MPLA-PT permitted favored members of the party to run the state bureaucracy, and nationalized businesses, schools, universities, and radio and television.[84]

The regime's success in building a one-party government was largely due to earnings from oil (after 1979, oil was the major source of government revenues) and military and technical assistance from Cuba and the Soviet Union. Cuba masterminded the plan to build up the armed forces, and provided military, educational, and technical expertise to the government. Oil money financed the over fifty thousand Cuban soldiers and technical personnel deployed in Angola by 1990. The Soviet Union played a crucial role in building up the government's armed forces, delivering nearly $1 billion annually in arms during the 1980s.[85] By the 1980s, FAPLA consisted of conscripts from the entire country, trained by Cuban and Eastern European–educated officers. It numbered two hundred thousand men and women and played a central role in maintaining the MPLA in power.[86]

The MPLA leadership argued that the role of the party was to transform Angola's population (more than 90 percent of whom were illiterate rural producers and former plantation workers) into "workers, peasants and revolutionary intellectuals." The party was also charged with fighting against "terrorists" both inside and outside Angola who were regarded as "stooges of foreign powers."

Apart from building up the army and the secret service, and placing party members at the head of various government agencies, the leadership also continued the ideological campaign to enhance the party image and advance their concept of Angolan nationality. The drive began with mass ideological campaigns in the urban centers where party officials emphasized slogans such as *poder popular* ("people's power") to stress the party's popular base, and "um só povo, uma só nacão" ("one people, one nation") to press the claims that the MPLA was a popular government and that all Angolans made up the nation. Throughout the cities and regions where MPLA control reached, especially in the schools, army barracks, and popular organizations, people learnt to identify with the new nation through these slogans.[87] Moreover, the party clamped down on dissidents and critics who accused the leaders of "bourgeois tendencies." Neto led the attack in February, 1976, warning that "there can be only one MPLA . . . with a single leader and no others."[88]

Yet the party was not open to everyone, for only individuals who went through rigorous re-education or participation in the various youth, women's, civil defence, and party satellite organizations (the labor unions, for example) became members. Thus, despite its success in taking over the government and placing its own appointees in the bureaucracy throughout the country, the MPLA-PT never became a national party. By 1985 only half of the party membership of 34,732 could claim peasant and working class roots, and the majority had origins in Luanda and the other Kimbundu regions. The 300,000 members in the various "mass organizations" were also of Kimbundu background,[89] and sixty to seventy percent of Angolans had no party affiliation. Furthermore, outside the Kimbundu areas, and especially in the central highlands where UNITA sympathies still ran high, people regarded the government and its organizations with distrust, believing that they were set up to deny them representation in ways similar to past Portuguese policies.[90] Indeed, Kimbundu and Afro-Portuguese dominance in the party hierarchy (as of 1987–88 only two Ovimbundu, Marcelino Moco who held the post of prime minister, and Faustino Muteka, held ministerial positions) and other organizations had discouraged the efforts of party representatives to recruit members from outside the Kimbundu region. City-bred Kimbundu and Afro-Portuguese party officials never seriously tried to overcome local resentments.

In the central highlands, the identification of the MPLA as the party of the Kimbundu was compounded by the resurgence of UNITA after 1977, with supporters throughout the region. Building a strong government and ruling party presence in the region proved difficult, in part because the local population was suspicious of a government identified with the Kimbundu and the urban elite. The Cuban soldiers' anti-UNITA campaigns and the government's counter-insurgency methods in the region also alienated most Ovimbundu from the party and state.[91]

By the 1980s, as the civil war intensified, guerrillas of the reborn UNITA increasingly infiltrated government-controlled regions, and gathered firsthand information about the MPLA-PT. UNITA planted Ovimbundu spies within the party and the government to furnish information on Cuban and Angolan troop movements, and recruited or conscripted new batches of recruits to join it in the bush. In addition, in 1983 UNITA's Radio *Vorgan* was able to supply its own nationalist propaganda.[92] This countered the government's efforts to expand its party's base in the Ovimbundu region. Thus, although many rural Ovimbundu moved to the cities, the government's efforts to recruit Ovimbundu into the ruling party and to reach out to the population had little success. Like the *assimilados* under the New State, Ovimbundu who became involved in the ruling party conformed to MPLA (Afro-Portuguese) cultural norms. For many, comformity to the party's program was the only way to improve their economic status and shield themselves from accusations that they were secretly supporting UNITA's ethnic politics. Their affiliation to the state however, stemmed more from their concern for their own security than from any conviction that the government represented their interests. The spectacle of public trials, executions, and intelligence gathering, which the government carried out to intimidate anti-government elements, distanced most Ovimbundu from the party and the state. Up to the late 1980s, Ovimbundu peasants and workers comprised a minority of the MPLA-PT membership and they remained under-represented in the state.[93]

But alienation from the party and the state was not confined to the Ovimbundu since the MPLA-PT never became a popular party. Indeed, by 1990, ruling party membership had fallen to about 31,000 persons out of a population of more than six million. The party was led by a 90 member Central Committee with an inner group who formed the Political Bureau.[94] In most regions under MPLA-PT control, particulary in the cities and centers with large concentrations of Kimbundu, most people accepted the head of the party as president of the nation, and obeyed the constitution which gave the party's Central Committee the right, when ratified by the membership, to run the government.

In the economic sphere, the government's socialist agenda failed to improve the welfare of all but a small minority of Angola's population. State management of the economy failed miserably. In the early days of the regime, MPLA officials quickly nationalized banks and insurance companies and negotiated new contracts with the oil companies to continue offshore operations and explorations in the Cabinda region. They also replaced the *escudo* with a new currency, the *kwanza*, and took over 85 percent of the plantations and lands, and industrial, mining, and trading enterprises that Portuguese settlers had abandoned. They set up farmers' cooperatives and producers' associations. The government also adopted a series of social welfare policies, dealing with the health and education of children (especially war orphans), war veterans, refugees, and displaced persons.[95]

Although on paper the initiatives strengthened the economy, the government did not have the trained management personnel to succeed in its massive nationalization. In the end, it came to rely for its revenues on the earnings of the foreign-managed national oil company, Sonangol, in which it had a 51 percent share, and the nationalized diamond industry, in which it held a 61 percent share.[96]

Until the mid-1980s, the government's policies did have some success in bringing about the first genuine social revolution for Africans in the country. For example, the number of Angolans enrolled in primary schools increased from fewer than half a million in 1974 to over two million children in 1980. The government also ran a widespread adult literacy campaign that spread literacy among an unprecedented number of adults, many of them in the armed forces. Thus, while adult literacy was estimated at only 12 percent in 1970, the literacy rate had risen to 36 percent by 1985.[97] Also, all areas of public health, especially infant mortality, had improved within a decade after 1974.[98]

Like the *bem estar* policies of the Salazar period, however, the socialist programs of the MPLA government did not have the long-term impact intended. By the beginning of the 1990s, most of the health and educational gains were reversed. Elementary school enrollment fell, while secondary school enrollment remained low by modern African standards.[99] Military and civilian casualties were so high that the advances in public health gained by the additional clinics and hospitals were slowed. In 1991 a sympathetic visitor to the country described the two major hospitals in Luanda, the Josina Machel and the Américo Boavida, as being "hell-holes."[100] This situation was a direct result of the continuing civil war.[101]

The downward spiral was also evident in the economy, since, according to United Nations estimates, between 1980 and 1990 the civil war caused $30 billion in material damage to the infrastructure.[102] Despite claims of a robust state sector that "accounted for 80 percent of the output of consumer goods and foodstuffs and 50 percent of heavy industry,"[103] the nationalization of industrial and agricultural enterprises (over 80 percent of the economy by the early 1980s) proved a complete disaster.[104] Except for oil, whose production increased from 140,000 barrels per day in 1975 to 500,000 in 1991, and diamonds which together with natural gas brought in $1 billion (U.S.) annually, all other sectors of the economy declined .[105] As was noted earlier, revenues from oil provided the government with most of the hard cash with which to fight the civil war, pay for the social programs, and finance the stay of (*cooperantes*) (foreign workers) to help manage the bloated bureaucracy.[106] The government was also heavily indebted to the Soviet Union by 1990.

The state of the economy was not only due to government policies but in large measure to the UNITA-led civil war which devasted the rural areas. The decline in the agricultural production was particularly noticeable in the plantation sector, where the government had taken over some of the older and better-managed plantations. By the late 1980s, state-owned farms run by party members produced only between 5 and 10 percent of the coffee, sisal, cotton, and sugar cane formerly produced by settlers. Coffee production, for example, which in 1973 made Angola the fourth largest producer in the world, dropped from 241,000 tons in the 1970s to 4500 tons by the end of the 1980s.[107] The peasant sector fared worse. Although in 1985 the country was supposed to have over 4,000 peasant associations and 400,000 peasants in cooperatives,[108] by 1990 peasant food production had collapsed. The flow of maize from the highlands stopped completely, and production for Angola as a whole declined precipitously, going from 500,000 tons in the mid-1970s to only 180,000 tons in the early 1990s.[109] Moreover, although 70 to 75 percent (700,779) of Angolan families were still listed as peasants, most of them had been displaced from their farms due to land mines and government and UNITA resettlement programs.[110]

In addition to the effects of wastage caused by the government's socialist economic policies, the human capital of the country was wasted in the vicious civil war between the government and UNITA. By 1990, more than five hundred thousand Angolans had died and more than one million had become refugees as a result of the civil war. Added to this was a foreign debt that totaled $6.5 billion, and a government supply system that could not keep up with basic demand. As a result, informal markets (*candongas*) flourished, and basic goods smuggled into the cities or stolen from government warehouses were sold at exorbitant prices, while shelves in government-run shops remained empty. Furthermore, urban sprawl had become uncontrollable as frightened and starving peasants crowded into the cities. By the early 1990s, Luanda's population stood at 927,867 and accounted for about 15 percent of the country's total population, while other urban centers such as Huambo, Lobito, and Benguela had also witnessed substantial population gains.[111] The economic decline was noticeable even in areas like Cabinda, that were not touched by the war. The party had succeeded in building up a party structure and in retaining control of the state but had lost the economic war due to the effectiveness of UNITA's campaign of economic sabotage.[112]

The government's political achievements also fell far short of what the intellectuals of the party had anticipated, as the MPLA-PT remained overwhelmingly urban and ethnically Kimbundu in its leadership and membership. The promotion of a one-party state with a single ideology turned the party into an exclusive club protecting the interests of party and state bureaucrats, instead of meeting the needs of Angola's rural and urban masses. Moreover, collectivization of agriculture after independence, and the killing, arrest and intimidation of those suspected of supporting UNITA or of other anti-MPLA activities alienated significant segments of the Angolan population.

Distrust of the government began in 1977 with political reprisals against those supporting the Nito Alves faction within the MPLA-PT. This group came out in support of a more African-centered focus in the party,

against what they argued was its mulatto-dominated leadership.[113] In response, the party purged the pro–Nito Alves faction in the Central Committee and armed forces, dismantled the evolving popular democratic structures, and consolidated power in the party. In 1984 when it established the
Defense and Security Council, (DISA) and reorganized other organs of the
party, it widened the gap between the government and its critics. Even in
1989–90 when the MPLA leadership took steps to introduce a multi-party
system, the leaders still envisioned a situation in which the MPLA-PT would
continue to shape Angolan nationalism. Mateus Júlio Paulo, a member of
the Political Bureau, emphasized the government's strategy when he observed that the purpose of the government's dealings with UNITA was to
encourage its supporters to lay down their arms and "rejoin your people,
who, led by the MPLA-PT, are tackling the task of national rehabilitation."[114] This statement was made at a time when the party apparatus was
still dominated by Afro-Portuguese intellectuals who represented less than
one percent of the population, with Kimbundus making up the core of the
party membership and government. The party had also failed women who,
although they comprised a significant segment of the membership, held
few decision-making positions. In 1990, of the ninety members of the
Central Committee, only six were females, and only one woman was on
the Political Bureau.[115] Furthermore, the government's dismal record on
incorporating rural Angolans into the administration had not changed. In
fact, Cabinda, the contested region that supplied most of the oil (thus the
government had strong motives for bringing its population fully into the
party), was the only non-Kimbundu region that had a fair number of representatives in the party.[116]

Government and party policies had also alienated major segments of
the population, including churchgoers and the traditional rural leadership
that had survived the colonial period. This made attempts at reconciliation
between the MPLA-PT and UNITA frustrating. Chester Crocker, recalling the many failed attempts to reach a settlement between the two parties
during the late 1980s, concluded that the government was weak as a result
of the many ideological factions in the party and because of its "dependence on and vulnerability to its external allies."[117] For these reasons, many
in the ruling party feared UNITA.

In his 1990 May Day speech President José Eduardo dos Santos, who
had succeeded Agostinho Neto as party head after the latter's death in 1979,
publicly acknowledged the difficulties he faced keeping the many ideological and racial factions together. He denounced members of the party and
government who were "reactionary and corrupt bourgeois elements" and

who were "attempting to undermine the unity and cohesion of the party and state."[118] Two years later, in anticipation of the scheduled 1992 elections, he again berated party members and officials for their alienation from the people, pointing out that it was time to "abandon the comfort of our own offices and conference rooms and to actively live with the people where they are."[119]

Local Administration and the UNITA Menace

MPLA-PT's failure was the result not only of its socialist programs and the uncompromising and corrupt position of some of its leadership, but of the successful guerrilla war that Jonas Savimbi and the UNITA organization waged against the MPLA-PT government from 1975 to 1991. During these years, Savimbi's powerful personality and the UNITA movement which he led symbolized Ovimbundu and rural nationalism contesting against the Kimbundu and mulatto-dominated postcolonial state. The acts of economic sabotage that UNITA's guerrillas carried out (including the operations of some units that targeted civilians) thwarted the government's programs in the rural countryside and in the cities. Their activities, along with their widespread military confrontations against the government's forces, helped to derail MPLA-PT's efforts to have total control over the postcolonial state. UNITA's survival under Savimbi's leadership and its co-optation of the aspirations of the Ovimbundu and other rural populations help to explain the problems the MPLA-PT faced in dealing with these populations.

In the beginning of the civil war, many Ovimbundu regarded Jonas Savimbi as their representative in dealings with the postcolonial state. They admired his charisma, leadership skills, and geopolitical expertise and flexibility. It was these qualities that allowed him to be the dominant force in UNITA and to develop the movement into a creditable opposition force. By the 1980s UNITA had emerged with an organizational structure and leadership that represented Ovimbundu nationalism.

The major reason Savimbi came to play such a crucial role in the transformation of UNITA was because of the links he developed with the South African regime.

Disregarding the view of his many critics that the "manipulative and condescending Afrikaner regime" was black Africa's worst enemy, Savimbi strengthened his ties with the South Africans, who helped him rebuild UNITA and come back as a formidable force against the MPLA-PT by the mid-1980s.

Apart from retaining his core Ovimbundu base, Savimbi expanded the war against the MPLA-PT and enhanced UNITA's multi-ethnic appeal by attracting other Angolans who remained wary of the MPLA. He also repackaged his own image, changing from Maoist to anti-imperialist to democrat as his political fortunes improved.

As he had demonstrated between 1974 and 1976 when he was maneuvering to become a legitimate contender for state power, Savimbi's ideological metamorphosis between 1976 and 1992 rested on his ability to tap into the deeply entrenched regional and ethnic sentiments in Angola. He was supported by a small core of loyal followers who believed in his version of Angolan nationalism. When the Cuban-MPLA forces drove him out of the highlands, the charismatic Savimbi made an emotional appeal to his followers, calling on them to defend the Angolan homeland from Cuban and Russian invaders. He emphasized the ideals of freedom and human dignity, promising that a day would come when Angolans would be able "to live as free men with the right to choose our own leaders and system of government in our country."[120] He also warned skeptics that "those who doubt us never believed in the creative capacity of men when inspired by noble and just ends."[121] Savimbi achieved a cult-like stature among his supporters, being referred to with the honorific titles of *Molowini* ("son of the people"), *Muata da Paz* ("leader of peace"), and *Jaguar Negro das Jagas* ("black jaguar of the hunters").[122]

Between 1976 and 1992, when UNITA participated in the first general elections in Angola, Savimbi kept his promise. The first strategy was to rebuild his guerrilla force. Here the arms and aid he received from Morocco, Saudi Arabia, and Senegal, but particularly from South Africa, which re-deployed soldiers in Angola in 1979 to stop the infiltration into Namibia of MPLA-supported SWAPO guerrillas, was invaluable. With South African technical and military assistance he built his movement's fighting capacity to a level which some estimates put as high as 71,000 men and women in guerrilla and units by the early 1990s.[123] His guerrillas and regular forces (including rogue elements that terrorized and exploited the population) fought battles against combined Cuban and government forces, and brought the war to the cities and rural areas all over Angola.

Paradoxically, the economic sabotage campaign which UNITA waged against the MPLA-PT government also forced many among the rural population to look to UNITA and not to the government for support and security. The campaign had begun in 1977 in response to the MPLA's socialist shift, and by 1983 when UNITA again began receiving direct support from

South Africa, the leadership broadened its strategy aimed at economic sabotage of Angola. Its guerrillas roamed all over Angola, hitting transport routes in the north and east, especially the diamond-producing Lunda Province, with the aim of pressuring the MPLA government into a negotiated political settlement.[124] Some generals also became involved in diamond trading (an activity that after 1992 became crucial to UNITA's survival as a well-equipped military force able to fight against the MPLA army).

By 1988 UNITA's military capacity had improved substantially, despite heavy losses in battles with Cuban and government forces. The movement's strategy of economic sabotage throughout the country exacted an astounding political and human toll.[125] The perseverance of UNITA's guerrillas, who successfully harassed government forces in the five provinces in the southern part of the country, attracted growing support for the movement in the West. Leon Dash of *The Washington Post* reported that he had traveled more than 2,100 miles with the guerrillas during a seven and a half months in 1977. He concluded that UNITA's war of "attrition, sabotage, economic disruption and terrorism" against MPLA and Cuban troops was wreaking havoc on the country.[126]

UNITA began to expand the war against the MPLA regime in 1983 as a result of the material support and training that the movement received from South Africa; it accelerated the pace after 1985 when the repeal of the Clarke Amendment brought in United States aid. By 1989 the United States had become the major military supporter of UNITA, providing the movement with anti-aircraft and anti-tank missiles and training worth up to $50 million (U.S.).[127] South African support was estimated to total some $80 million dollars.[128] Savimbi's most crucial military victory against the MPLA-PT came in May, 1990, when UNITA forces, with South African support, defeated a combined Cuban-MPLA force and regained control over the strategic southeastern town of Mavinga. This campaign, the costliest in the civil war, forced the government to spend an estimated $400–800 million and resulted in between 4,000 and 6,000 government casualties.[129]

UNITA's well-staged attacks on vital economic and military targets inside government-controlled areas of Angola catapulted the movement back into the international limelight. Its relationship with South Africa, its ability to regroup its forces, the determination of its soldiers who defended strategic bases like Mavinga and other areas of the south, and its bold acts of economic sabotage made UNITA a credible alternative to those whom MPLA-PT policies had alienated. Although the press was far from sympathetic (Savimbi especially came under attack for human rights violations among the civilian population),[130] UNITA played a crucial role in the proxy war between the Soviet Union and the United States and found support among many leaders and groups in the West.

UNITA also went a long way towards rebuilding the party structure, which had almost collapsed, and the regional base that it had lost to the MPLA in 1976. Savimbi expanded the movement's political base, converting UNITA into a party with a Central Committee, military, youth, and women's organizations and local committees or cells, which paralleled the MPLA-PT's structure and made UNITA a more populist and centralized organization, comparable to the MPLA-PT.[131] By 1979, the UNITA leadership was so confident that they took the ambitious step of establishing their own autonomous region, the "Republic" at Jamba, in the "lands at the end of the world" in southeastern Angola. In 1989 Jamba covered 470,000 square kilometers and had a population of eight hundred thousand to a million.[132] Although a large number of its people had been forcibly removed from rural villages surrounding UNITA-controlled regions and were war refugees, they came to rely on the health, educational, and social services UNITA offered. At that time, Savimbi's claims that UNITA controlled a significant segment of Angola's population could not be dismissed.

A 1989 U.S. government-sponsored mission to assess conditions in areas controlled by UNITA provided the first detailed look at the political administration of UNITA-controlled areas. UNITA party structure was composed of a 35–member Political Bureau and Central Committee, regional commissioners, village committees, and cells. The military and the civil administration completed the bureaucracy. Like the MPLA-PT, the party's membership was small, totalling only thirty thousand persons and including senior members of the military and other departments.

Several ministries delivered services to the population, including health and social welfare and education. The civilian villages outside the central area of Jamba that were under UNITA control were not local cells sowing the seeds of democracy. To build support for the movement, the traditional village structure was left intact, with sekulus chosen by the villagers in charge of affairs. These elders were responsible to a chief elder who was appointed by the party, and who was also the main contact between the villagers and the party representative.[133]

Indeed, the basic administrative pattern did not depart much from the indirect administrative structure that most of Angola's rural population had been accustomed to under both the colonial and precolonial regimes. While the MPLA's policies aimed at re-educating the rural leaders alienated member of this group and led some to label the period from 1977 to 1992 as "the worst period lived by the sekulu in Angola,"[134] UNITA's strategy of "mobilizing rather than re-educating," by organizing cells and working through village committees under traditional leadership, brought them closer to the movement. UNITA had the support of loyal local leaders who brought their people into its fold.[135] UNITA's social, health, agricultural, and educational policies in the central Jamba administrative region provided some essential services to the refugee population.[136] For all its emerging organizational structure, however, the movement remained a guerrilla organization, and the leadership lagged far behind the MPLA's in terms of formal education and adminstrative experience.

During the period of the civil war, Savimbi and the UNITA leadership conveniently shifted their political ideology as they attempted to attract popular support in Angola and expand their international base of support. Leon Dash's 1977 perceptive appraisal of Savimbi as "an enigma, . . . brilliant . . . Machiavellian, opportunistic lying, nationalist, Marxist, Maoist, pro-Western and socialist"[137] was a fitting description of the mishmash of ideas which characterized Savimbi and the movement. Although during the 1980s the leadership attempted to transform UNITA from a guerrilla movement into a political party, Savimbi's ideology still comprised a mixture of ideas, ranging from socialist doctrines borrowed from the Chinese and North Korean models, to Négritude, liberal democracy, and precolonial African ideology.[138] UNITA's publications and Savimbi's pronouncements hammered away at the MPLA-PT, alleging that it was a minority party with an alien ideology articulated by urban Afro-Portuguese and *assimilados*.[139]

Savimbi's attempts to transform UNITA into an effective military force and a political organization with a nationalist ideology shaped by Angolan experience had both contradictions and detractors. By the early 1980s, opposition arose within the movement and led to deep dissension in what had been a clearly knit guerrilla movement. Some members of the UNITA, especially leaders from Cabinda and the Guanhamas, increasingly resented the power of an inner circle of ethnic Ovimbundu loyal to Savimbi.[140]

The most damaging accusation against Savimbi and his inner circle concerned acts of political repression and political murders which resulted from attempts to bring about conformity and support for Savimbi's policies. The factionalism came to the attention of the world in 1989, after an international outcry against Savimbi for the arrest of the popular Tito Chingunji, a high-ranking representative who had manned the Washington office. Tito was killed in 1991, and Savimbi was accused of being responsible for his death.[141]

Additionally, former high-ranking leaders like the Cabindan António Fernandes accused UNITA of exploiting some of the antidemocratic elements of precolonial political ideology, including witchcraft trials and the dismemberment, drowning, and burning as witches and sorcerers of political critics. Detractors charged that some of these activities had been going on as early as the early 1980s. Furthermore, it was rumored that long-time members of the organization, such as the former foreign secretary Jorge Sangumbe, and the leading Ovambo (Guanhamas) commander António Vakulukutu, who had criticized Savimbi's South African links, had actually been murdered.[142] Such incidents, which demonstrated Savimbi's penchant for exercising unbridled authority, also illustrated his ability to retain control over the rural population. Among rural Angolans, Savimbi's penchant for spicing his speeches with a range of local proverbs and other cultural motifs in order to better communicate was legendary, and his manipulation of folk beliefs, especially those dealing with witchcraft, united him with rural supporters.[143] Thus despite the outcry from the Western press, the accusations of witch burning had little effect on Savimbi's political standing among his supporters, and may even have enhanced it.[144]

Savimbi's ability to rebuild UNITA and survive politically was largely due to the support of a hard core of Ovimbundu and other rural people. The continued presence in leadership positions of a number of non-Ovimbundu southerners, as well as northerners, also bolstered UNITA's political fortunes. The movement relied on South African and United States military support, and used economic sabotage and enforced recruitment which caused unparallelled suffering among the rural population. However, the movement's ability to challenge the MPLA-PT ultimately rested on the fact that it had the support of a significant portion of the Ovimbundu and other rural Angolans. UNITA became the opposition party, offering people what appeared to be a more inclusive party, an ideology that stressed Angola's position as an African country, and a economic model based on free market principles.[145]

Conclusion

As 1991 began, the end of the war seem to be in sight for Angolans, as the collapse of the Soviet Union brought about the end of the cold War and South African and Cuban troops no longer needed to fight a proxy war in Angola. On May 30, the world waited with bated breath as Savimbi and Dos Santos signed United States/Soviet Union/Portugal brokered Peace

Accords. On the surface the signing was a partial victory for both sides, as the MPLA retained control of the state but finally acceded to a negotiated political settlement it had long resisted, and Savimbi, although still powerless, viewed the signing as a personal triumph, vindicating the fifteen years of unrelenting guerrilla attacks and conventional war against the MPLA government. At the signing of the Peace Accords, Savimbi and dos Santos both committed themselves to the creation of a multi-party democratic government and to the holding of fair and internationally supervised elections.[146] How much Savimbi and the rest of the UNITA leadership were willing to set aside their personal ambitions to bring the larger Ovimbundu population and the rest of their rural supporters closer to the state as a result of the planned democratic elections was anyone's guess.

EPILOGUE

The 1991 Peace Accords and planned 1992 United Nations–supervised elections provided the forum in which the MPLA and UNITA leaderships openly contested for popular support to control the state—a scenario that the Alvor Agreement had set in motion, but which had been derailed by the politics of the Cold War and the seventeen-year old civil war. Despite the hopes of the Ovimbundu and other rural Angolans that the election would bring unity to Angola, in fact it laid bare all the contradictory tendencies in Angolan nationalism, as appeals to class, ethnicity, party, personality, and regionalism dominated the election rhetoric. More than anything, the election brought to the center of Angolan politics the contest between UNITA and the state. Again here, the UNITA leadership sidestepped the aspirations of the people they represented in pursuit of the goal of controlling the state.

The contest took center stage because of Savimbi/UNITA's decision to run a strident "us" against "them" campaign—poor and/or rural versus educated and urban—which exposed the fissures created by the history of regionalism and ethnicity. By adopting a strategy more suited to rural Jamba than to urban and politically sophisticated Luanda, Malange, or Benguela, the UNITA leadership alienated the urban elite, the workers, and the disaffected sectors of the population, who were ready for a change but whose support had to be won through a campaign of inclusion. Assured of UNITA and rural support, however, Savimbi and the UNITA leadership once again short-changed their supporters, subordinating the interests of the

Ovimbundu masses and other rural populations to party, personality, and region rather than working to promote national unity and integration.

The MPLA, on the contrary, relying on its control of the state treasury, the National Electoral Commission (NEC), and the mass media took the high road and ran a campaign of inclusion, even welcoming into the party Tony Fernandes and Miguel N'zau Puna, who had recently broken with UNITA. The Brazilian public relations firm that the MPLA hired to run its campaign had much to do with its success. They de-emphasized the party's Marxist-Leninist image and projected a wholesome image of dos Santos as a healer and a symbol of national unity. As a result dos Santos represented a positive alternative to Savimbi, who still had to defend himself against accusations that he was responsible for the murders of his trusted aides Tito Chingunji and Wilson dos Santos, that he had sold out the country to the white settlers and South Africans, and that he was the main reason for the killings, human rights abuses, and extensive violence that marked the civil war

The "us" versus "them" rhetoric that dominated the campaign that Savimbi and UNITA ran increased people's suspicions of the UNITA leadership. This was also the case with the ethnic and other biases which dominated the campaign and which were evident in all the parties contesting the elections.

The issues which refocused interest on the conflict between the Ovimbundu and the state surfaced in the early weeks of the campaign, and continued unabated after the polls closed. Observers who traversed Angola between May 31, 1991, and September 29, 1992, in preparation for the elections, noted the trend. They reported that although Marxist, Socialist, Chinese, and other imported ideologies were absent from the campaign rhetoric, each one of the eighteen parties contesting the elections was seeking to mobilize supporters using ethnic ties, regional identities, and personalities.

With a winner-take-all election set for September 29–30 and with more than 4.6 million voters or 92 percent of the eligible voters registered to vote, the stakes were high for the MPLA and UNITA parties which fielded the majority of the candidates. As was noted above, the MPLA control of government agencies, including radio, television, and the Electoral Commission worked in favor of the ruling party, whose leaders did their best to limit the air time of the opposition parties and to frustrate their campaigning. Nevertheless, all parties which fielded candidates ran heated campaigns. UNITA candidates campaigned intensely throughout the country, including Luanda, where Savimbi addressed a rally of fifty thousand people. Here and in other urban centers, however, candidates from both MPLA and UNITA parties confronted popular distrust. Many potential voters were skeptical of candidates who promised a rosy future, since they blamed the leadership of both parties for the terrible state of the economy and the suffering caused by the prolonged civil war. Indeed, graffiti that often appeared on the walls in Luanda which read "MPLA Rouba" ("MPLA steals"), "UNITA Mata" ("UNITA kills") went to the heart of the people's contempt for both the MPLA and UNITA leaders.[1] Ironically, despite the disagreements between these parties, they created a situation in which no other party emerged as a significant alternative.

Although both parties spread party and ethnic propaganda, in the rural areas of the central highlands UNITA's candidates presented the campaign as a contest between an MPLA party dominated by a corrupt urban Afro-Portuguese elite and UNITA, a genuinely rurally-based, African party which they argued represented the only hope for Africans. In densely populated Ovimbundu centers, UNITA's candidates increasingly geared their message to an ethnic Ovimbundu electorate.[2] Savimbi led the way here, often delivering his campaign speeches in Umbundu, or peppered with Umbundu proverbs, to audiences he presumed were sympathizers with UNITA. While many of Savimbi's Ovimbundu supporters defended the tactic, arguing that Savimbi "protects them and loves all Angolan," non-Ovimbundu heard only the slogan "é nossa vez," "it's our turn", and not the turn of all Angolans.[3] Although this strategy strengthened UNITA's support among committed Ovimbundu, it alienated the non-Ovimbundu, especially urban Afro-Portuguese who were alarmed by the racial rhetoric that came through.[4] This stridency not only distanced many non-Ovimbundu from Savimbi and the UNITA leadership, but also pushed back into the government's fold many Ovimbundu who had cause to resent the MPLA's handling of the economy.

The charged atmosphere generated by the ethnically-run campaign did not subside following the closing of the polls. The days of uncertainty between the closing of the polls and the anouncement of the election results on October 16 only raised the level of concern that nothing but victory would satisfy Savimbi and the UNITA elite. On October 16, an anxious world and war-weary Angolans received the news of the MPLA's victory. With fifty-four percent of the votes cast, the MPLA received 129 of the National Assembly's 220 seats to UNITA's thirty-four percent and 70 seats, and thus retained control of the state. But José Eduardo dos Santos, having achieved only 49.57 percent of the presidential vote compared with Jonas Savimbi's 40.07 percent, had failed to secure the 50 percent vote necessary to become president and faced a run-off against Savimbi.

Despite the MPLA's victory, participation in the elections did much to advance Savimbi's and UNITA's status among Angolans. For one thing, UNITA had demonstrated that it had a strong organization and was capable of fielding candidates and gaining substantial support throughout the country. At its party heaquarters in Luanda, for example, two of its major organizers who worked on the elections were Fatima Roque, a rich, well-educated Portuguese woman, and Waldemar Correia, a Mbundu attorney from Malange. For another, the party showed that it could win by sizeable majorities in some core provinces. UNITA had carried the provinces of Benguela, Huambo, and Bié (its traditional areas of support) with 60, 81, and 84 percent of the presidential vote, had respectable showings in Uige and Cabinda, and gained an average of 15 percent of the votes cast in MPLA areas.[5]

The party's strong showing nothwithstanding, the UNITA leaders were unprepared for the role of members of the opposition. Even before the election results were made public, Savimbi accused the a government of conspiracy to defraud UNITA of victory. He first made his allegations against the MPLA public on October 2, two days after the polls closed, claiming that the electoral process was characterized by "fraud and irregularities, in a massive systematic, and generalized way" and that this had substantially weakened UNITA's electoral strength as a result.[6] He charged the MPLA leadership with fearing a multi-party democracy despite agreeing to the United Nations–monitored elections, since they viewed open elections as a "capitalist fetish . . . not suitable for Africa." UNITA's leadership also accused MPLA officials of wanting the party "to be synonymous with Angola", and of fearing the prospects of a loss to opposition parties.[7] Even as the UNITA leadership broadened its accusations against the MPLA, they reassured Angolans that "a recourse to force is not part of the framework of options proposed by UNITA." Party spokesmen also vowed that they were committed to join in a coalition government, and noted that Savimbi was ready to face off dos Santos in a run-off presidential election as stipulated by the Bicesse Accords.[8]

UNITA's leaders also worked to unify the opposition, in order to strengthen their charges against the MPLA. On October 7, they joined with leaders from six other parties and, calling themselves the Angolan Democratic Opposition, warned that they would reject any announcement regarding the results of the elections made before the end of investigations looking into allegations of irregularities.[9] Later that month, ten of the other thirteen political parties who had fielded presidential candidates also joined with UNITA to condemn the elections as fraudulent. In the days up to

October 30, the opposition, excluding the MPLA-supported Democratic Renewal Party (PRD), began to build up its case against the MPLA.

UNITA's newspaper, *Terra Angolana*, published numerous stories detailing the massive electoral fraud which it alleged the MPLA had committed. For example, UNITA officials charged that in Huambo and Bié provinces, UNITA's margins of victory would have been one hundred percent had the government-controlled NEC not arbitrarily cut off voter registration on August 10, despite the protests of Russia, Portugal, the United States, and the United Nations. They estimated that as a result over five hundred thousand potential UNITA voters had been denied a vote.[10] Furthermore, they identified irregularities in Bengo and other provinces, questioning the way the elections were handled. The most glaring of their accusations focused on rigging of votes. In a case concerning presidential votes, they presented evidence purporting to show that President dos Santos had received exactly the same number of votes (11,456) in places as ethnically and geographically distinct as Lunda-Norte, Bié, and Kwanza-Norte. Other claims of fraud involved the charge that foreigners had been allowed to vote—Namibians in Cunene and Zairians in the north; the existence of more than a hundred polling stations of which the opposition had no knowledge; and intimidation of voters by riot police and members of the secret service (MINSE).[11] These reports helped to keep the rumor mill in the capital fed and heightened fears of an Ovimbundu coup d'état.

The UNITA leadership also used the party's radio station, *Vorgan*, to combat what they perceived as the reluctance of western journalists to run stories emanating from UNITA. Much of this reluctance stemmed from the fact the journalists were still skeptical about Savimbi, an attitude fueled by their belief in his complicity in the killings of Tito Chingunji and Wilson dos Santos.[12] *Vorgan* ran particularly vicious rumors against Margaret Anstee and the United Nations verifying team (UN Angola Verification Mission) because they had refused UNITA's request to delay the announcements of the election results until the United Nations had undertake a thorough investigation of UNITA's charges against the MPLA.[13] When the UNITA leadership withdrew its generals from the Angolan Armed Forces (FAA), and Savimbi left Luanda secretly for Huambo, purportedly to rein in the more militant members of the party who were denouncing the MPLA and Anstee, most observers concluded that the party was preparing to return to war to remove the government.[14] The continued presence of other UNITA members who were working to lay the legal groundwork in the hope of presenting the case of fraud against MPLA to the Angolan supreme court, did little to reduce the ethnic tensions in the capital. Fátima Roque and Waldemar Correia, for example, who were in Luanda, spent a great deal of time attempting to reach out, too late, to some of the disaffected members of the urban elite. Their actions, however, only confirmed the suspicion of UNITA's critics that the party was exploiting ethnic divisions.[15] The activities of Abel Chivukuvuku, Jerimias Chitunda, Elias Salupeta Puna, and other representatives, who worked in conjunction with members of the UN verifying team, the Joint Political/Military Commission, the NEC and Margaret Anstee to help gather the evidence that they hoped would bolster their claims and convince world opinion that MPLA had carried out a "bloodless electoral coup," also increased the level of ethnic hostility against Ovimbundu in the capital.[16]

In the days following the elections, when early returns showed them winning handily, the MPLA gave the appearance of being magnanimous in victory and willing to put aside the ethnic and regional differences which had marked the campaign. For example, the secretary-general of the party, Marcelino Moco, played down talk of war and insisted that the MPLA leadership was interested in forming a government of national unity. Dos Santos also made conciliatory statements, pointing out that opposition leaders like Jonas Savimbi and Holden Roberto had a fundamental role to play in Angola's reconstruction, and inviting them to meet with him. Many in the leadership, however, publicly demonstrated their disdain for UNITA.[17]

The MPLA leaders were eager to protect their positions, and acted in ways that also promoted party, regional and ethnic ties over national reconciliation. Their belief that Savimbi and the UNITA leadership were merely power-hungry Ovimbundu attempting to gain control of the state by rejecting the results of the elections, exacerbated the ethnic and regional tensions which the campaign had fostered.[18]

MPLA officials refused to respond to UNITA's accusations and, as they had in 1975, maneuvered to counter any support for Savimbi and the opposition by appealing to the international community to validate their victory and condemn UNITA's actions. They hoped to convince the world that they had met all the conditions laid down by the United Nations, had run a fair election, and therefore were the rightful elected government of Angola.

In the meantime, Minister of Foreign Relations Pedro de Castro Van Dunem Loy was despatched on missions, first to Portugal and then to the United States, to get international support. The aim was to win Security Council approval of the government's handling of the elections and to get Portugal, the European Community, South Africa, and the United States to pressure Savimbi to accept the election results.[19] The party leadership also allocated funds and personnel (particularly to its spokesmen and press agents partial to it in Portugal) to give the official response to the opposition's allegations.

MPLA won the international validation it sought on October 16, when the United Nations confirmed that despite the problems that had surfaced during the elections, they had been free and fair. UNITA also sent a letter to the United Nations on October 16 stating its own acceptance of the election, but the crisis over the state did not abate.

As in the crucial months following the Lisbon coup of April 1974, the attitude of the international community again pushed the Angolans to war. In 1992 a post-Cold War community, led by the United Nations with major input from the United States, was eager to resolve the "Angolan problem". The decision of Alioune Blondin Beye, the Malian United Nations Secretary General's Special Representative to Angola, the United Nations Angola Verification Mission, and other international observers to verify the fairness of the elections and thus concede the state to the MPLA added to the ethnic and regional divide which the election rhetoric and UNITA allegations had fueled. In their eagerness to point to Angola's move towards democracy as a justification for the United Nations southern African agenda, the representatives of the international community hailed the MPLA's victory as the triumph of Western democratic principles, while ignoring the election irregularities which had caused UNITA to lose some votes. The decision to declare the elections fair, while ignoring UNITA's real grievances, exacerbated the deep regional and ethnic divide which had simmered throughout the election.[20] Margaret Anstee made a passing reference to this gulf when she remarked of Dr. Valetim, who headed the UNITA delegation to the Abidjan Protocol, that he "moved in a very different world from most of the rest of us."[21]

Jill Jolliffe, foreign affairs reporter and an open critic of UNITA's human rights violations, noted a few months after the elections that the United Nations officials were content to monitor elections in Angola with "the lowest budget in . . . its peace-keeping history." Citing confidential United Nations reports, she concluded that "there were irregularities discovered in the electoral process which could have affected the overall outcome of the victory," but the United Nations took no action and stamped the results with UN approval.[22]

Thus, despite sending an additional four-man supervisory team to examine the charges that UNITA and the opposition had brought against the MPLA, the United Nations rejected UNITA allegations of electoral fraud. Their local representatives, undermanned and unarmed, with only 350 unarmed military observers, 126 police observers, 400 election observers and 40 planes to monitor the elections in a war-torn country the size of France, Germany, and Spain combined, were unable to conduct a thorough investigation. Perhaps, as critics charged, the overworked members of the mission did not want to be bothered, and expected UNITA would eventually "sign-on" to what they regarded as another successful "democratic" coup in southern Africa. Although elections conducted under similar circumstances in the West would certainly have warranted further scrutiny, the elections in Angola however, were no different from some others that had taken place in the Third World.[23]

Portugal and the United States, the other members of the Troika, also gave the MPLA their stamp of approval, and thus encouraged the ethnic and regional divisions which had surfaced in the country. These two members of the Troika with the most interest in stabilizing the Angolan situation disregarded UNITA's call for an investigation into the alleged election fraud. Instead, their negotiators attempted to convince UNITA to accept the United Nations-verified results. According to some reports Portugal's mediators, who, the UNITA leadership hoped, would lean towards them, were reluctant to accept its demands since they believed that an MPLA government would allow Portugal to expand its economic and other interests in the country.[24] Some commentators believed that Savimbi's anti-foreign posture during the elections had also served to tighten the bond between the MPLA leadership and Portugal.

Official United States reaction to Savimbi's accusation of fraud also helped fuel the crisis over the state. Personnel and policy changes in the State Department following presidential elections in November 1991 badly undercut Savimbi's efforts to gain official United States support. Chester Crocker, who during his eight years at the State Department Africa desk was widely regarded as being partial to Savimbi and skeptical of the MPLA's Marxist leadership, was handing over the Africa desk to his deputy Herman Cohen. The latter's early advice to Savimbi was to end the rhetoric and "stop saying the election was fraudulent."[25] According to critics of the Clinton administration's policy towards Savimbi, Cohen believed that Savimbi's "personality traits" and the desire for personal power which had led him to execute rivals within UNITA were preventing him from accepting an electoral loss. Others interpreted UNITA's posture as another example of Savimbi's duplicity and desire to impose his form of authoritarianism on the Angolan population.[26] The support that some election observers from Germany, France, Portugal, and Switzerland gave to UNITA's allegations of electoral fraud was not sufficient to turn the tide; Savimbi found out that the world was tired of the Angola problem.[27]

Meanwhile inside Angola, MPLA leaders, once more emboldened by the stamp of legitimacy from the international community, moved to re-consolidate their position over the state. They began by shifting from their earlier conciliatory position and adopting more militant anti-UNITA initiatives. They delayed a proposed meeting between dos Santos and Savimbi, declaring that since UNITA's generals had walked out of the FAA, UNITA had essentially broken the Bicesse Accords. Moreover, the MPLA's Political Bureau, noting that the actions of UNITA had prevented the presidential run-off from taking place, accused UNITA of waiting for a good time to begin the war again. The Bureau called for the disarming of UNITA, the return of UNITA's generals to the FAA, and the extension of central administration throughout the whole of Angola. The MPLA leaders also came out against any collaboration with UNITA when they announced that for a government of national unity to exist, the MPLA would have to choose, from among the opposition parties, qualified individuals whom the government could trust. Furthermore, the Bureau at its meeting on 23 October recommended that delegates elected to the Assembly should be seated, and that individuals named as members of the government should begin their duties. When the 129 MPLA delegates along with ten members from the other parties took their seats at the first session of parliament on October 28, all seventy delegates belonging to UNITA boycotted the session.[28]

The accusations which Savimbi and the rest of the UNITA leadership leveled against the MPLA and their boycott of the Assembly demonstrated once again the central role they had come to play in the continuing estrangement of the Ovimbundu from the state. Although Savimbi and the UNITA leadership had gambled and lost on the rural/urban and ethnic partisanship campaign they had run, they refused to accept their place as a legal opposition representing the interests of the Ovimbundu and other rural population. In effect, they believed that opposition status deprived them of the power over the state that they had come to believe was their right. Their rejection of the election results, fueled by the ethnic estrangement that the campaigning had encouraged, made those Ovimbundu and other rural peoples whom UNITA represented hostage to a party whose leaders were more interested in debating the role of the elite than in national reconciliation and inclusion.

Indeed, well before the United Nations-supervised elections the goal of controlling the state had come to supercede UNITA's leadership's stated goal of leveling the playing field in Angola for the Ovimbundu and the rest of the country's rural population. Thus, as in the earlier crisis over the state following the 1974 coup, local prerogatives, this time in the form of personality politics, regional, and ethnic tensions, pushed the parties into open conflict. Savimbi acknowledged this years later, pointing out that both UNITA and the MPLA had tried to use the cover of the United Nations–supervised elections as a way of winning legitimacy for their control of the state. According to him, neither party at the time had any strong commitment to a political program that would devolve power and achieve a balance between the authoritarian state and the estrangement of the population from the state, nor were the leaders thinking of how to build a democratic Angola.[29]

As the leadership of the MPLA and UNITA failed to resolve the impasse after the elections, and the international community refused to take UNITA's complaints seriously, the two parties became locked in a vicious round of fighting to gain control over the state. It would take assassinations, hundreds of thousands of civilian casualties, and the almost total economic destruction of the country for the leadership to find a way to salvage the peace and make the state represent national unity and inclusion.

On October 31, when violence erupted in Luanda, the MPLA raised the stakes against UNITA by publicly denouncing the behavior of its officials and the military actions of UNITA's forces in various regions of central and southern Angola, arguing that it was nothing less than an attempt to take power by force. Moreover, FAPLA generals in the FAA army denounced the decision of the UNITA generals to withdraw from the joint army, pledging that they would take steps to stop any efforts by UNITA to take power by force or to interfere in the functioning of the joint armed forces. In this atmosphere of recriminations, the MPLA blamed UNITA for the random acts of violence in Luanda, outbreaks of fires at munitions stores, and attacks against outlying villages which were occurring. These developments together with leaks by government officials, raised the level of ethnic tension in Luanda as the government discussed what actions would be necessary to stop UNITA, and the MPLA party publicly discussed strategies to prepare its supporters for the impending coup attempt.[30]

The crisis exploded on October 31, less than two weeks after the announcement of the MPLA's victory, when MPLA and UNITA army units using light and heavy weaponry faced each other in the streets, after MPLA reported that UNITA forces had started attacks on the airport and the television station. During the next three months the violence spread, as military trucks manned by government soldiers and armed civilians (*ninjas*) took up strategic positions in neighborhoods where UNITA committees had established their headquarters, guarded by their own soldiers, according to the Bicesse Accords. MPLA supporters, including armed government soldiers, former agents of the secret service (MINSE), demobilized soldiers, and the youth arm of the party (JMPLA), fired into the buildings occupied by UNITA committees, and also attacked and killed civilians they believed had voted for UNITA or were identified as UNITA supporters.[31] By November 20 more at least a thousand people had died, many of whom had been executed by firing squad and dumped in mass graves in Luanda.

Two months after the Luanda massacre, during the week January 2–9 1993, the civil war proper started. with a series of urban attacks by UNITA forces. By February 1993, the number of dead in Luanda rose to 6,000, including Kongo, government and UNITA soldiers, and Kimbundu civilians caught in the crossfire.[32] UNITA would later claim that more than 20,000 of its civilian supporters died in Luanda from the end of October.[33] In addition, the government had arrested more than 2000 UNITA officials, members, and guards, thus effectively wiping out official UNITA representation in Luanda.[34] One estimate put the number of arms in the hands of MPLA partisans in the capital at 700,000.[35]

The battle for Luanda almost wiped out the UNITA leadership resident in the capital. Among the dead were vice-President Jeremias Chitunda and Elias Salupeta Pena, who were members of the UN-supervised JPMC (Joint Political Military Commission), secretary-general of the party General Adolosi Mango Aliceres, and Eliseu Sapitango Chimbili, all of these had been elected as deputies to the Angolan parliament. They were in Luanda negotiating the second round of the elections, the demilitarization of the parties, the demobilization of the anti-riot police, and the formation of the joint army when the fighting broke out.[36]

Similar acts of violence, death, destruction, and imprisonment occurred in many other urban areas, including Malange, Lubango, Benguela, and Catumbela, where MPLA and UNITA partisans fought open battles during the same period.[37] Estimates for the number killed in what some observers referred to as "ethnic cleansing" (*limpeza*) in the streets of Benguela and Catumbela by January 1993 ranged from one thousand to two thousand.[38]

Although initial reports said that the UNITA leadership had been indifferent to signs of arms distribution and meetings of MPLA adherents in the days preceding the October 31 Luanda massacre, the leaders responded with their own killings, violence, and destruction to what their supporters believed was state-sponsored ethnic cleansing in order to "eliminate the Ovimbundu throughout Angola."[39] Whether or not UNITA had ignited the October 31 events in Luanda or was in control of nearly 50 percent of the country by November 20, as MPLA officials charged,[40] it was not until a full two months later that UNITA went on full offensive in areas outside of the capital, thus resuming the civil war.[41] As its members and supporters fled the MPLA urban enclaves for the central highlands and other areas of UNITA support, Savimbi unleashed his forces, which he had not fully demobilized before the elections. UNITA's guerrillas and soldiers made rapid sweeps in crucial provinces, taking over territory they hoped to use as bargaining tools in negotiations.

UNITA kept up its pressure on the government and took control of even more areas as its soldiers consolidated their positions in others. By March 1993 UNITA's troops occupied Huambo and Soyo, while their siege of Cuito, considered a strategic city by both parties, would last sixteen months and cost more than thirty thousand lives—at least a third of the city's population. By September, UNITA controlled more than 70 percent of Angola and about a quarter of the provincial capitals.[42] Savimbi then declared a unilateral cease-fire on September 20, and demanded that the MPLA government make concessions so that UNITA could play a prominent role in the government.

Although both parties blamed each other for the chaos and the renewed fighting which followed the Luanda battle, UNITA's decision to return to war brought to the fore the distrust between the leadership of the MPLA and UNITA. More importantly, it also revealed the role that personality politics had come to play in the Angolan situation, and the extent to which regionalism, personality, party, and ethnicity had come to epitomize the struggle for control of the Angolan state. The losers here were the majority of Ovimbundu and other rural peoples, whose quest for local autonomy Savimbi and the UNITA leadership had co-opted.

Savimbi and the UNITA leadership were not alone in putting ethnicity, party, personality, and region above the desires of the population for peace and prosperity. Initially, the MPLA was unable to prevent UNITA's military onslaught in the rural areas and provinces because a large percentage of the press-ganged soldiers in FAPLA had simply walked away, leading to the disintegration of the army outside of the capital and some other urban centers. FAPLA's best units, however, had not disbanded but had been transferred to the Rapid Intervention Force or remained in elite units. The presence of elite units allowed the MPLA to reconstitute its army and launch an effective counter attack against UNITA.

The MPLA's success against UNITA was due to the ethnic, partisan, and regional appeals they made in their urban strongholds while consolidating their claims over the state. They attacked UNITA on three fronts. First, they moved to weaken UNITA organizationally through a propaganda war at home and abroad, and by intimidation and co-option of younger leaders who were dissatisfied with the old guard. Second, they attempted to undermine the base UNITA had built up among the smaller parties in the post-election period by detaining, imprisoning, and even assassinating their leaders and supporters. Finally, they envisioned a military victory over UNITA in the areas FAPLA had overrun or besieged.

Between October 30, 1992, and November 1994, the MPLA leaders achieved most of their goals. On the political front the government ran two campaigns, one for international consumption and the other to recapture the political edge at home. For international consumption, MPLA officials attempted to distance the party from the events of October 30, especially against the charge that the authorities had made arms available to demobilized soldiers—*ninjas* and MINSE—and that this had resulted in the massacre and imprisonment of thousands of UNITA officials and supporters. They defended their handling of the situation by arguing that the killings were the spontaneous revenge of angry civilians.[43] Furthermore, they laid part of the blame for the chaos on the United States and the United Nations, noting that the United Nations had failed to disarm demobilized soldiers before the elections, and had done nothing to prevent the war from breaking out again.[44] They also contended that the Kongo were killed because UNITA had used Zairian soldiers and white mercenaries to capture Soyo.[45]

The MPLA won the diplomatic war against UNITA when the United States broke its nineteen-year old policy of not recognizing the MPLA-PT government and granted the victorious MPLA full diplomatic recognition in May 1993. Five months later, the United Nations imposed an arms and fuel embargo on UNITA, thus effectively cutting its military and fuel supply lines.[46]

Meanwhile, inside the country the government pursued several options, all intended to destroy UNITA as a political force and reimpose MPLA control. During the uprising, the government quickly welcomed into its ranks generals Adriano Makvela Mackenzie and Zacaria Mundombe who had defected from UNITA.[47] Moreover, in the wake of the Luanda battle, MPLA officials targeted for persecution opposition leaders and supporters from the Kongo and other areas who had allied with UNITA, as well as members of the press critical of official corruption. Some were killed, others managed to escape assassination attempts, and many were intimidated, imprisoned, or kept under house arrest.[48] Several opposition leaders who had been detained, and whom members of MINSE, the *ninjas*, and FAA soldiers had tortured, were forced to recant their support of UNITA on national television.[49] Georgina Sapalado, a UNITA deputy who, like other deputies, was kept in what was called protective confinement in Luanda, recalled that "UNITA deputies were forced to enter the National Assembly to prevent retaliatory attacks against UNITA members."[50] The government also tried to split the UNITA leadership by running a propaganda campaign detailing its deep divisions, and set up a radio station in Luanda, on which former UNITA members denounced the party publicly. Some reports had it that Savimbi had died, been critically wounded, or had other serious health problems.[51]

On the military front, the MPLA reconstituted its army with the specific aim of defeating UNITA and recapturing the territory under its control. During 1993, over 65 percent of government spending went to defense, to retrain and upgrade the army. Indeed, some estimates put military expenditure at $2.5 billion (U.S.). In 1994, military spending was estimated at 39 percent of the budget, and by 1995 the government had spent a total of $3.25 billion (U.S.) on the military since the war restarted.[52] To retrain the army while moving against UNITA forces, early in 1993 the government secretly agreed to a fourteen-month $20 million dollar contract with Executive Outcomes, a Pretoria-based mercenary recruitment company.

Within a year after the first agreement with Executive Outcomes, the more than five hundred South African mercenaries the firm brought into Angola, along with the elite corps that had never been disbanded, had helped the MPLA forces win back two-thirds of the territory UNITA had captured.[53] After the government signed a second $20 million contract with the firm in October, its troops dealt a major blow to the UNITA forces on November 10, 1994, when they captured the city of Huambo, UNITA's headquarters. In his official 1994 end of year message to the nation, dos Santos, reflecting on the government's achievements, praised the soldiers who had succeeded in "restoring the authority of the state throughout Angola," and warned his radio audience that "no foreigner will make reconciliation for us."[54] By February 1995, when UNITA's Eighth Ordinary Congress adopted resolutions calling for a strengthening of the peace process and national reconciliation, government troops had inflicted humiliating military defeats on UNITA's forces. The end to this phase of the renewed civil war came in March 1995, when government troops broke UNITA's siege of Cuito, and threatened to continue the offensive against the remaining UNITA strongholds in the central highlands and Lunda Norte Province.[55]

The ferocity of the war was a testament to the extent to which personality, partisan politics, regionalism, and ethnicity drove the contenders for power to put their interests above that of their supporters. Although MPLA reversed the advances UNITA had made on the military front, consolidating its hold over the state was a formidable task because of the astounding cost in lives and material. From October 30, 1992, to May 1995 an additional 150,000 Angolans had been slaughtered, and cities like Huambo and Cuito, which had largely been untouched during the previous years of civil war, lay in ruins. Journalists who visited Cuito following the end of the siege compared the level of destruction to of Berlin or Hiroshima in 1945.[56]

Moreover, the economic and social cost of the war was astounding. The more than $3 billion dollars the government had spent on arms (in 1993 alone more than 65 percent of the budget) and the upkeep of its 140,000–man force had created a hyper-inflated economy which negatively affected the masses of the population more than government officials. In 1993, the inflation rate stood at 1838 percent, and one year later it was still as high as 972 percent. At the same time the average monthly wage in 1994 for Angolans living in Luanda was 150,000 *novo kwanza* or $3 (U.S.), and domestic production had totally ceased. The health situation posed the greatest threat to MPLA attempts at reconstruction, since more than 70 percent of the health care system in the country been destroyed since 1992. The refugee crisis caused by the war also presented a major problem to the MPLA. The country had more than a million and a half displaced persons and refugees, and an additional three million persons who needed humanitarian assistance. Official government corruption was also a major issue which threatened to undermine the MPLA government. Local journalists accused the government of doing nothing to end the practice. For example, they decried the fact that the $400 million in humanitarian aid which was required to feed the three million Angolans left destitute by the war, along with the arms purchases were fueling corruption and profiteering by high government officials on a scale even worse than before.[57]

This crisis, which hindered MPLA leaders from fully consolidating their hold over the state, plus the military setbacks that UNITA had suffered, produced a stalemate which forced the leadership of both parties once again to return to the negotiating table.[58] Under the guidance of the Malian Alioune Beye, who had replaced Margaret Anstee in 1993, and with observers from the Troika states (United States, Russia and Portugal), representatives of the weakened UNITA leadership and of the victorious MPLA party drew up a formula intended to integrate Ovimbundu and other UNITA supporters into an MPLA-dominated state.[59]

At the time, however there was no guarantee that the power-sharing arrangements that the United Nations and the Troika favored would reduce the differences between the two parties. Instead of putting aside their differences in the interests of the Angolan nation, representatives of both parties still maneuvered to strengthen their position over the state. For example, MPLA officials insisted that UNITA recognize the government's legitimacy and right to rule, and reiterated their position that the party reserved the right to select, from among the opposition, individuals to bring into the administration.[60] As for UNITA's representatives, they hoped to get political concessions from MPLA, even demanding a prominent place in the government.

By November 20 1994, when representatives of both parties announced the Lusaka Protocol which was to initiate the conditions for peace and a return to the Bicesse Accords, the MPLA leadership had backed away from some of its demands and had agreed to a power-sharing arrangement. The government and the UNITA leadership agreed to a cease fire, to the deployment of a 7,000–man UN force to monitor the cantonment and demobilization of their two armies, and to the formation of a 70,000–strong national army. The Accords also called for UNITA's deputies to take their seats in parliament, for the party to have control of four ministries, three provinces, and numerous municipalities, and to have some diplomatic posts.[61]

UNITA's representatives were among the twelve hundred delegates from all eighteen provinces of Angola and from UNITA's offices in Africa, Europe, and America who formally accepted the Lusaka Peace Agreement.[62] By May 6, when Dos Santos and Savimbi held a historic meeting in Lusaka and embraced publicly, both leaders pledged to the international community that they would work as partners. Dos Santos also promised to extend a formal invitation to UNITA to become part of a Government of National Unity and Reconciliation (GURN).[63] Savimbi, for his part, publicly recognized dos Santos as "my president" and vowed to "cooperate and help consolidate peace in whatever way the president of the Republic may deem necessary."[64]

Yet for all the public pronouncements of unity, deep ethnic, regional, partisan, and other difficulties still plagued the relationship between the leaders of the MPLA and UNITA. For example, when UNITA held its Eighth Ordinary Congress in Bailundu on February 7–11 1995, the party still had an army of over fifty thousand men, most of whom were defending positions the organization still held. Moreover, although Savimbi had stressed, in a March 13 speech celebrating the twenty-ninth anniversary of the formation of UNITA, that the party represented the "oppressed and disinherited," most of the inner leadership were Ovimbundu who were fiercely loyal to Savimbi. Furthermore, many among the UNITA leadership remained convinced that it was *nossa vez* to run the state, and were less interested in helping to bring peace to Angola than they were in working to guarantee parity for UNITA and the Ovimbundu and rural populations in the state.

The leaders soon demonstrated their partisan position when UNITA representatives met with MPLA leaders to resolve some of the issues surrounding the Lusaka Protocol. They continued pressing for specific concessions from the MPLA, particularly insisting that UNITA should keep control of the diamond industry (which UNITA was using to fuel its war machine) if the government insisted on keeping control of the oil operations.[65] In a *Wall Street Journal* article published on June 16–17, Savimbi articulated UNITA's partisan bias when he stressed that "participation . . . should not mean the elimination of the identity of UNITA." He also demanded that the MPLA should address issues such as the "separation of powers, administrative decentralization, creation of a bill of rights and equal access to economic opportunities."[66]

Moreover, Savimbi declined the June 16 offer of the Central Committee of the MPLA to "share the country's vice-presidency with a member of the MPLA," claiming that it was merely a ceremonial. As he told dos Santos, "this is meaningless . . . it does not interest me to preside over a Council of the Republic made up of pastors, priests, and others. I am neither a pastor nor a priest." Again, Savimbi's refusal to play the role of elder statesman gave the appearance of continued Ovimbundu efforts to undermine the state. Savimbi's demand for a position such as coordinator of the economy, finance, social services, or international affairs was his way of guaranteeing that he would remain at the center of Angolan politics.[67] Furthermore, his refusal of a post which would have removed one of the last major barriers between the MPLA and UNITA was another indication of the depth of the ethnic, regional, and partisan divide between the leaders of MPLA and UNITA.[68]

The one development that kept the power-sharing arrangement from collapsing was the belated commitment of the United Nations and the observer states to the peace process. The members of the international community overseeing the implementation of GURN at last showed a determination to bring the Angolan crisis to an end. This was in contrast to the leaders of the MPLA and UNITA, who were in no mood to settle their differences and work for the good of the Angolan population.[69]

As 1997 heralded the fifth year of the post-election crisis, several major issues still separated the MPLA and the UNITA leaders.[70] The most important of these were the status of Savimbi, the extension of the GURN administration throughout the country, and matters of government policy. Although Savimbi accepted the government's offer to recognize him as the leader of Angola's largest opposition party, the UNITA leadership continued to send conflicting signals about full acceptance of the Peace Process and GURN. Savimbi, for example, absented himself from the ceremonies in Luanda held on April 18, 1997, for the seating of the seventy elected members of UNITA in the National Assembly. While President Eduardo dos Santos greeted the UNITA representatives with a "brotherly embrace" in front of President Nelson Mandela of South Africa and the presidents of Zimbabwe and Zambia, Savimbi remained in Mbailundu. Once again he blamed his absence on a lack of adequate security.[71]

This time, the threat of United Nations sanctions seemed to be the one weapon capable of compelling Savimbi and his inner circle to move beyond the ethnic, partisan, and personality politics which still dominated their thinking. An August 20, 1997, United Nations sanctions (implemented on October 29) banned the movement's leaders from international travel and imposed other harsh penalties on the group. This decision was meant to push the UNITA leadership to comply with the Peace Accords. At the time, Bill Richardson, the American representative, spelled out UNITA's failures by noting that the movement had "maintained its military force, brought the extension of state administration to a virtual standstill, and kept up a stream of anti-government propaganda through its Radio Vorgan."[72]

Within a few months the Angolan crisis seemed to be coming to an end. Although protesting the sanctions, by November 1997 the UNITA leadership could point to the eleven thousand members of the UNITA army which had been integrated into a new Angolan army, and had agreed to hand over large amounts of territory to comply with the United Nations demand that UNITA allow the GURN government to extend central administration throughout Angola. In addition, the party allowed its nominees to take up the four ministries and seven vice-ministries that UNITA had been allocated, thus partially fulfilling the mandate of the peace accord.[73]

The developments that had occurred since the elections once again highlighted the significance of the interplay of local imperatives, regional dynamics, national priorities, and international objectives in shaping Ovimbundu history over more than a century and a half. Although the ethnic, regional, partisan, and other local issues still loomed large in the Angolan landscape, the fact that in November 1997 representatives of the

Ovimbundu and other rural Angolans shared power with the other peoples of Angola in a democratically elected administration represented for them a partial victory.

But victory for the Ovimbundu and the rural masses proved elusive. As 1997 came to an end, Savimbi and some in the UNITA leadership still remained removed from the state, even as the presence of their representatives in GURN signaled that others had covered ground in narrowing the distance between the Ovimbundu and the state. The crucial role the MPLA's troops played in the fall of the Mobutu regime in neighboring Zaire and Congo Republic in 1997, and the continued threat of further United Nations sanctions against UNITA seemed to have lessened the possibility of another rupture.

Although the MPLA's critics argued that those UNITA representatives who joined GURN had no real power, since major policy initiatives still originated with the President and the MPLA party and not from the assembly, and that Ovimbundu officials in MPLA, like Marcelino Moco, Paulo Cassoma, and Faustinho Moco had either had been marginalized or lacked real power,[74] the future looked bright for the final integration of the Ovimbundu into the postcolonial state. The presence of Ovimbundu opposition in the assembly certainly appeared to be a counterweight to the unbridled use of power by the ruling MPLA.[75] Furthermore, the fact that the new FAA army included a significant number of Ovimbundu soldiers with no ties to UNITA, and that a number of UNITA army generals like Mackenzie and Mundombe supported the government augured well for the future.

But the postcolonial state had yet to face its most important challenge. This revolved around the issue of how to integrate members of the Ovimbundu (UNITA) elite into the state in a way that would lessen the alienation of the group and other rural Angolans, and still permit UNITA to function as a viable party in the country. The commitment of the MPLA to a One-Party State meant that they were unable to gain the allegiance of the Ovimbundu (UNITA won a majority of their votes in the 1992 election). Only a Multi-Party State would allow this. Between 1997 and 1998 the leaders of MPLA and UNITA failed once again to resolve their differences. By October 1999, war, which had broken out during the latter part of 1998, again dominated national politics in Angola. The aspirations of the Ovimbundu and rural populations to live in peace under a state that would represent their interests were a long way from being realized.

GLOSSARY

Angolar	Angolan currency
Assimilado	African who could speak Portuguese and who was acculturated to Portuguese culture and values
Aguardente	rum
Bem-Estar	well-being
Cantoneiro	road crew head
Capitão-mor	Portuguese civilian or military representative in the interior
Centavo	Unit of Portuguese money: one one-hundredth of an escudo
Chefe/Chefe de Posto	Portuguese local administrator
Cipão (pl. cipães)	African policeman
Circumscrição Civil	Small Portuguese colonial administrative unit
Concelho	Large Portuguese colonial administrative unit
Conto	One thousand escudos (Portuguese money)
Dizimo	Portuguese-imposed tax
Epia	Plot in the forest
Escudo	Portuguese currency
Estado Novo	New State/Salazar dictatorship
Estatuto das Indigenas	Native Law
Feira	Slave market in the interior
Fuca	Debt
Gremio de Milho Colonial	Colonial Maize Board
Imposto (pl. impostos) de Cubata	Hut Tax
Indígena	Native, nonassimilated African
Junta de Exportação Cereais	Cereal Export Board
Katanga	Shaba Province in the Democratic Republic of the Congo in colonial times
Kesila	Law
Mucano	Accusation and fining
Mulambo	Tribute

Ocibanda	Gift, tax, toll
Ocimbanda or kimbanda	Religious practitioners
Ocumbu	House garden
Olosoma	Ovimbundu ruler
Ombala	Head village, capital
Ombanda	Plot along bank of river
Onaka	Plot along stream
Onjango	Central male meeting place in the village
Otingo	Gift, advance payment, debt
Panno	Piece of imported cloth measuring seventeen yards
Pombeiro	Caravan supervisor and recruiter
Posto Civil	Colonial Administrative Unit
Presídio	Portuguese fort in a conquered region
Quitandeira	Small Portuguese outlet in the interior
Regedor	African civil official in colonial administration
Reis	Portuguese unit of currency and/or account
Sekulu	Elder, village head
Servical (pl. serviçães)	Slaves/servants
soba/soba grande	Portuguese term for African rulers
Sobado	Large colonial administrative unit
Soveta	Precolonial district/colonial village unit
Vieyno/Bieno	Subject of Viye/Bié

NOTES

Notes to Introduction

1. See, for example, Basil Davidson, *The Black Man's Burden: Africa and the Curse of the Nation-State* (New York: Times Books, 1992); Crawford Young, *The African Colonial State in Comparative Perspective* (New Haven: Yale University Press, 1994); Ali Mazrui and Michael Tidy, *Nationalism and New States in Africa from about 1935 to the Present* (London: Heinemann, 1984).

2. László Magyar, *Reisen in Süd-Afrika, 1849–1857* (Pest: Lauffer and Stopl, 1859, reprint, New York: Kraus, 1974); Antonio da Silva Porto, *Viagens e apontamentos de um Portuense em África: Excerptos do Diário de António Francisco da Silva Pôrto*, ed. by José de Miranda and António Brochado (Lisbon: Agência Geral do Ultramar, 1942).

3. Maria Emília Madeira dos Santos, ed., *Viagens e apontamentos de um Portuense em África: Diário de António Francisco Ferreira da Silva Porto*, Vol. 1 (Coimbra: Biblioteca Geral da Universidade de Coimbra, 1986); *idem*, "Perspectiva do comércio sertanejo do Bié na segunda metade do século XIX," *Studia* 45 (1981): 65–129.

4. I was able to study this corpus during my stay in Luanda (1979–80). As a *cooporante* with responsibility for reorganizing the official colonial documentation for the central highlands, I was in a unique position to get an insider's view of the working of the colonial bureaucracy from the level of the Governor-General, and from the lowest civil servants to the African agents of the colonial regime.

Notes to Chapter 1

1. Ralph Delgado, *Ao Sul do Cuanza: Ocupação e aproveitamento do antigo reino de Benguela* (Lisbon: no. publisher given, 1944), 1: 597.

2. Jean-Luc Vellut, "Notes sur le Lunda et la frontière luso-africaine, 1790–1900," *Études d'histoire africaine* 3 (1972): 61–166.

3. Santos, *Viagens e apontamentos*, 95–96, 159.

4. António de Oliveira de Cadornega, *História geral das guerras angolanas (1680–81)* Ms. of 1680–81. Ed. by José Matias Delgado and Manuel Alves da Cunha, 3 vols. (Lisbon: Agência Geral do Ultramar, 1940–42, reprint, 1972) 3: 168–74, 218, 250.

5. For more on the Imbagala see Joseph C. Miller, *Kings and Kinsmen: Early Mbundu States in Angola* (Oxford: Clarendon Press, 1976).

6. Joseph Miller, *Way of Death: Merchant Capitalism and the Angolan Slave Trade, 1780–1830* (Madison: University of Wisconsin Press, 1988), 28–30.

7. Cadornega, *História* 3: 168–74, 218, 250.

8. Alfredo de Albuquerque Felner, "Derrota de Benguela para o sertão," in *Angola: Apontamentos sôbre e colonização dos planaltos e litoral do sul de Angola* (Lisbon: Agência Geral das Colónias, 1940), 2: 15.

9. Elias Alexandre da Silva Corrêa, *História de Angola* (Lisbon: Editorial Atica, 1937) 2: 48–66; Arquivo Histórico Ultramarino, Lisbon (AHU), Cx. 61, doc. 18, António de Lencastro, 1 July 1776.

10. For a review of the history of the states see Gladwyn Murray Childs, *Umbundu Kinship and Character* (London: Oxford University Press, 1949), Chap. 12.

11. As quoted by Childs, *Umbundu*, 22.

12. A word on spelling and plurals. The first chapter uses Umbundu spelling for Umbundu words. For example, here the term olosoma is the Umbundu term for ruler; the Portuguese term is soba. Subsequent chapters adopt the Portuguese spelling for Umbundu terms. Rather than using the Umbundu system of plurals, which is complex, I have decided to use English rules by adding "s" to the singular of all Umbundu words (Umbundu and Portuguese spellings) to form the plural.

13. Magyar, *Reisen*, 159, 277–79, 386–87, 415 n. 16; Anibal dos Santos Brandão, "Vanuambo, nominação de um seculo e seus cargos," *Mensário Administrativo* 5 (Luanda, 1952): 38–39; Centro de Documentação e Investigação Histórico (CDIH, now named Arquivo Histórico Nacional de Angola) Luanda: Angola, Est. 33, Cx. 20, Secção 7, no. 2 (1946) "História dos Postos," n.p.

14. Magyar, *Reisen*, 280, 499; D.A. Hastings, "Ovimbundu Customs and Practices as Centered around the Principles of Kinship and Psychic Power" (Ph.D. dissertation, Hartford Seminary, 1933), 126, 150.

15. Felner, "Derrota de Benguela," 2: 15.

16. Gladwyn Murray Childs, "The Kingdom of Wambu (Huambo): A Tentative Chronology," *Journal of African History* 5, no. 3 (1964): 367–79.

17. Linda Heywood and John Thornton, "African Fiscal Systems as Sources for Demographic History: The Case of Central Angola, 1799–1920," *Journal of African History* 29 (1988): 218–19.

18. For the latest literature see Eric Hobsbawm, *Nations and Nationalism since 1780: Programme, Myth, Reality* (New York: Cambridge University Press, 1990); Benedict Anderson, *Imagined Communities: Reflections on the Origin and Spread of Nationalism* (New York: Verso Press, 1983).

19. Heywood and Thornton, "African Fiscal Systems," 213–28.

20. Magyar, *Reisen*, 279; Childs, *Umbundu*, 228.

21. René Pélissier, *Les Guerres grises: Résistance et révoltes en Angola, 1845–1941* (Orgeval: Pélisser, 1977), 135, 144, 147. See also Delgado, *Ao Sul do Cuanza*, 1: 603–4, 624, and *passim*.

22. Magyar, *Reisen*, 293, 312; Joaquim Rodriques Graçã, "Expedição ao Muatayanvua, 1843," *Boletim da Sociedade Geographia de Lisboa* (Hereafter referred to as *BSGL*), 9 (nos. 8–9): 387; H. Capello and E.R. Ivens, *From Benguela to the Territory of the Yacca*, trans. A. Elwes. 2 vols. (London: S. Low, Marston, Searle, and Rivington, 1882), 2: 107.

23. Childs, *Umbundu*, 174–76; Merlin Ennis, *Umbundu Folk Tales from Angola* (Boston: Beacon Press, 1962), 117, 202, 303; Anibal dos Santos Brandão, "O grande Soma Huambo Kalunga o terrivel antropófago," *Mensário Administrativo* (Luanda, 1953).

24. For an 1845 Portuguese description of the practice see George Tams, *Visit to Portuguese Possessions in South-Western Africa*. (New York: Negro University Press, 1969), 179–81; Magyar, *Reisen*, 261–65, 305–12.

25. W. D. Hambly, *The Ovimbundu of Angola*, (Chicago: Field Museum of Natural History, Anthropological Series, 21, 1934), 142; Silva Porto, *Viagens*, 174; Eugenia W. Herbert, *Iron, Gender, and Power: Rituals of Transformation in African Societies* (Bloomington: Indiana University Press, 1993), 164–87; Jan Vansina, *Paths in the Rainforests: Toward a History of Political Tradition in Equatorial Africa* (Madison: University of Wisconsin Press, 1990), 74, 78, 276–77.

26. Sociedade Geografia de Lisboa (SGL), Lisbon, Reservados 2-C-6, Silva Porto, "Apontamentos de un Portuense em Africa," vol. 1, Bihé 15 de Março a Bihé Setembro 1858–Costumes dos Gentilicos," p. 97. (Hereafter referred to as Silva Porto, "Apontamentos," vol. 1.)

27. Magyar, *Reisen*, 390; Alfred Hauenstein, "La Royauté chez les Ovimbundu," in Manuel Laranjeira Rodrigues de Areia, ed., *Angola: Os símbolos do poder na sociedade tradicional* (Coimbra: Centro de Estudos Africanos, 1983), 28; A.G. Mesquitela Lima, *Os Kyaka de Angola*. 3 vols. (Lisbon: Edições Távola Redonda, 1988), 1:142–44.

28. Graça, "Expedição," 387, 409; Magyar, *Reisen*, 71–72, 79, 293, 312. Heywood and Thornton, "African Fiscal Systems," *passim*.

29. Magyar, *Reisen*, 249–50.

30. Response to Questionaire, Bernardo Bongo, Italy, 8/1/97, Ms. in author's possession.

31. Childs, *Umbundu*, 28.

32. Ovimbundu informant, Personal Correspondence, 19 June 1997, in author's possession.

33. SGL: Res. 146-C-6, Silva Porto, "Apontamentos," vol. 1, fols. 102–4. Magyar, *Reisen*, *passim*; Ennis, *Umbundu*, 36.

34. Magyar, *Reisen*, 249–66.

35. National Library of Scotland, Scotland (NLS), Cameron Diary, entries for 10 October 1875; Adrian C. Edwards, *The Ovimbundu under Two Sovereignties: A Study of Social Control and Social Change among a People of Angola* (London: Oxford University Press, 1962), 65–66; E. R. Vieira da Costa Botelho, "Agriculture no distrito de Benguela," *BSGL*, 8a serie, 3–4 (1888–89): 225.

36. SGL, Reservados 145-c-6, vol. 11, "Apontamentos" 1884–85, 1886–87, n.p.; National Archives of Zambia, Zambia (NAZ), Diaries of Walter Fisher, 1889–1903, n. f., 1890; NAZ, Mrs. Fisher diary, 1891, fol. 28; Magyar, *Reisen*, 30.

37. Graça, "Expedição," 384; Magyar, *Reisen*, 297.

38. Magyar, *Reisen*, 213.

39. *Ibid.*, 256–57. Silva Porto, *Viagens*, 178; NAZ, HM8/F12/3/1 Diary of W. Fisher, 282–83; NAZ, Mrs. Fisher Diary, 1891, fols. 40–41; Canadian Council of Foreign Missionary Societies (Canada) (CCFMS) also known as United Church of Canada (UCC), Angola Mission, File 6, "The Canadian Independent," (1886), Mrs. Stover Letter, 286.

40. Magyar, *Reisen*, 210–13, 282–83.

41. *Ibid.*, *passim*; Ennis, *Umbundu*, 36, 152, 157.

42. Magyar, *Reisen*, 249–58.

43. *Ibid.*, 249–50.

44. *Ibid.*, 287–90; Interview, Maria Chela Chikuela, Maryland, U.S.A., 1993; Lawrence Henderson, *Angola: Five Centuries of Portuguese Conflict* (Ithaca: Cornell University Press, 1979), 92.

45. José Curto, "The Legal Portuguese Slave Trade from Benguela, Angola, 1730–1838: A Quantitative Re-Appraisal," *África: Revista do Centro de Estudos Africanos* 16–17, no. 1 (1993–94): 101–16.

46. Isabel de Castro Henriques, *Commerce et changement en Angola au XIX siècle: Imbangala et Tschokwe face à la modernité* 2 vols. (Paris: Editions Harmattan, 1995), 1: 81–85; Vellut, "Notes," 66–166.

47. Henriques, *Commerce*, 81–85.

48. José Curto, "The Anatomy of a Demographic Explosion: Luanda, 1844–1850," Unpublished Ms., May 1996.

49. National Archives of the United States (NAUS), Washington, D.C. RN 84, report of May 1874.

50. Judith Listowel, *The Other Livingstone* (New York: Scribners, 1974), 137–40.

51. Silva Porto, *Viagens*, 84, 172; Santos, *Viagens e apontamentos*, 70–71.

52. Silva Porto, *Viagens*, 96; Magyar, *Reisen*, 27–30; Santos, *Viagens e apontamentos*, 70.

53. Santos, *Viagens e apontamentos*, 143–50, 200, 224–400 *passim*.

54. For the transformation, see Heywood, "Slavery and Forced Labor in the Changing Political Economy of Central Angola, 1850–1949," in Suzanne Miers and Richard Roberts, eds., *The End of Slavery in Africa* (Madison: University of Wisconsin Press, 1988), 415–36.

55. Santos, *Viagens e apontamentos*, 170 and *passim*.

56. NLS, Cameron Journal, entries of 1, 8, 10, and 16 September 1875.

57. Santos, *Viagens e apontamentos*, 86–87, 172, 177.

58. *Ibid.*, 171–74.

59. *Ibid.*, 172.

60. Vernon L. Cameron, *Across Africa*, 2 vols. (New York: Harper & Brothers, 1877).

61. NAUS, RN 84, Report of 2 May 1874.

62. Santos, *Viagens e apontamentos*, 152–60; Cameron, *Across Africa*, 141; G.E.S. Tilsley, *Dan Crawford: Missionary Pioneer in Central Africa* (New York: Fleming H. Revel, 1929), 68.

63. Heywood and Thornton, "African Fiscal Systems," 213–28; *Idem.*, "Demography, Production and Labor: Central Angola," in Dennis Cordell and Joel Gregory, eds., *African Population and Capitalism: Historical Perspectives* (Madison: University of Wisconsin Press, 1987), 241–54.

64. Tilsley, *Dan Crawford*, 63.

65. Silva Porto, *Viagens*, 184–87; SGL Res. 146-C-6, Silva Porto, "Apontamentos," vol. 2 (1884–86), fol. 2.

66. ABCFM, WCA Woman's Board of Missions, doc. 99, Annie M. Fay to Friends, 6 June 1889, p. 3; ABCFM, vol. 24 (1902–29), Supplementary docs., no. 133, "The Social Life of the Native Christian," fols. 1–2; Frederick Stanley Arnot, *Garenganze or Seven Years Pioneer Mission Work in Central Africa* (London: J.E. Hawkins, 1889), 115–16.

67. Tilsley, *Dan Crawford*, 90–91.

68. Silva Porto, "Novas jornadas de Silva Porto nos sertões africanos," *BSGL*, 5a Sér. (1885): 18; John T. Tucker, *A Tucker Treasury: John T. Tucker: Reminiscences and Stories of Angola, 1883–1958*, ed. by Catherine Tucker Ward (Winfield, B.C.: Wood Lake Books, 1984).

69. Heywood and Thornton, "African Fiscal Systems," 218–19; Magyar, *Reisen*, 242; SGL, 145-C-48, "O Diário . . . de Capello e Ivens," 18–19.

70. Tucker Ward Collection, Letters of Ardell Henry Webster, 1887–1889 (Ms. in author's possesion, on loan from Catherine Tucker Ward, Mississauga, Ontario; Linda Heywood, "Production, Trade and Power: The Political Economy of Central Angola, 1840–1930" (Ph.D. dissertation, Columbia University, 1984), 230–37; Musée des Beaux-arts de Montréal, Canada (MBAM), Sanders Letters, 16 February 1886.

71. Heywood, "Production," 235–37; NLS, Cameron Journal, entry of 8 October 1875; James Johnston, *Reality versus Romance in South Central Africa*, 2nd. ed. (London: Frank Cass, 1969), 96.

72. Tucker Ward Collection, Letter dated 11 October 1888.

73. NAZ HM9/F12/1/1, Fisher Dairy, H. Arnot, Letter of 1 February 1890, fol. 147; Tilsley, *Dan Crawford*, 89.

74. Tucker Ward Collection, Ms. Webster letter no. 7, 21 July 1888.

75. NLS, Cameron Journal, entries of 28 August and 2 October 1875.

76. Magyar, *Reisen*, 260. István Fodor, *Introduction to the History of Umbundu: L. Magyar's Records (1859) and the Later Sources* (Hamburg and Budapest: Helmut Buske and Akadémiai Kiadó, 1983), 21–26.

77. Santos, *Viagens e apontamentos, passim.*

78. *Ibid.*, 155–56.

79. Silva Porto, *Viagens*, 170–71; SGL Res. 2-3-6, Silva Porto, "Apontamentos," vol. 1: 139; MBAM, Sanders Letters, 8 May 1886; A. A da Rocha de Serpa Pinto, *How I Crossed Africa*, trans. Alfred Elwes (Philadelphia: Lippincott, 1881), 155.

80. Graça, "Expedição," 382; Santos, *Viagens e apontamentos*, 65–66; MBAM, Sanders letters, 22 September 1885, Minnie Sanders to friends.

81. *Annaes do Conselho Ultramarino* (parte não oficial), 3a serie (Lisbon, 1862), 47; Graça, "Expedição," 396; Santos, *Viagens e apontamentos*, 95–96, 159.

82. CDIH, Estante 78, No, 4, Letter from D. Ecuhique Sobba do Bailundo to ILmo Sen. Cheffe d'Concelho da Catumbella, Bailundo, 18 Dec. 1886.

83. Delgado, *Ao sul do Cuanza*, 1: 381.

84. CDIH, Est. 73, Cx. Bié, no. 165, 1884, Dom Soba Pedro Neto Calumbo Jemina to Gov. of Benguela, 18 May 1884.

85. MPLA, *A História de Angola* (Luanda: Centro de Estudos Angolanos, 1975), 101.

86. Maria da Conceição Neto, "Comércio, religião e política no sertão de Benguela: O Bailundo de Ekwikwi 11 (1876–1893)," in *Fontes & estudos: Revista do Arquivo Histórico Nacional*, 1 (Nov. 1994): 101–18.

87. MBAM, Sanders letters, 10–22 April 1885; Lawrence Henderson, *A Igreja em Angola: Um rio com várias correntes* (Lisbon, Editorial Além-Mar, 1990), 67.

88. AHU, Angola, 1a Repartição, Relatório.

89. NAUS, RN 84, 1885, 12 January 1885, R.S. Newton, V. Consul to Hudson Smith, esq.

90. Arthur da Paiva, *Expedição ao Bihé* (Lisbon: Agência Geral das Colonias, 1890) 1, 224–25; Tucker, *A Tucker Treasury*, 120.

91. Fola Soremekun, "Religion and Politics in Angola: The American Board Missions and the Portuguese Government, 1880–1922," *Cahiers d'études africaines* 3 (1971): 83–84, 341–77; AHU, Silva Porto, "Exploraçoes Cientificas." Vol. 11, doc. 14, 1887; CDIH, Est. 78, Cx. 11, "Bailundu," Sova of Bihé to Governor of Benguela, 12 January 1885.

92. NAZ, HM9/F13/1, Arnot Diary, 15 April 1890; Pélissier, *Guerres grises*, 358.

93. Da Paiva, *Expedição ao Bihé*, 1: 178.

94. The term comes from the article "To Rise with One Mind: The Bailundo War of 1902," by Douglas Wheeler and C. Diane Christensen, in Franz W. Heimer, ed., *Social Change in Angola* (Munchen: Weltforum Verlag, 1973), 53–92.

95. Pélissier, *Guerres grises*, 360.

96. Da Paiva, *Expedição ao Bihé*, 1: 209–10; NAZ, HM9/F13/1/1, Arnot Diary, fol. 43, 4, December 1890; UCC (CCFMS), J.J. Tucker, papers & corr. L.S. Tucker to Friends, 29 November 1929.

97. Delgado, *Ao sul do Cuanza*, Doc. no. 88, officio do governo de Benguela to Governador Geral, 15 May 1890, p. 628.

98. For changes in Portuguese policy in central Africa during the period see Eric Axelson, *Portugal and the Scramble for Africa, 1875–1891* (Johannesburg: Witwatersrand University Press, 1967); Richard Hammond, *Portugal and Africa, 1815–1910: A Study in Uneconomic Imperialism* (Palo Alto: Stanford University Press, 1966).

99. Childs, *Umbundu, passim*.

100. No systematic study of this process in the central highlands exists. For developments in the Kimbundu region see Jill Dias, "Changing Patterns of Power in the Luanda Hinterland: The Impact of Trade and Colonization on the Mbundu, ca. 1845–1920," *Paideuma* 32 (1985): 285–318.

101. CDIH, Est. 78, Cx. 64, Huambo (1896), Martin Teixeira da Silva, "Relatório da Columna d'operações ao Huambo," 10 October 1896, fol. 1.

102. Wheeler and Christensen, "To Rise with One Mind," 53–92.

103. Pélissier, *Guerres grises*, 367–76.

104. Wheeler and Christensen, "To Rise with One Mind," *passim*.

105. Pélissier, *Guerres grises*, 368–71; Arquivo Histórico Militar, Lisbon, (Hereafter known as AHM), Cx. 7, doc. 21, Paes Brandão, "Relatório das Operações no Bailundu" (1902).

106. AHU: Repartição Militar, Maço 966, Confidential "Plano de Campanhia"; AHM, Cx. 8, Amorim, "Operações," 78.

Notes to Chapter 2

1. AHU, Cx. 9, Telegram from merchants to Governor General, 14 June 1914.

2. AHM, Cx. 47, no. 17, Telegram from Governor General to Governor of Benguela, 12 June 1917; AHM, Telegram no 245, from Governor of Benguela to Chief of Staff in Luanda, 12 June 1917; Telegram from Governor of Benguela to Governor General, 14 July 1917; Confidential letter from Quartel Geral to Governor of Benguela, 14 July 1917; note of 15 July, 1917, "Instruções relativas aos auxiliarios recrutados em Benguela," by Chief of staff; AHM., Cx. 47 no. 17, "Revolta do Selles e Amboim," 2 vols. Confidential letter from Governor General to Minister of Colonies, 2 August 1917; see also Pélissier, *Guerres grises*, 392–94.

3. AHM, Cx. 47, no. 17, note of 15 July 1917, "Instruções relativas aos auxiliaries recrutados em Benguela," from Chief of Staff; AHM, Cx. 47, no. 17, "Revolta do Selles e Amboim," 2 vols. Confidential letter from the Governor General to Minister of Colonies; Pélissier, *Guerres grises*, 192–94.

4. AHU, Maço 806, Norton de Matos, "Relatório Confidential, para . . . Ministro das Colonias," 12.

5. Douglas L. Wheeler and R. Pélissier, *Angola* (New York: Praeger, 1971), 100–128.

6. AHU, Repartição Militar, Angola, Maço 968, F. Gonçalves, "Relatório das operaçoes nos Luchazes na região de Canasse, 1904." See Pélissier, *Guerres grises*, 377–93.

7. The highlands accounted for a sizeable part of the 2,916,000 hectares of arable land in the colony. See Dino Taruffi, *L'altipiano de Benguela (Angola) ed il sua avenire agricolo* (Rome: Instituto Agri-Colonial Italiano, 1916) 24.

8. AHU, Repartição Militar, Angola, Maço 968, Eduardo Romeras do Macedo, "Copia do relatório do Capitão-mor do Bailundu, sobre a visita aos postos militares, d'aquela capitania em Julho 1903 até de 7 de Agosto."

9. Heywood and Thornton, "Demography, Production and Labor," *passim*. See Walter Currie's enthusiastic remarks about the new *soba* of Bié at the time, ABCFM, vol. 18, doc. 16, Currie letter, 3 September 1909; AHU, Angola, 2a Repartição, la Secção, Maço 807, Norton de Matos to Chefes, 9 August 1912; AHU, Same to District Governors, 9 July 1912.

10. ABCFM, vol. 18, doc. 16, Currie letter, 3 September 1909; AHU, Angola, 2a Repartição, 1a Secção, Maço 807, Norton de Matos to Chefes, 9 August 1912; AHU, Governor General to Governors of Districts, 9 July 1912.

11. For this issue in colonial Malawi and Zambia see Martin Chanock, *Law, Custom and Social Order: The Colonial Experience in Malawi and Zambia* (London: Cambridge University Press, 1985).

12. *A Reforma* (Lisbon) 10 June 1910, 3.

13. *Boletim Oficial da Colonia de Angola (BO)*, 12 (25 May 1911): 177–78, Potario no. 328.

14. *BO*, no. 12 (23 March 1911): 177–78; AHU, Junta Consultivo, Livro 237; Angola, la Repartição, la Secção, Cx. 23, Maço 807 (1913), Relatório creating Secretary of Native Affairs; CDIH, Est. 70, Cx. 1, Huambo to Chefe do Posto de Quipeio.

15. *BO* 1st series, 10 (17 March 1917): 102, Potario no. 51; *BO* 1st series, 35 (29 September 1917): 227, Potario no. 139.

16. José de Oliveira Ferreira Diniz, *Negócios Indigenas, Relatório do ano de 1916* (Lisbon, 1917).

17. Heywood, "Production," Chapter 8. See also Wheeler and Pélissier, *Angola*, 113–18, 120–21; and F. Clement C. Egerton, *Angola in Perspective: Endeavour and Achievement in Portuguese West Africa* (London: Routledge and Kegan Paul, 1957), 101–3.

18. José de Oliveira Ferreira Diniz, *Populações indígenas de Angola*, (Coimbra: Imprensa da Universidade, 1918).

19. CCFMS, UCC WMS, Box 2, File 32, V. Waln to Tucker, p. 24.

20. *BO*, no. 42 (20 October 1906) for the general decree and *A Defesa da Angola* (Angola), (13 October 1906), (11 December 1907) for its introduction into Angola and the District of Benguela.

21. José Capela, in *O Imposto de palhota e a introdução do modo de produção capitalista nas colónias* (Porto: Afrontamento, 1977), saw the introduction of the hut tax as a way for the introduction of a capitalist mode of production in the colonies).

22. Capela, *O Imposto*, 86.

23. *A Provincia de Angola* (Angola), 9 November 1918, p. 1; *BO* 1919.

24. *A Provincia de Angola* (Angola), 22 May 1928, p. 2.

25. Armando Augusto Gonçalves de Morais e Castro, *As Colónias Portugueses* (Porto: Companhia Editora, 1927) 55.

26. Heywood, "Production," Chapter 8.

27. *Ibid.*, 408.

28. *Ibid.*, 384–85. CDIH, Est. 78, Cx. 1, Report of Secretary of Arrolamento e cobrança dos impostos, Chipembe, 1912; CDIH, Est. 78, Cx. 1, no. 38, Administrador, concelho de Huambo to Secretary, Governor of Benguela, 1913; *A Provincia*, 30 August 1915, p. 2.

29. Heywood, "Production," 400.

30. Colonia de Angola, *Censo geral da população, 1940* (Luanda, Imprensa Nacional, 1941), Vol. 1.

31. Wheeler and Pélissier, *Angola*, 110.

32. Heywood, "Production," 381–83; for a discussion of the effects of early Portuguese social policies in the Kimbundu region see Douglas Wheeler, "Angola in Whose House? Early Stirrings of Angolan Nationalism and Protest, 1822–1910," *International Journal of African Historical Studies* 2, 1 (1969): 1–23.

33. Heywood, "Slavery and Forced Labor"; CDIH, Agriculture survey of 1923, Uncatalogued survey 1926.

34. Heywood, "Production," 381–83.

35. *Ibid.*, 407–10.

36. Egerton, *Angola*, 106–9.

37. They rejected the plans that Portuguese investors submitted. See AHU, CFB, Maço 467, Sala II; *A Provincia*, 28/9/1934, p. 3. See also Adelino Torres, *O Império português entre o real e o imaginário* (Lisbon: Escher, 1991), 53–54.

38. *Jornal das Colonias* (Lisbon), 23 August 1902, p. 2; *Ibid.*, 6 December 1902, p. 2. Heywood, "Production," Chapter 7. Initially some colonial officials believed that the penetration of a rail line would speed up their control of the Benguela hinterland, as had been the case in the Luanda hinterland when the Ambaca rail line was built.

39. In the Lunda region, however, South African and European investors were allowed to develop the diamond industry. Armado Castro, *O Sistema colonial portugues em África* (Lisbon: Editorial Caminho, 1959), 47–48.

40. See Leroy Vail and Landeg White, *Capitalism and Colonialism in Mozambique: A Study of the Quelimane District* (London: Heinemann, 1980).

41. Gerald Bender, *Angola under the Portuguese: The Myth and the Reality* (London: Heinemann, 1978), 94–102.

42. Heywood, "Production," Chapter 7.

43. The hectic pace of road building and city construction led to hundreds of deaths, "hands beaten to a pulp, arms torn out," according to eyewitnesses. See Tucker Ward Collection, Letter of 21 February 1921.

44. Heywood, "Production," 366–67.

45. Linda Heywood, "Porters, Trade and Power: The Politics of Labor in the Central Highlands of Angola, 1850–1914," in Catherine Coquéry Vidrovitch and Paul Lovejoy, eds., *The Workers of African Long Distance Trade* (Beverly Hills: Sage, 1985), 243–68.

46. Tucker Ward Collection, Letters of 6 August 1920 and 21 February 1921.

47. A bushcar was a two–wheel cycle that was carried or pushed by two porters. A tipoia was a carriage made of two poles attached to a heavy duty material.

48. Samuel Nelson, *Colonialism in the Congo Basin, 1880–1940* (Athens: Ohio Uni-

versity Press, 1994); Bruce Berman, *Control and Crisis in Colonial Kenya: The Dialectic of Domination* (Athens: Ohio University Press, 1990).

49. J. A. David de Morais with Hermann Pössinger, "Transformação occoridas na sociedade Umbundu desde do colapso do comercio das caravanas até ao fim da era colonial" (unpublished Ms, n.d [1978]), pp. 77–79; See W. Gervase Clarence–Smith, *Slaves, Peasants, and Capitalists in Southern Angola, 1840–1926* Cambridge: Cambridge University Press, 1979), and Dias, "Changing patterns of Power," 285–318.

50. Benguela Railway Company (BRC), *Relatório e contas* (Lisbon, 1915), 52.

51. Agência Geral de Angola, *A agricultura em Angola: Breve resumo sobre os recursos agrícolas da provincia de Angola* (Lisbon, 1922), 14, 73 (total cultivable land in highlands); Colonia de Angola, *Plano geral de propaganda e desenvolvimento da cultura de milho entre os indigenas* (Luanda, 1913), 5; José F. de Sousa Monteiro, "Breve noticia das riquezas naturais de Angola: Possibilidades da sua produção e aspectos regionães," in Província de Angola, *Boletim de agricultura*, série 4, separata 3 (1920): 151 (total planted in maize).

52. Afonso Costa Valdez Tomaz dos Santos, *Perspectivas económicas de Angola* (Lisbon: Agência Geral das Colónias, 1949), 122.

53. CDIH, Est. 11, Cx. 23, *Relatório* (Huambo, 1923); CDIH, Est. 69, Cx. 2, Huambo, no. 28 (1920); *O Districto de Benguela* (Angola), 3 March 1923, p. 6.

54. Alexandre Malheiro, *Chronicas do Bihé* (Lisbon: Livaria Ferreira, 1908).

55. Taruffi, *L'altipiano*, 30–31.

56. Heywood, "Production," 374; Heywood, "The Growth and Decline of African Agriculture in Central Angola 1890–1950," *Journal of Southern African Studies*, 13, no. 1 (April 1987): 355–71; Morais, "Transformação," 82.

57. Tucker, *Tucker Treasury*, 169.

58. *Ibid.*, 199.

59. Agência Geral de Angola, "Agricultura em Angola," 62; CDIH, Est. 11, Cx. 23, Relatório do Circumscrição Civil do Bailundo, January 1924.

60. CDIH, Est. 11, Cx. 23, Huambo, "Relatório do Administrador, Circimscrição Civil Bailundo," January 1924.

61. Tucker, *Tucker Treasury*, 99.

62. CCFMS, Angola, General Correspondence, File 45, W. H. Sanders to Mr. Tucker, Bié, 23 November 1919.

63. ABCFM, WCAM, vol. 2, doc. 514, W. H. Sanders to Dr. Barton, 2 April 1920.

64. *O Districto de Benguela*, 23 August 1924, p. 5.

65. Archives Génerales de R. Pères du St.–Espirit, France (AGSE) Boîte 485 B, Keiling to Monseigneur, 1 January 1925, p. 3.

66. *Ibid.*

67. ABCFM, WCAM, vol. 3, Una Jean Minto to Folks, Dondi, 1 May 1926, p. 5.

68. CDIH, Est. 70, Cx. 1 (1880–1951), Bié, Paiva Couceiro to Governor of Benguela, 5 February 1890; CDIH, Est. 74, Cx. 1, Bié, Capitão-Mor to Secretary of Governor of Benguela, 2 December 1895.

69. Gervase Clarence–Smith, *The Third Portuguese Empire, 1825–1925: A Study in Economic Imperialism* (Manchester: Manchester University Press, 1985), 117–18, for the metropolitan role.

70. Tucker, *Tucker Treasury*, 163

71. *Ibid.*, 191; AGSE, Boîte 485 B, Keiling to Monseigneur, 10 November 1915.

72. Heywood, "Slavery," 425.

73. *Ibid.*

74. Heywood, "Production," 368; Heywood, "Slavery."

75. F. Jaspert and W. Jaspert, *Through Unknown Africa: Experiences from the Jaspert African Expedition of 1926–1927* (London: Jarrolds, 1928), 72–73. W. Jaspert later mentioned that slave caravans still arrived in Benguela, *Ibid.*, 138.

76. Tucker, *Tucker Treasury*, 190.

77. For the problem of Africans holding and selling slaves see, CCFMS, File no. 25, 18 August 1927, "Kamundongo Report."

78. A group of Luba, Luba Kasai, Lunda, and Kanjok slaves who belonged to the Protestant convert Kanjundu and who were freed in 1914 did return to Luba region in modern Democratic Republic of the Congo. Their descendants are still living there today. See John C. Yoder, *The Kanyok of Zaire: An Institutional and Ideological History to 1895* (London: Cambridge University Press, 1992), 116–20; see also CCFMS, File no. 45, 1916, Report from C. Gordon Cattel.

79. Heywood, "Slavery," *passim.*

80. Heywood, "Production," 390, 421.

81. *Ibid.*, 381–83.

82. Heywood and Thornton, "Demography," *passim*; Heywood, "Production," 414–15.

83. Heywood, "Production."

84. Public Record Office, London, (PRO) FO371/11136/52, Letter of denial by Pauling and Company, 4 November 1925.

85. CDIH, Est. 24, Pasta 16, 1926, Confidential Circular to Administrator, Circumscrição Civil of Huambo.

86. ABCFM, WCAM, 1920–1929, Vol. 2, Letters A–G, Doc. 6x, Letter of W. C. Bell, 10 November 1925; CDIH, Est. 24, Pasta 16, 1926, Confidential Circular to Administrator, Circumscrição Civil of Huambo.

87. *O Jornal de Benguela* (Angola), 23 August 1918, p. 3.

88. CDIH, Uncatalogued Survey, 1923.

89. *BO*, no. 2 (17 January 1925): 46.

90. Otto Jessen, *Reisen und Forschungen in Angola* (Berlin: D. Reimer, Andrewa & Steiner, 1936), 210–11; CDIH, Est. 11, Cx. 23, Relatório of the Circumscrição Civil of Bailundo, January 1924; in fact, population estimates for the same area indicated a population of only fifteen thousand men between the ages of sixteen and forty–five who were available.

91. CDIH, Uncatalogued survey, 1923.

92. Heywood, "Porters."

93. Egerton, *Angola*, 106.

94. BRC, *Relatório do Alfandega* (Lisbon, 1915), 83–84; AHU, Maço 260, Comisário do governo, no. 380, 1913–14.

95. *Relatório do Alfandega*, 83–84; AHU, Maço 260, Comisário do governo, no. 380, 1913–14.

96. Taruffi, *L'Altipiano*, 31–32; Tucker, *A Tucker Treasury*, 119.

97. Clarence–Smith, *The Third Portuguese Empire*, 107.

98. Heywood, "Production," 373–74; Heywood, "Agriculture."

99. Heywood, "Slavery," 420–22. The Catholic priest Father Fisher noted that in Bailundu his work could not progress because many villagers stayed up to four months in

the interior, and there were many others willing to take the place of those who died there. AGSE, Boîte 476, "Situation des Missions 1911–1933," p. 174.

100. CDIH, Est. 70, Cx. 1 (1880–1951), Bié, Paiva Couceiro to Governor of Benguela, 5 February 1890; CDIH, Est. 74, Cx. 1, Bié, Capitão Mor to Secretary of Governor of Benguela, 2 December 1895.

101. Tanganyika Concessions Ltd., London (TANKS), BR, 110, Benguela Railway Africa Report, Mr. Scrayens Report, 1918; *A Voz do Planalto* (Angola), 19 August 1933, pp. 6–7; *O Lobito* (Lobito, Angola), Numero Especial do fim do ano Decembro de 1936; *Ibid.*, 15 December 1934, p. 1 (the last two cited the first official census of Europeans of 1933).

102. See, for example, Delgado, *Ao Sul do Cuanza*, vol. 1, Doc. 81, p. 635, when local officials were forced to imprison some white merchants.

103. Taruffi, *L'Altipiano*, 29.

104. *Ibid.*

105. *Ibid.*, 32.

106. TANKS, ZEI, Report of Inspector, 11 August 1918.

107. TANKS, Land Concessions, Letter from H. Greenwood, 27 February 1922.

108. Clarence–Smith, *The Third Portuguese Empire*, 133.

109. BRC, *Relatório e Contas*, (Lisbon, 1918), 49, 77.

110. Clarence–Smith, *The Third Portuguese Empire*, 128–29.

111. *Ibid.*, 105–6.

112. Egerton, *Angola*, 107; A. Bastos, *Monographia de Catumbela* (Lisbon, Tip Universal, 1912).

113. See, for example, R. H. Carson Graham, *Under Seven Congo Kings* (London: Carey Press, 1930), and António da Almeida, *Relações com os Dembos* (Lisbon, 1935).

114. CCFMS, Angola, General Correspondence, File 45, W. H. Sanders to Mr. Tucker, Bié, 23 November 1919.

115. CDIH, Estante Bailundu.

116. *Jornal de Benguela*, 23 April 1920, p. 4.

117. Jaspert and Jaspert, *Through Unknown Africa*, 110.

118. *Ibid.*, 111.

119. Childs, "The Kingdom of Wambu," 377–78.

120. CDIH, Est. 78, Cx. 4, Capitão Mor of Bailundo to Secretary of Governor of Benguela, 1 May 1898; AHU, la Repartição, la Secção, Angola (1901–1904), "Relatório sobre ao Preposito para a reorganização do districto de Benguela"; *BO*, no. 3 (9 August 1912): 45; no. 12 (25 March 1911): 177–78; no. 35 (2 September 1911): 594.

121. ABCFM, WCA, vol. 3, Una Jean Minto to Folks, Dondi, 1 May 1926, p. 5; CDIH, Est. 40, Cx. 89 Bié, Confidential circular from Governor General, 17 January 1928; CDIH, Est. 103, 1921.

122. CDIH, "Relatório," Huambo, 1921–22.

123. Income schedules are given in *BO*, 7th series, no. 10 (16 May 1922): 118, Potario 87; Heywood, "Production," 368.

124. Taruffi, *L'Altipiano* 32. The dialogue in the fictional story "Jamba," as related by the missionary anthropologist Wilfred Hambly in the early 1930s, was no doubt based on contemporary practices. In it, one character taunted the other by reminding him that he was lucky because he did not "go to work for the Governor. You're a friend of the sekulu, headman of the village. The king invites you to his village. No one picks on you when a gang is wanted." W. D. Hambly, *Jamba* (Chicago: Pelligrini & Cudahy, 1947), 44.

125. Tucker, *Tucker Treasury*, 119.

126. CDIH, Agricultural survey of 1923, Uncatalogued survey of 1926.

127. *Ibid.*

128. Jessen, *Reisen*, 241.

129. Tucker Ward Collection, Selected Writings, p. 8.

130. Heywood, "Slavery," 428.

131. PRO, FO371, A4626/1588/52 confidential letter from Anti–Slavery and Ab-origines Protection Society to Secretary of State, 30 August 1926, citing correspondence from Bailundo.

132. ABCFM, WCAM, vol. 3, doc. 66, Letters of Henry S. Hollenbeck, 11 March 1921.

133. TANKS, BR 157, Letter from Machado to General Manager, 12 May 1925.

134. Heywood, "Production," 411–12.

135. AGSE, Boîte 485 B, Keiling to Monseigneur, 16 July 1927; AGSE, Keiling to Monseigneur, 1 January 1925, p. l.

136. AGSE, Boîte 485 B, Keiling to Monseigneur, 20 February 1922.

137. AGSE, Boîte 485 B, Keiling to Monseigneur, 27 April 1921.

138. AGSE, Boîte 476 B, Keiling to Monseigneur, 10 July 1918.

139. The missionary contribution to the social life of Angola's Africans has been widely studied. See, for example, Henderson, *Igreja*; also Douglas Wheeler, "Angola in Whose House," 1–23; Jill Dias, "Uma Questão de identidade: respostas intellectuais as transformações económicas no seio da élite crioula da Angola entre 1870 e 1930," *Revista Internacional de Estudos Africanos* 1 (1984): 61–94.

140. Henderson, *Igreja*.

141. David H. Gallagher, *Along African Trails*, (Toronto: United Church of Canada, 1952), 110.

142. AGSE, Boîte 485 B, Keiling to Monseigneur, 16 July 1927.

143. CCFMS, Box 3, file 25, Report from Chileso Station, May 1929, p. 2.

144. Tucker Ward Collection, document of 1912, pp. 8–9.

145. AGSE, Boîte 485 B, Keiling to Monseigneur, 20 September 1923, p. 11.

146. UCC, WMS, Box 3, File 43, "Angola: Portuguese Regulations Concerning Religious Teachings," 1914.

147. Leona Stuckey Tucker, "Some Early Letters from Africa," January/February 1920, Ms. owned by Catherine Tucker Ward (in author's possession).

148. *United Church Record and Missionary Review* (Canada), April, 1930, p. 11.

149. *Angola after Fifty Years* (Boston: ABCFM, 1930), 4.

150. For a brief history of the Chipenda family which began its association with the Protestants in 1902, see Henderson, *Igreja*, 94–97. Indeed in 1914 the Protestant mission station in Ndulu [Andulu] had on its staff "Avirahama, son of Mbemlele . . . [a sekulu], Mbapolo, an interior slave" and Kolenge a commoner from Chisamba. Among the females were "Nyani, a daughter of chief Nanjundu and Ndumbu, a local girl and another younger girl." See Tucker, *Tucker Treasury*, 76.

151. AGSE, Boîte 485 B, Keiling to Monseigneur, 20 September 1923, p. 11.

152. CCFMS, Box 5, File 75b WCC WMS, Angola, M. Dawson, 13 June 1959.

153. CCFMS, Box 2, File 32, Tucker Correspondence, 1958, Duane V. Waln to Tucker, p. 2. Tucker, *Tucker Treasury*, 77; see also Morais, "Transformação," for a critical assessment of the impact of this innovation.

154. Tucker, *Tucker Treasury*, 170.

155. *Ibid.*, 190.

156. Tucker–Ward Collection, Leona Stuckey to Family, 31 May 1919.

157. Tucker, *Tucker Treasury*, 4.

158. CCFMS, UCC, Tucker, 31 December 1920; Leona Stuckey, 13 December 1920.

159. Tucker, *Tucker Treasury*, 188, 189.

160. TANKS, Land Concessions, Letter from H. Greenwood, 27 February 1922.

161. Tucker–Ward Collection, Letters of 5 & 6 July, 1920.

162. Personal Correspondence, Lawrence Henderson, 24 February 1997.

163. Tucker, *Tucker Treasury*, 117.

164. See *Ibid.*, 169, 172, 192.

165. *Ibid.*, 172.

166. *Ibid.*

167. *Ibid.*, 176.

168. AGSE, Boîte 485 B, Keiling to Monseigneur, 25 October 1925 and 15 September 1925.

169. Tucker, *Tucker Treasury*, 179.

170. John J. Tucker, *Angola: The Land of the Blacksmith Prince* (London: World Dominion Press, 1933), 177.

171. *Ibid.*, 178.

172. AGSE, Boîte 485 B, Keiling to Monseigneur, 22 April 1921.

173. CCFMS, Box 2, File 228, "Minutes of the 4 Annual meeting of the Angola Missions Conference June 1–3, 1925."

174. *Ibid.*, 110, 172, 177.

175. *Ibid.*, 174.

176. ABCFM, WCAM, vol. 2, doc. 389, Extract of letter of Miss Miller, 1925, p. 5.

177. ABCFM, WCA, vol. 3, doc. 101, Letter of Henry S. Hollenbeck, 20 August 1926.

178. ABCFM, WCA, vol. 1, doc. 252, Bailundo Station Reports, 1925–26.

179. Tucker, *Blacksmith Prince*, 188–89.

180. *Ibid.*, 67.

181. Dia Kassembe, *Angola: 20 ans de guerre* (Paris: L'Harmattan, 1995), 38.

182. John T. Tucker, *Old Ways and New Days in Angola, Africa* (Ontario: F.C. Stepheson, n.d. [1935]), 8–14.

183. A description of Ovimbundu marriage in 1920 repeated descriptions produced in the 1880s. Tucker–Ward Collection, 6 August 1920.

184. Tucker, *Tucker Treasury*, 99.

185. CCFMS, Box 5, File 75, WCC, Angola, M. Dawson, 13 June 1959.

186. Tucker, *Tucker Treasury*, 68–69.

187. CCFMS, Box 5, File 75b, WCC, Angola, M. Dawson, 13 June 1959.

188. Tucker, *Tucker Treasury*, 191.

189. Wyatt MacGaffey, *Religion and Society in Central Africa: The BaKongo of Lower Zaire* (Chicago: University of Chicago Press, 1985).

190. Tucker, *Tucker Treasury*, 123.

191. Tucker, *Old Ways and New Days in Angola*, 102. For a more thorough discussion of the role of witchcraft, see Linda Heywood, "Towards an Understanding of Modern Political Ideology in Africa: The Case of the Ovimbundu of Angola," *The Journal of Modern African Studies* 36 (1) (1998): 139–67.

Notes to Chapter 3

1. For the impact of the Salazar dictatorship, see Peter Fryer and Patricia McGowan Pinheiro, *Oldest Ally: A Portrait of Salazar's Portugal* (London: D. Dobson, 1961); Bender, *Angola*; Clarence-Smith, *The Third Portuguese Empire*.

2. See H.D. Wiarda, "Towards a Framework for the Study of Political Change in Iberian Latin Tradition: The Corporate Model," *World Politics*, 25 (1973): 212.

3. José Hermano Saraiva, *História concisa de Portugal*, 3rd ed. (Lisbon: Europa-America, 1979), 349–59.

4. See the Estado Politico, Civil e Criminal dos Indigenas Angola, Guinea; the Colonial Act of 1930; the Imperial Organic Charter (1933); and the Overseas Administrative Reform Act of 1933.

5. Amadeu de Castilho Soares, *Política de bem-estar rural em Angola*, Estudo Científico Political e Social, no. 49 (Lisbon: Junta de Investigação do Ultramar, 1961), 25.

6. Wheeler and Pélissier, *Angola*, 144–48; Michael Cahen, ed., *"Vilas" et "Cidades": Bourgs et villes en Afrique lusophone* (Paris: L'Harmattan, 1989) 98–117.

7. Representatives of a small section of a municipality who were also employed as labor police.

8. CDIH, Est. 24, pasta 8, 1944; *Jornal de Benguela* (25 February 1944), p. 7; CDIH, Est. 33, Cx. 20, no. 2, 1944 Circular. Although some *regedores* were descendants of former titleholders, most were not, and failed to gain the respect of the population. "*Katamajila*" literally means "someone who sets fire along his path." The general meaning referred to "a person under someone else's thumb, doing a dirty job for almost no money." Communication of Jardo Muekalia, Ocimbundu, Washington, D.C., February, 1999.

9. CDIH, Est. 1, doc. 17, Relatório Annual, Concelho de Bailundo, 1938, p. 35.

10. Egerton, *Angola*, 123.

11. The *escudo* had replaced the *real* as the Angolan currency during the Republican period.

12. Clarence-Smith, *The Third Portuguese Empire*, 181–86.

13. Egerton, *Angola*, 109.

14. *Ibid.*, 123.

15. CDIH, Est. 25, Pasta 6, no. 5, 1938; *Annuario Estatístico de Angola* (Luanda, 1935).

16. Arquivo de União dos Bancos Ultramarinos (AUBU), Banco de Angola, Gerência de Nova Lisboa, *Relatório*, 1935.

17. AGSE, Boîte 485 B, Keiling to Monseigneur, 4 August 1932, and P. D. Junqueira to Monseigneur, 18 May 1939, p. 1.

18. PRO, FO371 11958, JP 1016/2/ Consular to Foreign Office, 26 February 1956, p. 1.

19. National Archives of the United States, Washington, D.C. (NAUS), RG 59, Box 5023, Diplomatic Records Division, Consul Walter C. Isenberg to State Department, Luanda, 19 January 1950; *New York Times*, 5 August 1956; António Pires, *Angola, Essa Desconhecida: Ensaio político económico* (Luanda: no publisher given, 1964), 78–79.

20. PRO, FO371 11958, JP 1016, Consular to Foreign Office. 26 February 1956.

21. Castro, *O Sistema Colonial*, 149. The author notes that much of this money went into public buildings. Calculations based on exchange rates for 1958—see Thomas

Okuma, *Angola in Ferment: The Background and Prospects of Angolan Nationalism* (Boston: Beacon Press, 1962), 37.

22. Eduardo de Sousa Ferreira, "La Transformación y consolidación de la economia em Angola, 1930–1974," *Estudos de Asia y Africa* 15/3 (1980): 584, 589.

23. *Ibid.*, 584.

24. Castro, *O sistema Colonial*, 145–46.

25. TANKS, BR 118, Reports for 1933, Major Bowdre to Zambezi Exploring Company, 29 March 1933; S. E. Katzenellenbogen, *Railways and the Copper Mines of Katanga* (Oxford: Claredon Press, 1973), 122–32; CCFMS, Box 6, File 106, Camundongo Report, p. 1; AUBU, Banco de Angola, Gerência de Nova Lisboa, *Relatório*, 1942, p. 3; NAUS, RG 165 62 Regional File 1933–44, Portugal 3000–3640, Box 3155, Office of Strategic Services, 25 September 1943, p. 1.

26. *BO*, 1a serie, 40 (15 September 1923): 376–78, document no. 360; BRC, *Relatório e Contas*, 1918, pp. 49, 77; AHU: Direcção Geral Colónias, Concessões de Terrenos, 1916–20, Sala 4, Est. IX, Maço 2573; *Jornal de Benguela* (5 November 1929): 3.

27. AUBU, Banco de Angola, Gerência de Benguela, *Relatório*, 1939, p. 22.

28. Egerton, *Angola*, 200–201.

29. Minister of Colonies, parts of Colonial Act, 1936.

30. Wheeler and Pélissier, *Angola*, 130.

31. AHU, Minister of the Colonies 1936; Bender, *Angola*.

32. AHU, Direcção Geral das Colonias Ocidente, Relatório no. 1, Benito Alves 9 April 1931, pp. 5–8.

33. AHU, Maço no. 2877, "Generalidades sobre Angola," 1935.

34. AHU, Sala 12, Maço 865 Governor da Provincia de Benguela, Relatório, 1936, p. 65; Bender, *Angola*, 102; TANKS, BR, Report of Alvaro de Melo Machado, Managing Director of Caminho de Ferro de Benguela on European Settlement, 29 March 1938; AUBU, Banco de Angola, Gerência de Benguela, *Relatório*, 1939, p. 22.

35. AUBU, Banco de Angola, Gerência de Nova Lisboa, *Relatório*, 1943, p. 7.

36. *Jornal de Benguela*, 1 October 1946, p. 6.

37. PRO, 371 27210, Portuguese File 187, Webster #73293.

38. Brazil, and not Angola, was and remained attractive to non-Portuguese immigrant whites. See Bender, *Angola*, 25–26.

39. Egerton, *Angola*, 237–41.

40. *Ibid.*, 241.

41. Bender, *Angola*; Bender, "Planned Rural Settlements in Angola 1900–1968," in Heimer, ed., *Social Change*, 235–79.

42. Alves da Rocha, Nelson Lourenço, and Armando Morais, "Angola nas vésperas da Independência (1)," *Economia e socialismo: Revista mensal de economia política*, 36, 37, 38 (1979): 27.

43. Colonia de Angola, *Recenseamento, 1940* (Luanda, Imprensa Nacional, 1941), 1: 78–95 and *Recenseamento, 1960* (Luanda, 1960), 1: 35–42; Estado de Angola, *Informação Estatistica, 1972* (Luanda, n.d.); Adelino Torres, "Le Processus d'urbanisation de l'Angola pendant la Période Colonial (années 1940–1970)," in Michel Cahen, ed., *"Vilas" et "cidades"* 101; John Marcum, *The Angolan Revolution: Vol. 1: The Anatomy of an Explosion (1950–1962)* (Cambridge, Mass.: M.I.T. Press, 1969), 104.

44. Egerton, *Angola*, 199; Marcum, *The Angolan Revolution*, 1: 104.

45. Childs, "The Kingdom", 378.

46. Egerton, *Angola*, 123.

47. Vasco Lopes Alves, "Apontamentos sobre Angola," *Boletim Geral do Ultramar*, ano XXXII, no. 267 (January 1956): 148–49.

48. AHU, 2a Secção, Sala 2, Maço 2805, "Relatório Sobre o Orçamento da Colonia para o ano económico 1935–1936 pelo Julio Garcia de Lencastre, Governador da Provincia de Luanda, fol. 20–21.

49. AHU, Sala 12, Maço 865, Governador da Provincia de Benguela, "Relatório Annual, 1938. Relatório do Governador da Provincia de Benguela," p. 12.

50. UCC, Box 3, File 47, Tucker Papers, *Labor in Angola*, "Colonia de Angola, Distrito de Benguela, copia Circular no. 4/123/1933."

51. Andrew Roberts, ed., *The Colonial Moment in Africa: Essays on the Movement of Minds and Materials, 1900–1940* (New York: Cambridge University Press, 1990), esp. 68–71 and 121–29.

52. UCC, Box 3, file 47, Tucker Papers, *Labor in Angola*. Translation of relevant section of the colonial Act Decree no. 18, 570 of 8 July 1930. See also República Portuguesa, *Acto Colonial* Decreto-Lei no. 18, 570 of 8/7/1930 (Luanda: Impensa Nacional, 1930).

53. NAUS, RG 948, Angola, Foreign Service, p. 2; AUBU, Banco de Angola, Gerência de Benguela, *Relatório*, 1949, p. 1.

54. AHU, Rui de Sá Carneiro, "Delegação a 1a Conferencia Economica," p. 27.

55. Grémio do Milho Colonial Português, *Relatório* (Lisbon, 1933).

56. See, for example, Agência Geral dos Productos Agrícolas, *Brêve Notícia sobre o Comercio de Milho* Folheta 2, (Luanda: Imprensa Nacional, 1928).

57. *Ibid.*, p. 7.

58. AUBU, Banco de Angola, Gerência de Nova Lisboa, *Relatório*, 1936, p. 42; António Barreto, *Algumas notás sobre a acção da Junta de Exportação de Cereais*, (Lisbon, 1957), 9–12.

59. Ivo de Cequeira, *Relatório, 1931–32* (Luanda: Direcção dos Serviços e Negocios Indigenas, 1933), 414–16. This was intended to avoid bankruptcy caused by the astronomical rise in Angola's foreign debt brought on by the Depression.

60. TANKS, Benguela Estates, Africa Office, 1937–38.

61. AUBU, Banco de Angola, Gerência de Nova Lisboa, *Relatório*, 1940, 21.

62. CDIH, Est. 24, Pasta 16, doc. 16, 1936; CCFMS, Box 6, file 105, Report of Prior, 1937, p. 6; *Annuario Estatítico de Angola*, (Luanda, 1942), 627.

63. *BO* no. 43, 1st Series, (22 October 1941): 449.

64. PRO, FO371 60249, Portugal, file 42, 2533/42/36.

65. PRO, Z1293, "Angolan Budget," 1948.

66. David H. Gallagher, *Along African Trails* (Toronto: The United Church of Canada, 1952), p. 70.

67. Kenneth Beaton, *Angola Now* (Toronto: Committee on Missionary Education, 1945).

68. *O Jornal de Benguela*, 23 August 1918, p. 3; José de Oliveira Ferreira Diniz, "De Política Indigena em Angola," *Boletim da Agência Geral das Colonias de Angola* 5, no. 44 (May 1929): 158; *Annuario Estatístico de Angola* (Luanda, 1950), 627.

69. CDIH, Est. 8, Cx. 3, Administrador de Concelho de Bailundo, Porto Balombo, 1925–36; Est. 78, Cx. 1, Bailundo, "Relatório do Administrador do Concelho de Bailundo; *Annuario Estatístico de Angola* (Luanda, 1942), 571.

70. CDIH, Est. 33, Cx. 19, Huambo, no. 15, "Chefes Indigenas," 27 December, 1948.

71. PRO, FO371 131649, JP 163 1/9, Africa Department, Portuguese Africa, Sir C. Stirling, "Impressions of the Portuguese Colonial Administration in Angola and Mozambique," p. 11.

72. AHU, Sala 2, Maço 2877 Relatório dum inquérito ao processo disciplina instuarado ao concelho do Bailundo contra Admin. José Feigueira de Sousa, *Ibid*; Adm. Amadeu Betancourt . . . Reis, "Relatório dum Processo disciplinar" (7/3/1936) AHU, Sala 2, Est. 2827, "Relatório da Missão do Presidente da Commissão de Cartografia das Colonias em 1933," 21 July 1935.

73. *Annuario Estatítico de Angola* (Luanda, 1937), 232.

74. *Jornal de Benguela*, 3 December 1946, p. 6.

75. *Ibid.*

76. United Nations Archives, New York (UNA), DAG 4/4.2/1, "Background Information on Angola," p. 3.

77. UCC, Box 2, File 37, Eduardo Jonatão Chingunji, "Report of a Visit to Mossamedes and Porto Alexandre," Feb/March 1943, pp. 1–8; CDIH, Est. 25, Pasta 16, no. 8, 12 December 1947, Despacho do Governador da Provincia.

78. UNA, DAG 4/4.2/1 "Background Information on Angola," p. 25.

79. *Ibid.*, 134.

80. Castro, *O Sistema Colonial*, 146; Egerton, *Angola*, 192–98.

81. See, for example, UNA DAG, 4/4.2-16, Meeting no. 76, Interview with Robert McGowan, 25 May 1962, p. 42, concerning his recollection of labor practices in the highlands in the 1950s. See also CDIH, Est. 77, Cx. 19, Huambo, no. 20, Correspondência Diversa, 1951, in which Governor Feirreira of Benguela Province wrote to the administrator of the *concelho* of Huambo, requesting him to use his good offices to recruit laborers for the fishing firm of José Domingo Antunes, which was experiencing difficulties in recruiting laborers.

82. AHU, 7/3/1936, Governor General to Minister, Relatório dum Processo disciplinario, pp. 27–30.

83. CDIH, Est. 76, Cx. 1, Bailundo Report, 1936.

84. AUBU, Banco de Angola, Gerência de Lobito, *Relatório*, 1935, p. 10.

85. TANKS, Benguela Estates, Africa Office Reports, 1936–1942.

86. UCC, Angola Mission, Personal Reports, 1961–64, Reuling, "Unknown Land," 4.

87. UNA, DAG 4/4.2-16, Meeting no. 66, Interview with Theodore Tucker (12 April 1962), p. 26.

88. One administrator had the tuition of his children (who were in private school in Lisbon) paid for by a businessman who relied on him for contract laborers. AUBU, Banco de Angola, Gerência de Benguela, *Relatório* 1945, p. 23.

89. Tucker, *A Tucker Treasury*, 119.

90. PRO, FO 371/90313, JP 2181/1, Africa Department, Portuguese Africa, S. P. House, "Angola: Native Affairs," 16 October 1951.

91. Mary Dewar, Interview, New York City, May 1987. Dewar, an American, served for five years, 1953–58, as a missionary nurse in the central highlands.

92. PRO FO 371/90313 JP 2181/1, Africa Department, Portuguese Africa, S. P. House, "Angola: Native Affairs," 19 October 1951.

93. UNA, DAG 4/4/.2-16, McGowan, p. 41; CDIH, Est. 24, pasta 16, no. 11, Administrator of Concelho of Bailundo to Governor General, 28 March 1938; CCFMS, Box 7, file 135, John Tucker, "Some Memories of Government Relations and Other Matters," January 1942, p. 8.

94. M.A.C. da Silveira Ramos, "Recruitamento de mão-de-obra indigena," in *I Congresso dos Economistas Portuguesas*, Parte III, (Lisbon, Instituto Nacional de Estatística, 1955), 15–16.

95. UCC, Angola Mission, Personal Reports, 1961–64, Reuling, "Unknown Land," p. 4.

96. *London Times* (21 June 1960), p. 13.

97. M.A.C. da Silveira Ramos, "A Industria de Pesca e a Mão de obra Indigena," in *I Congresso dos Economistas Portuguesas*, Parte III (Lisbon, Instituto Nacional de Estatística, 1955), 77–81.

98. *Ibid.*, 4.

99. CCFMS, Box 2, file 37, Eduardo Jonatão Chingunji, p. 7 "Report" Feb/March 1943; for an unofficial critique of the fishing industry, see Castro, *O Sistema Colonial*, 144–46.

100. UNA, DAG 4/4.2/1, "Background Information on Angola." See also Réné Pélissier, *La colonie du minotaure: Nationalismes e révoltes en Angola (1926–1961)* (Ogeval: Pélissier, 1978), 145–57 and Basil Davidson, *In the Eye of the Storm: Angola's People* (Garden City, N.Y.: Doubleday, 1973).

101. UNA, DAG 4/4.2/1, "Background Information on Angola."

102. NAUS, R.G. 59, Dec. File 1940–44, From 853L1561/Jacket 2 to 853m. 6363/69, Box 59, Memorandum on present situation in Angola by Gladwyn M. Childs, p. 1.

103. UCC, Box 8, file 145, Collins to Wilkerson, 2 June 1943, p. 2.

104. Dewar interview; UCC, Angola, Reports and Documents, 1969, Childs, "Mission and Church," p. 3; Pélissier, *La Colonie*, 357.

105. UCC, Box 2, File 38, Overseas Mission, Minutes of General Assembly, 13 January 1961, p. 12.

106. See UNA DAG 4/4.2/10, "Some Observations on the Committee Report of the ILO Concerning Labor Organization in Portuguese Africa," p. 5. The exploitation of village labor for the benefit of the state and settlers was confirmed in interviews with two Ovimbundu eyewitness; Interview with Paulo Figueiredo, Washington, D.C., U.S.A., June, 1986 and Aarão Cornelio, interview, Grove City, Pa, U.S.A, 5–6 July, 1986.

107. PRO, FO 371/11958, JP 1016/1, Extract of a meeting held at the British Embassy, Lisbon, 27 March 1956; *London Times*, 21 June 1960, p. 13.

108. AUBU, Banco de Angola, Gerência de Nova Lisboa, *Relatório*, 1936, p. 42; António Barreto, *Algumas Notás*, 9–12; Gremio de Milho, *Relatório*, (1943), 5; AUBU, Banco de Angola, Gerência de Benguela, *Relatório*, 1939, p. 29; AUBU, Banco de Angola, Gerência de Benguela, *Relatório*, 1940, p. 60.

109. CDIH, Est. 9, Cx. 4, 11 April 1932.

110. *A Provincia de Angola* (9 February 1929), p. 3.

111. *O Lobito*, 7 March 1943, p. 3; *A Provincia de Angola*, 7 November 1939, p. 3. (European farmers received part of the seeds as well.)

112. *O Lobito*, 7 March 1943, p. 3.

113. Barreto, *Algumas Notás*, Mappas.

114. "Relatório Annual da Del. Reg. dos Serviços Agricola de Benguela," Direcção dos Serviços de Agricola e Commercio, *Boletim*, 3 (8–12) (1930): 124–25.

115. TANKS, BR, Report of Alvaro de Mello Machado, 3 May 1938, p. 62.

116. *Annuario Estatístico* (Luanda, 1935), 191; Grémio de Milho, *Relatório*, 1949, 5.

117. TANKS, BR, Report of Alvaro de Mello Machado, Director of Caminho de Ferro de Benguela, European Settlement, 29 March 1938.

118. Soares, *Política de bem-estar*, 62.

119. AUBU, Gerência de Ganda, *Relatório*, 1942, p. 6.

120. *O Lobito*, 30 July 1941, p. 1.

121. AHU, Sala 2, 2 Feb 1939, Robert Hudson et al. to Presidente do Conselho e Ministeros, p. 2.

122. AUBU, Banco de Angola, Gerência de Nova Lisboa, *Relatório*, 1938, p. 8; *O Intransigente*, 22 June 1937.

123. *A Provincia de Angola* 2 January 1936, p. 2; *BO* no. 47 (30 November 1935): 787; AUBU, Banco de Angola, Gerência de Nova Lisboa, *Relatório*, 1936, p. 42; *BO*, 1st series, no. 46 (4 December 1937): 571–72.

124. *O Lobito*, 10 September 1940, p. 3; 27 November 1940, p. 1.

125. CCFMS, Box 7, file 130, Tucker Report, Dondi Station, 1941.

126. *O Lobito*, 23 November, 1943.

127. *A Provincia de Angola*, 2 January 1936, p. 2; *BO* no. 47 (30 November 1935): 787; AUBU, Banco de Angola, Gerência de Nova Lisboa, *Relatório*, 1936, p. 42.

128. Direcção dos Serviços de Agricola e Comerico, *Boletim* (1930): 125; *A Provincia de Angola*, 12 June 1930, p. 1.

129. PRO, FO 371 (1933 Political, Western Europe), #17418 Files 1073–1629–W3757/1315/36, Report of Consul General Bullock, 5 April 1933.

130. *Annuario Estatístico de Angola* (Luanda, 1935), 191.

131. Grémio do Milho Colonial, *Relatório* (Lisbon, 1949), 5.

132. Direcção dos Serviços de Agricola e Comerico, *Boletim* (1930): 125.

133. *Jornal de Benguela*, 25 May 1943, p. 12.

134. F. Correira Mendes Vidigal, *O Milho na Económia da Provincia de Angola*, (Lisbon: Escola Superior, Provincia de Angola, 1953–54), 13; AUBU, Banco de Angola, Gerência de Benguela, *Relatório*, 1949, p. 54.

135. *Boletim Geral do Ultramar* (Lisbon), p. 74.

136. Cornelio Interview, Dewar Interview.

137. *Boletim Geral do Ultramar* (Lisbon), p. 75.

138. Morais, "Transformação," 78–83.

139. *A Provincia*, 31 December 1931; AUBU, Banco de Angola, Gerência de Benguela, *Relatório*, 1950, p. 85; AUBU, Banco de Angola, Gerência de Nova Lisboa, *Relatório*, 1943, p. 35; Heywood, "Agriculture," 366.

140. Morais, "Transformação," 82–83.

141. Barreto, *Algumas Notas*, 42–43.

142. Morais "Transformação," 82–83.

143. Grémio do Milho Colonial, *Relatório*, p. 5.

144. Vidigal, *Milho*, 19.

145. CCFMS, Box 6, file 114, Mrs. S. R. Collins to Friends, 20 November 1938; CCFMS., Box 8, file 172, Chisamba Report, 1945, p. 1; PRO, FO 371 C48879/39/36, #39583, "Report on Labor Conditions Angola, February 1943," Letter from Merlin Ennis; CCFMS Box 6, file 105, Report by Prior, p. 4.

146. *Annuario Estatístico de Angola* (Luanda), 362.

147. TANKS, Benguela Estates, Africa Office Report, 1 April 1932–1 March 1933; Africa Office Report, 1936–42.

148. CCFMS, Box 7, file 16, Henry A Niepp to Friends, 30 January 1938; CCFMZ, Box 6, file 93, Chisamba Station Reports, 1933–34, p. 3; *O Intransigente*, 23 November 1937.

149. *O Lobito*, 5 July 1941.

150. CDIH, Est. Cx. 3, Huambo, no. 2, Report from Posto Civil de Vila Nova, 8 June 1934.

151. Cornelio interview. This Ocimbundu reported knowing of an incident involving workers who, on returning from contract labor, were kept in the store of a settler until they had spent all their wages. Cornelio lived in a Christian village and at the Protestant mission of Bungie, Ngalangi. He was born in Ngalangi in 1937 and left Angola in 1975. He knew the rural scene well, as he spent considerable time with his grandmother, who had been a member of the precolonial ruling group. His grandmother lived in a non-Christian village. Even though it might well be apocryphal, at least from the viewpoint of the Ovimbundu who suffered at the hands of the settlers, it is not so far-fetched. Davidson and Pélissier provide additional examples.

152. UCC, Angola, Reports and Documents, 1969, Gladwyn M. Childs, "Mission and Church in Angola," p. 3; see also Christine Messiant, "Luanda (1945–1961): Colonisés, société colonial e engagement nationaliste," in Michel Cahen, ed., *"Vilas" et "Cidades"*, 144.

153. UNA, DAG 4/4.2-9, Woodman Statement, p. 71; UNA, DAG 4/4.2-9, Henderson Interview, pp. 13–15.

154. For a similar but more comprehensive analysis of the process in Luanda see Messiant, "Luanda," 125–99.

155. UNA, DAG 4/4.2-16, Meeting no.17, Chipenda Hearing, p. 18; UNA, DAG 4/4.2-9, Henderson Interview, p. 41; UNA, Woodman Statement, p. 51; Okuma, *Angola in Ferment*, 37, quoting *Annuario Estatístico de Angola*, 1958.

156. AHU, Sala 2, Est, 2827, *Relatório*, pp. 15–16.

157. Fred Bridgland, *Jonas Savimbi: A Key to Africa* (New York: Paragon House, 1987), 26.

158. CDIH, Est. 4, no. 9, Posto Adm. de Vila Nova, 1930s; AHU, Processo Disciplinar.

159. CDIH, Est. 33, Cx. 19, doc. 25, 1950. Jonas Savimbi followed the same strategy when UNITA occupied rural regions in eastern Angola during the civil war.

160. Wheeler, *Angola*, 131; AHU, Processo Disciplinar.

161. CDIH, Est. 24, Pasta 33, no. 8, 1944; *Journal de Benguela*, 25 February 1944, p. 7.

162. CDIH, Est. 33, Cx. 19, Huambo, no. 15, "Chefes Indigenas," 27 December 1948.

163. UNA, DAG 4/4.2-10, Meeting no. 66, Tucker, p. 6; UNA, DAG 4/4.2-16, Tucker, p. 35; Interview, Adelia Cardoso, Charles County, Maryland, August, 1986; Interview, Aarão Cornelio, Grove City, Pa, U.S.A.

164. CDIH, Est. 33, Cx. 20, no. 2, Secção 7a, Processo 8, 1946, História dos Postos.

165. Interview with Adelia Cardoso, Charles County, Maryland, August 1986; Figueiredo interview.

166. Edwards, *Ovimbundu*, 31.

167. Pélissier, *La Colonie*, 318.

168. *Ibid.*

169. *Ibid.*

170. For some discussion of the Zimbabwe case see Ian Phimister, *An Economic and Social History of Zimbabwe, 1890–1948* (Harlow: Longman, 1988). See also Terrence Ranger, *Peasant Consciousness and Guerrilla War in Zimbabwe* (London: James Currey, 1985).

171. Soares, *Política de bem-estar*, 54–55.

172. PRO, FO 371 JP 1282/2, S. P. House to Secretary of Foreign Affairs, 14 November 1950.

173. Soares, *Política de bem-estar*, 63.

174. *Ibid.*, 43.

175. Cornelio interview.

176. O Intransigente, 22 June 1937. *O Lobito*, 23 March 1940; *Journal de Benguela*, 5 June 1942, p. 2; AUBU, Banco de Angola, Gerência de Nova Lisboa, *Relatório*, 1940, p. 19; CCFMS, Box 7, file 130, Dondi Station Report, 1941; PRO, FO 371 C48879/39/36, #39583, "Report," February 1944.

177. AUBU, Banco de Angola, Gerência de Nova Lisboa, *Relatório*, 1940, p. 19.

178. *A Provincia* (1 January 1936); CDIH, Est. 24 Pasta 33, doc. 8, Report from Concelho do Bailundo, 1941.

179. AUBU, Banco de Angola, Gerência de Caconda, *Relatório* 1940, p. 17.

180. AUBU, Banco de Angola, Gerência de Benguela, *Relatório* 1943, p. 40.

181. *Annuario Estatístico de Angola* (Luanda, 1941), 347.

182. *O Intransigente*, 28 November 1945, p. 5.

183. CCFMS, Box 3, file 25, 1927.

184. CDIH, Est. 8, Cx. 3, Huambo, Estatística Riqueza Indigena, 1935–36.

185. CCFMS, Box 5, file 71, Report of Currie Institute, 1932, p. 1; CCFMS, box 4, file 52, Station Reports, Chileso Station, May 1929.

186. ABCFM, doc. 221, Galangue Report, 1938.

187. AUBU, Gerência de Nova Lisboa, *Relatório*, 1944, p. 23.

188. ABCFM, 15.1, Angola Mission, 1940–49, Gates to Coodsell, p. 5.

189. John. J. Tucker, *Old Ways and New Days in Angola, Africa* (Toronto: F.C. Stephenson, n.d. [1935].

190. ABCFM, Report of the Agricultural Extension Committee, 1939.

191. ABCFM, 15.1, Angola Mission Station Reports, 1940–1949, File 3, doc. 6, Sidney F. Dart to Reuling, 31 December 1947, p. 2.

192. CCFMS, Box 8, File 186, Alan T. Knight to Arnup, 25 August 1947, p. 1. Cornelio Interview; UNA, DAG 4/4.2-16, McGowan Interview, p. 23.

193. In the late forties, fees ranged from $2.00 to $4.00 (U.S.) a pair, and it was not unusual for a farmer to bring in four oxen for training. See ABCFM, 15.1, Angola Mission Station Reports, 1940–1949, Station Reports, Galangue, 1948–1949, p. 2.

194. UCC, Angola, Box 4, File 72, E. Clark to Friends, November, 1960, p. 2.

195. *Ibid.*

Notes to Chapter 4

1. Gov. Geral de Angola, A.C. Valdez Thomas dos Santos, "A Few Words about Angola," Direcção dos serviços de Economia, 1948, p. 32.

2. This concept became popular in Brazilian intellectual circles in the post–World War II period.

3. For a description and defense by Portuguese officials of the colony's social structure as it was in the early fifties, see Egerton, *Angola*, 250–56.

4. F. W. Heimer, *The Decolonization Conflict in Angola, 1974–1976: An Essay in Political Sociology* (Geneva: IUHEI, 1979), 5–12.

5. Henderson, *Igrega*, 291.

6. AGSE, Boîte 485 B, Keiling to Monseigneur, 8 December 1929.

7. Henderson, *Igreja*, 292.

8. *Ibid.*, 291.

9. *Ibid.*, 291–92.

10. Soares, *Política de bem-estar*, 25.

11. Rui Pereira, "Antropologia aplicada na política colonial Portugues do Estado Novo," *Revista Internacional de Estudos Africanos* 4–5 (June–December, 1986): 191–235.

12. Soares, *Política de bem-estar*, 126.

13. *Ibid.*, 25.

14. Soares, *Política de bem-estar*, presented an elaborate critique of the work of the delegations intended to support the policy of rural well-being.

15. Pereira, "Antropologia aplicada," 191, 221.

16. See, for example, Edwards, *The Ovimbundu*.

17. Edwards, in *Ovimbundu*, pp. xv–xvii, publicized the "better village" programs which the Protestant missionaries had been implementing and underwrote some programs themselves. See Soares, *Política de bem-estar, passim*, and UCC, WMS, Box 2, file 38, Report on the Committee on Folk Betterment, 1956 and 1957.

18. AHU, *Relatório*, Processo Disciplinar, pp. 13–14; Alexandre Sarmento, "Contribuição para o estudo da antropologia dos Bailundos," *Anais do Instituto de Medicina Tropical* (Lisbon, 1957): 328; Sarmento, "Subsidios para o estudo demografico da população de Angola," *Anais do Instituto de Medicina Tropical* (Lisbon, 1957); Pereira, "Antropologia aplicada," 191–234.

19. AHU, Processo Disciplinar Administrador do Bailundo.

20. PRO, FO 371/11958 JP 1016/2, Consul to FO, 26 Feb. 1956, p. 1.

21. UCC, Angola, Joint Committee, Chilesso, Feb. 1966, Excerpts of Letters from Africa. UNA, DAG 4/4.2-16, Dr. Robert McGowan, Interview, 25 May 1962, p. 6; Manuel Nunes Gabriel, *Angola: Cinco séculos do Cristianismo* (Queluz: Literal Sociedade Editora, Lt.da, 1978), 511. Many Protestant villages also operated their own dispensaries and clinics and charged for the services. Dewar Interview, Cardoso Interview, Cornelio Interview. Nurses at these clinics received yearly refresher courses and medications at cost since they were not allowed to receive training nor purchase medicines openly. Dewar Interview.

22. CCFMS, Tucker Correspondence, Box 1, File 17, Occasional Paper no. 3. Alliança Evangélica de Angola, 26 March 1943, p. 1.

23. UNA, Angola, Political and Social Affairs, Ona Forest, "Economic Report (1962)," p. 10. In 1959 the government set aside 5 percent of the colonial budget for social overheads.

24. Bill Warren, *Imperialism: Pioneer of Capitalism* (New York: New Left Books, 1981). For an opposing view see Marc H. Dawson, "Health, Nutrition, and Population in Central Kenya, 1890–1945," in Dennis D. Cordell and Joel W. Gregory, eds., *African Population and Capitalism: Historical Perspectives* (Madison: University of Wisconsin Press, 1987), 201–17.

25. UNA, DAG 4/4.2-1, Background Information:, p. 49; UNA, DAG 4/4.2-16, McGowan Interview, pp. 26–27.

26. These specific statistics are found in the testimony given by the Protestant medical doctor, Dr. Robert McGowan, before the UN subcommittee on Angola. See UNA, DAG 4/4.2-16, McGowan Testimony. Mary Dewar, a nurse in the villages at the time the survey was undertaken, explained the methods used to compile the statistics in her interview with the author in 1987.

27. Henderson Interview, p. 17.

28. John Sender and Sheila Smith put infant mortality rates for Africa at the turn of the twentieth century at 500 per 1000 live births. See John Sender and Sheila Smith, *The Development of Capitalism in Africa* (New York: Mentheun, 1986), 64. The authors list no figures for Angola, but give the figures for Mozambique as 160 deaths per 1000 live births. Infant mortality in Angola was certainly no better than in Mozambique.

29. PRO, FO 371/11958 JP 1016/1, 27 March 1956.

30. CCFMS, UCC Box 2, file 37 "Aliança Evangelica de Angola," and "Report of the Honorable Secretary," 11 Aug 1944, p. 2.

31. Gabriel, *Angola*, 512.

32. Mary Floyd Cushman, *Missionary Doctor: The Story of Twenty Years in Africa* (New York: Harper & Brothers, 1944), 90.

33. UCC, File 1, Box 25, Thomas Okuma "Report of the Treasurer for the Year 1959," December 1959, pp. 1–2.

34. Soares, *Política de bem-estar*, 79–81.

35. UCC, Box 4, File 72, Edith Clarke, December 1957, Report, p. 2.

36. UNA, DAG 4/4.2-16, Dr. Robert McGowan Interview. Mary Dewar also confirmed the view that the people's health was very bad. Dewar Interview.

37. See, for example, Dewar Interview.

38. Mrs. Henderson, the wife of American pastor Lawrence Henderson, recalled for the UN committee that in 1955 "there were more water taps or more water outlets in my home than there were in all the Cizala [senzala-slum] for 30,000 people." She also recalled that garbage collection was once a month. UNA, DAG 4/4.2-9, Kitty Henderson, Statement before Committee, pp. 8–11, 17.

39. UNA, DAG 4/4.2-16, McGowan Interview, p. 6. Mary Dewar corroborated this statement in her interview with the author in 1987.

40. PRO, FO371/11958 JP 1016/2, 26 Feb. 1956.

41. The population data provided by the Portuguese government statistics for 1954–56 show growth rates around twenty per thousand. UNA, DAG, File, World Health Organization, "Information on Health," 18 August 1961, p. 4. Undoubtedly, Portuguese figures provided to the UN were not based on the 1950 census. Figures for 1900 cannot be calculated by means of a model life table (no other method would be available using the existing data), because of the peculiarities of the age-sex pyramid of those years; see Heywood and Thornton, "Demography, Production, and Labor," 242–49.

42. UNA, DAG 4/4.2-1, "Background Information," p. 49; UNA, DAG 4/4.2-16, McGowan Interview, pp. 26–27.

43. AGSE, Boîte 485 B, Keiling to Monseigneur, 16 July 1927; Henderson, *Igreja*, 169.

44. AHU, Sala 2, 2875 José Ribeiro da Cruz, "Porque é urgente tratamos da colonização de Angola por portuguesas," 1932.

45. AGSE, Boîte 485 B, Keiling to Monseigneur, 6 May 1931, p. 1.

46. AGSE, Boîte 485 B, P. Daniel Junqueira to Monseigneur, 18 May 1939, p. 1.

47. AGSE, Boîte 485 B, Moise Pinho, Bishop of Angola and Congo, to Monseigneur, 10 November 1939.

48. AGSE, Boîte 485 B, Keiling to Monseigneur, 4 August 1932.

49. Gabriel, *Angola*, 371, 478, 562.

50. Henderson, *Igreja*, 297.

51. Agência Geral Das Colónias, *A Diocese de Nova Lisboa* (Lisbon: Agência Geral Das Colónias, 1946), 5.

52. Henderson, *Igreja*, 297.

53. AGSE, Boîte 485 B, Keiling to Monseigneur, 27 August 1932.

54. "Diocese de Nova Lisboa," *Portugal em Africa* 20 (1944): 254.

55. Their names were Father Justino Chilombo Changoma and Sister Tereza do Minino de Jesus. Agência Geral Das Colonias, *A Diocese*, 11 and 20.

56. *Ibid.*, 6–18.

57. *Ibid.*, 11.

58. Ovimbundu informant, Personal Correspondence, 19 June 1997.

59. Edwards, Ovimbundu, 24; Henderson, *Igreja*, 192.

60. Agência Geral das Colónias, *A Diocese*, 22.

61. *Ibid.*, 25.

62. UCC, File 44, Box 3, Africa Committee, National Council of Churches in Christ, "Protestant Missions in Angola," 18 January 1951, pp. 1–2.

63. *Ibid.* See also Eduardo de Sousa Ferreira, *Portuguese Colonialsim in Africa* (Paris: UNESCO, 1974), 49–136.

64. UCC, File 44, Box 3, Africa Committee, National Council of Churches in Christ, "Protestant Missions in Angola," 18 January 1951, pp. 1–2.

65. Soares, *Política de bem-estar*, 112–16, referring to the Escola da Magestério Teofilo Duarte and the Missão Feminina da Bela Vista.

66. Gabriel, *Angola*, 500, 501.

67. UCC, Box 5 File 92, Report of Utting, pp. 1–2; Soares, *Política de bem-estar*, 114–17.

68. PRO, FO 371/131649 JP1631/7, Report of Sir Charles Stirling, 17 July 1958, p. 3.

69. PRO, FO 371/97261, Report of British Consulate, 22 February 1952, p. 3.

70. Henderson, *Igreja*, 273.

71. See, for example, Ferreira, *O Fim de uma Era*, 81–82.

72. Messiant, "Luanda 1945–1961," 156; Davidson, *In the Eye of the Storm: Angola's People* (Garden City, N.Y.: Doubleday, 1973); J.M. Da Silva Cunha, *O trabalho indígena: Estudo de direito colonial*, 2nd ed. (Lisbon, Agência Geral do Ultramar, 1955).

73. Agência Geral das Colónias, *A Diocese*, 8–20.

74. Henderson, *Angola*, 159.

75. UNA, DAG 4/4.2-1, Political and Social Affairs Council, UNESCO, no.7, September 1960, "Current Student Enrollment Statistics," p. 12. Among the students who were awarded high school diplomas were Julio Chinovola Cacunda, Aarão Kunga, Móses Shangolola, Maria Adela Cardoso, Aarão Kasoma, Mateus Chicola, Armando Cacunda, and Chibanda. See Marcum, *The Angolan Revolution* 2: 108–20; Figuereido Interview; Cardoso Interview; Cornelio Interview.

76. Gabriel, *Angola*, 515.

77. UNA, DAG 4/4.2-12, Statements and Testaments, "Statement of Kambundu, an African inhabitant of Angola," 23 July 1961. In the coffee growing areas of the province the treatment of people in Catholic villages was outrageous. One report to the United Nations complained that the "students are required to gather coffee, it being determined how much each ought to deliver. Anyone who did not obey was held to be disobedient, being immediately expelled and sent to the post, where he was obliged to pay the tax levied upon adults." UNA, DAG 2/4.2-13, Youth group, "Filhos dos Chamados Indigenas de Angola," p.1.

78. For the origins of the MPLA/Portuguese communist links, see Fernando J. Andresen Guimarães, "Origins and Development of the MPLA: Two Dissident Views," *Camões Center Quarterly* 5, nos. 1 & 2 (Winter 1993–94): 17–29. See also Marcum, *The Angolan Revolution*, 1: 15–48.

79. See Cahen, ed., *"Villas" et "Cidades"*. For developments in the north see Davidson, *In the Eye of the Storm*, 145–82, and Marcum, *The Angolan Revolution* 2: 49–100, and chapter nine.

80. This number is taken from Catholic sources. The number of Ovimbundu Catholics in official lists is 1,500,000. See, for example, Pélissier, *Colonie*; see also Gabriel, *Angola*, 492.

81. *United Church Record and Missionary Review* (1936): 21.

82. CCFMS, Box 3, file 36, Report of Chisamba Station, 1926–27, p. 4; CCFMS, Box 6, file 98, Chileso Station Report, 1936, p. 1; CCFMS, Box 6, file 98, Camundongo Report, 1936, p. 3; CDIH, Est. 9, Cx. 44, Relatório of Huambo, 15 February 1936.

83. CCFMS, Box 7, file 116, Henry A. Niepp to Friends, 30 January 1938.

84. UCC, Angola, Reports and Documents, Rutherford and Gilchrist, "Angola," p. 1.

85. John Tucker, *Men of Africa* (Toronto: United Chruch of Canada, n.d.), 19–38.

86. Cushman, *Missionary Doctor*, 42.

87. *Ibid.*, 106–7; 152.

88. Tucker-Ward Collection, Webster Letters, N6.

89. CCFMS, Tucker Papers, Box 1, file 14, Tucker to Friends 12 March 1934, p. 1;

90. CCFMS, Tucker Papers, Box 7, file 119, Reports.

91. CCFMS, Tucker Papers, Box 8, file 144, Camundongo Report, p. 2; CCFMS, UCC, WMS, Angola Box 5, file 75b, M. Dawson to Friends, 13 June 1959.

92. Beaton, *Angola Now*, 50–51.

93. *United Church Record and Missionary Review* (1930): 11.

94. Beaton, *Angola Now*, 42, 50.

95. Gallagher, *Along African Trails*, 110.

96. CCFMS, Tucker Papers, Box 8, file 144, Camundo Report, p. 2; CCFMS, UCC, WMS, Angola, Box 5, file 75b, M. Dawson to Friends, 13 June 1959.

97. Gallagher, *Along African Trails*, 112.

98. AHU, Processo Administrativo, 26 September 1935.

99. Tucker-Ward Collection, Webster Papers N6.

100. Tucker-Ward Collection, Selected Writings; Gallagher, *Along African Trails*, 110; Ovimbundu informant, Personal Correspondence, 19 June 1997.

101. Henderson, *Igreja*, 232.

102. CCFMS, Box 1, file 17, Tucker to Friends 4 October 1943.

103. CCFMS, Box 7, file 130, Dondi Station Report, 1941; Henderson, *Igreja*, 263 and Tucker, *Old Ways and New*, 42–43.

104. Ovimbundu Informant, Personal Correspondence, 19 June 1997.

105. Beaton, *Angola Now*, 50.

106. Tucker, *Men of Africa*, 27.

107. Cushman, *Missionary Doctor*, 39–40.

108. *Ibid.*, 39.

109. *Ibid.*

110. *Ibid.*, 88.

111. *Ibid.*, 103–4.

112. Yves Loiseau and Pierre-Guillaume de Roux, *Portrait d'un révolutionnaire en général: Jonas Savimbi* (Paris: La Table Ronde, 1987), 37.

113. Kassembe, *Angola: 20 ans de guerre*, 38.

114. Cushman, *Missionary Doctor*, 122.

115. Loiseau and de Roux, *Portrait*, 39–40.

116. UCC, Box 5, file 75, WMS, Overseas Mission, Angola, Missionaries—Margaret Dawson, E. Utting, and M. Dawson to Friends, Sept. 1953, p. 2.

117. Gallagher, *Along African Trails*, 40.

118. Cushman, *Missionary Doctor*, 62.

119. Beaton, *Angola Now*, 33.

120. Dewar Interview; Cardoso Interview; UCC, Reports and Documents, 26 May, 1961, p. 2. Two young Protestant teachers, Pedro Paulo and Benjamin Manyeka, had up to four hundred students in the schools they ran. Cornelio Interview.

121. Loiseau and de Roux, *Portrait*, 67.

122. UCC, Angola, Reports and Documents, 1969, Margaret Dawson, "Mission and Church in Angola, Educational Work Then and Now," (1959), pp. 1–2.

123. UCC, Box 5, file 92, Elizabeth Utting, Annual Report, 1955, p. 1.

124. Dewar Interview.

125. Beaton, *Angola Now*, 61.

126. CCFMS, Box 2, F 37 EM, Eduardo Jonatão Chingunji, "Report of a Visit to Mossamedes and Porto Alexandre, 1943."

127. CCFMS, Box 5, file 7, Camundongo Station, 1932, p. 2; CCFMS, Box 7, file 116, Henry A. Niepp to Friends, 30 January 1938; CCFMS, Box 8, file 144, Report on Coast Work, 1944, p. 4; CCFMS, Box 6, file 113, J. M. Singer to Jesse H. Arnot.

128. UNA, DAG 4/4.2-9, Henderson Interview, p. 7.

129. CCFMS, Box 5, file 7, p. 2.

130. CCFMS, Box 4, file 61, Collins to Endicott, 25 October 1931.

131. CCFMS, Box 8, file 163, Camundongo Report, 1941, p. 3.

132. CCFMS, Box 8, Report from Chisamba, 1942, p. 3; CCFMS, Box 8, file 163, Camundongo Report, 1941, p. 4.

133. AUBU, Banco de Angola, Gerência de Nova Lisboa, *Relatório*, 1940.

134. CCFMS, Box 3, file 36, Report of Chisamba Station, p. 4; CCFMS, Box 6, file 98, Chileso Station Report, 1936, p. 1; CCFMS, Box 6, file 98, Camundongo Report, 1936, p. 3.

135. CCFMS, Box 5, file 7, Camundongo Station, 1932, p. 2.

136. CCFMS, Box 2, file 37, "Aliança Evangelica de Angola, 10–15 August 1944, p. 7.

137. *United Church Record and Missionary Review* (1936): 21.

138. UNA, DAG 4/4.2-9, Henderson Interview, pp. 25–26; CDIH, Est. 77, Cx. 8, no. 31, Huambo, 1947.

139. CCFMS, Tucker Papers, Box 2, file 37, Alliança Evangelica de Angola, "Report of the Secretary," 1944, p. 4.

140. Henderson, Igreja, 263–64, 289–90.

141. NAUS, RG 59, file 190, 1944, 853L.1561, Jacket 2 to 853M 6363/69, Box 59, Irving N. Linnel (Consul of Luanda) to Secretary of State, 13 March 1943, p. 2; also see Heywood, "Slavery," 425–34.

142. CCFMS, Box 2, file 37, Tucker to Emory Ross, 11 January 1945, p. 1.

143. CCFMS, Tucker Corr., Box 1, File 17, Tucker to Friends, 4 Oct. 1943.

144. CCFMS, Box 1, file 15, Tucker to Endicott, 14 July 1934.

145. CCFMS Box 3, file 43, WMS notes of an Interview with His Excellency the Portuguese Minister to the U.S., Senhor J. Brandire, New York, 8 Dec. 1939, p. 4.

146. UNA, DAG 4/4.2-9, Henderson Interview, pp. 26–27.

147. Vasco Lopes Alves, "Apontamentos sobre Angola," *Boletim Geral do Ultramar* ano XXXII, 267 (1956): 148–49.

148. Pélissier, *Colonie*, 100–105.

149. UCC, Angola, Reports and Documents, 1969, G.M. Childs, "Mission and Church," pp. 1–2. See also Torres, "Le Processus," 98–117.

150. Torres, "Le Processus," 111–12.

151. UNA, DAG 4/4.2-9, Henderson Interview, pp. 38, 41.

152. Family funds and scholarships from the Protestant boards paid for their training. UCC, Box 23, file 1, Report of Treasurer, 1959, p.3.

153. See, for example, Marcum, *The Angolan Revolution* 1: 105–9; Henderson, *Angola*, 157; UNA, DAG 4/4.2-16, Meeting no. 77, Chipenda Hearing, pp. 3, 12.

154. CCFMS, Box 7, file 130, Dondi Station Report, 1941.

155. Agência Geral das Colónias, *A Diocese*, 19.

156. CCFMS, WCC, WMS, Angola, Box 5, file 77b, M. Dawson Collection, 1950s.

157. Obviously this might be explained by the fascination of researchers and officials with African customs. See, for example, Lima, *Os Kyaka de Angola*.

158. Agência Geral das Colónias, *A Diocese*, 18–19.

159. PRO, FO 371/97261 22/2/52, Report of Consul, p. 4.

160. Edwards, *Ovimbundu*, 43.

161. CCFMS, UCC, WMS, Angola, file 75b, letter of M. Dawson, 13 June 1959.

162. Dewar Interview; in a letter from Margaret Dawson and Elizabeth Utting to friends in 1956, they wrote that "the heathen still rage about us. They tell us about bad spirits which cause illness as they encourage us to try the 'treatment' of the witch doctors. They attempt to harm us in every way." UCC, WMS, Angola, Box 5, file 75b, Utting and Dawson to Friends, May 1956.

163. UCC, WMS, Angola, Box 4, file 72, Edith Clark to Friends, Dec. 1957, p. 2.

164. Dewar Interview; UCC, WMS, Angola, Box 4, file 72, Edith Clark to Friends, Dec. 1957, pp. 2–3; UCC, WMS, Angola, Box 5, file 75b, M. Dawson to Friends, 13 June 1959, pp. 1–2.

165. Of the thirty thousand Africans in Lobito in 1955, none could legally own property in the city, even though some were *assimilados*. Illiterate Portuguese who had built houses in the African area, however, had legal rights to their houses and land. See Henderson Interview, pp. 8–11.

166. UCC, WMS, Angola, Box 5, file 75b, M. Dawson to Friends, 13 June 1959, pp. 1–2. In 1960 Edith Clark wrote that Protestant men were still expected to pay a high

bride price, and that the weddings were a mixture of African and Christian customs. UCC, WMS, Angola, Box 4, file 72, E. Clark to Friend, November 1960, p. 1.

167. Interview, Ocimbundu Informant (Washington, Spring 1993).

168. Dewar Interview; Cornelio Interview.

169. Henderson, *Angola*, 175.

170. This is the impression that one comes away with after interviews with a number of Angolans.

Notes to Chapter 5

1. Marcum, *The Angolan Revolution*, 1.

2. See Marcum, *Angolan Revolution, Vol. 2: Exile Politics and Guerrilla Warfare, 1962–1976* (Cambridge, Mass.: MIT Press, 1978); Film, "The New Liberation Wars," (Toronto: Stornoway Productions, 1988).

3. Heimer, *Decolonization Conflict*.

4. See, for example, Marcum, *The Angolan Revolution*, 1.

5. See David P. Sandgren, *Christianity and the Kikuyu: Religious Divisions and Social Conflict* (New York: P. Lang, 1989); Frederick Cooper, "Mau-Mau and the Discourses of Decolonization," *Journal of African History* 29 (1988): 313–20; John Lonsdale, "Mau of the Mind: Making Mau and the Remaking of Kenya," *Journal of African History* 31, (1990): 393–41.

6. See Berman, *Control and Crisis in Colonial Kenya*; Thabitha Kanogo, *Squatters and the Roots of Mau Mau* (London: James Currey, 1987); Dane Kennedy, *Islands of White: Settler Society and Culture in Kenya and Southern Rhodesia, 1890–1939* (Durham, N. C.: Duke University Press, 1987).

7. For an exception see Soremekun, *Angola: The Road to Independence*.

8. Davidson, *In the Eye of the Storm*.

9. Marcum, *The Angolan Revolution*, 2.

10. Clarence-Smith, *Third Portuguese Empire*, 192–223. For a critical review of the literature up to 1980 see also his "Class Structure and Class Struggles in Angola in the 1970s," *Journal of Southern African Studies* 7 (1980): 109–26.

11. See the relevant sections of Henderson, *Angola: Five Centuries of Conflict*; Heimer, *Social Change in Angola*; Bender, *Angola under the Portuguese*.

12. Marcum, Bender, Pélissier, and other scholars have all stressed that the military strategies which officials followed in Angola from 1961 to 1975 were not a response to the increasing sophistication or success of the nationalist attacks against Portuguese military and civilian targets in the colony. They maintain that the Portuguese were intent on keeping control over the state. Marcum, *The Angolan Revolution*, 2; Bender, *Angola under the Portuguese*, 157–237; and René Pélissier, *Le Naufrage des caravelles: Etudes sur la fin de l'empire portugais (1961–1975)* (Orgeval: Pélissier, 1979), pp. 162–93.

13. See also D. Porch, *The Portuguese Armed Forces and the Revolution*. (London: Croom Helm, 1977).

14. For the role of the military before 1961, see Pélissier, *La colonie du minotaure, passim*.

15. See, for example, Marcum, *The Angolan Revolution*, 1; See also Keith Somerville, *Angola: Politics, Economics and Society* (London: Lynne Rienner, 1986), 29.

16. Pélissier, *Naufrage*, 162–63; NAUS, RG 59, Records of G. Mennon Williams, 1961–1966, Account of Richard Beeston of the Daily Telegraph; NAUS, RG 59, Box 28 Records of G. Mennon Williams, American Committee on Africa, George Houser, "A Report on a Journey through Rebel Angola," p. 11. See also, Marcum, *The Angolan Revolution*, 1; for a Portuguese view, albeit from a critic of the regime, see Orlando Ribeiro, *A colonização de Angola e o seu fracasso* (Lisbon: Imprensa Nacional, 1981), where the author gives as the losses: 400 plantations destroyed, 500 white civilians killed, 170 Portuguese soldiers and between 30,000 and 50,000 Afro-Angolans killed. Three quarters of the population of the Kongo provinces were refugees.

17. Ribeiro, *A colonização*.

18. See Marcum, *The Angolan Revolution*, 1.

19. PIDE first came to Angola in 1959. Douglas Wheeler and René Pélissier, *Angola* (New York: Praeger, 1971), 146.

20. René Pélessier, in *Explorar: Voyages en Angola et autres lieux incertains* (Orgeval: Pélissier, 1979), relates his frustrations with PIDE officials on a journalistic journey to Angola in 1966; Marcum, *The Angolan Revolution*, 2: 1.

21. See, for example, Marcum, *The Angolan Revolution*, 2; Heimer, *Decolonization Conflict*; Clarence-Smith, *The Third Portuguese Empire*; Pélissier, *Naufrage*.

22. Ferreira, *Portuguese Colonialism in Africa*, 104.

23. Clarence-Smith, the source for this figure, countered that this only represented 7.7 percent of the country's gross national product. See *The Third Portuguese Empire*, 194. According to Marcum, however, Portugal's economy was weakened by the war. The country had the highest inflation rate in Europe (23%) and $400 million a year trade deficit by the early 1970s. Marcum, *The Angolan Revolution*, 2: 241.

24. See Anthony Lake, *The "Tar Baby" Option: American Policy toward Southern Rhodesia* (New York: Columbia University Press, 1976), 276; see also George Wright, *The Destruction of a Nation: United States Policy toward Angola since 1945* (London: Pluto Press, 1997), 49–56.

25. Pélissier, *Naufrage*, 85.

26. Marcum, *The Angolan Revolution*, 2: 426, footnote 13. Marcum notes that between 1969 and 1971, the percentage of defense costs borne by the Overseas Territories rose from 25.2 percent to 32.3 percent and that plans were underway for each Territory to organize more and more of their defense.

27. Bender, *Angola under the Portuguese*, 161.

28. Pélissier, *Naufrage*, 149–66.

29. Marcum, quoting material presented by the American Committee on Africa in 1971, noted that the United States was the source of many of the herbicides which Portugal began using in the colonies from 1969. See Marcum, *The Angolan Revolution* 2: 409.

30. See Bender, *Angola under the Portuguese*, p. 162.

31. See Marcum, *The Angolan Revolution*, 2: 244.

32. Bender, *Angola under the Portuguese*, 158–96.

33. Pélissier, *Naufrage*, 178.

34. See, for example, Bender, *Angola under the Portuguese*, 200–237.

35. Gerald Bender and Stanley P. Yoder, "Whites in Angola on the Eve of Independence: The Politics of Numbers," *Africa Today* 21 (1974): 23–37; Heimer, *Decolonization Conflict*, 54–55.

36. Tom Gallagher, *Portugal: A Twentieth Century Interpretation* (Manchester: Manchester University Press, 1983).

37. William Minter, *King Solomon's Mines Revisited: Western Interests and the Burdened History of Southern Africa* (New York: Basic Books, 1986), 234.

38. Clarence-Smith, *The Third Portuguese Empire*, 194–95.

39. Banco de Angola, *Relatórios e Contas*, 1960–1968; *Actualidade Económica* (Luanda) 2 April 1970.

40. Clarence-Smith, *The Third Portuguese Empire*, 205. See also Pélissier, *Naufrage*, 85–88.

41. ACS, "African Scenario," (Loose leaf, manuscript), p. 1.

42. UNA, DAG 4/4.2-1, Ona Forrest, Economic Report . . . Angola," (1962), p. 15.

43. Rocha and Morais, "Angola," 39.

44. For the statistics of the impressive increase in mineral production, agriculture, and fishing between 1962 and 1970, see those complied by Pélissier in *Le Naufrage*, 83–89. See especially the work of Rameiro Ladeiro Monteiro, *A família nos musseques de Luanda: Subsidios para o seu estudo* (Luanda, Fundo de Acção Social no Trabalho em Angola, 1973), for work supported by state. Between 1960 and 1970 the urban population in Angola went from 396,383 or 8.2 percent of the entire population to 847,182 or 14.9 percent of the population. See Rocha and Morais, "Angola," 35.

45. Ferreira, *Portuguese Colonialism*, 96.

46. Eduardo de Sousa Ferreira, "The Present Role of the Portuguese Resettlement Policy," *African Studies*, 4, 21, 1 (1974): 53. One state-supported plan was the Cunene project designed to regulate the flow of the Cunene river. The plan aimed to bring five hundred thousand Portuguese to settle in the south of Angola. *Ibid.*, 50. See also Bender, *Angola under the Portuguese*, 107–31.

47. Clarence-Smith, *The Third Portuguese Empire*, 213.

48. High-ranking Portuguese still publicly expounded on the backwardness of African culture and the need for Africans to be led by the Portuguese. For example, in 1968 Salazar told an Argentine reporter that it would take another three hundred to five hundred years before Africans could govern themselves. Bender, *Angola under the Portuguese*, 207, note 10. Franco Nogueira, the Foreign Minister of Portugal, answered critics of Portuguese policy in Africa by pointing out that the Portuguese brought above all "human rights and racial equality" to Africa. Franco Nogueira, *The Third World* (London: Johnson, 1967), 11.

49. Clarence-Smith, *The Third Portuguese Empire*, 214–15.

50. UNA, DAG 4/4.2-1, "Recent Legislative Reforms Instituted in Angola, 1961."

51. This in effect doubled the tax which was US$5.00 at the time. See, for example, Marcum, *Angolan Revolution*, 1: 191; UNA, DAG 4/4.2-2, "English Translation of a Speech Delivered by Portuguese Minister for Overseas Territories in Oporto on August 28, 1961." See also UNA, DAG 4/4.2-1, "Recent Legislative Reports Instituted in Angola, 1961."

52. AHM, Caixa #52, no. 5, "A Situação Militar no sul de Angola pelo Governo Geral," 1918, p. 16.

53. See, for example, Davidson, *Eye of the Storm*; William Minter, *Operation Timber: Pages from the Savimbi Dossier* (Trenton, N.J.: Africa World Press, 1988).

54. Marcum, *The Angolan Revolution*, 1: 154–56.

55. *Ibid.*, 155.

56. Newspapers in Angola from the 1930s were subjected to intense scrutiny by state censors.

57. UNA, DAG 4/4.2-9, Statement of Holden Roberto to U.N. Sub-delegation, 1961, p. 9.

58. Bender, *Angola under the Portuguese*, 180.

59. *Washington Post*, 5 August 1974, A-16-1.

60. Pastor Marcos Fortuna, Response to Questionnaire Complied by Linda M. Heywood, May 1997.

61. Bridgland, *Savimbi*, 32–34; Loiseau and de Roux, *Portrait*, 37–39.

62. Although critics of UNITA suspected that Savimbi was cooperating with the Portuguese military because of his rift with MPLA, the evidence supporting the accusation became public only in 1982, when Portuguese military files were released to the press and Costa Gomes, the Portuguese commander in chief of the armed forces operating in Angola, detailed the relationship in several interviews. UNITA's leadership has never acknowledged that such a close relationship existed. See Heimer, *Decolonization of Angola*, 31; See also Minter, *Operation Timber*; John Stockwell, *In Search of Enemies: A CIA Story* (New York: W.W. Norton & Co, 1978), 151; Marga Holness, "The Struggle Continues," in David Martin and Phyllis Johnson eds., *Destructive Engagement: Southern Africa at War* (Harare: Zimbabwe Publishing House, 1986), 77–78.

63. Evidence from Marcos Fortuna, Response to Questionnaire, May, 1997.

64. Loiseau and de Roux, *Portrait*, 81.

65. Pélissier, *La Colonie du minotaure*, 534.

66. Irving Kaplan ed., *Angola: A Country Study* (Washington: American University Press, 1979), 77.

67. Unofficial estimates put the number at 100,000. See Rocha and Morais, "Angola nas Vésperas," 30, note 3.

68. *New York Times*, 20 March 1961, 3: 4.

69. Monteiro, *A Familia*, Table 6. See also Heimer, *Decolonization in Angola*, 21–22.

70. Henrique Guerra, *Angola: Estructura económica e classes sociais: Os ultimos anos do colonialismo português em Angola* (Lisbon: União dos Escritos Angolanos, 1979), 98–100. Linda Heywood, "History, Urbanization and Nationalism in Central Angola: The Case of Huambo/Nova Lisboa," Paper presented at the African Urban History Conference, School of Oriental and African Studies, London University, June, 1996).

71. For this period see Pélissier, *La colonie du minotaure*, 288–91; and Marcum, *The Angolan Revolution*, 1: 105–20.

72. Cornelio Interview; Loiseau and de Roux, *Portrait*, 82.

73. Pélissier, *La colonie du minotaure*, 288–90.

74. UNITA, *The UNITA Leadership* (Jamba: UNITA, 1990), 31.

75. *New York Times*, 9 March 1960, p. 3.

76. UCC, BWM, File 537, Correspondence, R.M. Bennett to Colleagues, 4 Dec. 1966; Marcum, *The Angolan Revolution*, 1: 148.

77. UNITA, *Leadership*, 32.

78. UCC, BWM, Angola, 1967, File 564, "A Partial List of Events . . . Central Angola, 1967," pp. 1–4.

79. UCC, BWM, Angola, 1965, File 502, Rev. and Mrs. Dille to Friends, Oct. 1965, pp. 1–3.

80. UNA McCowan, "Report to the United Nations," p. 16.

81. *Ibid.*, p. 7.

82. UCC, Angola, Documents, 1961, Murray MacInnes to J. A. Reuling, 13 June 1961. See also UCC, Reports and Documents, Angola, 1961; Thomas Okuma, "Report on Protestant Work in Angola," Confidential, N.Y., 6 November 1961, p. 2.

83. *Ibid.*

84. UCC, Personal Files, Angola 1961–1965, The Dilles to Friends, Camundongo, 27 May 1961; Henderson, *A Igreja*, 22. See also Marcum, *Angolan Revolution*, 1: 154–58.

85. Henderson, *A Igreja*, 301–38; Cornelio Interview.

86. UCC, File 502, BWM, Angola, 1965, Correspondence, Dilles to Friends, Oct. 1965, p. 3.

87. *Ibid.*, p. 2.

88. Henderson, *A Igreja*, 360. See also UCC, BWM, Angola, 1967, File 564, "A Partial List of Events . . . Central Angola, Jan.–May 1967.

89. The best analysis of this topic still remains Bender, *Angola under the Portuguese.*

90. UCC, Angola, Reports, May 1961, p. 1; UCC, Angola, Personal Files, 1961–1965, The Dilles to Friends, 27 May 1961, p. 1.

91. UCC, Personal Files, Angola 1965, Anonymous, "On This Rock," *Christian Herald*, April 1963.

92. UCC, Angola, Reports, Doc. 1961, Letter from Whitney Dalrymple to Floyd Honey, 30 April 1961; UCC, Personal Files, 1961–1965, "The Dilles to Friends," 27 May 1961, p. 1;

93. Marcos Fortuna, Response to Questionaire, May 1997.

94. UCC, Angola, Reports and Documents, 1966, Letter from Amy S., Chisamba, 11 Dec. 1967, p.2.

95. Heywood, "History, Urbanization, and Nationalism."

96. Cornelio Interview.

97. *Ibid.*

98. UCC, Reports and Documents, 26 Dec. 1964, Bailundu, p. 3; UCC Personal Files, Report for 1965, p. 2; UCC, Personal Files, Report for 1965, Letter from the Dilles, October 1965, p. 3.

99. Pélissier, *La Colonie du minotaure*, 288–90. Marcum, *The Angolan Revolution* 1: 105–08.

100. Marcum, *The Angolan Revolution* 2.

101. UCC, NWM, Angola, 1964, Correspondence, File 486, "The Baptist Missionary Society and Angola: A Statement, January 1964," p. 2.

102. Henderson, *Angola*, 219–20.

103. *Ibid.*, 220–21.

104. *Ibid.*, 219–20.

105. Bender, *Angola under the Portuguese*, 179.

106. *Ibid.*, 179–86.

107. *Ibid.*, 159–65.

108. *Ibid.*, 187.

109. Ernesto Neiva, *Missão é Evangelho: Angola busca de novas coordenadas evangélicas para a missão* (Lisbon: Editorial L.I.A.M, 1974), 134.

110. "Troubled Angola," *The Observer*, 15 June 1965, p. 14. Women received 2$50 escudos ($.10) per day for picking 200 lbs. of coffee, UCC, Angola, Reports and Documents, "The War in Angola," p. 23.

111. Cornélio Interview.

112. *The Observer*, "Troubled Angola," 15 June 1965, p. 14. The migrant was supposed to receive 500$00 ($16.00 U.S.) when he initially agreed to the contract, and 300$00 ($10.00 U.S.) per month for the period of his contract.

113. Bender, *Angola under the Portuguese*, 226 note 45.

114. *Washington Post*, 5 August 1974, A-16-1.

115. Bender, *Angola under the Portuguese*, 168; Neiva, *Missão e evangelho*, 140–47.

116. *Washington Post*, 5 Aug. 1974, A-16-1; A.J. Venter, *The Terror Fighters: A Profile of Guerrilla Warfare in Southern Africa* (Cape Town: Purnell, 1969), 79.

117. Cornelio Interview. The reforms of 1961 classified African lands as second class lands and presumably protected them against expropriation. See Bender, *Angola under the Portuguese*, 181.

118. Bender, *Angola under the Portuguese*, 182–84.

119. *Ibid*, 183.

120. *Ibid.*, 181–96.

121. Rocha and Morais, "Angola" 39. Ferreira, *La Transformación*, 594.

122. Morais, "Transformações," note 146.

123. *Ibid.*, note 163.

124. Bernard Rivers, "Angola: Massacre and Oppression," *Africa Today* 21 (1974): 47.

125. Cornelio Interview.

126. J.A. David de Morais *et al.*, *Subsídios para o conhecimento médico e antropológico do Povo Undulu (Angola)* (Lisbon: *Separata dos Anais do Instituto de Higiene e Medicina Tropical* 2, nos. 1–4 January/December, 1975).

127. UCC, Angola, Reports and Documents, 1970.

128. The works of Heimer, Marcum, and Henderson have greatly advanced our understanding of the social origins of some of the Ovimbundu who became associated with UNITA. Marcum in particular has provided insights into the early networking of many of the Ovimbundu nationalist leaders.

129. See Heimer, *Decolonization*, 31.

130. See Davidson, *Eye of the Storm*; Henderson, *Angola*.

Notes to Chapter 6

1. Besides Jonas Savimbi, who is an Ocimbundu, the founders were Miguel N'Zua Puna and Tony Fernandes (Cabindans), Ernesto Mulato, Antonio Dembo, and José N'dele (Kongos).

2. See Douglas Wheeler, "Origins of African Nationalism in Angola: Assimilado Protest Writings, 1859–1929," in R. Chilcote, ed., *Protest and Resistance in Angola and Brazil* (Los Angeles: University of California Press, 1972), 67–87.

3. For the links between Pan-Africanism and Angolan nationalism, see Marcum, *The Angolan Revolution*, 1: 21–22.

4. Messiant, "Luanda (1945–1961)," 143–99.

5. See Basil Davidson, *In the Eye of the Storm*, 148–50, and René Pélissier, "Origines du mouvement nationaliste moderniste en Angola," *Revue française d'études politiques africaines*, no. 126 (June 1976): 14–47.

6. For the early nationalists, see Marcum, *The Angolan Revolution*, 1: 13–48; See also Guimarães, "Origins and Development," 17–29.

7. Richard Gibson, *African Liberation Movements* (London: Oxford University Press, 1972), 211–25.

8. Marcum, *The Angolan Revolution*, 1: 53–60.

9. *Ibid.*

10. Daniel Ekundi, an early Ovimbundu Protestant, was imprisoned for ten years during the 1920s for anti-government activities. Bridgland, *Savimbi*, 30–31.

11. Pélissier, "Origines," 14–47.

12. Pastor Marcos Fortuna, Response to Questionnaire, May 1997.

13. Personal Correspondence, Rev. J. Murray MacInnes, 16 June 1997.

14. Culled from telephone interview with American missionary Rev. Joyce Myers Brown, who served as a missionary among the Ovimbundu from 1964 to 1975 when she was airlifted out. She visited Angola in 1995, and has maintained official contact with the Congregational Church there. Telephone Interview 12 June 1997.

15. César Pedro Kaliengue, "Testemunho para a História da U.N.I.T.A." Manuscript (Jamba 25 February 1986), 4.

16. Interview with Jaka Jamba, Vice President of the Commission of Foreign Relations and Umbundu scholar. Washington, D.C., 16 June 1997.

17. Kaliengue, "Testemunho," p. 4.

18. Loiseau and de Roux, *Portrait*, 39.

19. The author bases this conclusion on the more than twenty interviews she has conducted with Ovimbundu in the United States, Portugal, and Angola.

20. Kaliengue, "Testemunho," 6.

21. Some scholars may argue that this occurred as a result of a conscious policy of the liberation movements. See Timothy Luke, "Angola and Mozambique: Institutionalizing Social Revolution in Africa," *The Review of Politics* 44, no. 3 (July 1982): 413–36.

22. Somerville, *Angola, Politics, Economics*.

23. Cornelio interview.

24. Cornelio Interview. See also Marcum, *The Angolan Revolution*, 1.

25. Personal Communication, J. Murray MacInnes, 25 August 1997.

26. *Ibid.*

27. Cornelio Interview; Figueiredo Interview; Kaliengue, "Testemunho," p. 7.

28. Kaliengue, "Testemunho," 8.

29. *Ibid.*, 7.

30. See Marcum, *The Angolan Revolution*, 1; also Cornelio Interview; Rev. Joyce Myers Brown Telephone Interview; Kaliengue, "Testamunho," p. 8.

31. Some of these were the *Organização Cultural dos Angolanos* formed by Júlio Afonso and José Belo Chipenda, the *Grupo Ohio* in Lobito, and *L'Ologende* in Bailundu. See Pélissier, *La Colonie du minotaure*, 289–90.

32. Cornelio Interview; Cardoso Interview; Figueiredo Interview.

33. Marcum, *The Angolan Revolution*, 1: 111. Figueiredo Interview; Cornelio Interview.

34. Personal Correspondence, J. Murray MacInnes, 25 August 1997.

35. Figueiredo Interview.

36. Other members were Júlio and Armando Cacunda, Aarão Kunga, Luciano Kasoma, Aarão Cornelio, and Emelia Cardoso (Cornelio Interview; Cardoso Interview; Figueiredo Interview).

37. Rev. Joyce Myers Brown, Telephone Interview.

38. J. Murray MacInnes, Letter, 16 July 1997.

39. Kaliengue, "Testemunho," 10.

40. Augusta Conchiglia, *UNITA, Myth and Reality* (London: ECASAAMA, 1990), 6, 46.

41. UCC, BWM, Angola, 1968 Correspondence . . . Missionaries #571.

42. UNITA, Leadership.

43. Soremekun, *Angola: The Road to Independence*.

44. Bridgland, *Savimbi*, 38–43.

45. To develop a modern political consciousness that could support an effective counter state against the Portuguese colonial regime, the Ovimbundu had to have a party organization that could politicize subaltern classes and rural producers. See Luke, "Angola and Mozambique," *The Review of Politics*, 416.

46. See Cahen, ed., *"Vilas" et "Cidades"*, 125–99.

47. See Marcum, *The Angolan Revolution*, 1, for the social origins of the Kongo and Ovimbundu leadership.

48. See Bridgland's, *Savimbi*, 21–35, for a sympathetic view of Savimbi's youth. In Loiseau and de Roux's *Portrait*, 81–84, Savimbi reconstructs this phase of his life.

49. Marcum, *The Angolan Revolution*, 1: 138; Bridgland, *Savimbi*, 53–54. Savimbi received a scholarship from the American Protestant missionaries. With the outbreak of war, many of the African students in Portugal were under surveillance from *PIDE* and left Portugal for other European capitals.

50. Lawrence Henderson Interview, Estoril, Portugal, July 1990.

51. See Wheeler, "Angola in Whose House?" 1–23. See also Dias, "Uma Questão de identidade," 61–94, Marcum, *The Angolan Revolution*, 1; René Lemarchand, "The Bases of Nationalism among the Bakongo," *Africa*, 31 (October 1961): 344–54.

52. Loiseau and de Roux, *Portrait*, 82.

53. Pélissier, *La Colonie du minotaure*, 479–83. See also MPLA, *Angola: Exploitation esclavagiste, résistance nationale*. (Dakar: A. Diop, 1961).

54. UNITA, *Leadership*, 6, notes that Savimbi joined UPA in February 1961.

55. Bridgland, *Savimbi*, 55.

56. Before the break with UNITA, Miguel N'Puna held various posts, including secretary general of UNITA. Da Costa Fernandes served in many diplomatic capacities.

57. Bridgland, *Savimbi*, 63.

58. Personal Correspondence, J. Murray MacInnes, 25 August 1997.

59. UNITA, *Leadership*, 9.

60. J. Murray MacInnes, Personal Correspondence, 25 August 1997.

61. See, for example, Minter, *Operation Timber*. For another view, see Linda Heywood, "UNITA and Ethnic Nationalism in Angola," *Journal of Modern African Studies*, 27, 1 (1989): 47–66.

62. See Marcum, *The Angolan Revolution*, 1: 105–10.

63. Bridgland, *Savimbi*, 61–66. See also Marcum, *The Angolan Revolution*, 2: 160–64.

64. Gerald Bender, "The Eagle and the Bear in Angola," *The Annals of the American Academy of Political and Social Science*, 489 (Jan. 1987): 125.

65. Daniel's brother José Belo Chipenda attended seminary in the United States and remained strongly attached to his rural roots.

66. Marcum, *The Angolan Revolution*, 1: 108, 2: 86.

67. PIDE recruited from among all ethnic groups in Angola, but the Ovimbundu were the most numerous. This was not because the Ovimbundu were less nationalistic than other Angolans, but because they defined nationalist goals less ideologically than their Kimbundu and Kongo counterparts.

68. Cornelio Interview.

69. Bridgland, *Savimbi*, 66; UNITA, *Leadership*, 8.

70. See, for example, *Kwacha Angola* (Special edition, London, 1972).

71. Bridgland, *Savimbi*, 71.

72. For the formation of UNITA see Bridgland, *Savimbi*, 71–74,

73. See Minter, *Operation Timber*.

74. Bridgland, *Savimbi*, 67–76.

75. *Ibid.*, 67–76.

76. Conchiglia, *UNITA: Myth and Reality*, 9.

77. UNITA, *Leadership*, 9.

78. Bridgland, *Savimbi*, 75. See also Marcum, *The Angolan Revolution*, 2: 191–97.

79. "Excerpts of interview between Jonas Savimbi and François Soudan of *Jeune Afrique*," in UNITA, *UNITA: Identité d'un Angola livre* (Jaamba: UNITA, 1985), 139–44.

80. Bridgland, *Savimbi*, 65–101.

81. Henderson, *Angola*.

82. Marcum, *The Angolan Revolution*, 2: 191–97. See also Bridgland, *Savimbi*, 64–76.

83. Bridgland, *Savimbi*, 81–101.

84. *Ibid.*, 92–94. Bridgland notes that in 1971 Fritz Sitte, an Austrian journalist who traveled in UNITA-held territory, referred to UNITA members as black Chinese.

85. Marcum, *The Angolan Revolution*, 2.

86. General Board of Global Ministries (The United Methodist Church) [Henceforth GBGM], Film #900, Annual Meeting, 12 October 1971; GBGM, #900, WCC Task Force 13, 20 May 1971, J. Murray MacInnes to Rev. Zacarais Cardoso; American Committee on Africa [henceforward ACA], UNITA, 1969, Jonas Savimbi, "Open Letter to Protestant Missionaries Who Served in Angola," October 1969; ACA, "Re: Resolution Passed at the Seventh Annual Meeting of the Ohio Conference, United Church of Christ, 1970," Manuscript.

87. Personal Correspondence, J. Murray MacInnes, 25 August 1997.

88. Henderson, *Angola*, 234.

89. Marcum, *The Angolan Revolution*, 2: 239.

90. Kwadwo Oluwale Akpan, "Revolution and Reconstruction in Angola," *Black World* (May 1974): 1–8

91. Marcum, *The Angolan Revolution*, 2: 248; see also Heywood, "UNITA and Ethnic Nationalism," 47–66.

92. Kaliengue, "Testemunho," 12.

93. Cornelio Interview.

94. Conchiglia, *UNITA: Myth and Reality*, 9–15. Savimbi's adherents in the highlands certainly believed that his own network of supporters spirited him into the highlands without the knowledge of the Portuguese. See Cornelio Interview.

95. As recalled by Jaka Jamba. Jaka Jamba Interview.

96. Kalingue, "Testemunho," 14–20.

97. Marcum, *The Angolan Revolution*, 2: 69.

98. Marcum, *The Angolan Revolution*, 2: 191–97; Bridgland, *Savimbi*, 71–101; See Heywood, "UNITA and Ethnic Nationalism," 47–66.

99. Bridgland, *Savimbi*, 65–89.

100. For an overview of Portuguese strategies, see Marcum, *The Angolan Revolution*, 2: 191–21. Basil Davidson, *Walking 300 Miles with Guerrillas through the Bush of Eastern*

Angola. (Pasadena: California Institute of Technology, Munger Africana Library Notes, 1971). Bridgland, *Savimbi*, 77–101.

101. Bridgland, *Savimbi*, 68–69. Marcum, *The Angolan Revolution*, 2: 167.

102. Heywood, "Unita and Ethnic Nationalism," *passim*.

103. Marcum, *The Angolan Revolution*, 2: 196; Bridgland, *Savimbi*, 97–99.

104. Akpan, "Revolution and Reconstruction," 6–8.

105. Figueiredo Interview; Bridgland, *Savimbi*, 99–100.

106. Cornelio Interview; Cardoso Interview.

107. See Davidson, *In the Eye of the Storm*, *passim*; Roeland Kerbosh, *Angola: met eigen ogen* (Antwerp: A.W. Brun & Zoom, 1971).

108. See Conchiglia, *UNITA: Myth and Reality*, 13–18; also Minter, *Operation Timber*, 19.

109. For details of this collaboration see Minter, *Operation Timber*.

110. Bender, *Angola under the Portuguese*, 181, 185–86.

111. Marcum, *The Angolan Revolution*, 2: 199–205.

112. Conchiglia, *UNITA: Myth and Reality*, 13–18.

113. For the expansion of the guerrilla war, see Marcum, *The Angolan Revolution*, 2; Bridgland, *Savimbi*.

114. Bender, "The Eagle and the Bear in Angola," 126.

115. Marcum, *Angolan Revolution*, 2: 241–42.

116. See Fátima Roque *et al*, *Economia de Angola* (Lisbon: Betrand Editora, 1991), 66–76; see also John A. Marcum, "Angola: Twenty-Five Years of War," *Current History*, 85 (May, 1986): 194.

117. Angolan exile, personal correspondence, 5 April 1996.

118. Heywood, "UNITA and Ethnic Nationalism," *passim*.

119. Marcum, *The Angolan Revolution*, 2: 191–97.

120. For some discussion of the difficulties which UNITA faced in recruiting among the Ovimbundu peasants see Don Barnett and Roy Harvey, eds., *With the Guerrillas in Angola* (Richmond, B.C.: Liberation Support Movement Information Center, 1970); Cornelio Interview.

121. Sousa Jamba, *Patriots* (London: Viking Press, 1990).

122. See F.W. Heimer, *The Decolonization Conflict*.

123. *Ibid.*

124. Colin Legum and Tony Hodges, *After Angola: The War over Southern Africa* (London: Rex Collins, 1976), 49.

125. For the effects of the coup on Angola in 1974, see Bridgland, *Savimbi*, 102–10.

126. *Ibid.*, 76–101.

127. *Ibid.*, 103.

128. *Ibid.*, 104.

129. As quoted in Fola Soremekun, *Angola*, 64. See also Bridgland, *Savimbi*, 102–4.

130. For a discussion of this option see Soremekun, *Angola*, 44.

131. See, for example, Agostinho Neto, *Messages to Companions in the Struggle, Speeches by Agostinho Neto*, (Richmond, B.C.: Liberation Support Movement Information Center, 1972.)

132. Kaliengue, "Testemunho"; Savimbi's father, Loth Malheiro, was jailed between 1967–89. He was then put under house arrest and died in August 1973.

133. Personal Communication, J. Murray MacInnes, 25 August 1997.

134. Gregory Simpkins, *Angola: A Chronology of Major Political Developments February 1961–September 1996* (Virginia: Institute for Strategic Studies, 1996), 11–12.

135. See Marcum, *The Angolan Revolution*, 2; See also Minter, *Operation Timber*.

136. Marcum, *The Angolan Revolution*, 2: 249–53.

137. The two other factions were Agostinho Neto's true MPLA and Mário and Joaquim de Andrade's "Active Revolt."

Notes to Chapter 7

1. The full treatment of rural life in this period is impossible owing to the inaccessibility of local documentation and the inability to conduct interviews in the rural regions. The author made several attempts when she resided in Luanda (1978–80) to visit the central highlands to undertake research and conduct interviews. Interviews with foreign missionaries who worked in the interior, reports from journalists, and the reports of the United Nations and other political and Human Rights Organizations were useful in addressing this problem. Personal interviews that the author conducted with Ovimbundu pastors and other leaders with extensive knowledge of the local environment, and questionnaires they answered, provided valuable insights into the local situation. They inform the analysis in this chapter as well as the Epilogue.

2. *The Guardian*, 14 August 1975, p. 2; Bridgland, *Savimbi*, 113.

3. Chinsole, "A Second Crossing," (Unpublished Typescript, in possession of author), p. 2.

4. Basil Davidson, *The Black Man's Burden: Africa and the Curse of the Nation State* (New York: Times Books, 1992). See also Davidson, *The Search for Africa: History, Culture, Politics* (New York: Times Books, 1994). For an earlier statement see Davidson, *African Nationalism and the Problem of Nation-Building* (Lagos: Nigerian Institute of International Affairs, 1987). For other examples, see Alan Cowell, *Killing the Wizards: Wars of Power and Freedom from Zaire to South Africa* (New York: Simon & Schuster, 1992), and Jeremy Harding, *The Fate of Africa: Trial by Fire* (New York: Simon and Schuster, 1993).

5. Davidson, *The Black Man's Burden*, 302–9.

6. Cowell, *Killing the Wizards*; Daniel Spikes, *Angola and the Politics of Intervention: From Local Bush War to Chronic Crisis in Southern Africa* (Jefferson, N.C.: McFarland & Company, 1993).

7. Davidson himself is well aware of parallels between the African case and Europe's. See *The Black Man's Burden*, 266–89.

8. Their attitudes were similar to those of settlers in French Guinea who two decades earlier had deliberately destroyed both private and public buildings, vehicles, and the like, instead of allowing them to pass to the nationalists. See Michael Wolfers and Jane Bergerol, *Angola in the Front Line* (London: Zed Press, 1983), 38–39, 116–17.

9. Jardo Muekalia, UNITA Representative to the United States, Interview, Washington, D.C., April, 1995.

10. A. de Brança and I. Wallerstein, *The African Reader*, 2 vols. (London: Zed Press, 1982), 2: 107.

11. For the details of the Alvor Agreement and the conflicts surrounding it, see *Alvor and Beyond: Political Trends and Legal Issues in Angola* (Washington, D.C.: Angola Peace Fund, 1988). See also Marcum, *The Angolan Revolution*, 2: 255–56.

12. Wolfers and Bergerol, *Angola in the Front Line*, 131–34.

13. By June 1974, FNLA had a force of fifteen thousand men being trained by ten Chinese instructors at the movement's Kinkuzu base in Zaire, Bridgland, *Savimbi*, 108.

14. Guimarães, "Origins and Development," 29.

15. Interview, Armando Francisco, Press Attaché, Embassy of Angola, May 1995.

16. *The Guardian*, 11 August 1975, p. 2.

17. Fernando J. Andresen Guimarães, "The Collapse of the New State and the Emergence of the Angolan Civil War," *Camões Center Quarterly*, 5, nos. 1&2 (Winter 1993–94): 14.

18. Bridgland, *Savimbi*, 117; See also Interview with Coutinho, "The New Liberation Wars."

19. For an analysis of this paralysis see Guimarães, "The Collapse," 9–16.

20. See, for example, Gibson, *African Liberation Movements*, and Legum and Hodges, *After Angola*.

21. Porch, *The Portuguese Armed Forces*.

22. Chester A. Crocker, *High Noon in Southern Africa: Making Peace in a Rough Neighborhood* (New York: W.W. Norton, 1992), 46–52.

23. State Department Archives (SDA), Case no. 8601323 Sec. II, "Angola: US Secret Aid to the Insurgents," January 1985 to March 1986.

24. SDA, Case no. 8704129, "Angola: Soviet, Cuban, and South African Intervention, 1974–1987," 16 December 1975.

25. Bridgland, *Savimbi*, 168.

26. SDA, Case no. 8704129, "Angola: Soviet, Cuban, and South African Intervention, 1974–1987," 16 December 1975, 2–3. See also *Seis Portuguesas em Terras da UNITA* (Portugal: Venda Nova, 1988), 87.

27. The author, who was a graduate student of African history at Columbia University in New York City, attended most of the meetings on and off campus in fall 1975 when several representatives of the MPLA visited the United Nations and made speaking tours in the United States.

28. Basil Davidson, J. Slovo, and A. R. Wilkinson, *Southern Africa: The New Politics of Revolution* (Harmondsworth: Pelican, 1976).

29. For the independence celebrations and the preceding period see Marcum, *The Angolan Revolution*, 2.

30. Bridgland, *Savimbi*, 150.

31. Representative Dick Clark informed the author that, of the three leaders, Neto had the most presidential bearing. (Private conversation, Washington, D.C., February, 1994).

32. American Committee on Africa (ACA) New York, Letter from George Sangumba to Rev. Anderson, 17 July 1974, 2. Bridgland, *Savimbi*, 113.

33. Bridgland, *Savimbi*, 105.

34. *New York Times*, 24 November 1974, 7:1.

35. For contrasting views of the moves by the UNITA leadership, see Bridgland, *Savimbi*, 110–33, and Conchiglia, *UNITA*, 22–25.

36. *Alvor and Beyond: Political Trends and Legal Issues in Angola*.

37. Janatão (Tito) Chingungi, Interviews, 1990, Washington, D.C.

38. Jardo Muekalia, Interview, April 1995, Washington, D.C.

39. See Savimbi's speech praising Portugal for not encouraging racism in Angola, *A Provincia de Angola* (Luanda: 1 July 1974).

40. Crocker, *High Noon*, 174.

41. Muekalia Interview, April 1995.

42. Cornelio Interview; Chingunji Interview.

43. Bridgland, *Savimbi*, 117–35.

44. See, for example, Savimbi's visit to the Protestant Church headquarters in January, 1975, in Henderson, *Igreja*, 390.

45. See, for example, Minter, *Operation Timber*.

46. Muekalia Interview, Washington, D.C., April 1995.

47. *New York Times*, 24 November 1974, 7:1; see also issue of 25 April 1974.

48. "The View from UNITA: Angola, Unity or Struggle," *Black World* (October, 1972): 60; See also, *New York Times*, 16 January 1975, 12:1; UNITA, *Leadership, passim*.

49. UNITA, *Leadership, passim*. See also Henderson, *A Igreja*, 390.

50. Marcum, *The Angolan Revolution*, 2: 256; Cornelio Interview.

51. UNITA, Leadership, *passim*.

52. *New York Times*, 28 March 1975, 4:4; *Washington Post*, 1 November 1975, A–15–1.

53. Muekalia Interview, April 1995.

54. See, for example, Chester Crocker, *High Noon*, 43–57.

55. Cornelio Interview.

56. Personal Correspondence, J. Murray MacInnes, 25 August 1997; Rev. Maria Chela Chikueka, 5 April 1996.

57. Bridgland, *Savimbi*, 118–25.

58. See Bridgland, *Savimbi*, 108.

59. Marcum, *The Angolan Revolution*, 2: 246; Bridgland, *Savimbi*, 125.

60. For the debate about who was responsible for bringing in outsiders, see William Minter, *Apartheid's Contras: An Inquiry into the Roots of War in Angola and Mozambique* (London: Zed Press, 1994), 19–21.

61. Interview, Shaka Jamba, Luanda, Angola, 11 August 1997.

62. For a reconstruction of the events leading to the South African invasion of Angola, see SDA, Case no. 8601323, sec. II, "Angola: U.S. Covert Assistance to Insurgents, January 1985 to March 1986"; See also Bridgland, *Savimbi*, 142–62.

63. SDA, Case no. 8704129, Section II, Secret Report, December, 1975.

64. Somerville, *Angola: Politics, Economics and Society*, 41.

65. For South African involvement see Phyllis Johnson and David Martin, eds., *Destructive Engagement: Southern Africa at War* (Harare: Zimbabwe Publishing House, 1986).

66. Daniel Chipenda of the MPLA made the first contacts with the South Africans. See Legum and Hodges, *After Angola*.

67. *Africa Research Bulletin*, April 1975, 1–30.

68. Bridgland, *Savimbi*, 144.

69. *Seis Portuguesas em Terras da UNITA*, 60.

70. Marga Holness, "Angola: The Struggle Continues," in Johnson and Martin, eds., *Destructive Engagement*.

71. SDA, Case no. 8704129, Sec. II, "Angola: Soviet, Cuban, and South African Intervention, 1974–1987."

72. Bridgland, *Savimbi*, 134–36.

73. Conchiglia, *UNITA*, 21–31; See also Marcum, *The Angolan Revolution*, 2.

74. SDA, Case no. 8704129, sec. II, "Angola: Soviet, Cuban, and South African Intervention 1974–1987."

75. Bridgland, *Savimbi*, 168; Legum and Hodges, *After Angola*.

76. Prexy Nesbitt, "US Foreign Policy: Lessons from the Angolan Conflict," *Africa Today* (1st & 2nd Quarters 1992): 57.

77. Bridgland, *Savimbi*, 148. See also SDA, Case no. 8704129, sec. II, "Angola: Soviet, Cuban, and South African Intervention."

78. SDA, Case no. 8601323, sec. II, "Angola: U.S. Covert Assistance to Insurgents, January 1985 to March 1986."

79. See Bridgland, *Savimbi*, 187–218.

80. *Ibid.*, 218.

81. See Legum and Hodges, *After Angola*.

82. Some critics charge that, for all the rhetoric, the MPLA had made very little headway among the population in Eastern Angola. For a comparative discussion of social revolutions in contemporary Africa, see Timothy W. Luke, "Angola and Mozambique: Institutionalizing Social Revolution in Africa," *Review of Politics*, 44, no, 3 (July 1992): 413–36.

83. M.R. Bhagavan, "Establishing the Conditions for Socialism: The Case of Angola" in Barry Munslow, ed., *Africa: Problems in the Transition to Socialism* (London: Zed Books, 1986), 166–67.

84. For an overview of the party organization before 1986, see Bhagavan, "Establishing the Conditions," 140–76. See also Gerald Bender, "The Continuing Crisis in Angola," *Current History*, 82 (March, 1986): 124–38.

85. Chester A Crocker, "Southern Africa: Eight Years Later," *Foreign Affairs*, (Fall, 1989): 146.

86. SDA, Case no. 8601323, sec. II, "Angola: U.S. Covert Assistance to Insurgents, January 1985 to March 1986."

87. Armando Francisco, Press Attaché, Embassy of Angola, Interview, Washington, D.C., May 1995.

88. Daniel Spikes, *Angola and the Politics of Intervention: From Local Bush War to Chronic Crisis in Southern Africa* (Jefferson, N.C.: McFarland & Company, 1993), 311.

89. The Economist Intelligence Unit, *Country Study: Angola, São Tomé and Principé, 1992–1993* (London: The Economist, 1993), 7.

90. Muekalia Interview, April, 1995.

91. *Ibid.*, April, 1995.

92. One of the slogans went thus: "Menongue—pointe de partida, Luanda, pointe de chegada." Interview, Olga E. Mundombe, Assistant for External Affairs, Embassy of Republic of Angola, Washington, D.C., May 1995.

93. Until 1982, Faustino Muteka was the only Ocimbundu in a responsible position in the government. He was the transport minister. See Somerville, *Angola: Politics, Economics and Society*, 60. See also Bhagavan, "Establishing the Conditions," 165–69.

94. For the membership of the political bureau in 1986 see Marcum, "Angola: Twenty-Five Years of War," 194.

95. Somerville, *Angola*, 74–75.

96. *Ibid.*, 134–35.

97. Tony Hodges, *Angola to 2000: Prospects for Recovery* (London: The Economist Intelligence Unit, 1993), 60–61.

98. Luke, "Angola and Mozambique," 427.

99. Hodges, *Angola to 2000*, 60–61.

100. Personal communication from a political writer on Angola. I myself spent three

weeks in the hospital for contagious diseases in Luanda in 1979–1980 with typhoid fever, and can attest that crisis conditions existed even then, despite the presence of Cuban health personnel. I would like to take this opportunity to thank the Cuban and Angolan doctors and nurses whose professionalism and kindness resulted in my full recovery.

101. The numbers of Angolans attending university continued to expand despite the falling-off in the elementary and secondary grades. Some members of the MPLA leadership put little trust in the country's school system, however, and sent their children abroad for education.

102. *Africa Report* (March/April, 1992): 62. See also *New York Times*, 8 October 1991.

103. As quoted by W. James Martin III, *A Political History of the Civil War in Angola, 1974–1990* (New Brunswick, N.J.: Transaction Publishers, 1992), 211.

104. Piero Benetozzo, "Angola Paradox: Nation Loves, Hates Its East-West Patrons," *The Christian Science Monitor*, 29 January 1984, p. 12.

105. *Angola Update*, vol. 1, no. 9, 21 October 1991, p. 1.

106. I found out that the only way I could undertake research in Angola was to become a *coorporante*. In 1979–1980 I, like other *coorporantes*, received 50 percent of my salary in American currency.

107. *Angola Peace Monitor*, vol. 3, no. 7, 4 October 1991, p. 5.

108. Martin, *Civil War in Angola*, 211.

109. The Economic Intelligence Unit, *Angola, São Tomé and Principé*, 10–17.

110. *Ibid.*, 15.

111. *Ibid.*, 10.

112. *Angola Peace Monitor*, vol. 3, no. 7, 4 October 1991, p. 5.

113. See Somerville, *Angola*, 50 ff.

114. "A Landmark in Angolan History," *World Marxist Review* (March, 1989): 80.

115. *Angola News Brief*, vol. 5, no. 4 (December, 1990).

116. Bender, "The Continuing Crisis in Angola," 124.

117. Crocker, *High Noon*, 116.

118. Free Angola, "The Angolan Economy under the MPLA Administration: 14 Years Later," (Washington, D.C.: Free Angola, 1990).

119. Vicki Finkel, "Violence and the Vote," *Africa Report* 37, no. 4 (July/August 1992): 54.

120. UNITA, *Leadership*, 11. This pledge was made in May 1976, and was part of the Cuanza Manifesto.

121. *Seis Portuguesas*, 59.

122. Martin, *A Political History*, 137.

123. *Ibid.*, 97.

124. Crocker, *High Noon*, 171.

125. SDA, Case no. 8601323, sec. II, "Angola: U.S. Covert Assistant to Insurgents, January 1985 to March 1986."

126. Leon da Costa Dash, Jr. *Savimbi's 1977 Campaign against the Cubans and MPLA* (Pasadena: California Institute of Technology, Munger Africana Notes, 1977): 14.

127. Donald Rothchild and Caroline Hartzell, "Great and Medium-Power Mediations: Angola," *Annals* (November 1991): 51. For South African involvement in Angola see Martin, *Civil War in Angola*.

128. *Washington Post*, 16 April 1990.

129. Karl Maier. "Blueprint for Peace," *Africa Report* (March–April 1991): 22.

130. *Congressional Record*, 27 September 1989, E 3187, Hon. Howard Wolpe, "United States Foreign Policy toward a Peaceful Settlement of the Angolan Civil War."

131. Martin, *Civil War in Angola*, 89–128.

132. Sam R. Toussie, "War and Survival in Southern Angola: The UNITA Assessment Mission," MS. (International Rescue Committee, December, 1989), pp. 26–27.

133. Toussie, "War and Survival," 18–19.

134. Personal Correspondence, Bernardo Bongo, Italy, 1 January 1997.

135. See Sam R. Toussie, "War and Survival"; See also U.S. Congress: *New Reports of Human Rights Violations in the Angolan Civil War*, "Hearing of the House of Representative, 1st Session, 12 April 1989, John Marcum, Testimony."

136. See Toussie, "War and Survival," *passim*.

137. Dash, *Savimbi's 1977 Campaign*, 113.

138. UNITA, *Leadership*, 5–11.

139. Martin, *Civil War in Angola* 102.

140. William Minter, *The National Union for the Total Independence of Angola (UNITA) as Described by Ex-Participants and Foreign Visitors* (Washington, D.C., 1990) 13–14.

141. See Heywood, "Towards an Understanding."

142. Heywood, "Towards an Understanding"; Minter, *The National Union For the Total Independence of Angola*, 12–16; See also U.S. Congress, *New Reports*, 9–10.

143. On the MPLA's treatment of witchcraft see Henrique Abranches, *Reflexões sobre cultura nacional* (Lisboa: Edições 70, 1980), 63–102.

144. Heywood, "Towards an Understanding"; Interview, Larry Henderson, Washington, D.C., 1989.

145. See Linda Heywood, "UNITA and Ethnic Nationalism," 47–66.

146. *UN Chronicle*, 29, no. 2, (June, 1992): 33.

Notes to Epilogue

1. Inge Tvedten, *Angola: Struggle for Peace and Reconstruction* (Boulder, Colo.: Westview Press, 1977), 55.

2. Anthony W. Pereira, "Angola's 1992 Elections: A Personal View," *Camões Center Quarterly* 5, nos. 1 & 2 (Winter 1993/1994): 1–8.

3. Response to questionnaire, Jeremias Bandwa, Portland, Oregon, April 1997; Personal Correspondence, J. Murray MacInnes, 16 June 1997.

4. Personal Correspondence, J. Murray MacInnes, 16 June 1997.

5. Letter from Jardo Muekalia, Unita Representative to the United States, Washington, D.C., 16 May 1994; *Jornal de Notícias*, Lisbon, 12 May 1994. Interview given by Chester Crocker, former U.S. assistant Secretary for African Affairs.

6. UNITA, Communique, Huambo, 16 October 1992. Typescript.

7. UNITA, "Angola: Democracy on a Life Support," n.d. Typescript. Cícero Queirós, *Angola: Outubro de 1992: Um passo para o abismo* n.p. n.d.

8. UNITA, Communique, Huambo, 16 October 1992. Typescript.

9. UNITA, "Angola: Elections," (Luanda: Gabinete de Imprensa, 8 October 1992). Typescript.

10. See for example, *Terra Angolana*, 10, 17, 24 October 1992; *Washington Times*, 19 October 1992, p. 2.

11. *DataFile Portugal*, (Lisbon, Servipressa Lda, 1992); Margaret Calhoun, "Only Fair Elections Can Keep Angola's Peace," *Wall Street Journal*, European Edition, 21 October 1992.

12. *Datafile Portugal*.

13. Margaret Anstee, *Orphan of the Cold War: The Inside Story of the Collapse of the Angolan Peace Process, 1992–1993* (London: Oxford University Press, 1996), 248–49.

14. Queirós, *Angola*, 93–94.

15. Jill Jolliffe, "Captive Heart in Angola's Ordeal by Fire," *The European*, 18–21 February 1993, p. 12. Fátima Roque, "Media Statement," Lisbon, 22 February 1993.

16. See especially *Terra Angolana*, 17 and 24 October 1992.

17. The statement was made in the presence of party representatives, foreign observers, and Margaret Anstee, and was published in the Portuguese daily *Diário de Notícias*. Queirós, *Angola*, 68.

18. Impression gained from several interviews with UNITA representatives, Washington, D.C., 1996–1997.

19. Queirós, *Angola*, 67–77.

20. For the United Nations perspective see Anstee, *Orphan of the Cold War*.

21. Anstee, *Orphan of the Cold War*, 488.

22. Robert C. Schmults, "Bloodshed and Blame in Angola," *Insight*, 14 February 1993, p. 16.

23. *Ibid.*, 16, 31.

24. *Washington Times*, 24 September 1993.

25. Schmults, "Bloodshed," 30.

26. For the various journalistic accounts of Savimbi's recalcitrance see, for example, *Washington Post*, 20 November 1992, A 46; *The Guardian*, 19 November 1992.

27. Letter signed by French delegation to Dr. António Caetano de Sousa, President of National Electoral Council, Luanda, Angola, dated Luanda 30 September 1992, (Original Typescript in French in author's possession).

28. Queirós, *Angola*, 67–77.

29. For Jonas Savimbi's reflections on why the peace failed in 1992, see Free Angola Information Service, *Angola Update* 18, no. 3, 21 June 1995, pp. 3–6.

30. Xavier Figueiredo, "Angola: The Luanda Coup," *Africa Insight*, (1992): 1–4.; Alex Vines, "La troisième guerre angolaise," *Politique Africaine*, 57 (1995): 28.

31. "Testimony from Two Bakongos, Confidential," Lisbon, 11 October 1993, (Typescript, copy in author's possession); "Interview with Jose Manuel ("Jo-Jo") Saraiva Baptista," Lisbon 18 August 1993, (Typescript, copy in author's possession); Letter to President Clinton from Dr. Alberto Videira Bokula, international Jurist, Lisbon, 15 February 1993; Free Angola Information Service, "Ethnic Cleansing in Angola," 27 February 1993, (Typescript, copy in author's possession).

32. Karl Maier, "Angolans Say Grisly Discoveries Point to Executions by Police," *Washington Post*, 28 November 1992, A 46; Karl Maier, *Angola: Promises and Lies* (London: Serif, 1996), 74–127; Free Angola Information Service, "Ethnic Cleansing in Angola," Washington, D.C., 27 February 1993.

33. *Angola Update* 3, vol. 4, 23 April 1996, p. 6.

34. Fátima Roque, "An Appeal for Peace, Media Statement," Lisbon, 22 February 1992, (Typescript, copy in author's possession).

35. This was the estimate General Higino Caneiro, vice minister of Territorial Administration, gave during negotiations in the Ivory Coast. See Malik Chaka, "Angola's Government of National Unity," The Center for Democracy in Angola, Inc., Washington, D.C., 24 April 1997, p. 2.

36. "Message to the Nation from Dr. Jonas Malheiro Savimbi," Broadcast by *Vorgan* at 1 PM, 20 September 1993; *Washington Times*, 16 Nov. 1992, p. E2.

37. Several correspondents in Luanda and elsewhere reported on the violence, but so far no one has done a comprehensive analysis of the events. See, for example, Free Angola Information Service, "Ethnic Cleansing in Angola," 27 Feb. 1993; "Testimony from Two Bakongos, Confidential," Lisbon, 11 October 1993; Jill Jolliffe, "Situation of UNITA Deputies Elected to the Angolan Parliament," Lisbon, 9 November 1993, (Typescript, copy in author's possession).

38. Chris McGreat, "Vanquished Rebels Flee Angola's Killing Fields," *Guardian*, 18 January 1993.

39. Personal Correspondence, Bernardo Bongo, Rome, Italy, 8 January 1997.

40. Maier, "Grisly Discoveries."

41. According to a UNITA official who left Luanda on 14 October 1992, UNITA was in an untenable situation in the capital and would have been unable to go on the offensive in November 1992 as some critics have charged. Personal Correspondence, UNITA official, 23 December 1997. See also Maier, *Angola*, 97–141.

42. *Washington Post*, 7 February 1995, pp. A 1, A 19.

43. Chris McGreat, "Gravediggers Reveal Truth behind Angola Massacre," *Guardian*, 19 November 1992.

44. APIX, *Angola: A Country Profile* (Washington, D.C., April 1995), 4.

45. *New York Times*, 1 January 1993.

46. Africa Confidential, 24, vol. 34 (3 December 1993): 7.

47. Maier, *Angola: Promises and Lies*, 107.

48. Jill Jolliffe, "Testimony of Rui Oliveira," Lisbon, 18 July 1993. Typescript; Paul Taylor, "Muckraker's Death Chills Angolan Journalist," *Washington Post*, 8 February 1995, pp. A 23, 25; Free Angola Information Service, *News*, 9 March 1994.

49. Xavier Figueiredo, "Angola: The Luanda Coup," *O Público*, 6 January 1993.

50. *Angola Update*, 9, vol. 3, 16 August 1994, p. 7.

51. Free Angola Information Service, *News*, n.d.

52. Free Angola Information Service, *Angola Update* 3, no. 9, 15 August 1994, pp. 4–5; United Nations S/1995/588 17 July 1995, "Report of the Secretary-General on the United Nations Angola Verification Mission," (New York, Typescript); Victoria Brittain, "War is the Only Victor in Angola," *Guardian*, 28 July 1995; Shawn H. McCormick, *The Angolan Economy: Prospects for Growth in a Post War Environment* (Washington, D.C.: Center for Strategic and International Studies, 1994).

53. *Los Angeles Times* (Washington Edition), 10 October 1994.

54. [José Eduardo dos Santos], *Mensagem de fim de ano 1994 do Presidente da República* (Ms. in author's possession).

55. IPS Correspondents, "Africa Politics: Among Mercenaries, Mad Mikes Out, Trainers In," (Inter Press Service, 22 May 1995); Free Angola Information Service, *Angola Update* 3, no. 15, 16 March 1995, pp. 1–2.

56. *Washington Post*, 7 May 1995, A 32.

57. *Washington Post*, 8 February 1995; Associated Press, 2 July 1995; *Guardian*, 28 July 1995.

58. The civil war was taking at least 1,000 Angolan lives daily. *Globe and Mail* (Toronto), 16 November 1993.

59. *Globe and Mail* (Toronto), 6 November 1993; *Agence France-presse* International News via NewsNet, "Angolan Rivals Agree to Cease Hostilities, Free Prisoners," 10 January 1995; United Nations S/1995/588 17 July 1995, "Report."

60. Reuters, "Angolan Negotiators Convene for Session on Truce," 25 November 1993.

61. *Washington Post*, 29 November 1994, A12.

62. *Angola Update* 3, no. 15, 16 March 1995, p. 3.

63. *O Pensador* (Washington, D.C.), May 1995, p. 3.

64. *Ibid.*, p. 3.

65. *Agence France presse*, 23 May 1995.

66. *Wall Street Journal* (European Edition), 16–17 June 1995. See also *Angola Update* 3, no. 18, 21 June 1995.

67. Joseph Lamberga, "Angola: Savimbi Says He Does Not Want a Cosmetic Vice Presidency," Luso, 21 March 1997, Typescript.

68. Free Angolan Information Service, "The Angolan Peace Process: An Update on Critical Issues," Washington, D.C., 21 July 1995.

69. United Nations S/1995/588, 17 July 1995, "Report . . . Angola," (Typescript, copy in author's possession).

70. See, for example, "Statement by the President of the Security Council," 30 January 1997 (Typescript, copy in author's possession); Congressman Ed Ross to the Honorable George Moose, Assistant Secretary for African Affairs, 19 February 1997 (copy of letter in author's possession).

71. Angola, Home Page, 24 April 1997.

72. *New York Times*, A 8, August 28, 1997.

73. *Washington Post*, A 30, November 9, 1997; *Angola Now*, vol. 1, no. 6, 12 November 1997.

74. Personal correspondence, UNITA official, December 1997.

75. I spent a week in Angola (August 1997) and was able to witness at first hand Ovimbundu representatives at work in the assembly. I also had conversations with several UNITA representatives, all of whom expressed great enthusiasm for the work they were carrying out in the assembly.

BIBLIOGRAPHY

Manuscript Sources

1. Angola

Centro de Documentção e Investigação Histórico (CDIH), Luanda, Angola. Now known as Arquivo Histórico Nacional de Angola (AHNA).

2. Canada

Canadian Council of Foreign Missionary Societies (CCFMS), University of Toronto. Also known as United Church of Canada (UCC). All documents are from the section Angola Mission, General Correspondence.
Tucker Ward Collection, Mississauga.
Musée des beaux-arts de Montréal (MBAM), Montreal.

3. England

Public Record Office (PRO), London.
Tanganyika Concessions Ltd. (TANKS), London.

4. France

Archives Générales de R. Pères du St-Espirit (AGSE), Cheverly-la-Rue.

5. Portugal

Arquivo Histórico Ultramarino (AHU), Lisbon.
Caminho de Ferro de Benguela (Benguela Railway Company (BRC), Lisbon.
Sociedade de Geografia de Lisboa (SGL), Lisbon.
Arquivo Histórico Militar (AHM) Lisbon.
Arquivo de União dos Bancos Ultramarinos (AUBU), Lisbon.

6. Scotland

National Library of Scotland (NLS).

7. United States of America

American Board of Commissioners For Foreign Missions (ABCFM), Houghton Library, Harvard University, Cambridge, Mass.
American Committee on Africa (ACA), New York.
General Board of Global Ministries (GBGM), New York.
National Archives of the United States (NAUS), Washington, D.C.
State Department Archives (SDA), Washington, D.C.
United Nations Archives (UNA), New York.

8. Zambia

National Archives of Zambia (NAZ), Lusaka.

Periodicals and Newspapers

Africa Confidential
Africa Report.
Africa Research Bulletin.
Agence France presse.
Angola Home Page (http://www-personal.umich.edu)
Angola News Brief.
Angola Now.
Angola Peace Monitor (http://www.anc.org.za.angola)
Angola Update.
Boletim da Sociedade de Geografia de Lisboa.
Boletim Geral do Ultramar.
Boletim dos Serviços Agricolas.
Boletim Oficial da Colonia de Angola (BO).
Christian Science Monitor.
Congressional Record (Washington).
Datafile Portugal.
A Defesa de Angola (Luanda).
Diário de Notícias (Lisbon)
O Districto de Benguela (Angola).
Free Angola Information Service (Washington).
Grémio do Milho Colonial, Relatório.
Globe and Mail (Toronto).
Guardian (London).
Informação Estatística, 1972. Luanda.
O Intransigente (Angola).
O Journal de Benguela (*Jornal de Benguela*) (Angola).
Jornal das Colónias (Lisbon).
Jornal de Notícias (Lisbon).
Kwacha Angola. London: 1972.

O Lobito (Angola).
Los Angeles Times.
London Times.
Mensário Administrativo.
New York Times.
Observer.
O Pensador (Washington).
A Provincia de Angola (Luanda).
O Público (Lisbon)
A Reforma (Angola).
Reuters News
Terra Angolana (Jamba, Angola).
United Church Record and Missionary Review (Canada).
UN Chronicle (New York).
A Voz do Planalto (Angola).
Wall Street Journal.
Washington Post.
Washington Times.

Books and Articles

Abranches, Henrique. *Reflexões sobre cultura nacional.* Lisbon: Ediçoes 70, 1980.
Actualidade económica. Luanda, 1972.
Agência Geral das Colónias. *A Diocese de Nova Lisboa.* Lisbon: Agência Geral das Colónias, 1946.
Agência Geral de Angola. *A agricultura em Angola: Breve resumo sobre os recoursos agrícolas da Provincia de Angola.* Lisbon, 1922
Agência Geral dos Productos Agrícolas. *Breve notícia sobre o comércio de Milho.* Folheta 2. Luanda: Imprensa Nacional, 1928.
Akpan, Kwadwo Oluwale, "Revolution and Reconstruction in Angola." *Black World* (May, 1974): 1–8.
Almeida, António de. *Relações com os Dembos.* Lisbon, 1935.
Alves, Vasco Lopes. "Apontamentos sobre Angola." *Boletim Geral do Ultramar* ano XXXII, 267 (January, 1956.)
Alvor and Beyond: Political Trends and Legal Issues in Angola. Washington, D.C.: Angola Peace Fund, 1988.
Anderson, Benedict. *Imagined Communities: Reflections on the Origin and Spread of Nationalism.* New York: Verso Press, 1983.
Angola after Fifty Years. Boston: ABCFM, 1930.
Annaes do Conselho Ultramarino (parte não oficial) 3a serie. Lisbon (1862).
Annuário Estatístico de Angola. Luanda, 1935.
Annuário Estatístico de Angola. Luanda, 1937.
Annuário Estatístico de Angola. Luanda, 1941.
Annuário Estatístico de Angola. Luanda, 1942.
Annuário Estatístico de Angola. Luanda, 1950.

Annuário Estatístico de Angola. Luanda, 1958.

Anstee, Margaret. *Orphan of the Cold War: The Inside Story of the Collapse of the Angolan Peace Process, 1992–93.* London: Oxford University Press, 1996.

Apix. *Angola: A Country Profile.* Washington, D.C., April 1995.

Arnot, Frederick Stanley, *Garenganze; or, Seven Years' Pioneer Mission Work in Central Africa.* London: J. E. Hawkins, 1889.

Axelson, Eric. *Portugal and the Scramble for Africa, 1875–1891.* Johannesburg: Witwatersrand University Press, 1967.

Barnett, Don and Roy Harvey, eds. *With the Guerrillas in Angola.* Richmond, B.C.: Liberation Support Movement Information Center, 1970.

Barreto, Antônio. *Algumas notas sobre a acção da Junta de Exportação de Cereais.* Lisbon, 1957.

Bastos, A. *Monographia de Catumbela.* Lisbon: Tip. Universal, 1912.

Beaton, Kenneth. *Angola Now.* Toronto: Committee on Missionary Education, 1945.

Bender, Gerald. *Angola under the Portuguese: The Myth and the Reality.* Los Angeles and Berkeley: University of California Press, 1978.

———. "The Continuing Crisis in Angola." *Current History* 82 (March 1983): 124–25, 128, 138.

———. "The Eagle and the Bear in Angola." *The Annals of the American Academy of Political and Social Sciences* (January, 1987): 103–22.

———. "Planned Rural Development in Angola." In F. W. Heimer ed., *Social Change in Angola.* Munchen: Weltforum Verlag, 1973.

———, and Stanley Yoder. "Whites in Angola on the Eve of Independence: The Politics of Numbers." *Africa Today* 21 (1974): 23–37.

Benetozza, Piero. "Angola Paradox: Nation Loves, Hates Its East-West Patrons." *Christian Science Monitor*, January 29, 1984.

Benguela Railway Company. *Relatório da Alfandega.* Lisbon, 1915.

———. *Relatório e contas.* Lisbon, 1915.

———. *Relatório e contas.* Lisbon, 1918.

Berman, Bruce. *Control and Crisis in Colonial Kenya: The Dialectic of Domination.* Athens: Ohio University Press, 1990.

Bhagavan, M. R. "Establishing the Conditions for Socialism: The Case of Angola." In Barry Munslow, ed., *Africa: Problems in the Transition to Socialism.* London: Zed Books, 1986.

Botelho. Viera da Costa. "Agricultura no distrito de Benguela." *Boletim da Sociedade de Geographia de Lisboa* 8th series, 34 (1888–89).

Bragrança, A. de, and I. Wallerstein. *The African Reader.* Vol. 2. London: Zed Press, 1982.

Brandão, Anibal dos Santos. "O grande soma Huambo Kalunga, o terrivel antropofago." *Mensário Administrativo* 5 (Luanda, 1953).

———. "Vanuambo, nominação de um seculu e seus cargos." *Mensário Administrativo* 5 (Luanda, 1952).

Bridgland, Fred. *Jonas Savimbi, A Key to Africa.* London, 1986; reprint, New York: Paragon, 1987.

Cadornega, António de Oliveira de. *História geral das guerras angolanas.* (Ms. of 1680–81) 3 vols. Ed. by José Matias Delgado and Manuel Alves da Cunha. Lisbon: Agência Geral do Ultramar, 1940–42; reprint, 1972.

Cahen, Michel, ed. *"Vilas" et "Cidades": Bourgs et villes en Afrique lusophone.* Paris: L'Harmattan, 1989.

Calhoun, Margaret. "Only Fair Elections Can Keep Angola's Peace." *Wall Street Journal*. European Edition, 2 October 1992.

Cameron, Vernon L. *Across Africa*. 2 Vols. New York: Harper & Brothers, 1877.

Capela, José. *O imposto de palhota e a introdução do modo de produção capitalista nas colónias*. Porto: Afrontamento, 1977.

Capelo, Hermenegildo de Brito and Robert Ivens. *From Benguela to the Territory of the Yacca*. 2 vols. London, 1882.

Castro, Armando. *O Sistema colonial português em África*. Lisboa: Editoral Caminho, 1959.

Castro, Armando Augusto Gonçalves de Morais e. *As Colónias Portuguesas*. Porto: Companhia Portuguesa Editora, 1927.

Cequeiro, Ivo de. *Relatório 1931–1932*. Luanda: Direcção dos Serviços e Negocios Indigenas, 1933.

Chaka, Malik. *Angola's Government of National Unity*. Washington, D.C.: The Center for Democracy in Angola, Inc., 1997.

Chanock, Martin. *Law, Custom and Social Order: The Colonial Experience in Malawi and Zambia*. London: Cambridge University Press, 1985.

Childs, Gladwyn Murray. "The Kingdom of Wambu (Huambo): A Tentative Chronology." *Journal of African History* 5, no. 3 (1964): 367–79.

———. *Umbundu Kingship and Character*. London: Oxford University Press, International African Institute, 1949.

"Chinsole." Unpublished typscript. 22 pages [circa 1976]. In possession of author.

Clarence-Smith, W. Gervase. "Class Structure and Class Struggles in Angola in the 1970s." *Journal of Southern African Studies* 7 (1980): 109–26.

———. *Slaves, Peasants and Capitalists in Southern Angola, 1840–1926*. Cambridge: Cambridge University Press, 1979.

———. *The Third Portuguese Empire, 1825–1975: A Study in Economic Imperialism*. Manchester: Manchester University Press, 1985.

Colónia de Angola. *Censo geral de população, 1940*. Luanda: Imprensa Nacional, 1941.

———. *Plano geral de propaganda e desenvolvimento da cultura de milho entre os indígenas*. Luanda, 1913.

———. *Recenseamento, 1960*. Luanda, 1960.

Conceição Neto, Maria da. "Comércio, religião e política no sertão de Benguela: O Bailundu de Ekwikwi II, 1876–1893." *Fontes & estudos: Revista do Arquivo Histórico Nacional* no. 1 (November 1994): 101–18.

Conchiglia, Augusta. *UNITA: Myth and Reality*. London: ECASAAMA, 1990.

Cooper, Fredrick. "Mau Mau and the Discourses of Decolonization." *Journal of African History* 29 (1988): 313–20.

Cordell, Dennis, and Joel Gregory, eds. *African Population and Captialism: Historical Perspectives*. Madison: University of Wisconsin Press, 1987.

Corrêa, Elias Alexandre da Silva. *História de Angola*. 2 vols. Lisbon: Editorial Atica, 1937.

Cowell, Alan. *Killing the Wizards: Wars of Power and Freedom from Zaire to South Africa*. New York: Simon & Schuster, 1992.

Crocker, Chester A. *High Noon in Southern Africa: Making Peace in a Rough Neighborhood*. New York: W.W. Norton, 1992.

———. "Southern Africa: Eight Years Later." *Foreign Affairs* (Fall, 1989).

Cunha, J. M. da Silva. *O trabalho indígena: Estudo de direito colonial*. 2 ed. Lisbon: Agência Geral do Ultramar, 1955.

Curto, José. "The Anatomy of a Demographic Explosion: Luanda, 1844–1850." Unpublished Ms. May 1996.

———. The Legal Portuguese Slave Trade from Benguela, Angola, 1730–1838: A Quantitative Re-Appraisal." *Africa: Revista do Centro de Estudos Africanos* (São Paulo, Brazil) 16–17, no. 1 (1993–94): 101–16.

Cushman, Mary Floyd. *Missionary Doctor: The Story of Twenty Years in Africa*. New York: Harper & Brothers, 1944.

Dash, Leon da Costa Jr. *Savimbi's 1977 Campaign against the Cubans and MPLA*. Pasadena: California Institute of Technology, Munger Africana Library Notes, 1977.

Davidson, Basil. *African Nationalism and the Problems of Nation-Building*. Lagos: Nigerian Institute of International Affairs, 1987.

———. *The Black Man's Burden: Africa and the Curse of the Nation-State*. New York: Times Books, 1992.

———. *In the Eye of the Storm: Angola's People*. Garden City, N.Y.: Doubleday, 1973.

———. *The Search for Africa: History, Culture, Politics*. New York: Time Books, 1994.

———. *Walking 300 Miles with Guerrillas through the Bush in Eastern Angola*. Pasadena: California Institute of Technology, Munger Africana Library Notes, 1971.

Davidson, Basil, J. Slovo, and A.R. Wilkinson. *Southern Africa: The New Politics of Revolution*. Harmondsworth: Penguin, 1976.

Dawson, Marc H. "Health, Nutrition, and Population in Central Kenya, 1890–1945." In Dennis Cordell and Joel Gregroy, eds. *African Population and Capitalism: Historical Perspectives*. Madison: University of Wisconsin Press, 1987.

Delgado, Ralph. *Ao sul do Cuanza: Ocupação e aproveitamento do antigo reino de Benguela*. 2 vols. Lisbon: no publisher given, 1944.

Dias, Jill. "Changing Patterns of Power in the Luanda Hinterland: The Impact of Trade and Colonization on the Mbundu, ca. 1845–1920." *Paideuma*, 32 (1985): 285–318.

———. "Uma questão de identidade: respostas intelectuais se transformações económicas no seio da élite crioula da Angola portuguesa entre 1870 e 1930." *Revista Internacional de Estudos Africanos* 1 (1984): 61–94.

Direcção dos Serviços de Agricola e Commercio. *Boletim* (Lisbon, 1930).

The Economist Intelligence Unit. *Country Study: Angola, São Tomé and Principé, 1992–1993*. London: The Economist, 1993.

Edwards, Adrian C. *The Ovimbundu under Two Sovereignties: A Study of Social Control and Social Change among a People of Angola*. London: Oxford University Press, 1962.

Egerton, F. Clement C. *Angola in Perspective: Endeavor and Achievement in Portuguese West Africa*. London: Routledge & Paul, 1957.

Ennis, Merlin. *Umbundu Folk Tales from Angola*. Boston: Beacon Press, 1962.

Estado de Angola, *Informação estatística, 1972*. Luanda, n.d.

Felner, Alfredo de Albuquerque. "Derrota de Benguela para o sertão." In *Angola: Apontamentos sôbre a colonização dos planaltos e litoral do sul de Angola*. vol. 2. Lisbon: Agência Geral das Colónias, 1940.

Ferreira, Eduardo de Sousa. *Portuguese Colonialism in Africa*. Paris: UNESCO, 1974.

———. "The Present Role of the Portuguese Resettlement Policy." *African Studies* 4, 21, 1 (1974).

———. "La transformación y consolidación de la economia em Angola, 1930–74." *Estudos de Asia y Africa* 15/3 (1980).

Ferreira Diniz, José de Oliveira. "De político indigena em Angola." *Boletim de Agência Geral de Angola* 5, no. 44 (May 1929).

————. *Negócios indigenas: Relatório de ano de 1913*. Luanda: Imprensa Nacional de Angola, 1914.

————. *Negócios indigenas: Relatório do ano de 1916*. Lisbon, 1917.

————. *Populações indigenas de Angola*. Coimbra: Imprensa da Universidade, 1918.

Figueiredo, Xavier. "Angola: The Luanda Coup." *Africa Insight*. Lisbon, 1992.

Finkle, Vicki. "Violence and the Vote." *Africa Report* 37, no. 4 (July/August 1992).

Fodor, István. *Introduction to the History of Umbumdu: L. Magyar's Records (1859) and the Later Sources*. Hamburg and Budapest: Helmut Buske and Akadémiai Kiadó, 1983.

Free Angola. Washington: UNITA, 1990.

Fryer, Peter, and Patricia McGowan Pinheiro. *Oldest Ally: A Portrait of Salazar's Portugal*. London: D. Dobson, 1961.

Gabriel, Manuel Nunes. *Angola: Cinco Séculos de Cristianismo*. Queluz: Literal Sociedade Editora, Lt.da, 1978.

Gallagher, David H.. *Along African Trails*. Toronto: The United Church of Canada, 1952.

Gallagher, Tom. *Portugal: A Twentieth-Century Interpretation*. Manchester: Manchester University Press, 1983.

Gibson, Richard. *African Liberation Movements*. London: Oxford University Press, 1972.

Graça, Joaquim Rodrigues. "Expedição ao Muatayanvua, 1843." *Boletim da Sociedade Geografia e da História de Lisboa* 9, nos. 8–9 (1890): 365–468.

Graham, R.H. Carson. *Under Seven Congo Kings*. London: Carey Press, 1930.

Grémio de Milho. *Relatório*. Lisbon, 1933.

Grémio de Milho, *Relatório*. Lisbon, 1943.

Grémio de Milho, *Relatório*. Lisbon, 1949.

Guerra, Henrique. *Angola: Estrutura económia e classes sociais: Os ultimos anos do colonialismo português em Angola*. Lisboa: União dos Escritos Angolanos, 1979.

Guimarães, Fernando J. Andresen. "Origins and Development of the MPLA: Two Dissident Voices." *Camões Center Quarterly*, 5, nos. 1&2 (Winter 1993–94).

————. "The Collapse of the New State and the Emergence of the Angolan Civil War." *Camões Center Quarterly* 5, nos. 1&2 (Winter 1993–94).

Hambly, W. D. *The Ovimbundu of Angola*, Chicago: Field Museum of Natural History, Anthropological Series, 21, 2, 1934.

————. *Jamba*. Chicago: Pelligrini & Cudahy, 1947.

Hammond, Richard. *Portugal and Africa, 1815–1910: A Study in Uneconomic Imperialism*. Palo Alto: Stanford University Press, 1966.

Harding, Jeremy. *The Fate of Africa: Trial by Fire*. New York: Simon & Schuster, 1993.

Hastings, D.A. "Ovimbundu Customs and Practices as Centered around the Principles of Kinship and Psychic Power." Ph.D. dissertation, Hartford Seminary (1933).

Hauenstein, Alfred. "La royauté chez les Ovimbundu." In Manuel Laranjeira Rodrigues de Areia, ed. *Angola: Os símbolos do poder na sociedade tradicional*. Coimbra: Centro de Estudos Africanos, 1983.

Heimer, F. W. *The Decolonization Conflict in Angola, 1974–1976: An Essay in Political Sociology*. Geneva, IUHEI, 1979.

————. *Social Change in Angola*. Munchen: Weltforum Verlag, 1973.

Henderson, Lawrence. *Angola: Five Centuries of Conflict*. Ithaca: Cornell University Press, 1979.

————. *A Igreja em Angola: Um rio com várias correntes*. Lisbon: Editorial Além Mar, 1990.

Henriques, Isabel de Castro. *Commerce et changement en Angola au XIX Siècle: Imbangala et Tschokwe face à la modernité*. 2 vols. Paris: Editions Harmattan, 1995.

Herbert, Eugenia W. *Iron, Gender, and Power: Rituals of Transformation in African Societies.* Bloomington: Indiana University Press, 1993.

Heywood, Linda. "The Growth and Decline of African Agriculture in Angola, 1890–1950." *Journal of Southern African Studies* 13, no. 1 (1987).

———. "History, Urbanization and Nationalism in Central Angola: The Case of Huambo/Nova Lisboa." Paper Presented at the African Urban History Conference, School of Oriental and African Studies, London University, June 1996.

———. "Porters, Trade and Power: The Politics of Labor in the Central Highlands of Angola, 1850–1914." In Catherine Coquéry-Vidrovitch and Paul Lovejoy, eds. *The Workers of African Trade.* Beverly Hills: Sage, 1985.

———. "Production, Trade and Power: The Political Economy of Central Angola, 1850–1930." Ph. D dissertation, Columbia University, (1984).

———. "Slavery and Forced Labor in the Changing Political Economy of Central Angola, 1850–1949." In Suzanne Miers and Richard Roberts, eds. *The End of Slavery in Africa.* Madison: University of Wisconsin Press, 1988.

———. "Towards an Understanding of Modern Political Ideology in Africa: The Case of the Ovimbundu of Angola." *Journal of Modern African Studies* 36, 1 (1998).

———. "UNITA and Ethnic Nationalism in Angola." *Journal of Modern African Studies* 27, 1 (1989).

Heywood, Linda, and John Thornton. "African Fiscal Systems as Sources for Demographic History: The Case of Central Angola, 1799–1920." *Journal of African History* 29 (1988).

———. "Demograpyhy, Production and Labor: Central Africa." In Dennis Cordell and Joel Gregory, eds. *African Population and Capitalism: Historical Perspectives.* Madison: University of Wisconsin Press, 1987.

Hobsbawm, Eric. *Nations and Nationalism since 1780: Programme, Myth, Reality.* New York: Cambridge University Press, 1990.

Hodges, Tony. *Angola to 2000: Prospects for Recovery.* London: The Economist Intelligence Unit, 1993.

Holness, Marga. "The Struggle Continues." In David Martin and Phyllis Johnson, eds. *Destructive Engagement: Southern Africa at War.* Harare: Zimbabwe Publishing House, 1986.

Jamba, Sousa. *Patriots.* London: Viking Press, 1990.

Jaspert, F., and W. Jaspert. *Through Unknown Africa: Experiences from the Jaspert African Expedition of 1926–1927.* London: Jarrolds, 1929.

Jessen, Otto. *Reisen und Forschungen in Angola.* Berlin: D. Reimer, Andrews & Steiner, 1936.

Johnson, Phyllis, and David Martin, eds. *Destructive Engagement: Southern Africa at War.* Harare: Zimbabwe Publishing House, 1986.

Johnston, James. *Reality versus Romance in South Central Africa.* 2nd ed. London: Frank Cass, 1969.

Jolliffe, Jill. "Captive Heart in Angola's Ordeal by Fire." *The European,* 18–22 February, 1993.

Kaliengue, César Pedro. "Testemunho para a História da U.N.I.T.A." Manuscript. Jamba, 1986.

Kanogo, Thabitha. *Squatters and the Roots of Mau Mau.* London: James Currey, 1987.

Kaplan, Irving, ed. *Angola: A Country Study.* Washington: American University Press, 1979.

Kassembe, Dia. *Angola: 20 ans de guerre.* Paris: L'Harmattan, 1995.

Katzenellenbogen, S.E. *Railways and the Copper Mines of Katanga*. Oxford: Clarendon Press, 1973.

Kennedy, Dane. *Islands of White: Settler Society and Culture in Kenya and Southern Rhodesia, 1890–1939*. Durham, N.C.: Duke University Press, 1987.

Kerbosch, Roeland. *Angola: met eigen ogen*. Antwerp: A.W. Brun & Zoom, 1971.

Kitching, Gavin. *Class and Economic Change in Kenya: The Making of an African Petite Bourgeoisie, 1905–1970*. New Haven: Yale University Press, 1980.

Lake, Anthony. *The "Tar Baby" Option: American Policy toward Southern Rhodesia*. New York: Columbia University Press, 1976.

———. "A Landmark in Angolan History." *World Marxist Review* (March, 1989).

Lamberga, Joseph. "Angola: Savimbi Says He Does Not Want a Cosmetic Vice Presidency." Luso, 21 March 1997. Typescript.

Lan, David. *Guns and Rain: Guerrillas and Spirit Mediums in Zimbabwe*. Berkeley: University of California Press, 1985.

Legum, Colin, and Tony Hodges. *After Angola: The War over Southern Africa*. London: Rex Collings, 1976.

Lemarchand, René. "The Bases of Nationalism among the Bakongo." *Africa* 31 (October, 1961): 344–54.

Lima, A.G. Mesquitela. *Os Kyaka de Angola*. 3 vols. Lisbon: Edições Távola Redonda, 1988–92.

Listowel, Judith. *The Other Livingstone*. New York: Scribner, 1974.

Loiseau, Yves, and Pierre-Guillaume de Roux, *Portrait d'un révolutionnaire en général: Jonas Savimbi*. Paris: La Table Ronde, 1987.

Lonsdale, John. "Mau Mau of the Mind: Making Mau Mau and the Remaking of Kenya." *Journal of African History* 31 (1990): 393–423.

Luke, Timothy. "Angola and Mozambique: Institutionalizing Social Revolution in Africa." *Review of Politics* 44, 3 (1992): 413–36.

Lusaka Protocol. Washington, D.C.: Free Angola Information Service, 1995.

MacGaffey, Wyatt. *Modern Kongo Prophets: Religion in a Plural Society*. Bloomington: Indiana University Press, 1983.

———. *Religion and Society in Central Africa: The BaKongo of Lower Zaire*. Chicago: University of Chicago Press, 1985.

Magyar, László. *Reisen in Sud-Afrika, 1849–1857*. Pest: Lauffer & Stopl, 1859; reprint, New York: Kraus, 1974.

Maier, Karl. *Angola: Promises and Lies*. London: Serif, 1996.

———. "Blueprint for Peace." *Africa Report*, March–April, 1991.

Malheiro, Alexandre. *Chrónicas do Bihé*. Lisbon: Livraria Ferreira, 1903.

Marcum, John. "Angola: Twenty Five Years of War." *Current History* 85 (May 1986).

Marcum, John. *The Angolan Revolution, Vol. 1: The Anatomy of an Explosion, 1950–1962*. Cambridge, Mass: MIT Press, 1969.

———. *The Angolan Revolution, Vol. 2: Exile Politics and Guerilla Warfare, 1962–1976*. Cambridge, Mass: MIT Press, 1978.

Martin, W. James III. *A Political History of the Civil War in Angola, 1974–1990*. New Brunswick, N.J.: Transaction Publishers, 1992.

Mazrui, Ali, and Michael Tidy. *Nationalism and New States in Africa from about 1935 to the Present*. London: Heinemann, 1984.

McCormick, Shawn H. *The Angolan Economy: Prospects for Growth in a Postwar Environment*. Washington, D.C.: Center for Strategic and International Studies, 1994.

Messiant, Christine. "Luanda (1945–1961): Colonisés, société colonial et engagement nationaliste." In Michael Cahen, ed., *"Vilas" et "Cidades": Bourgs et villes en Afrique lusophone*. Paris: L'Harmattan, 1989.

Miller, Joseph. *Kings and Kinsmen: Early Mbundu States in Angola*. Oxford: Clarendon Press, 1976.

———. *Way of Death: Merchant Capitalism and the Angolan Slave Trade, 1730–1830*. Madison: University of Wisconsin Press, 1988.

Minter, William. *Apartheid's Contras: An Inquiry into the Roots of War in Angola and Mozambique*. London: Zed Press, 1994.

———. *King Solomon's Mines Revisited: Western Interests and the Burdened History of Southern Africa*. New York: Basic Books, 1986.

———. *The National Union for the Total Independence of Angola (UNITA) as Described by Ex-Participants and Foreign Visitors*. Washington, D.C., 1990.

———. *Operation Timber: Pages from the Savimbi Dossier*. Trenton, N.J.: Africa World Press, 1988.

Monteiro, José Firmo de Sousa. *Agricultura em Angola: Breve resumo sobre os recursos agrícolas da Província de Angola*. Lisbon: Agência Geral de Angola, 1922.

Monteiro, Rameiro Ladeiro. *A família nos Musseques de Luanda: Subsidios para o seu estudo*. Luanda: Fundo de Acção Social no trabalho em Angola, 1973.

Morais, J.A. David de, *et al*. *Subsídios para o conhecimento médico e antropológico do Povo Undulu (Angola)*. Lisbon: Separata dos *Anais do Instituto de Higiene e Medicina Tropical* 2, nos. 1–4 (January–December, 1975).

Morais, J.A. David de, with Hermann Pössinger. "Transformações occoridas na sociedade Umbundu desde do colapso do comércio das Caravanas até ao fim da era colonial." Unpublished Ms., n.d. [1978].

MPLA. *Angola: Exploitation esclavagiste, résistance nationale*. Dakar: A. Diop, 1961.

———. *A História de Angola*. Luanda: Centro de Estudos Angolanos, 1975.

Munslow, Barry, ed. *Africa: Problems in the Transition to Socialism*. London: Zed Press, 1986.

Neiva, Ernesto. *Missão e evangelho: Angola busca de novas coordenadas evangélicas para a missão*. Lisbon: Editorial L.I.A.M. 1974.

Nelson, Samuel. *Colonialism in the Congo Basin, 1880–1940*. Athens: Ohio University Press, 1994.

Nesbitt, Prexy. "US Foreign Policy: Lessons from the Angolan Conflict." *Africa Today* (1st & 2nd quarters, 1992).

Neto, Agostinho. *Messages to Companions in the Struggle: Speeches by Agostinho Neto*. Richmond, B.C.: Liberation Support Movement Information Center, 1972.

Nogueira, Franco. *The Third World*. London: Johnson, 1967.

Okuma, Thomas. *Angola in Ferment: The Background and Prospects of Angolan Nationalism*. Boston: Beacon Press, 1962.

Paiva, Arthur de. *Expedição ao Bihé*. 2 vols. Lisbon: Agência Geral das Colónias, 1890.

Pélissier, René. *La Colonie du minotaure: Nationalismes et révoltes en Angola, 1926–1961*. Orgeval: Pélissier, 1978.

———. *Explorar: Voyages en Angola et autres lieux incertains*. Orgeval: Pélissier, 1979.

———. *Les Guerres grises: Résistance et révoltes en Angola, 1845–1941*. Orgeval: Pélissier, 1977.

———. *Le Naufrage des caravelles: Études sur la fin de l'empire portugais, 1961–1971*. Orgeval: Pélissier, 1979.

————. "Origines du mouvement nationaliste moderniste en Angola." *Revue française d'études politiques africaines* no. 126 (June 1976): 14–47.

Pereira, Anthony W. "Angola's 1992 Elections: A Personal View." *Camões Center Quarterly* 5, nos. 1 & 2 (Winter, 1993/94): 1–8.

Perreira, Rui. "Anthropologia applicada na política colonial portuguesa do Estado Novo." *Revista Internacional de Estudos Africanos* 4–5 (June–December, 1986): 191–235.

Phimister, Ian. *An Economic and Social History of Zimbabwe, 1890–1948.* Harlow: Longman, 1988.

Pires, António. *Angola: Essa desconhecida: Ensaio político-económico.* Luanda: no publisher given, 1964.

Porch, D. *The Portuguese Armed Forces and the Revolution.* London: Croom Helm, 1977.

Provincia de Angola. Direcção dos Serviços de Estatísticas, *Censo Geral da População.* vol. 3. Luanda: Imprensa Nacional, 1941.

————, *et al. III recenseamento geral da população, 1960* Vol. 1. Luanda: Imprensa Nacional, 1964.

————, *et al. III recenseamento geral da população, 1960* Vol. 2. Luanda: Imprensa Nacional, 1967.

Queirós, Cícero. *Angola: Outubro de 1992: Um passo para o abismo.* n.d. n.p.

Ranger, Terence. *Peasant Consciousness and Guerrilla War in Zimbabwe.* London: James Currey, 1985.

República Portuguesa, *Acto Colonial,* Decreto-Lei no. 18, 570 of 8/7/1930. Luanda: Imprensa Nacional, 1930.

Ribeiro, Orlando. *A colonização de Angola e o seu fracasso.* Lisbon: Imprensa Nacional, 1981.

Rivers, Bernard. "Angola: Massacre and Oppression." *Africa Today* 21 (1974).

Roberts, Andrew ed. *The Colonial Moment in Africa: Essays on the Movement of Minds and Materials, 1900–1940.* New York: Cambridge University Press, 1990.

Rocha, Alves da, Nelson Lourenço, and Armando Morais. "Angola nas vésperas da independência (I)." *Economia e socialismo: Revista mensal de economia política* 36, 37, 38 (1979): 25–49.

Roque, Fátima *et al. Economia de Angola.* Lisbon: Betrand Editora, 1991.

Rothchild, Donald, and Caroline Hartzell. "Great and Medium-Power Mediations: Angola." *Annals* (November 1991).

Sandgren, David P. *Christianity and the Kikuyu: Religious Divisions and Social Conflict.* New York: P. Lang, 1989.

Santos, Afonso Costa Valdez Tomaz dos. *Perspectivas económicas de Angola.* Lisbon: Agência Geral das Colónias, 1949.

[Santos, José Eduardo dos]. *Mensagem ao fim do ano 1994 do Presidente da Republica.* Ms. in author's possession.

Santos, Maria Emília Madeira dos, ed. *Viagens e apontamentos de um Portuense em África: Diário de António Francisco Ferreira da Silva Porto.* vol. 1 Coimbra: Biblioteca Geral da Universidade de Coimbra, 1986.

————. "Perspectiva do comércio sertenejo de Bié na segunda metade do secúlu XIX." *Studia* 45 (1981): 65–129.

Saraiva, José Hermano. *História concisa de Portugal.* 3rd ed. Lisbon: Europa America, 1979.

Sarmento, Alexandre. "Contribuição para o estudo da antropologia dos Bailundos." *Anais do Instituto de Medicina Tropical.* Lisbon, 1957.

————. "Subsidios para o estudo demografico da população indigena de Angola." *Anais do Instituto Medicina Tropical.* Lisbon, 1957.

Schmults, Robert C. "Bloodshed and Blame in Angola." *Insight,* 14 February 1993.

Seis Portuguesas em Terras da UNITA. Venda Nova: Bertrand Editora, 1988.

Sender, John, and Sheila Smith. *The Development of Capitalism in Africa.* London: Metheun, 1986.

Serpa Pinto, A. A. da Rocha de. *How I Crossed Africa.* Trans, by Alfred Elwes. 2 vols. Philadelphia: Lippincott, 1881.

Silva Porto, António da. *Viagens e apontamentos de um Portuense em África: excerptos do Diário de António Francisco da Silva Porto.* Ed. by José de Miranda and Antonio Brochado. Lisbon: Agência Geral das Colónias, 1942.

————. "Novas jornadas de Silva Porto nos sertões africanos." *Boletim da Sociedade de Geografia de Lisboa.* 5a ser. (1885).

Silveira Ramos, M.A.C. da. "A Industria de Pesca e o mão de obra indigena." In *I Congresso dos economistas Portuguesas.* Parte III. Lisbon: Instituto Nacional de Estatística, 1955.

————. "Recrutamento de mão-de-obra indigena." In *I Congreso dos economistas portuguesas.* Parte III. Lisbon: Instituto Nacional de Estatística, 1955.

Simpkins, Gregory. *Angola: A Chronology of Major Political Developments—February 1961– September 1996.* Virginia: Institute for Strategic Studies, 1996.

Soares, Amadeu de Castilho. *Política de bem-estar rural em Angola.* Estudo Científico Político-cal e Social, no. 49. Lisbon: Junta de Investigações do Ultramar, 1961.

Somerville, Keith. *Angola: Politics, Economics, and Society.* London: Lynne Rienner, 1986.

Soremekun, Fola. *Angola: The Road to Independence.* Ile-Ife, Nigeria: University of Ife Press, 1983.

————. "Religion and Politics in Angola: The American Board Missions and the Portuguese Government, 1880–1922." *Cahiers d'études africaines* 3 (1971): 341–77.

Sousa Monteiro, José F. "Breve noticia das riquezas naturais de Angola: Possibilidades da sua produção e aspectos Regionais." *Província de Angola. Boletim de Agricultura,* série 4, separata 3 (1920).

Spikes, Daniel. *Angola and the Politics of Intervention: From Local Bush War to Chronic Crisis in Southern Africa.* Jefferson, N.C.: McFarland & Company, 1993.

Stockwell, John. *In Search of Enemies: A CIA Story.* New York: W.W. Norton & Co., 1978.

Tams, Georg. *Visit to the Portuguese Possessions in South-Western Africa.* 2 vols. New York: Negro Universities Press, 1969.

Taruffi, Dino. *L'altipiano de Benguela (Angola) ed il sua avenire agricolo.* Rome: Instituto Agri-colonial Italiano, 1916.

Tilsley, G.E.S. *Dan Crawford: Missionary and Pioneer in Central Africa.* New York: Fleming H. Revell, 1929.

Torres, Adelino. "Le Processus d'urbanisation de l'Angola pendant la période coloniale (années 1940–1970)." In Michael Cahen, ed. *"Vilas" et "cidades": Bourgs et villes en Afrique lusophone.* Paris: L'Harmattan, 1989.

————. *O Império portugûes entre o real e o imaginário.* Lisbon: Escher, 1991.

Toussie, Sam R. "War and Survival in Southern Angola: The UNITA Assessment Mission." Unpublished Ms. International Rescue Mission, December 1989.

Tucker, John T. *A Tucker Treasury: John T. Tucker, Reminiscences and Stories of Angola, 1883– 1958.* Ed. by Catherine Tucker Ward. Winfield, B.C.: Wood Lake Books, 1984.

————. *Angola, the Land of the Blacksmith Prince.* London: World Dominion Press, 1933.

————. *Men of Africa*. Toronto: The United Church of Canada, n.d.

————. *Old Ways and New Days in Angola, Africa*. Toronto: F.C. Stephenson, n.d. [1935].

Tvedten, Inge. *Angola: Struggle for Peace and Reconstruction*. Bolder, Colo.: Westview Press, 1977.

UNITA. "Angola: Democracy on a Life Support." n.d. Typescript.

————. *Angola Elections*. Luanda: Cabinete de Imprensa, 8 October 1992.

————. "Communique." Huambo, 16 October 1992. Typescript.

————. *The UNITA Leadership*. Jamba: UNITA, 1990.

————. *UNITA: Identité d'un Angola libre*. Jamba: UNITA, 1995.

US Congress. "New Reports of Human Rights Violations in the Angola Civil War." *Hearings of the House of Representatives*. 1st Session (12 April 1989). John Marcum Testimony.

US State Department, Case No. 8601323, sec. II. "Angolan US Covert Aid to the Insurgents, January 1985 to March, 1986.

Vail, Leroy, and Landeg White. *Capitalism and Colonialism in Mozambique: A Study of the Quelimane District*. London: Heinemann, 1980.

Vansina, Jan. *Paths in the Rainforests: Toward a History of Political Tradition in Equatorial Africa*. Madison: University of Wisconsin Press, 1990.

Vellut, Jean Luc. "Notes sur le Lunda et la frontière luso-africaine, 1790–1900." *Études d'histoire africaine* 3 (1972): 61–166.

Venter, A. J. *The Terror Fighters: A Profile of Guerrilla Warfare in Southern Africa*. Cape Town: Purnell, 1969.

Vidigal, F. Correia Mendes. *O milho na economia da provincia de Angola*. Lisbon: Escola Superior, Provincia de Angola, 1953–54.

Vines, Alex. "La troisième guerre angolaise." *Politique africaine* 57 (1995): 27–40.

"The View from UNITA: Angola, Unity or Struggle," *Black World* (October 1972).

Warren, Bill. *Imperialism: Pioneer of Capitalism*. New York: New Left Books, 1981.

Wheeler, Douglas. "Angola in Whose House? Early Stirrings of Angolan Nationalism and Protest, 1822–1910." *International Journal of African Historical Studies*, 2, no. 1, (1969): 1–23.

————. "Origins of African Nationalism in Angola: Assimilado Protest Writings, 1859–1929." In R. Chilcote, ed., *Protest and Resistance in Angola and Brazil* (Los Angeles: University of California Press, 1972).

Wheeler, Douglas, and C. Diane Christensen. "To Rise with One Mind: The Bailundu War of 1902." In Franz W. Heimer, ed., *Social Change in Angola*. Munchen: Weltforum Verlag, 1973.

Wheeler, Douglas, and René Pélissier. *Angola*. New York: Praeger, 1971.

Wiarda, H. D. "Towards a Framework for the Study of Political Change in Iberian Latin Tradition: The Corporate Model." *World Politics* 25 (1973).

Wolfers, Michael, and Jane Bergerol. *Angola in the Frontline*. London: Zed Press, 1983.

Wright, George. *The Destruction of a Nation: United States' Policy towards Angola since 1945*. London: Pluto Press, 1997.

Yoder, John C. *The Kanyok of Zaire: An Institutional and Ideological History to 1895*. London: Cambridge University Press, 1992.

Young, Crawford. *The African Colonial State in Comparative Perspective*. New Haven: Yale University Press, 1994.

INDEX

Contested Power in Angola, 1840s to the Present shows that the Ovimbundu of central Angola have been key players in the history of modern Angola. The work focuses on the tensions between the centralizing forces of the state and the local, regional, and ethnic tendencies that have characterized the modern history of Angola. The study begins by highlighting the relationship between relatively weak precolonial Ovimbundu state systems and the autonomous local economic, political, and social institutions that functioned in the villages. The book also examines how both state and local systems adapted to the commercial, political, and cultural imperatives of industrializing Europe and America. Subsequent chapters explore the emergence and transformation of the Portuguese colonial state in central Angola, including issues of pacification and colonialization, the Estado Novo, and the politics of subjugation. They illustrate the contradictions between the rhetoric of racial democracy of the apologists of the colonial state and the reality of rising ethnic and regional tension. The book concludes by tracing the evolution of Ovimbundu nationalism during the colonial and postcolonial periods. Heywood argues that the divisions of the Cold War and continuing ethnic and regional divisions frustrated the Ovimbundu leadership in its efforts to make the state more inclusive. This quest to reshape the state remains a salient feature in the relationship between the Ovimbundu and the state.

Linda Heywood is Associate Professor of History at Howard University. She has published several articles on the political and economic history of modern Angola and on the history of the African Diaspora, and is presently coauthoring a book on the first generation of central Africans in North America and the Caribbean.

DATE DUE